Withdrawn from
Barnard College
Library

Disgraceful Matters

Disgraceful Matters

*The Politics of Chastity
in Eighteenth-Century China*

Janet M. Theiss

UNIVERSITY OF CALIFORNIA PRESS
Berkeley   ·   Los Angeles   ·   London

University of California Press
Berkeley and Los Angeles, California

University of California Press, Ltd.
London, England

© 2004 by the Regents of the University of California

Library of Congress Cataloging-in-Publication Data

Theiss, Janet M., 1964–
    Disgraceful matters : the politics of chastity in eighteenth-century China / Janet M. Theiss.
       p.   cm.
    Includes bibliographical references and index.
    ISBN 0-520-24033-2 (alk. paper)
    1. Chastity. 2. Women—China—Social conditions. 3. China—Social conditions—1644–1912. I. Title: Politics of chastity in eighteenth-century China. II. Title.

BJ1533.C4T49   2004
176'.0951—dc22   2004009186

Manufactured in the United States of America
13 12 11 10 09 08 07 06 05 04
10 9 8 7 6 5 4 3 2 1

Printed on Ecobook 50 containing a minimum 50% post-consumer waste, processed chlorine free. The balance contains virgin pulp, including 25% Forest Stewardship Council Certified for no old growth tree cutting, processed either TCF or ECF. The sheet is acid-free and meets the minimum requirements of ANSI/NISO Z39.48–1992 (R 1997) (Permanence of Paper).

For
Norman Theiss and Judith Eheim Theiss,
my first and foremost models of virtue and
scholarship

Contents

Acknowledgments ix

A Note on Textual Conventions xiii

A Note on Dynasties and Reigns xv

Introduction 1

PART ONE · *The Chastening State: The Qing Chastity Cult in Ritual, Law, and Statecraft*

Prologue: A Chaste Barbarian Martyrs Herself on the Imperial Frontier 17

1. Defining Gender Orthodoxy for a Multiethnic Empire 25
2. Statecraft and Gender Order in the Qianlong Reign 39

PART TWO · *Female Virtue and the Politics of Patriarchy*

Prologue: A Righteous Husband Plays the Politics of the Wifely Way 57

3. Enforcing Gender Order: Between the Ancestral Hall and the *Yamen* 65

4. Divided Loyalties: Natal Families and the Exercise
   of Patrilineal Authority   82
5. Adultery, Incest and the Multiple Meanings of Patriarchy   98

   PART THREE · *Mapping Chastity across Boundaries
   of Body, Mind, and Space*

   Prologue: A Compromised Widow Sacrifices Her Body
   to Defend Inner Virtue   121
6. The Wages of Wanton Mixing: Violation
   and Gender Disorder   133
7. "Accommodating Sages": Gender Separation
   in Social Practice   154

   PART FOUR · *"Being a Person": Female Humiliation
   and Social Power*

   Prologue: Male Impropriety and Female Outrage Lead
   to a Tragic End   167
8. The Problem of Female Moral Agency   177
9. The Logic of Female Suicide   192
   Epilogue   211

   Notes   219
   A Note on Archival Sources   259
   Character List   261
   Bibliography   265
   Index   275

Acknowledgments

Over the many years of this project's evolution from dissertation to book, I have benefited immeasurably from the encouragement, wisdom, and moral support of numerous people. I am immensely grateful to my mentors and teachers at Berkeley, who, over the years of my graduate study and the writing of this book, molded my historical instincts and habits in countless ways, seen and unseen. With her uncanny ability to see my point, even when it was lost on me, Yeh Wen-hsin has deeply influenced the progress of this book and the way I think about history. Frederic Wakeman, with his boundless intellectual energy and his keen eye for the unanswered question, has been a constant source of inspiration and confidence through many moments of writing when my imagination was failing me. Between the two of them, I learned to appreciate good stories and savor taking them apart. David Keightley remains for me a model teacher and exemplar of how to meld intellectual rigor with creativity. At Swarthmore College, Lillian Li introduced me to the field of Chinese studies and, with her wise advice during a moment of uncertainty, inspired me to enter it.

Several people have read this manuscript in its entirety at various stages and offered the most constructive criticism one could hope for. This book has been greatly improved by the detailed comments and suggestions of William Rowe and another anonymous reader for the press, Joan Judge, Melissa Macauley, Paul Ropp, Matthew Sommer, and Norman Theiss, who have helped me to hone my arguments and clarify my assumptions.

I owe much of my understanding of female suicide in China and the evolution of the chastity concept in general to many stimulating conversations with Paola Zamperini, Katherine Carlitz, Harriet Zurndorfer, and Grace Fong, my co-participants in a fateful panel at the Association for Asian Studies in the year 2000 and a special issue of the journal *Nan Nü*. This book and my exploration of Qing history have also been greatly enriched by the friendship of Tobie Meyer-Fong, whom I thank for years of inspiring conversation, provocative criticism, merciless editing, and unflagging confidence in me and this project, even when it was floundering in purple prose and trapped in the anecdotal abyss.

Many other people have commented on earlier incarnations of various chapters or the conference papers that spawned them, offered critical advice, or suffered through long conversations about violations of chastity and other disgraceful matters. They include Megan Armstrong, Samuel Cheung, Elizabeth Clement, Bruce Dain, Nadia Durbach, Norman Kutcher, Susan Mann, James Millward, Patricia Moore, Susie Porter, Wesley Sasaki-Uemura, Carol Summers, and Yi-li Wu. I was privileged go through my education in Chinese history at Berkeley with a fabulous community of scholars. With their friendship, wisdom, and humor, Carlton Benson, Susan Glosser, Andrea Goldman, Guo Qitao, Mark Halperin, Eugenio Menegon, Ruth Mostern, Allison Rottman, Brett Sheehan, Yu Maochun, and Paola Zamperini taught me much about sinology and helped me survive the stresses of academic life.

Over the years I have had the pleasure and good fortune to be surrounded by wonderful colleagues on my research trips to China: Iwo Amelung, David Coulson, Brian Dott, Pat Giersch, Richard Horowitz, Yasuhiko Karasawa, and Paola Vanzo helped me to discover the archives and enlivened my research trips with their friendship. I am deeply grateful to the staff of the Number One Archives in Beijing, especially Qin Guojing and Zhu Shuyuan, who made my many months there productive and enjoyable. The faculty and students of the Qing History Institute at People's University, especially Cheng Chongde, Guo Chengkang, Dong Jianzhong, and Yin Tongyun, graciously hosted me during my yearlong sojourn in the archives in 1994–95 with research support, friendship, and critical logistical help in difficult moments. At the University of California Press, Reed Malcolm, Mary Severance, and Elisabeth Magnus have deftly and cheerfully guided me through the publication process. I remain grateful to Sheila Levine for her patient commitment to this book over more years than I would like to admit.

I would also like to thank the many organizations that provided financial support for the various stages of this project. My initial research was made possible by a Fulbright-Hays Doctoral Dissertation Research Fellowship, and I received a Mabel McLeod Lewis Dissertation Fellowship and a Dean's Dissertation Fellowship at the University of California, Berkeley to support the writing of the dissertation. Subsequent research and revision of the manuscript was supported by a Tanner Humanities Center Post-Doctoral Fellowship and a Faculty Research Grant from the University of Utah, and leaves were granted by the History Department at the University of Utah.

My parents, Judy and Norm Theiss, to whom this book is dedicated, my sisters Jennifer Theiss Sharp and Tamara Theiss, and my brother-in-law Mark Sharp provided the comic relief, patient indulgence, affectionate nagging, and reality checks to keep me balanced and mindful of the joys of family duty throughout the long years of this project. My niece Lily arrived in the final harried phase of this manuscript's completion, just in time to remind me that there is life beyond the book. Finally, Bradley Parker has shared all the most intimate frustrations and hidden satisfactions of writing a first book. He is an exemplar of the husbandly way, without which wives might never finish books, or at least not stay sane and healthy doing so. Thanks for centering me in my distraction, cheering me in my blues, and encouraging me always as my most loyal fan and partner.

And last but not least, I would like to recognize the special contribution to the final stages of this book's creation made by my daughter, Tabitha Parker-Theiss, who arrived just in time to be acknowledged.

Salt Lake City, August 2003

A Note on Textual Conventions

Most of the women who appear in this book are referred to as they are in legal cases, with their husband's surname, followed by their natal family surname and the term *shi,* the equivalent of *née.* Thus Du Song Shi (or Du née Song) is the wife of Mr. Du and the daughter of Mr. Song. Occasionally the husband's surname is dropped, leaving, for example, Gao Shi (née Gao).

Ages are given in Chinese *sui* rather than years. By Chinese count, a person is one *sui* old at birth and then two *sui* at the following turn of the New Year. So, depending on the month one was born, one's age in *sui* would be anywhere from one to two years older than one's age in Western years. Thus, a person who was thirty *sui* would be twenty-eight or twenty-nine years old by the Western count.

A Note on Dynasties and Reigns

MAJOR CHINESE DYNASTIES

Zhou (ca. 1045–256 B.C.E.)
Qin (221–206 B.C.E.)
Han (202 B.C.E.–C.E. 220)
Tang (618–906)
Song (960–1279)
Yuan (1279–1368)
Ming (1368–1644)
Qing (1644–1911)

REIGNS OF THE QING DYNASTY AND THEIR ABBREVIATIONS

Shunzhi SZ (1644–62)
Kangxi KX (1662–1722)
Yongzheng YZ (1723–36)
Qianlong QL (1736–96)
Jiaqing JQ (1796–1820)
Daoguang DG (1820–51)
Xianfeng XF (1851–61)
Tongzhi TZ (1861–75)
Guangxu GX (1875–1908)
Xuantong XT (1908–12)

Introduction

This book engages the most familiar and most thoroughly researched topic within Chinese gender and women's history: the cult of female chastity in the Qing dynasty (1644–1911). The institutionalized veneration of chaste widows and chastity martyrs first came to the attention of historians in the 1930s, who approached it from the perspective of the radical critiques and transformations of the old Confucian family system in their day. These scholars described the late imperial chastity award system as a religious cult, invoking associations with superstitious beliefs, unquestioned ritual prescriptions, and rigid patriarchal hierarchy. In one of the earliest attempts to trace the evolution of the "chastity concept" *(zhenjie guan)* from antiquity through the twentieth century, Liu Jihua described its intensification in the Song dynasty (960–1279) with the influence of Neo-Confucianism, the steady expansion of the state canonization system from the Yuan dynasty (1279–1368) onwards, and the culmination of the cult under China's last dynasty, the Qing. By that point, she asserted, "a chastity concept that had become increasingly rigid, superstitious, and religious became extremely popular throughout society." For Liu and her generation, the chastity concept was the inevitable product of the patrilineal clan system. As she explained, "Men all see chastity as the essential behavioral expression of the wifely way for women and also as an eternally unchangeable value from the Classics." She therefore concluded that "the chastity concept, having completely lost any rationality and out of touch with reality, has become a religion for women."[1]

Over the decades, scholars have complicated this picture of a rigid gender orthodoxy with nuanced depictions of the shifting stakes that states, literati elites, family authorities, and women themselves had in the promotion and practice of chastity. Most recently historians have discovered that while chastity was certainly part of state orthodoxy and integral to dominant gender norms, it was also a component of women's personal identities and an object of intense and perennial elite male fascination.[2] They have identified a complex matrix of factors that spurred the widening relevance of chastity in elite and popular culture in the late imperial period, culminating in its eighteenth-century heyday. At its height, the culture of chastity was marked not only by dramatic increases in the numbers of canonized women but also by the eruption of widespread debate over all aspects of chastity-centered female virtue, including the propriety of widow suicide and the requirements of female moral education.[3] Chastity was clearly a touchstone for rising concerns with orthodoxy on the part of both the morally conservative Manchu rulers of the Qing dynasty and the Han Chinese governing elites who promoted ritual revival in the wake of the Manchu conquest.[4] Threats to female virtue were also a compelling metaphor for the many disruptive social changes brought on by processes of commercialization that began in the late Ming dynasty (1368–1644) but continued to be a source of social problems and unease in the mid-Qing. Emphasizing this context of growing social instability and normative uncertainty, scholars have interpreted the promotion of chastity in the Qing as part of a larger state and literati project to reinvigorate Neo-Confucian family values and shore up a patriarchal order that was diversely threatened by the rise of a rogue male population, the increasing fragility of elite and commoner male status, and the stresses of geographic and social mobility on family hierarchy.[5]

These approaches to chastity, shaped largely by readings of social commentaries and hagiographic biographies of women written by literati men, and the writings of late imperial elite women themselves, offer a flexible model of the relationship between norm and practice that accounts for both the reproduction of orthodox values and structures and the diversity of accepted gender practices and interpretations of female virtue. Dorothy Ko's study of elite women poets in the formative period of urban print culture in the seventeenth century brings her to the conclusion that "the resilience of the seventeenth century gender system depended . . . on the opportunities it allowed for diversity and plurality of expression. . . . [It] was able to perpetuate itself by allocating a new social space for women to write, publish, and build communities."[6] Exploring the lives of elite women and the evolving gender discourse on women's education, family roles, and labor that accompanied the classical revival in the eighteenth century, Susan Mann identifies a conservative turn in gender norms reflecting the influence of the Qing dynasty's efforts to promote a "familistic moralism" among its Chinese and non-Chinese subjects. The successful propagation of patrilineal family values, among elite women at least, was due, in large part, to their ability to use dominant precepts about their educational and moral roles in the family to shape emotionally and intellectually fulfilling lives for themselves. The resilience of late imperial gender norms derived from the fact that in an era when "contradiction . . . seems to lie at the heart of every gender issue," they still offered women and men the resources to make sense of their complicated lives.[7]

This study began by applying these insights about the fluidity of the late imperial gender system and the contested, contradictory, and shifting meanings of female virtue to the examination of the only sources that show us the lives of nonelite, nonliterate women: criminal cases. I started this project by reading 866 central criminal cases preserved in the form of Board of Punishments routine memorials *(xingke tiben)* from the Number One Historical Archive in Beijing. The memorials come from six years of the Qianlong period (1736–96), randomly selected from years with large numbers of preserved cases to cross the span of the whole reign.[8] All from the archival category of "marriage and sex cases" *(hunyin jianqing)*, these memorials record the final stages of the extensive review process for serious criminal cases: that is, those involving a sentence greater than temporary banishment, usually a death penalty.[9] Used extensively by historians in recent years to examine many aspects of legal, social, and gender history, these cases document the practical interaction of the state's officials with its subjects through the judicial system, which, as we will see, served complex political and pedagogical functions while it adjudicated social conflicts. Rich as they are in details about the lives and views of ordinary women and men, these sources depict them only at the moment of their interaction with the state. Combing them for information about women's lives and the implications of gender norms in practice, one is compelled to pay attention to the Qing state's constructions of female virtue and the political context within which officials dealt with sexual assault, spousal homicide, adultery, and female suicide. Reading these cases in the context of the palace memorials (preserved in the archives as *zhupi zouzhe* and *lufu zouzhe*) through which governors, Board of Punishments officials, and provincial judicial commissioners made suggestions for changes in the law or reported local social problems, I began to see how the routine adjudication of such "disgraceful matters" fit with the broader set of state policies to regulate gender norms.

At the height of the Qing Empire's fluorescence, the chastity ethos permeated the processes and institutions of imperial state building and the dynamics of family and community life to an unprecedented degree. As chastity became more deeply implicated in state, family, and personal politics than it had ever been or would ever be again, it was intensely contested and entangled with issues of state power and legitimacy, family and self-interest, identity, status, and reputation. At the heart of the messy gender politics at every level of mid-Qing society was a struggle to define and implement a coherent and consensually accepted model of patriarchal family order. For as the promotion of chastity became an ever greater priority, it became increasingly clear to officials and ordinary people that the defense of chastity all too often worked against the interests of family authorities. Conflicts over female chastity starkly revealed the tensions between generational and conjugal notions of patriarchy and the fragmented nature of family authority in practice. A focus on this political aspect of chastity—its entanglement with power in the family, the local community, and the state—moves us away from the polarities of practice and precept, rigidity and fluidity, that structure much of the analysis of Chinese gender norms by highlighting the process through which norms were defined, enacted, enforced, and contested. From this perspective, the reproduction of the gender system was not simply a matter of the normative paradigm being adapted and negotiated by people in their social practice. Instead, the meaning of the norms shifted and varied in the midst of policy making and implementation, adjudication, social conflict, and the ordinary encounters of everyday life.

The very structure of case memorials, which document moments of state-society interaction and social conflict, suggests this emphasis on the dynamic instability of the gender system rather than its resilience. Like all routine memorials, *xingke tiben* were structured to reflect the document transmission process and bureaucratic procedure that produced them. At every step in the process of investigation, trial, and preparation of memorials, judicial officials, from county magistrates to prefects, provincial judicial commissioners, and board officials, were guided by detailed regulations governing rules of procedure, structure, composition, and even wording. Each memorial quotes extensively the original report on the case submitted by the county magistrate who first tried it and the reports of each level of the judiciary that reviewed the case: the prefect and the provincial judicial commissioner *(anchasi)* for memorials in the first stage of review and the Three High Courts *(sanfasi)* for memorials in the next stage. The magistrate's initial report usually includes transcripts of the initial plaint that was filed; the coroner's report, including descriptions of wounds suffered by all injured parties; a summary of the magistrate's investigatory procedure; excerpts from the statements and testimonies of critical witnesses and case participants, including, sometimes, the magistrate's questions to them in the courtroom; the defendant(s)' confession; and the magistrate's final summation of the case with recommended sentences. The reports of the higher levels reviewing the sentence usually include only the case summary and sentencing recommendations but occasionally also present further evidence from the requestioning of the defendant(s) and witnesses.

Structurally and linguistically, *xingke tiben* are hybrid documents that incorporate the written vernacular testimonies of case participants into the rigid structure of memorials in formal bureaucratic language. Juxtaposed to this official commentary, vernacular testimonies convey the impression that one is "hearing the voices" of the common people participating in the case. However, these testimonies were subject to several forms of editing. First, when legal secretaries recorded testimony in the course of on-site investigations and trials, they translated Chinese spoken in a local dialect (or minority languages) into a written form of vernacular speech that was standardized according to the northern dialect we call Mandarin. Second, the rules governing the construction of testimony mandated that it avoid wordiness, vulgar language, and localisms whose meaning was not readily apparent. Finally, the Qing rules of judicial procedure mandated that there be a precise match between the evidence presented from the investigation (numbers, sizes, and locations of wounds, details of timing and place, etc.), the various testimonies, and the final summation of the case, and they placed a great emphasis on application of the appropriate statute or substatute. The multifaceted processes of translation and editing affected not only vocabulary and phrasing but also sometimes the very "facts" of the case when divergent versions of events as seen by various case participants were molded into one consistent story that fit under the rubric of one statute or substatute.[10]

Despite the "fictional" aspects of these archival materials, historians can still decipher sufficient traces of the individual views of case participants to address questions about social life and mentalité.[11] They contain rich information about matters that are less tainted by the judicial construction of the case, like household structure, the day-to-day habits and leisure and work patterns of men and women, and these patterns' spatial contours. Read with attention to the context of their production, the cases also indicate where fissures of opinion occurred within families and communities and which aspects of the normative order and gender structure were contested in everyday life. They reveal discrepancies between popular and state views and values and show how officials applied and adapted the state's orthodoxy in practice. Though the picture of society presented in these cases may be circumscribed and distorted, it is not false.[12] Whatever their value as resources for social history, *xingke tiben* highlight the constructed and contentious nature of social realities in ways that compel us to question the fictions that historians take for orthodoxy and to wonder about the human interactions that create social phenomena like a cult of female chastity.

These kinds of judicial records are no longer extant for dynasties prior to the Qing, and they exist in significant numbers only from the middle of the eighteenth century onward. Nevertheless, the patterns of courtroom interaction and the complex functions of the adjudication process as a mechanism for state legitimation, propaganda, and social reform were no doubt similar in earlier eras. What was new in the mid-Qing was a political context within which routine adjudication of "disgraceful matters" was part of a larger normative agenda that aimed to reshape the relationship between the imperial state and its subjects. Part One of this study examines the nature of the state that people encountered in the eighteenth century as they entered the courtroom. Like many earlier foreign conquerors of China, the Manchu rulers of the Qing dynasty admired many aspects of Han Chinese culture and recognized the political necessity of patronizing and promoting it. Yet their approach to Chinese tradition, like that of the Mongol Yuan dynasty (1279–1368) rulers, was inevitably quite different from that of native dynasties for three critical reasons. However deep their identification with Chinese civilization, they were committed to preserving their distinct ethnic identity and culture; they governed empires that were multiethnic; and as borrowers and adapters of Chinese tradition, they were far more inclined to challenge cherished ideals and break with long-standing custom.[13]

Numerous scholars have shown how such a flexible cultural strategy was critical to the successful consolidation of Qing rule.[14] By the early eighteenth century, having pacified their opposition and returned China to a path of prosperous economic development and cultural efflorescence, Manchu rulers turned their political ambitions toward the expansion of the empire and the perfection of the state's control over its resources, personnel, and society at large. Qing policies toward the chastity cult reflected the cultural and moral impulses that accompanied this broader agenda of conquest and state building. Under the Yongzheng (1723–36) and Qianlong Emperors (1736–96), the state became, for the first time, the chief patron of the cult of chastity, avidly promoting female virtue through a diverse set of policy initiatives beyond the granting of chastity awards. With the support of reform-minded officials committed to the enforcement of ritual orthodoxy and the reinvigoration of social hierarchy, the dynasty developed an array of institutional mechanisms for state engagement with local society and radically transformed the nature of the chastity cult and its role in the political order: the reward system that had for several centuries functioned by distantly inspiring chastity through example became a thoroughly bureaucratized tool of moral reform, deployed within a complex set of policies designed to expand the state's regulation of society.

Unprecedented in their focus, scope, and complexity, these initiatives were a critical component of the imperial civilizing project that aimed to transform the customs of both newly incorporated non-Han peoples on the frontiers and Han subjects in the heartland. It touched on many of the key areas of traditional statecraft concern: law, ritual regulation of marriage and state honors, reform of local customs, the suppression of heterodox religious sects, education, acculturation of non-Han peoples, economic development, and even management of the penal system. In shrines, temples, and schools run by local magistrates and through judicial proceedings, public rites honoring the virtuous, and public readings and performances of the Kangxi Emperor's Sacred Edict, imperial subjects regularly experienced the state's civilizing presence and were reminded of the canon of state-sanctioned values, including chastity, filiality, and frugality.[15] Yet despite the apparent conservatism of this agenda, these policies reflected a new activist and interventionist approach to the promotion of female virtue that aimed to enhance state legitimacy and cultural hegemony by making it the central arbiter of gender order. In the ongoing process of defining and redefining a state gender orthodoxy, Qing rulers upheld many elements of the existing Chinese gender order but also showed a willingness to oppose or undermine customs that they found abhorrent or politically problematic. Moreover, the expanded eighteenth-century chastity cult represented a profound innovation in the technologies that structured state-society interactions. The dynasty's assertion of the state's prerogative to control the interpretation and practice of female virtue fundamentally transformed the modes and meanings of ruler-subject relations. Paradoxically, this assertion of an expanded normative relevance for the state did not result in straightforward state control of the process of defining and enforcing behavioral norms in local society. Indeed, an account of the significance of the Qing chastity cult must reconcile the state's hegemonic claim as ultimate framer and arbiter of the moral and social order with the copious evidence of the limits of its authority at the local level.

Up to this point, my study affirms the broadest conclusions reached by Matthew Sommer in his study of the judicial construction of illicit sex in late imperial China. Interpreting the state's promotion of a universal standard of female chastity in the context of the Yongzheng Emperor's elimination of debased-status categories, Sommer argues that Qing statutes on illicit sex heralded a new paradigm for the regulation of sexual behavior. The state's goal was no longer the preservation of a status hierarchy characterized by varying norms of sexual propriety but rather the maintenance of a gender order based on common moral standards defined in relation to the fulfillment of family roles. Sommer associates this shift in emphasis from status to gender performance with the expanded reach of the judicial system into family life to enforce its own norms of gender order, which focused on protecting the "settled peasant family," assumed to be the foundation of social order, from the sexual predations of "antisocial" males who threatened it from the outside.[16] Thus, although they were part of a larger state-building agenda that included a civilizing mission to enforce conformity with state norms, these developments reflected, at least in principle, a focus on the interests of common peasant families as the state envisioned them. Yet, Sommer concludes, the disjuncture between this new state orthodoxy and the lived experience of poor peasant families, especially women, ultimately limited the state's ability to transform the values of its subjects. Nevertheless, "The cumulative thrust of these initiatives [to regulate illicit sex] was to extend a uniform standard of sexual morality and criminal liability to all. This uniform standard, based on rigid interpretation of the normative marital roles expected of commoners, left less room for variation and exception than before."[17]

Shaped by questions about how the state defined and regulated illicit sex, Sommer's study emphasizes the coherence of the state's agenda and its effects. In contrast, I begin by looking for process rather than paradigm, asking questions of why and how chastity became politically important in the Qing, what it meant to rulers, officials, moralists, and ordinary women and men, and how it influenced political culture and social practice. By examining not just how the state imagined moral order but how the concept of chastity actually worked in policy making, courtroom interactions, and family and community conflicts, this study highlights the contradictions in the state's goals, the messiness of their implementation, and their unintended consequences. I see state initiatives, including the creation of new substatutes, developed and asserted from the outset through subtle negotiation between state and society as officials and ordinary subjects encountered one another directly in the courtroom and indirectly through the allocation of ritual honors and the implementation of educational and economic programs at the local level. A focus on these processes reveals that while the state certainly desired to impose a uniform vision of gender order, its own laws and policies were fraught with contradictions and reflected compromises with popular mores, most critically with women's own views of virtue. The remarkable political prominence and popularity of the cult of chastity in this period, I argue, can best be explained not as the imposition of a uniform state orthodoxy but as the motley outcome of a complex interplay among imperial agendas, elite priorities, and the views and values of ordinary people, especially women.

Part Two analyzes the complexities of these interactions and their implications for the practice of chastity and the exercise of patriarchal authority on the local level. The state played a critical yet circumscribed role in structuring the local communities immediately involved in the interpretation and enforcement of gender norms. It is clear in the case record that people at every level of society were aware of state-defined orthodoxy with regard to female virtue. However, the state was not the only, and usually not the primary, arbiter active on a daily basis in the discursive communities that coalesced to mediate disputes and adjudicate transgressions. As it promoted its orthodoxy and enforced its laws, the state was one of many sources of normative authority at the local level and asserted itself through continual processes of negotiation not only with local elites but also with common people through the judicial system. Despite the limitations on its normative role, the state figured prominently in people's minds and in social practice as an option for seeking punishment of transgression or revenge. Moreover, even when county magistrates were not directly engaged in arbitrating conflicts over female virtue and enforcing orthodox norms, their very presence as embodiments of orthodox authority and sources of serious punishment altered local processes of conflict mediation and retribution. Although its impact on society rarely took the form desired by statecraft thinkers, the state's presence, imbricated in diverse aspects of local life, worked to reproduce its legitimacy as the keeper of socioethical order.

Qing policy makers, as many scholars have noted, were deeply concerned about the health of the patriarchal family and hoped that the promotion of chastity would bolster proper family hierarchy. Within the rhetoric on the civilizing project, the restoration of a gender order based on female chastity and gender separation was, indeed, inseparable from the revitalization of family and community authorities. In reality, though, there were multiple contradictions between the goals of promoting chastity and invigorating patriarchal authority. Moreover, the crisis of patriarchy, as perceived by mid-Qing officials and revealed in social practice, was due not primarily to external threats but, even more critically, to tensions within the family and the moral paradoxes inherent in norms of family practice. Although judicial discourse on sexual assaults of all kinds often invoked the threat of rootless male outsiders preying upon women and children of good families, officials were far more deeply and frequently disturbed by the weakness, corruption, and compromised authority of fathers, husbands, lineage leaders, community elders, and even local magistrates. These patriarchal authorities, imagined by the architects of the civilizing project to be pivotal local players in the promotion, defense, and vindication of state-defined gender orthodoxy, turned out to be problematic partners. The desire of Qing policy makers for an effective patriarchal authority that could provide the foundation for a civilized social order was continually thwarted by the fragmentation and contestation of that authority in practice. While in some contexts fathers, husbands, and lineage leaders promoted chastity to augment their authority, in others women or state officials defended female virtue against the perceived interests and opposition of patrilineal authorities. The legitimacy of lineage and family authorities as arbiters of moral norms was frequently challenged. Transgressions of married women's virtue implicated not only their husbands' families but their own, resulting in the frequent contestation of patrilineal prerogatives by women's natal families. Contrary to the assumptions of much judicial discussion on rape, most cases of sexual assault and adultery involved not male outsiders but neighbors, friends, and quite often even relatives. Cases of incest between fathers- and daughters-in-law or brothers- and sisters-in-law often set the defense of chastity in direct conflict with the exercise of patriarchal authority, placing the adjudicating officials and policy makers in an unresolvable quandary that eroded the foundational assumptions of the chastity cult.

Complicating still further the project of revitalizing and strengthening a patriarchal family order was the ongoing tension between patrilineal and conjugal notions of family patriarchy within state policy and social practice. Conflicts over female virtue, especially those involving incest and disputes over widows' management of their husbands' property, often pitted loyalty and obedience to a husband against the interests of his patriline.[18] As Sommer describes it, the shift from status to gender performance implied a new emphasis on the marital bond as the primary familial relationship, since the chastity that defined proper womanhood meant sexual loyalty to one's husband first and foremost. Both the impassioned conjugal focus of nonstate rhetoric on the chastity cult and the rising popularity of ideals of companionate marriage similarly augured the emergence of a new gender order centered on marital patriarchy. The ample evidence in the case record of social tensions arising from the divergent interests and competing authority of husbands and their patrilines suggests that this transition was incomplete. The instability of patriarchy as norm and practice was the subject of considerable discussion and legislation throughout the Yongzheng and Qianlong reigns. Yet, as their floundering in the face of incest cases indicates, most officials were neither willing nor able to assert a consistent definition of patriarchy, caught as they were between their own ideals of social order and the unintended implications of their commitment to the defense of chastity.

Similar gaps between the state's ideals and the working logic it applied to social policy and adjudication characterized the legislation on sexual assault. Part Three presents a reading of the rape statute as the expression of a profound misrecognition of the sources of gender disorder whose implementation resulted in continual compromises of state norms. The statute codified a definition of chastity as the linchpin of a gender order constructed around the separation of the sexes and threatened primarily by the moral weakness of women and the predations of rogue males cut off from the strictures and benefits of the family system. To differentiate consensual from coerced illicit sex, the rape statute homed in on the problem of proving the chastity of a woman's intent. But women themselves struggled to define and maintain their chastity in a society in which the boundary between the inner realm of the family in which they were supposed to be cloistered and the outer world was usually permeable and subject to local and personal interpretation. More often than not, the inner-outer paradigm functioned not as a spatial or social divide but as a fluid rubric for propriety in the interactions between women and men that were commonplace for most people. Given the importance of chastity for reputation, it was women themselves who had the greatest stake in upholding propriety in these social encounters. Coping with perpetual compromises of idealized gender norms in their living and work situations, women maintained the inner-outer distinction by cultivating a "sense of shame" that guided them in "avoiding suspicion" of impropriety in their inevitable interactions with men. Violation of chastity was, for them, not merely an assault on their bodies and certainly not an assault on their husbands' sexual monopoly, but a humiliation that undermined their sense of personhood. The unworkable contradictions of the rape statute forced adjudicating magistrates to focus on women themselves as the chief defenders of chastity and thus to respond to their understandings of violation, which quite often prevailed in the final analysis of sexual assault cases. Far from being a fixed behavioral norm, the chastity affirmed through this dialectical interaction between would-be chaste women and the state was a purity of intent that could be manifested in diverse ways.

State recognition of women's perspectives on chastity culminated in the proliferation during the Qianlong reign of a plethora of new substatutes to deal with women's suicides in the wake of assault, unwanted flirtation, or insult. Anxious about the collapse of inner-outer dichotomy in social life and confronted with epidemic numbers of women committing suicide after being assaulted, physically or verbally harassed, or even accidentally humiliated, judicial officials elaborated the rape statute into a tangled web of laws intended to punish every possible violation of chastity. Part Four examines the controversy surrounding this legitimation of female outrage and its implications for women's agency and the family politics of female suicide. The new substatutes made women's perceptions of insult or impropriety the defining element in crimes that resulted in very serious punishments for the offender, ranging from flogging at the very least to death. Ironically, they did so at a time when most officials, moral commentators, and even male popular opinion held very disparaging views of women's potential for moral agency, seeing them as irrationally oversensitive to insult, prone to temptation, or ignorant of true ritual propriety.

At the height of the chastity cult, women thus faced profoundly contradictory expectations about their virtue: they were required to uphold the strictest standards of chastity, yet they were assumed to be morally weak-willed and prone to overreaction. Such assumptions together with the new substatutes created the complex family and community politics that surrounded women's humiliation and suicide and efforts to deal with the disgrace they caused. Women and men, and women and their family authorities, had very different understandings of and stakes in chastity-centered virtue. A woman's chastity could bring her family status, social leverage, and sometimes state honors, while the perceived lack of chastity could result in family disgrace. For women themselves, a chaste reputation was inextricably bound up with individual notions of femininity, moral integrity, and personhood. Case records indicate that women usually chose suicide when their humiliation was not requited or as an act of revenge upon their assailants. For while women almost always sought public vindication of their virtue and often demanded that the incident be reported to the magistrate, their husbands, fathers, and parents-in-law were usually reluctant to "spread disgraceful matters outside" by involving the state. In the political, ritual, and legal context of the High Qing, women's suicides could be powerful public statements and aggressive acts that ensured severe judicial, ritual, and symbolic consequences. For the women themselves, suicide was more fundamentally a redemption of personhood.

Paradoxically, the Qing chastity cult itself had profoundly destabilizing consequences for a late imperial gender order based on the dichotomy of the inner domestic realm and the outer public realm. To an unprecedented degree, private female virtue became meaningful only through a very public process of interpretation that made it inseparable from public reputation and integral to public discourse on the nature and aims of the state. Women of the inner quarters were the most public of women. Their bodies and the most intimate aspects of their lives were among the most prominent issues in public discussion, whether statecraft debates, trial proceedings, or community conflicts. The shape and content of the chastity cult shifted to fit the changing needs, interests, agendas, and obsessions of the day, but the political apotheosis of chastity in the High Qing in its turn had transformative effects not only on gender order but on political culture, law, and state-society relations. As the imperial state reached into the inner quarters of family life, seeking to mold behavior and moral intent, it placed women at the center of political culture, making female virtue integral to imperial state building and the civilizing project that legitimated it.

PART ONE

The Chastening State

*The Qing Chastity Cult in Ritual,
Law, and Statecraft*

Prologue: A Chaste Barbarian Martyrs Herself on the Imperial Frontier

In 1752, the eighteenth year of the Qianlong reign, a twenty-*sui*-old Miao woman named Wang Aguan, from a walled village in the Puan District of southwestern Guizhou Province, committed suicide after being sexually assaulted by her cousin, Wang Ali. Her suicide embroiled their family in a court case that resulted in a death sentence for her assailant, lesser punishments for various relatives who had failed to report the crime, and Wang Aguan's official canonization by the Qing state as a chastity martyr, the first Miao woman thus honored in the district.[1] Although the case was set in a remote frontier region of the Qing Empire, the circumstances of the suicide and the nature of the ensuing encounter between the imperial state and a local community were typical for the latter half of the eighteenth century. The encounter was structured by the complex institutions and practices of a state chastity cult that in the mid-Qing consisted not only of a system for awarding chastity but also of laws and educational, economic, and cultural policies designed to promote chastity-centered female virtue as the foundation of family and community order.[2] The case dramatizes the curious convergence of the agendas of state building, imperial expansion, and promotion of female chastity that was a hallmark of the High Qing era.

Aguan's life, like the lives of many Chinese women in this period, was complicated and rather transgressive from the standpoint of dominant norms of gender propriety. She had been married for two years to a Miao man from a neighboring village but often came home to her natal village to live for prolonged periods of time because, according to her brother, her husband's family was very poor. But it is highly likely that the poverty explanation masked the fact that this was a delayed-transfer marriage. This form of marriage, in which the wife remained with her natal family for up to three years after the marriage rites, was common among the Miao in Puan District in the mid–eighteenth century, but it incurred the strong disapproval of Han Chinese authorities. The district gazetteer described the practice as "bestial."[3] Like most Miao women and quite a few Chinese women, especially in the South, Aguan worked in her family's fields, engaging in a kind of farm labor widely considered improper for women because it took them outside the walls of the family compound and even the village. Such compromised work and living circumstances provided the context for many incidents of casual flirtation, adultery, harassment, and assault by male relatives or neighbors. In Aguan's case, the incident occurred when she was out alone one day releasing water into a distant field in a mountain hollow and gathering grasses for the pigs. Her cousin Wang Ali came up to her, grabbed her hand, put his arm around her neck, and began to "flirt" with her. She bit his finger and screamed, attracting the attention of a Han Chinese man from a neighboring village who was working in his own fields nearby. That man accompanied her back home, where she tearfully told her brother Wang Axiang and her sister Amian what had happened. Amian asked the village headmen, who were also their uncles, to confront Ali and seek an apology. But when the uncles went to his house, Ali was not home, and his father, Ahai, denied the accusation, saying, "They are cousins. How could there be such an incident? What's there to discuss?"

The next day Aguan's brother and sister went again to confront Ali, telling him that if he came out to kowtow and apologize, the matter would come to a close. Ali's father, however, counseled him not to admit anything and accused Aguan of inventing the sexual assault because she and Ali had fought over the use of water in the fields. He called her "a monster who does not care about honor." Humiliated, Aguan hanged herself the next day. Her brother reported her death to the headquarters of the army brigade stationed in the district, as the law required him to do. When Ali's father learned of this, he, too, hanged himself—according to his wife and sons, out of dread at the prospect of official involvement, which was widely seen to compound the disgrace caused by such incidents.

As in many such cases, the precise nature of the interaction between Aguan and Ali was initially unclear, and there was conflict over the appropriate course of action to take in response. Ali first claimed that Aguan was lying, and his family filed a counterplaint accusing her of provoking his father's suicide by intimidating him with the assault accusation in order to get the upper hand in a conflict over water rights. Later, under threat of torture, he confessed that he was "possessed by demons and wanted to have illicit sex with her."[4] In the end, he was sentenced to strangulation after the assizes for attempted rape resulting in the suicide of the victim.

Whatever transpired in the fields that day, Ali's father's intense fear of state intervention was not unwarranted in this heavily garrisoned province. Direct Qing administration of the largely non-Han region had been forcibly established under the *gaitu guiliu* policy (replacing local headmen with regular officials), which subsumed the previously Miao-administered area under Nanlong Prefecture in 1728.[5] The region had been heavily militarized ever since: in Puan, such local criminal matters were reported first not to a civil official but to the local brigade commander. The Chinese civil magistrate who tried the case interrogated his Miao defendants, victims, and witnesses with a tone of mixed suspicion, contempt, and paternalism. He repeatedly berated the participants for their ignorance of propriety and the law, prompting each witness to end his testimony with some variation of the disclaimer that "we are barbarian people and do not know about ritual propriety and obligation." In his interrogations, the magistrate focused first on trying to establish whether the relationship between the victim and the offender was within the grades of mourning and thus whether the offense was incestuous.[6] One after another, family members protested their ignorance of such matters, insisting that only the lineage elders could explain their relationships in Chinese kinship terms, since "we barbarians do not know anything about mourning relations."

The magistrate then turned to the nature of Aguan's suicide, saying to her brother in a patronizing tone, "Your sister was weeping and wailing in rage and humiliation. You people should have had someone keep watch, fearing she would be shortsighted [and rashly want to kill herself]. Why is it that you failed to keep watch, . . . causing her to hang herself?" Her brother defended the integrity of the family's actions, emphasizing their sense of honor:

Our whole family tried to console her with kind words and told her not to be upset because Ali would come out and admit his guilt and apologize.... We couldn't help it that Ahai protected his son so that he was unwilling to admit fault and they just stood by the wayside and didn't care. He even slandered my sister saying she was some kind of demon who had no sense of honor and tried to slander him. This caused my sister to become even more upset. [The next day] she hanged herself. It was a busy agricultural season and my family had to go to the fields. We didn't take precautions against her developing this short-sighted view and killing herself. Please be the judge of our actions.

Interrogating the village headmen, the magistrate pursued the possibility that the assault accusation had been intended as a form of intimidation:

This incident of Ali attempting to rape Aguan happened on the 19th. If Aguan was really humiliated and outraged, she should have killed herself on that very day. Why did she wait until the 21st to hang herself? When her brother informed you, why didn't you immediately come to report the case to the authorities for investigation and punishment? And also, if Ali is suspected of rape, then he alone must come to court and bear the burden of guilt. It has nothing to do with Ali's father. So why would Ahai go and hang himself? This must have to do with someone using the illicit sex incident as an excuse to force him to commit suicide.

Another village elder claimed he had intended to report the case but events had developed too quickly. He denied that anyone had pressured Ahai into killing himself. Finally, he said simply, "We ignorant Miao people have no knowledge [of these things]. I can only beg for your mercy" *(Xiaode men yu miao wuzhi. Zhi qiu kai en)*.

At a time when the cult of female chastity was in its heyday, it was not uncommon for women to commit suicide in response to sexual insults that were not redressed.[7] In Han society, such suicides were widely valorized as acts of heroism that incontrovertibly vindicated a woman's assertion of chastity. With thousands of women across the empire being honored each year by the state or their local communities as chastity martyrs or chaste widows, the sexual virtue of women was a critical element of individual and family reputation. Even the remote, largely non-Han district of Puan had its own local paragons of female virtue. Six Han Chinese chastity heroines from the Ming were recognized in the district gazetteer for defending their chastity to the death in the face of Miao rebel attacks. In 1744, Governor-General Zhang Guangsi made the first request during the Qing for imperial canonization of a Puan woman who had drowned herself to avoid violation in a rape attempt.[8] Her chaste heroism was publicly commemorated in twice-yearly sacrifices in the district's first Shrine to the Chaste and Filial *(jie xiao si)*, constructed by imperial instruction in 1733 near the Confucius Temple *(wenmiao)*, just outside the north gate of the district town.

It is impossible to know for sure what a Miao woman like Aguan knew of these Han Chinese heroines. Perhaps on her journeys from her husband's to her natal home she had passed by the shrine with its giant stone arch where her own name would soon be inscribed. The case testimonies indicate that her family and the elders in her village knew something of Chinese customs and law. Both the case participants and the magistrate judged behavior with reference to assumed standards of Han orthodoxy that were never clearly defined. The filing of the countersuit suggests some degree of familiarity with the Qing legal system and acceptance of its usefulness for the pursuit of personal grievances.[9] Although this Miao family cleverly used their "barbarian" status as an excuse for ignorance of Chinese norms, they, like their Han counterparts in hundreds of other cases, ultimately explained their actions using the language of honor. Both suicides were prompted by loss of face. Reputation was a more salient motivation than adherence to law or ritual orthodoxy.[10]

The moral and cultural content of this orthodoxy, as it was presented to local villagers through the judicial system or state-sponsored shrines and schools, was inseparable from the authority and institutional presence of the Qing state. Because the magistrate in Aguan's case assumed the ignorance and impropriety of his non-Han constituents, he was more explicit and patronizing than most in articulating the requirements of law and the expectations of state orthodoxy. However, his multifaceted responsibility here as judge, moral reformer, and propagator of the dominant cultural values was not substantially different from that of magistrates dealing with cases involving transgressions of gender norms among Han people in the heartland. Nor was the content of his missionizing concern unique: judicial officials routinely used the adjudication of cases of sexual assault, harassment, adultery, and domestic violence as an opportunity to explain and attempt to enforce normative expectations about family relationships, gender roles, virtuous behavior, and the role of the state as the primary source of vindication, punishment, and moral authority. In the most influential magistrate's handbook of the mid-Qing, Wang Huizu (1731–1807) emphasized this civilizing role of the magistrate and the educational effectiveness of court proceedings:

In the big courtroom no fewer than several hundred people gather to watch [the proceedings]. Through the adjudication of only one matter, . . . the true and the false will be amplified for all who stand within hearing distance. Those not involved in lawsuits will be forewarned and litigants will be mollified. Thus, chastising [only] one person, you must continue repeatedly to educate and enlighten. If you make an example of the person being chastised, then the hidden feelings of those who have not been chastised will be imperceptibly transformed. . . . Moreover, the issues behind lawsuits deal for the most part with everyday matters of the five relationships. So adjudicating lawsuits extends filiality, friendliness, and social harmony, . . . facilitating moral transformation.[11]

Such prescriptive visions of magisterial duties suggest that the judicial system worked in concert with the cult of chastity to promote orthodox norms of behavior among the Han Chinese in the heartland and among newly conquered peoples on the "uncivilized" frontiers.

But did it? In this case, the Qing state granted its highest honors for chastity to a Miao woman whose quite unorthodox marriage and work practices were the immediate context for her humiliation. What, precisely, was being venerated in the twice-yearly sacrifices and rites honoring her tablet in the local chastity shrine? The magistrate recommended state canonization as a chastity martyr for "this Miao woman, Aguan, who was righteous and unable to endure humiliation and, vehement in her chastity, sacrificed her life." Although it would seem that he found the chastity of this young Miao woman, which she had asserted in an orthodox Han manner, to be extraordinary, such melodramatic language was typical of the encomiums with which judicial officials recommended chastity martyrs for imperial honors. In accordance with dynastic regulations promulgated in 1654, the state bestowed thirty taels of silver on Aguan's family to construct a stone arch outside their gate as an impressive and constant reminder for her community not only of her virtue but of the state's benevolence and the prestige of the cultural values it represented. In accordance with regulations from 1723, her name would also be inscribed on a tablet placed in the Puan district's Shrine to the Chaste and Filial and on a giant stone arch outside its gate. The prayer presented by the local magistrate to the spirits of chastity martyrs during twice-annual rites at this shrine offered "wholehearted respect" for their "resolve to perfect chastity and preserve the integrity of the inner quarters." These rites, the prayer asserted, will "make manifest the models of virtue in the inner quarters." But the prayer also praised imperial benevolence in establishing such shrines "to display the laws and regulations [of the dynasty]." The shrine and the rites conducted within it advertised Aguan's martyrdom as a fulfillment of state-defined orthodoxy and an affirmation of Qing cultural and moral authority.¹²

In dealing with Aguan's suicide, the magistrate was, in principle, upholding Chinese orthodox standards of kinship relations and female virtue. But what he in fact enforced in this case was a particular, complicated set of state-defined expectations and rules about how chaste women and their families should behave; how family authorities should deal with disgraceful matters like affronts to chastity and consequent women's outrage; when and how proper suicides should take place; and how they should be handled. He asserted, indeed imposed, not just a set of cultural norms but the presence of the state as the central arbiter and definer of virtue and its proper behavioral expression.

Both the magistrate's mission and the state-defined "orthodoxy" underlying this set of expectations were contingent products of a particular moment in a long process of enacting a new normative role for the state through the creation of a new state discourse on moral transformation *(jiaohua)*, bureaucratic institutions, and laws. That process began with the consolidation of Qing rule and culminated in the state-building and civilizing projects of the Yongzheng (1723–36) and Qianlong (1736–96) Emperors, which shaped the institutions and political culture of state-society interactions well into the nineteenth century.

CHAPTER I

Defining Gender Orthodoxy for a Multiethnic Empire

INTERPRETING TRADITION

Chinese dynasties had for centuries issued awards for extraordinary virtue to the chaste and filial to provide exemplars for the moral cultivation of their subjects and to enhance their own image of virtue and benevolence. Shortly after the founding of their new dynasty, Qing rulers announced their reestablishment of the traditional imperial award system to canonize "filial sons, obedient grandsons, righteous husbands, and faithful widows." The clichéd wording of the edict was intended to invoke the age-old link between imperial benevolence, moral authority, and the dynasty's mandate to rule. However, this ritualized pronouncement masked the dramatic and, for Qing rulers, disturbing shift in the imperial award system over the course of the preceding Ming dynasty. Rhetoric about filiality, obedience, and righteousness aside, the state canonization system had come to focus mostly on awarding chaste widows and widow suicides who martyred themselves after the deaths of their husbands.

As numerous scholars have observed, the elevation of chaste widows as the ultimate models of gender orthodoxy originated in the Song and was first enshrined in state policy in the Yuan dynasty. But the chastity exemplified by Song and Yuan models was quite different from that expressed by their late Ming descendants. The emerging discourse on chastity among Neo-Confucian scholars in the Song justified it explicitly in terms of the economic interests of the husband's patriline. Song women, like their ancestors in many previous dynasties, inherited substantial property in the form of dowry that remained separate from the property of their husbands' families and under their own control. Widows typically returned to their natal families with their dowry and any other property they had accumulated during the marriage, all of which would accompany them if they remarried, as they often did. Although women's property rights were supported in Song law, Neo-Confucian scholars were increasingly critical of them as subversive of the prosperity and ritual integrity of the male patriline, whose reinvigoration was key to their social agenda. Their rhetoric on widow chastity emphasized the virtue of women who used their dowry to support their husbands' families and served them even after the death of their husbands.[1]

Bettine Birge explains how this radically new idea that a woman should remain with her husband's patriline until her own death came to be enshrined in law for the first time in the Yuan period, when a complex and confusing interplay between Mongolian and Chinese marriage customs prompted the state's repeated attempts to regulate marriage and inheritance practices. As the influence of Neo-Confucian philosophy grew among Yuan rulers and elites, an odd congruence emerged between the Mongol practice of the levirate and the Neo-Confucian ideal of widow chastity, with its emphasis on retaining women's property and labor for the husband's patriline. This commonality of emphasis on marriage as a permanent transfer of a woman's body and property to her husband's family fostered the institutionalization of state support for widow chastity in the form of awards for chaste widows and laws prohibiting women from taking any property out of a first marriage if they returned to their natal families or remarried.[2]

The Ming state carried over both the laws and the ritual regulations that encouraged widow chastity. But as the notion of chastity became widely popular as a cultural ideal and in social practice, its meaning began to shift away from its moorings in the principle of patrilineality. The virtue of chaste widowhood was gradually overshadowed in the popular imagination by the much more extreme expression of wifely chastity through suicide. Whatever accolades and state recognition it may have won, this practice of "following [a husband] in death" *(xunsi)*, in practical terms, subverted the interests of the husband's family. In the name of loyalty to the husband alone, widows who joined their husbands in death abandoned their responsibilities to care for children and in-laws. Katherine Carlitz and Fei Si-yen have shown how the biographies and eulogies of chastity martyrs written by the literati men who were the primary patrons of the chastity cult in the Ming were increasingly tinged with the pathos of fathers, brothers, and uncles grieving for beloved female relatives.[3] Even when the men had never met the subjects of their commemorations, as was often the case, they identified passionately with these self-sacrificing heroines, who represented the loftiest form of the loyalty that was the heart of literati ethics in this period. By the end of the Ming, the "chastity concept" was thoroughly infused with *qing*, the passion or sentiment praised by fiction writers and philosophers alike as an ideal of cultural sensibility. The often gruesome depictions of the suicides of widows and betrothed maidens highlighted their defiance of family elders and their essentially romantic devotion to their husbands or fiancés. Such chastity was not about the economic or ritual interests of the patrilineal family unit; rather, it was an expression of the emotional primacy of the patriarchal family centered on the conjugal relationship.

Over the course of the dynasty, as the numbers of chastity heroines increased dramatically, the Ming state attempted to exert greater control over the definition of canonizable chastity and the process of identifying worthy women. It expanded the categories of recognized chastity and furthered the bureaucratization of the cult by tightening eligibility criteria and systematizing award procedures. But while the Ming state cult worked to enhance the prestige of female chastity and, to some degree, to standardize its definition, the state did not make the promotion and enforcement of the values associated with the chastity cult a critical priority. The state was not the main impetus for the wider social popularity of chastity, nor was it interested in shaping the practice or meaning of chastity.[4] The state canonization system in the Ming served merely to affirm and provide dynastic prestige to this highly localized cult of chastity that was inspired and promoted primarily by literati men to honor women in their families and local communities.[5]

By the time early Qing rulers took up administration of the award system, the passionate conjugal devotion of the chastity martyr had become the dominant metaphor for literati loyalty to the dying Ming regime. The political dangers of this linkage were not lost on early Qing rulers. Shortly after the conquest, they attempted to refocus expressions of chastity on the more prosaic practice of lifelong widowhood by issuing the first of many bans on widow suicide and prohibitions of its canonization. Yet they also approached the management of the chastity cult with a new understanding of the imperial state's cultural role and the political function of orthodoxy in its interactions with society. They took seriously the notion of the civilizing role of the ruler, his duty to reform barbaric and inhumane customs, and linked it to an evolving idea of universal rulership that guided them in consolidating control over their multiethnic empire.[6] The civilized culture they promoted varied, however, across the empire's diverse ethnic groups and shifted over time in response to changing imperial priorities and circumstances.[7] The Qing state cult of chastity became one among a diverse array of tools for the civilizing project of the universal empire. Under the first two Qing emperors, Shunzhi (1644–62) and Kangxi (1662–1722), the dynasty expanded the state's canonization system, granting monies for commemorative arches *(pailou, paifang)* and designating non-Han groups for eligibility. Placing equal stress on the universality of the emperor's benevolence and the particularity of his patronage of distinct ethnic groups with varying political status, Qing regulations stipulated that Han subjects, Manchu, Mongol, and Han martial bannermen, and members of the imperial clan would all be equally eligible for awards but that each group would be subject to different, parallel procedures and that the forms of award would vary.[8]

This flexible and essentially political approach to state orthodoxy worked a subtle transformation of the normative content of the state chastity cult and its relation to literati culture and patronage. With their bans on footbinding, widow suicide, and *gegu* (the practice of cutting off a piece of flesh, usually from the thigh or liver, to make medicinal soup to cure a dying parent), early Qing rulers attempted to eradicate practices with visceral links to foundational Han cultural values: feminine virtue, loyalty, filiality.[9] Though the bans met with uneven success, they established the dynasty's claim to be the primary definer and arbiter of norms governing gender roles and family life, thus undermining the effective monopoly of literati and local elites over definitions of orthodoxy in these areas.[10] Kangxi's edict announcing the ban on widow suicide exemplifies this assertion of a new normative role for the state:

> Recently we have noticed that there are still many women in the capital region and in the provinces who are following in death *(congsi)*. The consequences for human life are tremendous. Death is really a pitiable thing. Nature takes its course in determining the length of a lifetime. How can one recklessly sacrifice one's life? Taking life lightly by following in death *(qingsheng congsi)* is uncanonical. If we continue to commend [such behavior], then I fear that many more lives will be destroyed. If from now on there are no longer any honors for following in death, then [the practice] should cease. Following in death is forever forbidden for everyone from princesses of the imperial clan down to commoner women. If there is a woman who feels she must sacrifice her life out of principle *(shenxun)*,

then she should plead her case to appropriate officials of the Board [of Rites] and seek their permission.[11]

The emperor claims that there is nothing admirable or canonical about widows unnecessarily sacrificing their lives to follow their husbands to the grave. The ban on such suicides and their canonization will ideally prevent such abhorrent, inhumane, and needless deaths. Although his final caveat to the ban appears to contradict this goal, he carefully uses another term to distinguish this acceptable suicide from the unacceptable *congsi*, which is characterized as "reckless" *(wang)* and "taking life lightly" *(qingsheng)*. This term, *shenxun*, refers to the sacrifice of one's life for one's beliefs or principles. Principled suicide undertaken after careful deliberation is thus understood to be categorically different from taking life lightly, and, the emperor asserts, only the state can judge whether a suicide is principled.

Over the course of the dynasty, the official definition of acceptable expressions of chastity was continually in flux, but the state's assertion of its prerogative in normative matters remained constant. Precedent-setting exceptions were granted under Kangxi for canonization of women who died or killed themselves resisting rape if they were not actually raped; betrothed girls who performed the highest level of three-year mourning by the side of their fiancé's grave and then killed themselves; betrothed girls who, upon hearing of the death of their fiancé, were so resolved to maintain chastity that they starved themselves to death; and widows committed to raising their sons and maintaining their chastity who killed themselves after being pressured by relatives to remarry.[12] Yongzheng began canonization of women who committed suicide in response to a proposition.[13]

This expansion of categories of state-sanctioned chastity suicides served as a politically benign and pragmatic gesture of support for the values of Han literati, whose movement for revival of ritual and moral orthodoxy was gaining momentum over the first half of the eighteenth century.[14] Yet it also made the state the effective arbiter of what was and was not an orthodox expression of chastity. Exceptions to the ban on suicide honors were framed by the distinction between reckless and principled suicide. All were justified on the basis that these women were fundamentally "unlike those who ordinarily take life lightly" *(yu xunchang qingshengzhi bu tong)* or that their suicides "were not committed out of an extremist desire to take life lightly" *(yuan fei jilie qingsheng)*. These suicides were carefully and long-considered acts committed some time after the death of the husband or fiancé. They were inspired, not in the heat of the moment by irrational passion, but by an immediate and severe threat or a well-thought-out sense of familial duty, manifested in observance of the full mourning period or the raising of sons. By establishing the principle of distinguishing between acceptable and unacceptable suicides, the dynasty asserted the state's prerogative to set the conceptual boundaries for the interpretation, not only of female martyrdom, but of gender norms in general.

BUREAUCRATIZATION OF THE CHASTITY CULT UNDER YONGZHENG

If the first two reigns of the dynasty saw the creation of a new state discourse on female virtue, it was the Yongzheng Emperor who constructed the institutional edifice to promote and enforce the evolving state orthodoxy. While in the early Qing the chastity cult was caught up in the political dynamics and priorities of dynastic consolidation, under Yongzheng it became a tool for state building and imperial expansion, emblematic of a mid-Qing vision of statecraft *(jingshi)* that wedded institutional reform with the moral transformation of society. As they crafted strategies to enhance the efficiency and central government control of administration, fiscal management, famine relief, frontier management, bureaucratic communications, and policy-making procedures, Yongzheng and his top officials assumed that the improved exercise of state power required the moral reform of officialdom and the general populace.[15] At the same time, the ultimate success of this civilizing project depended upon extending the reach and influence of the state on the expanding frontiers and in the Han heartland.[16] Inspired by this mission to chasten society, to purify and discipline it, Yongzheng dramatically transformed the institutional nature of the chastity cult and its role in the political order: the reward system that had functioned as a symbolic hallmark of dynastic virtue, distantly inspiring chastity through example, became a thoroughly bureaucratized tool of moral reform, deployed within a complex set of policies designed to engineer social transformation.

Within the first year of his reign, the Yongzheng Emperor issued numerous regulations, unprecedented in quantity and detail, and intended to enhance the reach, prominence, efficiency, and integrity of the state's system for awarding chastity.[17] He ordered every provincial, prefectural, county, and district seat in the empire to construct a Shrine to the Chaste and Filial *(jiexiao ci)* where the ancestral tablets of officially canonized

Defining Gender Orthodoxy

women would be placed and officials would preside over sacrifices twice a year. Yongzheng set guidelines for the shrines' location and design, designated local tax monies to fund construction and maintenance, and called for regular oversight by the Board of Works. He ordered local officials to ferret out models of virtue in the poorest, most remote regions of the empire and submit rosters of those eligible for honors in these shrines on a fixed yearly schedule. Finally, the emperor laid out detailed procedures for families wishing to apply for canonization of their women, requiring affidavits from relatives and neighbors and review at various levels of the bureaucracy.[18]

The aim of this bureaucratization of the chastity cult was twofold. On the one hand, the new regulations and procedures would tighten central state control of the award process and ensure its integrity, efficiency, and thoroughness, goals that the Yongzheng Emperor pursued in all of his bureaucratic reforms. On the other hand, a state cult that bestowed honors and recognition on large numbers of ordinary women and maintained an active ritual and physical presence in local communities would enhance the prestige of the values associated with state orthodoxy and, at the same time, work to legitimate the role of the state as a source of normative authority at the local level. Explaining the need for such state-maintained shrines in addition to the usual private arches, the emperor was explicit about their propagandistic function: "[W]hen silver is granted for construction of commemorative arches, the common people often take this to be a mere formality and never construct the arches. I fear that as time goes by [such examples of virtue] will vanish without a trace and there will be nothing to provide visual moral inspiration for the people." The shrines would thus serve to "illuminate hidden virtue and pass it on forever."[19] Stipulating that these shrines be freestanding edifices, with a huge commemorative arch standing outside the gate, inscribed with the names of all local chaste women, the emperor made clear his intention that they be seen by the broadest possible audience of men and women. In contrast, the Shrines to the Loyal, Righteous, and Filial *(zhongyi xiaodi ci)* established for virtuous men by the same edict were to be built inside the grounds of the local Confucian Temple and have, not an arch, but merely a stone stele placed inside the gates. Their audience would be limited to the literati men and aspiring male students who were most likely to visit such temples. Chastity heroines thus became the most numerous and the most widely publicized models of state-defined virtue. The impact of the new bureaucratized chastity cult over the latter half of the eighteenth century was evident in local communities across the empire in the phenomenal increase in the numbers of chaste widows and chastity martyrs. Yongzheng's policies propelled the chastity cult to the peak of its popularity. Arches and shrines honoring chastity models were constructed in unprecedented numbers in villages and towns across the empire as the numbers of chaste widows and chastity martyrs officially awarded each year reached into the thousands, while tens of thousands more were recognized locally, their names recorded in local gazetteers.

Gazetteer descriptions of these shrines and the history of their construction indicate that the particular meanings and implications of this state presence in local communities varied. In a largely non-Han frontier region like Puan District, Guizhou, where literati elites were scarce and state authority was tenuous, local officials spearheaded the building of schools, shrines, and temples promoting Confucian cultural values as part of the civilizing project that accompanied and facilitated military conquest and administrative incorporation into the empire. The imperial state's cultural presence was inseparable from its military occupation. In such regions, the state-sponsored chastity shrines and arches were often the first public memorials to chaste women. The state's assertion of its cultural presence would have carried very different local meanings in a mainly Han area like Shanhua County, Hunan. Near the capital of a province that was devastated in the Qing conquest, it had developed, by the mid-eighteenth century, a thriving commercial economy with the help of central state investment and support of immigration from other provinces.[20] In contrast with Puan District's eight women recognized for chastity by 1758, Shanhua's gazetteer of 1747 boasted 102 chaste women, including one from the Song dynasty and nine from the Ming. Yet its Shrine to the Chaste and Filial, built next to the Confucian Temple in 1723 to comply with Yongzheng's edict, was the first chastity shrine in the county, and there was no mention of privately constructed arches honoring chaste women.[21] Here too, though chastity had long been revered, the chastity cult as a ritual and institutional phenomenon was created by the central state, albeit without the association with military conquest by a culturally alien regime.

Wuxi County, Jiangsu, in the heartland of the Ming chastity cult, offers yet another pattern. By the end of the Qianlong reign, it had at least eight privately built shrines and eight private arches honoring chaste women. When the edict mandating the establishment of local chastity shrines was issued, Wuxi already had a shrine to honor local chastity heroines. It had been established in 1716, when the local magistrate placed the tablets of fifty-two women who had not received imperial honors in an already existing shrine to one martyr at a local temple. Since the shrine was small, a local donor sponsored the construction of a new one that included tablets for twenty-two more women. In 1728 a so-called "new chastity shrine" was built at the same temple in compliance with Yongzheng's edict.[22] Here, as in counties all over Jiangnan, which produced hundreds of chaste widows and chastity martyrs in the Ming, the Qing state cult enhanced imperial authority by affirming values that had long been at the heart of local elite identity. Yet the chastity cult was also an arena of contestation between a central state imposing its authority to define cultural and moral norms and local literati who continued patronage of private shrines and stubbornly commemorated hundreds of women who were not eligible for imperial canonization by honoring them in these shrines and listing their names in gazetteers. Ultimately, though, while it left room for local benevolence toward ineligible women, a policy that was consistent with the dynasty's flexible definition of state orthodoxy, the state cult succeeded in establishing the imperial center as the most prominent and most consistent patron of female chastity in local society. Not only did it incorporate local shrines for its own use, but it effectively shifted the emotional and symbolic center of the cult away from widow suicides and toward chaste widowhood.[23]

CHASTITY MODELS AS EXEMPLARS OF THE IMPERIAL CIVILIZING MISSION

As he expanded the reach and effectiveness of the state chastity cult and enhanced its physical and ritual presence in local communities across China, Yongzheng cast the chaste woman, epitomized as a lifelong widow, as a model of the proper subject of his civilizing empire. For him, the chastity exemplified in the lives of canonized women was the heroic extreme of a quotidian virtue to which every woman could aspire. In a 1728 edict reinforcing the dynasty's ban on widow suicide, he explained:

> Widow martyrs *(liefu)* die to martyr themselves for their husbands *(yi si xunfu)*, nobly following them down under the earth. This is certainly difficult for people to do. Yet if widow martyrdom is difficult, then chaste widowhood is even more difficult. For those who follow in death *(congsizhe)* show resolve only for a moment, while those who maintain chastity [for a lifetime] must have perpetual regard for their husbands. Those who follow in death sacrifice their lives and that is the end of it. Those who maintain chastity must be prepared to undergo hardships. Moreover, the circumstances under which widow martyrs martyr themselves for chastity and sacrifice their lives *(xunjie juanqu)* vary. Some suicides are pressured by

poverty and lack of means of support. Some occur out of indignation and failure to think about the future. [These women] do not realize that after the husband has died, the duties that a wife must fulfill are even greater [than before]. Above her are her parents-in-law, whom she must serve and nurture as a substitute in the way of the son. Below her are her descendants, whom she must educate as a substitute in the way of the father. If she prepares the sacrifices and manages household affairs, her duties are countless. How can it be that her responsibilities cease as soon as she dies? This is why the honoring of chaste widows is stipulated in the laws and regulations [of the dynasty]. But widow martyrs are not mentioned in the statutes.[24]

Yongzheng asserted that the critical issue in assessing the legitimacy of a suicide was not the particular form of women's expressions of virtue, suicide or lifelong widowhood, but the implications of their behavior for social order.[25] Like his father, the Kangxi Emperor, he saw following-in-death as essentially an expression of individual emotional fervor or personal distress. Given the magnitude of the widow's ritual and familial duties after her husband's death, suicide was not merely irrational and unnecessary but fundamentally selfish and irresponsible. Although he co-opted the language of the conjugal bond with his reference to perpetual regard for the husband, he emphasized that wifely duty, properly understood, was not about impassioned personal devotion and loyalty to one's husband. Rather, it had much broader social and indeed political implications as obedient lifelong service by the living to the patrilineal family interest as a whole and thus, implicitly, to the social order.[26]

This edict reveals Yongzheng's unease with the tendency in the popular culture of chastity to privilege the conjugal family over the patriline. His attempt to link chastity more closely to patrilineal interests did not, however, represent a return to the older chastity paradigm. Within Qing state discourse, lifelong widowhood became an expression of a much broader notion of chastity-centered female virtue that focused not only on every woman's fulfillment of familial duties but also on the maintenance of proper gender distinction in every aspect of social life. The dutiful wife as chaste widow, the most publicly and widely touted of exemplars, was the model of the proper subject, female or male: civilized by a benevolent ruler, she expressed absolute loyalty to the new imperial social and political order through obedience and service to family and state. There are revealing parallels between Yongzheng's approach to moral reform and his treatment of bureaucratic inefficiency and corruption through fiscal reform. Underlying both policies was a practical assessment of human foibles combined with an optimistic expectation that under the right circumstances with the right incentives all of his subjects were capable of assisting him in the grand project of perfecting imperial civilization. Women's ignorance of propriety and official extortion were problems to be solved through the state's provision, respectively, of education and assurance of adequate income.[27] Yongzheng's emphasis on women's duties, like the focus on local fiscal discretion that marked the reforms of the meltage fee system, implied that subjects who had their virtue properly nourished by the state could be entrusted with substantial responsibility for the order of the realm.[28]

The newly bureaucratized chastity cult embodied the Yongzheng Emperor's understanding that the ruler was not a model for emulation but a civilizer: chastising, regulating, and transforming the values and practices of the people. His civilizing mission was not simply about the promotion of conformity to a particular set of norms but was intended instead to forge a new dynamic for the relationship between the ruler and his subjects, the loyal objects of his civilizing benevolence. The nature of this idealized relationship between ruler and subject, imperial state and society, was captured in the notion of *jiaoyang*, the "teaching and cultivation" of the people, or *jiaohua*, the "transformation of customs through education." The concept of *jiaohua* was an old staple of Confucian statecraft discourse, but it acquired a distinctly paternalistic and bureaucratic cast in the eighteenth century as emperors and officials basking in the peace, prosperity, and imperial might of the High Qing formulated new ambitions for the state's role in society.

In his edict on widow suicide, the Yongzheng Emperor juxtaposed the concept of *jiaoyang* with another term: *aiyang*. Expounding on his explanation for the perpetuation of suicidal expressions of "ignorant virtue," he blamed the failure of local officials to "enlighten and guide the common people by educating them on the ethical way of the sages and worthies and on the state's commitment to loving support *(aiyang)*." In its most common usage in Qing imperial discourse, *aiyang* was a translation of a Manchu term for fatherly support that invoked notions of paternalism and loyalty based on a master-slave model of ruler-subject relations, emphasizing an exchange of total service for protection and affection.[29] This kind of paternalism and absolute loyalty contrasted subtly but significantly with the ethically inspired understanding of hierarchy in Confucian tradition, in which the ruler inspired loyalty and wielded authority by setting a virtuous example for his subjects' emulation.[30] Consistent with the dynasty's eclectic approach to culture and ritual in other policy realms, the Qing model of female virtue, in a sense, grafted Manchu notions of loyalty and duty onto Chinese models of chastity and martyrdom. While conventional Neo-Confucian discourse on moral reform assumed proper familial relationships (father-son, husband-wife) to be the foundation of moral and political order, the Qing notion of *jiaohua* inspired by *aiyang* assumed that normative order required the intervention of the state, embodying the paternalistic intent of the ruler, in local social and family life.

Yongzheng elaborated on the implications of *jiaohua* for the ruler-subject relationship as he concluded his edict on widow suicide. He commanded that

> all local officials should broadly proclaim and strive to instruct every family and household in the most isolated and backward areas, so that ignorant people all realize that one can be a filial son or a chaste widow only by taking the long road and that preserving one's life is in accordance with orthodox principles. Then family relationships will be in harmony with cosmic order and will not go against the teaching and cultivation through which the state shows compassion for and protects [the people]. If, after the issuing of this edict, there are still those who do not love life and imperil themselves, we will generally no longer canonize them, which would allow this to become a fanatic craze in the countryside or prolong the custom among ignorant people of taking life lightly.[31]

The emperor suggests here that the relationship between the paternalistic ruler and his obedient, loyal subjects is to be forged and mediated by the bureaucracy. Officials are to function as agents of a paternalistic imperial state whose intervention is necessary to rectify family relationships, raise its subjects out of ignorance, and save them from the tragic consequences of their fanatic beliefs. The imperial state, not the family, is presented here as the source of moral order, and it fulfills its normative function not by setting an example but by regulating social interaction with ever more precision.

Yongzheng's high expectations for the depth and effectiveness of state intervention in local society are evident in an edict of 1734, in which he chastised the governors of Zhili and Jiangsu, Li Wei (1687?–1738) and Gao Qizhuo (1676–1738), for submitting some ten requests for widow suicide honors within the space of a few days.[32] He noted that the state's ban on suicide honors had been so effective that "for many years ... the number of requests for honors for chastity martyrs has been very small, so I have shown benevolence and granted honors as exceptions." But, he concluded, such a spate of widow suicides indicated that "obviously, local officials have not spread knowledge of my edicts broadly enough and ignorant villagers still do not know how . . . we cherish their lives. Thus the number of commoner women who sacrifice their lives in extremist fashion is even greater than before. If I continue to generously grant honors, I fear that people will revert [to this bad custom] in imitation."[33] Yongzheng saw the state, through the agency of its officials, as directly responsible for the persistence of individual widow suicides, yet readily capable of stopping the practice. He thus ordered more thorough propaganda efforts among the populace and announced that he would no longer grant any such exceptions, to prevent "the development of a zealous craze in the countryside."

For the Yongzheng Emperor, then, the state's "loving support" for his subjects was not merely a gesture of moralizing rhetoric but was to be enacted through bureaucratic institutions designed, in the case of the chastity cult, to promote state-defined models of female virtue and social order in every corner of the expanding empire. Thoroughly bureaucratized and thrust into unprecedented political prominence, this micromanaged state chastity cult became central to Qing policies of imperial expansion and consolidation, promoting the chaste woman as a model of imperial subjecthood in the Han heartland and in non-Han frontier regions. The pacification of rebellious non-Han peoples in the Southwest was accompanied by civilizing policies that included the establishment of local chastity shrines and official promotion of state orthodoxy with regard to marriage practices, kinship systems, and household economics.[34] Canonizations of Inner Asian women followed in the wake of the conquest of Xinjiang, although the feasibility of extending the chastity award system among the nomadic peoples of the region appears to have been in question in the late eighteenth century.[35]

Over the course of the Yongzheng, Qianlong, and Jiaqing reigns, there would be many instances of strategically timed recognition of chastity martyrs at critical junctures in the process of imperial expansion and in the suppression of rebellions. In 1726, Ortai (1680–1745), then leading campaigns against the Tai in southern Yunnan as governor-general, requested special honors for the wife and concubine of a government student *(jiansheng)*, normally ineligible because of the student's degree status, who had killed themselves to preserve their chastity in the face of a bandit attack. The same memorial requested honors for commoner women in Yunnan who had martyred themselves *(xunnan)*, leaving sons behind. Committed as he was to the civilizing mission of the Qing, Ortai seemingly saw chastity martyrs as useful symbols of loyalty in the context of imperial conquest. The Yongzheng Emperor agreed with him, granting the honors.[36] In 1738, the Qianlong Emperor granted the request of Zhang Guangsi (d. 1749), governor-general of Guizhou, who had just successfully led the campaign to suppress the Miao Rebellion, for honors for a woman and her two daughters who had killed themselves to defend their chastity in the midst of a Miao bandit attack.[37] The Qianlong Emperor made similar awards in the context of suppression of the Wang Lun Uprising in Shandong in 1774.[38] After the conquest of new territories or pacification of tribal groups within the borders of China proper, chastity honors were often inaugurated for newly incorporated non-Han peoples, providing local models of the dutiful loyalty expected of Qing subjects. In 1782 and 1783, for example, shortly after the suppression of the aboriginal Jinchuan rebels in Sichuan, Qianlong set precedents for granting chaste widow honors to "barbarian women" *(fanfu)* in the families of native officials *(tusi)* "in order to demonstrate the intention to pacify barbarians with impartial kindness."[39] The canonization of the righteous Miao chastity martyr Aguan in 1753 and the placement of a tablet in her name in the district's Shrine to the Chaste and Filial worked not only to create a native exemplar of orthodox virtue for her community to emulate but also to establish and normalize the presence and the legitimacy of the imperial state as the source of normative authority in a local society that had only recently been incorporated into the Qing realm.

CHAPTER 2

Statecraft and Gender Order in the Qianlong Reign

Although the state chastity cult constructed by Yongzheng was a particularly effective and visible example of imperial state penetration of local society, it was only one of many statecraft incarnations of the empire's civilizing ambitions. Indeed, its full political and cultural significance comes into focus only when we look beyond the award system itself to the web of state technologies developed in the latter half of the century to mold society and transform customs. The intertwined agendas of moral transformation *(jiaohua)* and state building shaped much of the social policy making of the Yongzheng and Qianlong years, indicating that commitment to the Qing vision of the thoroughness, precision, and intimacy of the state's loving support for its subjects was widely shared by Han and Manchu officials alike. In numerous edicts and memorials on the reform of customs and rectification of morals in localities throughout the empire, emperors and policy-making officials expounded their views of how to routinize the civilizing mission in bureaucratic practice. These wide-ranging discussions produced new laws and policies to intervene in diverse realms of social life and promote chastity, frugality, and respect for social hierarchy throughout the empire.

Memorialists advocated improving local education, creating new punishments and incentives, and enhancing the reach of hortatory imperial pronouncements like the Sacred Edict to address diverse moral and social problems. These included declining filiality and respect for familial hierarchy; female infanticide; excessive lawsuits; excessive rowdiness at operas; lack of interest in the primary occupations of farming for men and weaving for women;[1] heterodox religious sects that promoted disorder and immoral behavior, particularly wanton mixing of the sexes; improper and extravagant marriage and funerary rituals; kidnappings of women for marriage; inappropriate behavior of stepmothers; prostitution; incest; slander leading to suicides; the social disorder and conflicts caused by unscrupulous matchmakers; widow chastity; women going to temples; and the maintenance of sex segregation and propriety in prisons and among those exiled as punishment for crimes.

Whatever the specific problem at hand, the participants in the discourse of *jiaohua* commonly advocated two strategies for improving customs, both of which enhanced the local presence of the state: mandating regular magistrate tours of their districts to investigate conditions and educate people and refining the law as a tool for local magistrates to transform local customs. In 1743, the ninth year of Qianlong's reign, these strategies became the focus of a campaign to mobilize local officials and make them more accountable for concrete progress in promoting the moral transformation of the people.[2] The theme of magistrates' neglect of their normative duties was hardly new, but the specific measures bandied about in this discussion originated in the Yongzheng Emperor's attempts to solicit yearly reports from provincial officials on their efforts to carry out the policies mandated by his edicts at the local level. The point initially was not to promote moral transformation per se but to increase general accountability and control of the bureaucracy and enhance the effectiveness of local government, both favorite issues for Yongzheng. Early in the Qianlong reign, officials took up the issue of bureaucratic efficiency and melded it with the project of transforming customs in a campaign to expand the state's normative role in local communities. Representing, in many ways, the culminating incarnation of Yongzheng's *jiaohua* vision in policy, this campaign undoubtedly developed in large part because of the continuity of personnel in the Inner Court and provincial administration across the regnal transition: many of Yongzheng's most powerful and closest imperial advisors, the men who first articulated and implemented his civilizing mission, constituted the core of Qianlong's Grand Council and dominated the highest levels of the bureaucracy.[3] However, the proliferating rhetoric on *jiaohua* in the wake of the campaign increasingly reflected Qianlong's distinctive priorities, paranoias, and approach to his subjects.[4]

The campaign gathered force in the eighth year of the Qianlong reign (1743) as the emperor issued at least one edict calling for officials to pay more attention to the dynasty's civilizing mission. Setting the context for this renewed focus on moral transformation, he noted that both moral education *(jiao)* and nurturance *(yang)* were important components of governance. But surveying the state of his realm, he observed that the dynasty had "diligently emphasized [the promotion of] agriculture and sericulture and lowered labor and land taxes for the nurturance *(yang)* of the people. I fear, however, that this is not sufficient. Rectifying the people's hearts and strengthening customs *(zheng renxin hou fengsu)* are also great missions of the dynasty that it is time for us to eagerly embrace." After reviewing the efforts of his grandfather and father to improve customs and morals, he emphasized that local-level officials were not doing enough to fulfill their roles as teachers and models for the people. They thus needed more guidance from provincial-level officials. He concluded by ordering these higher-level officials to be more conscientious in carrying out the emperor's directives on moral transformation, communicating imperial policies to the lower levels, and keeping track of the successes and failures of their cultural reform efforts.[5]

At the end of that year, Censor Shi Jiqi submitted a memorial suggesting much more concrete bureaucratic measures to promote the state's civilizing mission. Although he did not reference a specific imperial edict, his memorial opened with an echo of the emperor's statement about why the time was right for a concerted effort to promote moral transformation. "I think that the way of governance includes nurturing and moral education. Nurturing strengthens the people's livelihood. Moral education rectifies the people's morals. The two require each other and we cannot do without either one.... Successive peaceful reigns have already improved the people's livelihood. So moral transformation is [now] a priority." Despite the dynasty's benevolent and concerted efforts to instruct the people in the ways of propriety, Shi argued, "the people are not sufficiently upright in their conduct." Offering examples of the persistent degeneracy of customs, he stated, " In recent years, there have been frequent cases of younger brothers killing older brothers and nephews killing uncles. Now, filiality and respect for older brothers are innate to the common people. Yet cruelty and violence are suddenly overcoming fathers and elder brothers. This is fundamentally about the degeneration of human relationships *(lunchang)*." Such breakdown of proper hierarchy in local communities was for him at the root of the two most nagging problems of local governance: excessive litigation and corruption in the sub-bureaucracy. Local bullies who misused litigation, as well as corrupt clerks and runners (who carried out nonclerical tasks) for the county magistrate's office *(yamen)*, proliferated when village authorities and officials did not fulfill their duties to provide moral tutelage and manage local affairs.

To restore social and moral order, Shi suggested that the throne instruct governors to order magistrates to conduct regular investigatory tours of their districts and compile detailed portraits of local social, economic, and cultural conditions and their own efforts to improve customs and mores. Such routinized "closeness to the people," Shi argued explicitly, would serve a dual function of enhancing surveillance of the populace and regularizing the normative presence of the state at the local level. Only if magistrates kept close tabs on social and economic trends, improper local customs, and potential troublemakers could they intimidate "wicked elements and corrupt runners" into giving up their violent and unsavory ways and thus avoid losing control of their districts. As part of these investigatory tours, magistrates were also to make routine visits to villages to

> summon the local elders and inspire their sympathy by inquiring into their problems and the people's hardships. Select from among them those who are especially experienced, sincere, and honest, and order them to teach the villagers filiality, respect for elders, faithfulness, and honesty. If the elders respect the words of officials, then they will not need to recoil from them out of fear and desire to avoid suspicion. When the village youth see that [the elders] are respected by the officials, they will want to serve and obey them and will more readily listen to them.[6]

Commonly referred to as father and mother officials, county magistrates were not merely to educate and provide models for the people but to mobilize their active participation in their own moral transformation by winning over community leaders, soliciting their advice about local problems, and enhancing their authority by publicly linking them to the state. By integrating themselves into local authority structures, magistrates would ensure the constant presence of the state in local communities and win the sympathy and cooperation of local leaders with the imperial civilizing project. Moral transformation in this context was decidedly not a process of self-cultivation; rather, as Yongzheng had insisted, it required the intervention of state authorities.

Intriguingly, Shi quoted as precedents the exemplary efforts of the Song statecraft thinkers Cheng Hao (1032–85) and Zhang Zai (1020–77) when they served as magistrates to promote moral transformation and solve local problems by enhancing the authority of community elders and establishing the *wubao* system of mutual aid and responsibility. In the

Song, advocacy of such local community building, albeit with the state as catalyst, was part of ongoing debates about the decentralization of political authority and the proper limits of state intervention in society. But Shi's invocation of these Song examples in the context of discussions in the Yongzheng and early Qianlong periods about how to enhance the effectiveness of state policies imbued them with state-building aims that would have made Song statecraft thinkers uneasy. His proposal did not augur a nostalgic revival of age-old paradigms for community self-governance but took up instead the emerging vision of an intrusive, activist state binding local communities more tightly to itself by mobilizing the people to participate in *jiaohua*. Like many statecraft thinkers of his day and the Qianlong Emperor himself, Shi believed that normative order could be restored only through the reinvigoration of local patriarchal authority, yet he was deeply ambivalent about the moral and political capabilities of elders, lineage leaders, and magistrates to fulfill their responsibilities.[7] The only way to civilize society was therefore to strengthen central control of local bureaucrats and thus the state's influence in community life.

This memorial was followed early in 1744 by two edicts. In the first, dated in the first month of the new year, Qianlong expounded again on the crucial role of local magistrates, the officials most intimate with the sufferings and foibles of the people, in the project of moral transformation. He issued very general instructions for governors-general and governors to report on problematic customs in their regions, monitor their subordinates' efforts to transform them, and correct their mistakes.[8] In the second edict, issued the following month, the emperor replied explicitly to Censor Shi's suggestions. He castigated governors-general and governors for not implementing his past edicts on "teaching the people and improving customs" and ordered them to submit yearly reports on the success or failure of their civilizing efforts.[9] After further procedural refinements suggested by the president of the Board of Personnel and grand secretary, Nuoqin (d. 1749), Censor Shi's proposed *jiaohua* campaign was set in motion. Magistrates were ordered to make field trips to the villages within their jurisdiction, assess local conditions, and develop strategies for dealing with local problems. They were specifically instructed to promote schools, correct local elite behavior, improve popular customs, and work to eradicate gambling, litigation, violence, heterodox sects, banditry, and vendettas. They were to compile detailed progress reports on what they discovered on their tours, the local projects they initiated, and their results or the lack thereof. They were to submit these to their provincial governors on a yearly schedule. The governors would then synthesize them into a single report on conditions in the province at the end of every year. They were also ordered to censure any magistrate who did not show "sincere energy" in carrying out these civilizing efforts.[10]

Qianlong's call for more concerted bureaucratic focus on moral transformation spurred voluminous memorials from capital and provincial officials duly filing their required annual reports on problematic local customs or making ad hoc suggestions for reform. Typical of the flood of memorials on the subject of *jiaohua* was one from the investigating censor of the Jiangnan Circuit, Ou Kanshan, in 1744. He began by framing his specific policy suggestions with reference to the concept of *aiyang*: "In investigating officials and pacifying the people, Your Majesty the Emperor, like Heaven, cherishes life, establishes the path of uprightness, and bestows favor on excellent conduct, all to show loving support *(aiyang)*. To mold and educate the common people and set the scholars in order, government officials perfect the law and make policies appropriate."[11] In this context, Ou set forth a few policies and laws that could still be perfected "in order to rectify morals, enrich the livelihood of the people, improve customs, and enhance the way of governance." His far-ranging suggestions included curbing the extravagance of wedding and funeral ceremonies, tightening up regulations on holders of purchased degrees, improving the quality of teachers in government academies, establishing local charity schools "to provide moral education for the rustic and ignorant," curbing lawsuits among the people, and improving the effectiveness of officials. Officials, scholar-elites, and the common people were all equally the object of the ruler's loving support and, as the reforms outlined by Ou suggested, equally in need of the ruler's guidance and education.

Although Shi Jiqi did not mention women or the issue of chastity explicitly in his memorial, gender separation was often a defining element of civilization in memorialists' reports and policy suggestions. Indeed, with their concern about the integrity of family rituals, memorialists like Ou Kanshan implied that promotion of female and male virtue was integral to the rectification of morals and improvement of customs. Shi himself was explicit that what was at stake in the *jiaohua* campaign was not only the effectiveness of social and political hierarchy but the integrity of patrilineal authority. In a memorial of 1746 requesting "prohibition of vulgar and ignorant marriage and funerary customs in order to rectify customs and morals," Hunan Judicial Commissioner Zhou Renji

Statecraft and Gender Order

articulated the gender logic behind the civilizing project by showing how one form of gender disorder was implicated in cultural degeneracy that corrupted patriarchal authorities, resulting in social disorder and criminal behavior. Of particular concern to him were improper funerary and marriage rites. The problem with funerary customs, he explained, was that

> [f]amilies in mourning not only invite [Buddhist] monks and Daoists to officiate but also gather their relatives together for seven days to watch opera and have banquets. Men and women mix indiscriminately from dawn to dusk every day in funerary revels. The latter is especially untoward. Inevitably, neighboring clans, relatives, and friends band together and drink wine. One person sings while the whole crowd claps until the whole crowd sings together. Inevitably most people sing throughout the entire night for days. It is hardly surprising that such vulgar customs of night singing get passed down. Commoners follow them and the degree holders also do not avoid them. Your minister has patiently exhorted and instructed [them], but the stain of these practices is deep and long-standing and they are difficult to change. Truly this greatly concerns the transformation of morals. I think that when uneducated, foolish people knowingly engage in vice like this, it is because the people of learning do not teach them ritual propriety. So if we want to restore debased customs, we must start with the gentry.[12]

Zhou expressed a contempt for popular customs in the Han heartland that sounds much like the paternalistic hostility of the Chinese magistrate investigating the Miao woman's suicide. Yet ignorance of propriety, Zhou argued, was not the problem here, for "the rites emphasize marriages and funerals, and all the particulars of what is allowed and what is forbidden in ceremonial etiquette are detailed in the ritual texts and codified in the statutes and substatutes. Yet the customs of Hunan are still degenerate." He concluded that those at the top of the social hierarchy had abrogated their duties as moral exemplars. He was thus far more critical of the local elites who, he believed, should know better, than he was of the common people, whose ignorance he assumed. Faced with the failure of the tutelary approach to *jiaohua*, he argued that "long-standing practices that are passed down from one generation to the next must be strictly banned." He requested the emperor to forbid these practices and ordered local magistrates to forward the names of any degree holders who after one year still failed to comply, subjecting them to removal of their titles and punishment for contravening imperial orders. "When the degree holders have been warned and know what to watch out for, then an impression will be made on the common people."[13] When local elites failed to cultivate their own morality, the state should intervene with new regulations specifying punishments that undermined the basis of local gentry status, in effect manipulating their self-interest.

Hunan marriage customs posed a different kind of problem for Zhou. Since most families in the province betrothed their children at a very early age, he explained, it was all too common for brides' families to renege on marriage contracts after some change in fortunes of one family or the other. This often resulted in the groom's family "stirring up a mob to kidnap [the bride]." Widows were also frequent victims of such kidnappings for marriage when their natal and marital families competed for access to their brideprice and betrothed them to different people. "Proper human relationships begin with husbands and wives," Zhou noted, "and kidnapping is the degeneracy of the mob." After dealing with countless such cases, he found the statutes punishing these crimes to be insufficient because they did not specifically target the problem of inciting mob action. In a telling comparison with strategies used to combat the "disorderly behavior" of mobs among the "Miao barbarians," Zhou suggested a more flexible application of the existing statutes to punish such mob kidnappings explicitly and more severely than ordinary bride stealing. He reiterated the barbarian analogy in his conclusion, again invoking a term often used to describe the savage tribal peoples of the frontier: "If laws are a bit more severe, then barbaric *(manye)* customs can gradually be transformed. Your minister has himself been given the duty to assist with moral transformation *(bijiao)*. Seeing for myself that the customs of Hunan greatly need to be put in order, I offer my absurd and limited opinions. Whether they are appropriate or not, I beg the emperor to judge." Judicial Commissioner Zhou's memorial illuminates the Qing paradigm of imperial civilization with unusual clarity, equating Han and non-Han, gentry and common people, women and men, and even, finally, albeit formulaically, himself, as subjects in need of the normative influence of the dynasty, an influence best imposed through law.

Clarification or expansion of the law was the single most commonly advocated strategy for promoting reform. Memorials on *jiaohua* resulted, among other things, in a dramatic expansion of the Qing Code, honing its function as a bureaucratic tool for moral transformation.[14] The most prominent focus of new laws was the promotion of chastity-centered virtue among women. Numerous officials called for increasing punishments for adultery, incest, sexual assaults and harassments leading to suicide, and prostitution. Over the course of the Yongzheng and Qianlong reigns, huge numbers of new substatutes were created in the sections of the code dealing with illicit sex, illegalities in the contracting of marriages (some twenty-five substatutes), homicides arising out of sexual assaults, adultery and prostitution (altogether over forty substatutes), and causing a woman to commit suicide through improper behavior (some twenty-five substatutes).[15] The meaning of chastity in this diverse legislation expanded to include not just sexual loyalty to one husband but proper female behavior in social interactions with men in general. The new substatutes also defined with ever greater precision—indeed, with hair-splitting detail—the parameters of proper family behavior and gender relations.

Collectively, these myriad new substatutes reflected widespread anxiety among mid-Qing elites about increasing challenges to fidelity and a heightened distrust both of women's moral fortitude and of the integrity of the local patriarchal authority that should have been the first defense against such improprieties. In their responses to requests for canonization of chastity martyrs who did not fit the imperially sanctioned model, the Qianlong Emperor and his officials evinced a subtle shift in the visions of human nature that underlay the *jiaohua* project.[16] The dynasty's paradigm of proper and improper suicides was applied increasingly to dissect the motives of potential awardees. Expressing a deep distrust of women's virtuous intent, memorialists and the emperor suggested that many allegedly chaste women who committed suicide acted out of selfish desire for fame, moral weakness, or irrational fury. Denying a 1775 canonization request for a concubine who had followed her husband in death, Qianlong asked, "How can we know that she did not have conflicts with the first wife and kill herself because she feared future insult and abuse from her?"[17] Similarly disparaging views of women's moral integrity inspired Henan Judicial Commissioner He Wei to suggest in 1765 that honors for women who killed themselves in response to harassment be limited to those who acted purely out of humiliation or desire to prove their chastity. The emperor rejected this proposal with an edict that articulated his divergence from his father's approach to the moral reform of his subjects:

> Women who take life lightly may perhaps do so because they wish to assuage their fury and use this as a pretext to obtain hidden merit. But they are not so different from those who become vegetarians and recite Buddhist scriptures. Within the women's quarters sincerity and insincerity are obscured. There is no consistent pattern. Sometimes wives and daugh-

ters originally do not want to die but are pressured by husbands or parents to do so. And we cannot protect them from doing so. How is it benevolent to promulgate a statute to distinguish [these motivations] clearly?[18]

Although he insisted on the moral superiority of chaste widowhood over martyrdom, Yongzheng maintained a tone of respect for the integrity of the female suicide and extended canonization to humiliation suicides. He attributed "reckless" suicide to circumstantial and remediable problems like social and economic pressures, impulsiveness, and ignorance of duty. However, he did not link these to any inherent moral weakness in women, nor did he question women's capability for moral perfection. In fact, he emphasized the vital role of women in preserving social order and extolled chastity heroines as model subjects. In contrast, Qianlong, though known for being far more "lenient" and "compassionate" than his father,[19] was consistently suspicious of the loyalty and moral integrity of his subjects.[20] His distrust of officialdom and gentry elites and his belief that only careful monitoring and control could keep them in line have been well documented by historians.[21] In his edicts on the chastity cult and *jiaohua* more generally he revealed a similar cynicism about his commoner subjects. His response to He Wei's proposal suggested that since women were incapable of full moral transformation, the benevolent state had to show tolerance for their incorrect expressions of chastity. Beyond this, the behavior of commoners, like that of officials, could be shaped and regulated through the law.

The dramatic expansion of the Qing Code overseen by Qianlong was thus intended not simply to enforce a more rigid standard of virtue but, perhaps more critically, to forge a new relationship between the state and its subjects. The application of these substatutes and the process through which they were created worked to implement the new interventionist role of the state envisioned by mid-Qing emperors and their officials.[22] In two memorials written on the same day in 1747, Hubei Governor Chen Hongmou demonstrated common assumptions about the nature and effectiveness of state intervention in society through the judicial system. He complained that local magistrates in the province consistently failed to deal promptly with cases of "abduction for illicit sex," resulting in de facto appeasement of adulterers, since "licentious men and women see an opportunity to knowingly engage in vice" by, in effect, staging kidnappings to run off illicitly together.[23] He called for more swift and consistent prosecution and then, in a separate memorial, suggested some clarifications of the substatutes on illicit sex. He framed his discussion of the statutes and their social effects with a broad statement about the grave consequences of sexual misconduct that was typical of many such memorials: "I think that the rectification of morals and customs is the first priority of government and illicit sex and licentiousness is the source of all vice. As for those who first engage in illicit sex and then [carry out] an abduction, they corrupt family morals and destroy proper kinship relations and the feelings they involve." He criticized the existing substatutes for failing to recognize that usually the man and the woman were equally guilty. They required that one party be named as the principal and sentenced to military exile on the northern frontier for life and that the other be named as the accessory and sentenced to a lesser punishment of banishment for three years. Since women automatically had sentences of exile reduced to flogging with the heavy bamboo and a fine, Chen argued that "after [they] are caught, what adulterous man would not enjoin the adulterous woman to confess to having wanted to escape [her husband] so as to avoid serious punishment [for himself].... Convicting the woman as the principal offender results in the man evading punishment, which leads inevitably to the gradual weakening of the law.... This is destructive of customs and morality." Sharing Qianlong's disdain for women's moral integrity, he noted that "in the majority of cases of abduction for illicit sex, it is the woman who initiates the idea."[24] He advocated stronger punishments for the men so that they would have something to fear and would refuse to go along with a woman who initiated the idea of an abduction. "Then the practice of abductions for illicit sex will gradually diminish."[25] Positing an intimate state intervention in local society through the mechanism of the law, he implied that through laws that embodied certain normative values and created incentives and punishments to uphold them, the state directly influenced the choices individuals made.

The law functioned here not primarily as a source of punishment but as a tool for molding behavior. Indeed, some memorialists noted the limited usefulness of law as an instrument of coercion in the *jiaohua* project. Censor Sun Zongpu, in a memorial of 1751, differentiated the process of *jiaohua* from both punitive sanction and education in the context of a discussion of how to curb the extravagance of wedding, funerals, and other rituals among the people. "The emperor has issued an edict exhorting officials and the common people to pursue the reform of vulgar customs and work together to achieve benevolent and enduring governance. This is the goal of teaching and cultivating the people *(jiaoyang)*." After explaining his particular concern with wastefulness and extravagance in the performance of rituals, Sun argued that reform of such practices "cannot be forcibly compelled through the coercion of law and punishments. Nor can widespread proclamations and education cause the people to suddenly become enlightened [about this problem]." The remedy, he suggested, lay with the local authorities,

> the county and prefectural magistrates who are closest to the people and have a responsibility to reform and enlighten them. But there are no rules to guide them in fulfillment of their duty to regulate the daily affairs of the people. . . . So it is necessary to develop a set of regulations to provide restrictions that can be the basis for action by local authorities and a standard for the people to follow.

He suggested that local magistrates investigate the sources of excess in their own areas and compile this information for provincial authorities so that they could formulate new regulations to curb ritual expenditures and eliminate improper ritual activity (like operas and festivities surrounding local deities).[26]

What is striking here is the careful differentiation of a bureaucratic process of *jiaohua*, expressed in regulations, from both Legalist punishments and conventional Confucian education.[27] Sun suggested that the imperial state should be the central arbiter of the normative order, not merely by setting an example and punishing egregious transgressions, but by regulating social interaction with ever more precision. Of course, Legalists had long advocated using rewards and punishments to encourage upright behavior. What was new in this articulation of the state's normative role, particularly in the larger context of mid-Qing legislation, was the level of precision and effectiveness expected of state intervention to shape individual motivations and behavior. The state was meant to be not merely an exemplar or even a source of punishment but a social engineer, mobilizing local officials, who in turn would mobilize local elites and elders to change the values and behavior of the common people.

LEGISLATING CHASTITY

The evolution of the substatutes used in the case of Aguan's suicide and the policy discussion surrounding them demonstrates the practical workings of the new relationship between the civilizing state and its subjects: the honing of legislation to respond to social problems and change behavior. The magistrate found the defendant, Ali, guilty of attempted rape leading to suicide of the victim, sentencing him to strangulation after the assizes. He was sentenced according to a substatute created in 1733 (YZ 11), when the Yongzheng Emperor initiated canonization for women who killed themselves in response to a sexual proposition. The substatute reads:

> Those who rape a woman and then kill her immediately shall be sentenced to immediate decapitation. Those who accomplish the rape of a woman, causing her to commit suicide out of humiliation, shall still be sentenced in accordance with [the substatute] on causing a person to commit suicide because of illicit sex, to decapitation after the assizes. As for those who cause a woman to commit suicide out of humiliation after attempting rape without accomplishing it, or only by flirting, they shall be sentenced to strangulation after the assizes.[28]

This substatute replaced a more general one left over from the Ming (1588) that, for the first time in Chinese law, mandated punishments for causing a person to commit suicide in connection with illicit sex, very vaguely defined. The 1733 substatute specified, for the first time, punishments for causing suicide through attempted rape or unwanted flirtation, thus in effect criminalizing sexual harassment if it led to a woman's suicide.[29] Between 1733 and the end of the Qianlong reign, some fifteen new substatutes were appended to the statute on "causing a person to commit suicide." Among these, a dozen or so dealt with women committing suicide under various circumstances in the wake of rape, attempted rape, or unwanted propositions; unintended sexual insult or "improper familiarity;" "indecent remarks," "dirty jokes," or "obscene gestures" made in her presence, in the context of an argument with her, or about her; adultery; or gossip arising out of any of these incidents.[30] Chaste women who killed themselves under such circumstances were all deemed eligible for canonization.

In a memorial of 1745, the head of the capital Office of Transmission, Zhang Ruoai (d. 1746, son of Zhang Tingyu, 1672–1755) described the social consequences of these substatutes. On the basis of his experience processing incoming documents from the provinces, he noted the large number of women who committed suicide in response to a verbal insult and then reviewed the creation of new substatutes in the Yongzheng and Qianlong periods to punish men who had caused a woman's suicide with verbal harassment. But after noting that "punishments aid [the process of] moral transformation," and praising the benevolence and wisdom of these particular laws, he launched into a litany of cases in which women killed themselves only after a prolonged delay of some days or even weeks after an insult. He observed that in these cases delay or failure of the family, neighbors, or village leaders to report the verbal harassment to the local magistrate for punishment, or the magistrate's own delay or failure to punish the offender, caused the women to feel that "their grievance went unredressed and because of this to take life lightly." Zhang suggested that officials inform people that they should report such cases to the magistrate and that he be required to arrest the offender within three days and punish him with the cangue.³¹ "In this way, the woman's humiliation and anger can be assuaged and the offender can avoid having to atone with his life. . . . The laws of the dynasty have reached into popular sentiment. [When the people] know fear and feel ashamed of their customs, then perhaps such customs can gradually be eradicated and one aspect of the emperor's benevolence can be extended."³²

Echoing the condescending view of the common people's motivations that prevailed across the Qianlong reign, Zhang adopted the tone of a paternalistic official calling for the state to protect women from the worst effects of their frail, irrational, and hypersensitive natures. He implied that such suicides were neither moral nor heroic but merely the helpless gestures of women too readily prone to outrage. Assuming, like Zhou Renji and Chen Hongmou, that the state was capable, through laws, of "[reaching] into popular sentiment" to assuage the humiliation of individual women, he suggested honing the law to be a more effective instrument for dissuading women from suicide. In the spirit of the *jiaohua* campaign, he also suggested that local officials should supplement patriarchal authority, educating family and community elders about the fulfillment of their legal and moral duties.

His memorial resulted in the creation of a new substatute in the same year, the one used to sentence the headmen in Aguan's village to eighty strokes of the heavy bamboo for failing to report the assault to the authorities immediately. This substatute reads:

> In all [cases of] flirtation or attempted rape that is not accomplished, if the woman informs her relatives or village headmen and they immediately report it to the local official, he shall investigate, conduct interrogations, and, if there is proof, then judge the severity of the crime and punish [the offender] with the cangue or flogging with the heavy bamboo, as appropriate. . . . If [the woman's] family has already informed the local headman and [he] does not report to the magistrate, or he reports, but the magistrate does not investigate and settle [the case], and this results in the woman harboring outrage and killing herself, then the village headman shall be sentenced . . . to eighty strokes of the heavy bamboo. The local magistrate shall be punished.³³

This substatute, for the first time, mandated specific punishment for sexual harassment itself and criminalized the failure to report any incident of sexual assault or harassment to state authorities. It directly implicated family and community authorities in the preservation of chastity and redress of its violation. Yet the creation of the new substatute alone appears not to have been sufficiently effective in preventing women's suicides, for an edict of 1759 instructed local officials to inform people clearly that

> families and relatives must try to comfort [women who have been insulted] and refrain from exacerbating their humiliation. If [a woman] originally does not want to die, then even more so, they should not do anything to incriminate her and cause her to take life lightly. If any of these improper things occur, they should be punished accordingly. As for county and district officials, if they fail to investigate and try such flirtation cases thoroughly, then the governor should investigate and issue punishment.[34]

Recent scholarship has noted the emergence in eighteenth-century discourses on law and social reform of an emphasis on the individual as an autonomous moral actor defined by his or her own virtuous intent and behavior. Matthew Sommer, for example, documents the shift in judicial discourse from a status-based construction of sexual morality to a gender-based standard that applied different criteria of sexual virtue to men and women but disregarded differences of status. Accompanying this new emphasis on gender performance was a focus on the individual moral responsibility of women and men, whose virtue was increasingly measured by intent rather than status.[35] As they dealt with the growing social problem of women's suicides, the Qianlong Emperor and his officials intended the law to reach into the family and forge links with individual subjects as independent moral actors, strangely bypassing all the mediating family and community authorities whose prerogative as arbiters and enforcers of moral standards was central to the paradigms of social order that underlay the *jiaohua* discourse.[36] As we will see in later chapters, the pervasive mistrust of these authorities, combined with the focus on individual moral integrity as the key to *jiaohua*, began to reconfigure the relationship between chastity and patriarchal hierarchy in unexpected ways that made state authorities extremely uncomfortable. For, allying itself with women like Aguan, the Qing state committed its power to defend them, and their personal definition of virtue and its violation, against family authority and local officials as well as their harassers. While this asserted intimacy between the ruler and would-be chaste women did not represent the emergence of a notion of individualism per se, it suggested a subtle but significant shift in patterns of state-society interaction and the values that informed them. Although Qianlong may have retreated from his father's most ambitious state-building aims, as many scholars contend, the development of the civilizing project in law and social policy during his reign shows the legacies of Yongzheng's vision of a morally activist state that would rectify its subjects to conform to an imperially defined normative order.

PART TWO

Female Virtue and the Politics of Patriarchy

Prologue: A Righteous Husband Plays the Politics of the Wifely Way

In 1768, an aspiring literatus named Chen Shiwan of Jintan County, Jiangsu, stabbed his wife, Gao Shi, to death and was sentenced perfunctorily to strangulation after the assizes.[1] At the heart of the marital conflict was Shiwan's claim that Gao Shi had abrogated the most sacred duty encompassed in the "wifely way" *(fudao)* by refusing to pay proper respects to his parents and continually fighting with them.[2] The elders of the Chen and Gao families, their affinal relatives, the Dings, and two magistrates in succession tried unsuccessfully for years to mediate the dispute. The case elucidates the workings of family and local politics surrounding a woman's alleged violation of gender norms, norms that Shiwan himself identified with "people who read books." Headed by Shiwan's father, who at age fifty-seven was still only a government student *(shengyuan)*, the Chen family was at the margins of the educated elite. Shiwan, the eldest son, was employed in the neighboring prefecture, Jiangning, as a teacher in a private village school, a low-paying, low-status job for a thirty-five-*sui*-old would-be literatus with aspirations to respectability.

Marital tensions had emerged the moment Gao Shi entered the house as Chen Shiwan's second wife after the death of his first wife some five years earlier. The conflict began because Gao Shi and her stepmother-in-law quarreled continuously. In their testimonies, Chen and his father, Chen Jichuan, attributed this conflict to Gao Shi's "lazy temperament and refusal to do household chores."[3] Shiwan claimed that his stepmother "often instructed and admonished my wife, but [she] did not listen and often wrangled with Stepmother and argued with me." Gao Shi's father, Gao Shenghe, who intervened frequently to defend his daughter's interests, deflected blame from her and implicated Chen's mother in the conflict, noting that "from the time [my daughter] entered the household, Chen Jichuan's second wife, Fan Shi, and my daughter were not harmonious, so my son-in-law also did not get along with my daughter."

Such accusations of bad temperament and bland references to personality conflicts were common in marital homicide cases as the defendant-husband and his wife's relatives competed to construct the dead wife as either provoking the murder or falling victim to a vicious husband.[4] As was often the case, though, the context for the failure of this marriage was complex. Gao Shi, only twenty-one at the time of her death, was some fifteen *sui* younger than her husband.[5] Moreover, various testimonies indicate that the Gaos were much wealthier than the Chens. A few months into the marriage, Gao Shi's father provided the couple with moving expenses when Shiwan decided to bring his wife to live with him in Jiangning to put an end to the squabbling between his wife and stepmother. Two days before their departure, however, Gao Shi and her stepmother-in-law had yet another quarrel, this time over the daughter-in-law's demand to eat rice rather than more plebian congee.

Chen testified, "I shouted at her to stop, but my wife ignored me and I slapped her face." Although the testimonies do not make this explicit, this was apparently the first time that Chen Shiwan had hit his wife, for her father was incensed when he heard about it. The very next day, he marched over to his in-laws' house and confronted his son-in-law, who said sarcastically, "Such a good daughter you've raised!" Angered that his son-in-law "spoke disrespectfully" to him, Gao Shenghe slapped Chen and grabbed Chen's father to force him to report his son's behavior to their lineage leaders. Gao also accused him of wasting the travel money he had provided and not moving to Jiangning as intended. The Chen family leaders counseled both sides to stop fighting, but the truce lasted only a couple months longer before Shiwan's father decided that since Gao Shi "stirred up trouble over trifling matters" his son should divorce her and send her home "to avoid more quarreling in the family."

Gao Shi remained with her natal family for over two years, but her father felt that "since my daughter had already been married out there was no reason to remarry her." So he brought suit against the Chen family with the county magistrate, who then ordered them to take her back. A delegation consisting of six leaders of both the Chen and Ding families, the Dings being the natal family of both Chen Shiwan's mother and Gao Shi's mother, approached Shiwan's father and convinced him to accept the court's judgment. Shiwan himself testified, "I thought that since my wife had been living at her mother's house for over two years, maybe her personality would have improved a little." To keep the contentious daughter and mother-in-law separated, one of his maternal uncles allowed the reunited couple to live in his compound.

The feelings of husband and wife, however, had not changed over the years. Soon after moving, Shiwan suggested that they go together to pay respects to his parents, but Gao Shi refused. His maternal uncles persuaded him to be patient with her. One month later, Shiwan suggested to his wife that since the Mid-Autumn Festival was nearing, they should go and pay respects to his parents. According to his confession, Gao Shi replied, "I don't recognize this mother-in-law." As they undressed for bed, he said to her, "I have never seen such a wife as you, not even recognizing your parents-in-law." He claimed his wife started to scream and swear at him, and, pulling his queue, told him that he and his parents were "humiliating her and were completely worthless." "Now I want to have it out with you. If it's not you, it'll be me," she reportedly said to him. As the two struggled, Shiwan grabbed a nearby knife and stabbed her to death as the Dings came running into the room. Explaining his actions to the magistrate, he said, "I am a person who reads books. Since Gao Shi had been divorced and then returned, it was proper for us to go and pay respects to my parents."

In his testimony, Shiwan constructed his violent response to his wife's fury as a frustrated, last-ditch effort to uphold a set of family values that were integral to his identity and aspirations. He associated these values with a textual orthodoxy that he invoked as a paradigm for moral judgment of his and his wife's behavior. No doubt, he assumed that the magistrate would share his values and commitment to propriety. As Susan Mann has shown, many people who read books in the eighteenth century shaped their ethical standards and expectations of family life, especially women's behavior, with reference to a canon of advice books and family instructions that were published in unprecedented quantities in the mid-Qing.[6] Handbooks for women reflected a clear consensus on a daughter-in-law's duty to respect and obey her husband's parents. While often quite realistic about the obstacles to true affection between mothers- and daughters-in-law, they consistently emphasized the obedience and respect that young wives always owed their husbands' mothers. Tang Yi, the author of one popular advice book, suggested that "[the relationship between] mothers and children thrives on affection, while ritual propriety is most important for [the relationship between] mothers- and daughters-in-law." He noted that if relations between wives and mothers-in-law were fraught with difficulties and potential conflict, stepmothers-in-law posed even greater challenges for family harmony. He advised, inferring the frequency of such conflicts, that it was vital for both sides to treat each other with politeness, but he warned that daughters-in-law must be "sincerely respectful without showing the slightest bit of affection" in order to win over their mothers-in-law to treat them kindly. For "if, in their hearts, daughters-in-law make the slightest distinction between the former [mother-in-law] and the latter, even if this is undetectable in their utterances and expressions, . . . there will be no way to avoid becoming recalcitrant."[7]

So consistent was the consensus on this issue that no one in this case, including Gao Shi's father, disputed that it was her moral duty to serve and obey her stepmother-in-law and, at a minimum, to offer her and Shiwan's father the ritually mandated obeisance on festival days. Nor did any of the witnesses deny Gao Shi's lack of respect for her mother-in-law and her abrogation of her proper duties as wife and daughter-in-law, though her father and husband's family offered different explanations for her hostility: the former emphasized personality conflict with an equally unaffectionate stepmother-in-law, while the latter highlighted Gao Shi's "recalcitrant nature" and her resentment of being married into a family of less wealth.

Yet Shiwan and his father were alone in their moral rigor as they demanded Gao Shi's conformity to the wifely way and, when she resisted, demanded the ritually and legally sanctioned punishment of divorce. Despite her failure to meet commonly accepted standards of wifely virtue, Gao Shi's father was sympathetic to her unhappiness and often intervened on her behalf. He was, in fact, less concerned with the impropriety of her behavior per se than with the possibility of a divorce, which would bring disgrace to his family and make it difficult for his daughter to marry again. Similarly, the Chen and Ding descent group leaders and the local magistrate were more interested in resolving the conflict than they were in labeling wrongdoers or punishing immorality. Gao Shi's unfiliality toward her parents-in-law constituted legal and ritual grounds for divorce, yet the magistrate pursued a compromise by ordering the Chens to take her back. The family leaders not only complied readily but offered alternative housing for the couple to facilitate a harmonious resumption of the marriage. Presumably they wished to bring closure to a potentially disgraceful prolonged legal battle over private family problems.

Although the case memorial does not reveal the larger context of the relationship between the Chen, Gao, and Ding families, the intervention of the husband's affinal relatives and the wife's natal family highlights the impotence of patrilineal authority to resolve this domestic dispute. In the end, none of the putative patriarchs in the case—husband, fathers, lineage leaders, magistrates—carried the clout to dictate a resolution: each phase of response to this normative crisis required negotiation and even compromise among those who felt they had a stake. Both the magistrate and the descent group leaders appear in a decidedly reactive role, hardly the staunch upholders of orthodox norms that one might expect them to be. In reversing the divorce decision, the local magistrate acted as a catalyst initiating the resolution of the dispute, much like the judicial officials examined by Philip Huang in his analysis of the interplay between judicial and nonjudicial procedures in the resolution of local conflicts.[8] Although this preliminary settlement demonstrates the operation of Huang's "third realm of justice," the ultimate failure of the mediation suggests that the critical dynamic of conflict resolution here was not simply the interaction between formal state authority and informal local leadership.[9] The magistrate played his catalytic role only at the behest of Gao Shi's father, who chose the court as only one of several avenues of mediation. Indeed, the court's directive could be implemented only with the assent and assistance of the Chen and Ding descent group leaders, who were also involved at the request of Gao Shi's father. Yet Gao Shenghe himself entered the case only because his daughter drew him into the fray by informing him of her plight. It was finally the acceptance or rejection of mediation efforts by husband and wife that was most crucial. The conflict began and ended with the two of them. And they summoned the intervention of various family leaders not as respected elders in a functioning patriarchal hierarchy but as alternative sources of leverage that could be played off against one another.

From the perspective of mid-Qing statecraft reformers, the Gao-Chen case demonstrates the consequences of the failure of state and family authorities to carry out moral transformation. *Jiaohua*, as we saw in Part One, was supposed to be the process through which the state would both propagate its orthodoxy and edify and control local family and community authorities, mobilizing them to fulfill their putative duties to uphold the patriarchal underpinnings of imperial social order. Here tragedy and social chaos resulted when parents, husband, lineage leaders, and magistrates failed to educate a young woman in the ways of wifely propriety and then failed to exercise their rightful authority to deal decisively with the familial conflict surrounding her impropriety. In social practice, as in statecraft discourse, questions about the meaning, practice, and implications of female virtue were inseparable from questions about the nature and effects of patriarchal authority. The architects of the civilizing project understood chastity-centered female virtue to be both a fitting metaphor for patriarchal social order and a vital tool for its regeneration. Wifely unfiliality, adultery, improper encounters between women and men, and sexual assault challenged that order not only because they violated the patriarchal prerogative of fathers and husbands but also because their very occurrence and the conflicts they spawned pointed up the failures of family leaders to control and educate those under their authority.

But statecraft ideals and ambitions aside, was the promotion of female virtue in practice consistent with the promotion of patriarchal hierarchy? What was the relationship of officials to family and community authorities as they dealt with moral transgressions in everyday life? Was there widespread consensus over a set of "orthodox" norms of virtue codified by the state? What kind of practical normative authority did the state really wield in local society? The Gao-Chen case opens up the possibility that the *jiaohua* model describing the transmission of cultural and moral norms does not fully account for the social processes by which improprieties and immorality were identified and addressed. In dealing with such "disgraceful matters," as they were often called, the stem family rarely functioned in isolation, but the patterns of authority that facilitated its resolution of such matters rarely resembled the linear, patriarchal hierarchies of state and lineage imagined by reformers. Moral crises and conflicts over the behavior of women activated people who, for one reason or another, claimed the prerogative to assess women's virtue and intervene in domestic affairs, including not only patrilineal kin networks and the state but also affinal kin networks and neighbors.

Yet if all of these local players were potentially implicated in transgressions of chastity, they did not necessarily see the strict enforcement of normative standards as their first priority. Despite broad consensus on the value of chastity and filial obedience, the normative and judicial rights and roles of each of these players were subjects of great contention.

Instead of galvanizing them to uphold moral order, transgressions of female virtue often set these local players in conflict as they maneuvered to protect personal and family reputation and control their interaction with state authority represented by the county magistrate's office *(yamen)*, a constant, if not always decisive or welcomed, figure in processes of conflict resolution. The local politics of chastity fractured patriarchal authority, distracting attention away from questions of right and wrong and thwarting the statecraft desire for a unitary social hierarchy upholding an orthodox normative consensus. The next three chapters will exam ine the modes and implications of this fragmentation of authority through an exploration of the normative and judicial roles of lineage leaders and women's natal families and the judicial conundrum posed by incest.

CHAPTER 3

Enforcing Gender Order

Between the Ancestral Hall and the Yamen

Ideologically and politically associated with the state through their degree status or aspirations, while at the same time occupying local positions of power through involvement in lineages or less formal village associations, family and community authorities were supposed to be catalysts for moral transformation. They were expected to share the state's normative priorities, to serve as effective mediators between state and society, and to transmit and enforce the values associated with state orthodoxy.[1] But although mid-Qing emperors and officials hoped that local elites and lineage leaders would function as "models and leaders for the common people, by respectfully obeying established regulations so as to be standard bearers for emulation in village lanes,"[2] they would not have been surprised by the appeasing and reactive role of the Gao, Chen, and Ding lineage leaders in the case just described in the Part Two Prologue. Nagging concerns about the weakness or corruption of local magistrates, local elites, and community elders haunted their proposals and reports, and they were especially ambivalent about the effectiveness and commitment of lineage leaders to the imperial state's agenda.

To some extent, lineage leaders did fulfill Qing officials' vision of their role. In the mid-Qing period, they produced unprecedented quantities of family instructions, morality handbooks, and ledgers of merit and demerit elaborating in great detail the behavioral standards and duties fitting for men and women, husbands and wives, daughters and sons.[3] They reinforced the values of filial piety and chastity through patronage of ancestral rites and ritual performances of morality tales like the Mulian saga, sponsored by lineages and village associations.⁴ Criminal cases widely confirm the effectiveness of such efforts to propagate standards of female virtue and family values, attesting that awareness of a shared set of norms extended to the poorest segments of society and the most remote regions of the country.⁵

But if official *jiaohua* discourse emphasized the importance of the alliance between the state on the one hand and family and community authorities on the other in the management of moral affairs, advice books on family governance and female behavior suggest the divergence of state and family interests and the potential for conflict between them. Focusing exclusively on the patrilineal family as the site of normative authority, they marginalized the state if they mentioned it at all. For example, despite Chen Hongmou's often strident insistence in his discussions of law and social policy on the critical role of the state in reforming customs, including the behavior of women, reference to the foundational linkage between the family order and political order is completely and strikingly absent from the handbooks for women's education he compiled in his "Bequeathed Guidelines for Instructing Women" *(Jiaonü yigui)* and from his own commentaries on them. Lan Dingyuan (1680–1733) did begin his handbook "Lessons for Women" *(Nüxue)* by reiterating the classical paradigm of moral transformation that informed these sets of instructions and their textual precedents. "The governance of all under heaven relies on customs. The rectification of customs relies on the ordering of the family. The way of ordering the family must begin with women."⁶ If all people under heaven rectified their families, he asserted, they would "silently assist the imperium's solemn and harmonious [moral] transformation."⁷ In this formulation, moral order began in the family with the proper regulation of gender relationships and then emanated out to influence the realm.

Wang Huizu, in his manual of advice to his sons on the regulation of family life, entitled "Simple Precepts from the Hall Enshrining a Pair of Chaste Widows" *(Shuangjietang yongxun)*, described a morally self-sufficient patriarchal stem family that kept outsiders, including the state, at bay. Although he asserted that "the court provides officials in order to regulate social hierarchy *(zhi zunbei)*," he did not grant the state any role in family life. On the contrary, he suggested avoidance of unnecessary intimacy or influence with local officials and outlined strategies for displaying respect for state authority by paying taxes on time, strictly obeying the law, and offering strategic salutations and praise to the local magistrate, precisely in order to avoid the meddling and harassment of officials and *yamen* staff.⁸ He warned his sons not only to avoid settling family matters through litigation but also to avoid the appearance of having influence with the *yamen* lest they unwittingly become community leaders prone to "incitement" by local people to lead resistance against the magistrate or to entanglements in their lawsuits.⁹ Wang emphasized that the regulation of the family was entirely the responsibility of family elders—a view that, as we shall see, was widely shared by family leaders across the empire—and identified women as the primary source of familial tension. "Within a family, the tenor of blood ties and marital relationships differs, and temperaments vary from the stubborn to the pliant. Only the discipline of family elders can forge unity. Without this, the wanton destruction of propriety will be endless as brothers' wives compare the splendor of their wealth and wives and sisters develop animosities over unfriendliness."¹⁰

Chen Hongmou, Lan Dingyuan, and Wang Huizu were all respected and influential statecraft thinkers who in their memorials or essays on administration eloquently articulated the normative functions of the state in local society and in their administrative careers worked to extend the state's moral influence ever deeper into local community life. Of course, it was not at all uncommon for men as influential and widely published as these to express contradictory views as they wrote for different audiences at different points in their careers. William Rowe has nevertheless argued that in the case of Chen Hongmou such seemingly contradictory ideas about the role of the state and local lineage leaders in the regulation of moral order reflect a disjuncture between his ideals and the political realities he faced as an official.¹¹ But far from being idiosyncratic, such contradictions were rife in statecraft proposals, legislation, and law in this period. They were symptomatic of the unease of emperors and officials with the absence of pure and reliable patriarchal authority with which the imperial state could ally itself in its civilizing project.

PROBLEMS WITH PATRIARCHS

With the proliferation of formal lineage organizations and their increasing influence in local affairs during the seventeenth and eighteenth centuries, the normative and judicial role of lineage leaders became a prickly issue for the expanding Qing state. The copious memorials, edicts, and legislation surrounding the issue consistently failed to get past the paradox that, from the state's perspective, lineage authorities had a legitimate and potentially useful role as arbiters of morality within their families but that their effectiveness as defenders of social order was all too often compromised when family or personal interest conflicted with the state's priorities. In his study of Qing lineage law, Zhu Yong traces a series of attempts to harness the de facto power of lineages for the state's agenda, demonstrating the dynasty's increasingly explicit recognition of the judicial authority and responsibilities of lineage heads *(zuzhang)* and the legitimacy of clan rules.[12] In 1689, in response to a case of a woman who beat and cursed her mother, the Kangxi Emperor established a standard of *zuzhang* accountability for the crimes of lineage members by ordering punishment for the lineage head for failure to morally educate the younger generation. Yongzheng formalized the judicial duties of lineage leaders in 1726 with the creation of the position of *zuzheng*, a lineage leader deputed by the magistrate to report criminal activities within the lineage to supplement the surveillance activities of the *bao* headman.[13] Three years later he ordered that lineage leaders and household heads who failed to intervene in family conflicts that then resulted in homicides be punished with eighty strokes of the heavy bamboo. Finally, in an edict of 1727, Yongzheng went so far as to authorize that

> in dealing with wicked lawbreakers who have been punished by the magistrate but remain obdurately unrepentant and are detested by their entire lineage, lineage members are allowed, after informing the magistrate, to banish them to a distant region to remove the threat to the lineage. Or, if punishment is carried out according to family rules and results in death, [the responsible lineage members] will be exempted from paying with their lives.[14]

Although these initiatives, especially the condoning of extrajudicial punishments, appear at first glance to enhance lineage autonomy at the expense of central state control, on closer reading they represent a careful delegation of authority intended to expand state control, a strategy that was fully consistent with Yongzheng's approach to state building and with the ethos of *jiaohua*. Lineage leaders were not granted autonomous judicial authority but were deputed to be agents of the state: their expanded judicial prerogative was circumscribed by the greater surveillance of the state and their increased accountability to state authorities for their adjudicatory actions. The new substatute that codified the emperor's order gave lineage members the right, with the prior permission of the magistrate, to mete out sentences of exile for recidivist criminals. It then clarified the very specific circumstances under which extrajudicial executions of such lineage criminals could be considered for lesser punishment, mandating thorough investigation by the magistrate of the circumstances of the killing. If lineage members executed a convicted criminal for a capital offense but did not inform the *yamen* until afterwards, they were to be punished with one hundred strokes of the heavy bamboo, according to the substatute on illegally arrogating the authority to punish a criminal. If the offense for which the lineage execution was carried out was not a capital crime, those responsible were to be punished one degree less than the criminal would have been but were still exempted from a death penalty.

The Yongzheng Emperor's vision of the place of lineage authorities in the imperial order paralleled his construction of chaste women as models of dutiful subjects.[15] Inspired by a profound optimism about the moral potential of his subjects and their loyalty to the state's civilizing agenda, he attempted to mobilize them to fulfill their duty as participants in the creation of imperial moral and social order. Such optimism, however, appeared increasingly misplaced as instances of extrajudicial lineage killings and violent feuds multiplied over the latter half of the eighteenth century, reflecting not only the growing numbers and power of lineages but the divergence between their priorities and those of the imperial state.[16] Faced with such threats to social order and the judicial prerogative of the state, the Qianlong Emperor rescinded his father's substatute on lineage executions, explaining,

> Although [this substatute] is intended to punish the wicked and in its essence accords with human sentiment, it is difficult to distinguish the wise from the foolish among lineage leaders. There are those who incur general animosity with their parsimonious handling of wealth; some arouse widespread hostility by being tough-minded and upright; sometimes one person stirs up a group to go along with him; or they all share a grudge over a trifling matter and seek revenge. [Thus] false accusations that cause harm are common. If the local magistrate cannot investigate thoroughly, then it is difficult to guarantee that injustices do not occur. Moreover, [decisions] about life and death are still the sovereign prerogative of the court. If the law has been broken, then [the court] itself must publicly carry out an execution in accordance with the law. It is not appropriate to exercise this power through the hands of lineage members.[17]

Underlying Qianlong's opposition to the delegation of judicial authority were two assumptions that differentiated his approach to state-society relations from that of his father. First, he argued, aptly as we will see, that most lineage leaders were incapable of fulfilling the responsibilities of adjudication either because of their own foibles or because their authority was not fully accepted by lineage members. Less confident of his subjects' (not to mention his officials') identification with his values and political agenda than Yongzheng, Qianlong also saw in the delegation of judicial authority not an extension of sovereignty working to enhance state influence but rather a retreat of the state from local society that undermined the state's prerogative to make and enforce the law.

Doubts about the integrity of local patriarchal authority and concerns about maintaining the state's role in local society emerged even more clearly in a 1789 edict rejecting the suggestion of a memorialist to expand *zuzheng* powers to proscribe and charge lineage members who broke the law. The majority of *zuzheng*, Qianlong asserted, were "gentry bullies," not law-abiding people interested in the common good. *Zuzheng* would also, inevitably, be prone to nepotism and would protect their own family members from punishment. Furthermore, investigation of crimes and apprehension of criminals were the job of the magistrate. "What's the use of establishing local officials if *zuzheng* are investigating thieves and bandits and arresting criminals?" he argued. Finally, given this modicum of judicial authority, *zuzheng* were likely to arrogate even more power to themselves. In this case, he asked, "How would they be different from hereditary native officials *(tusi),*" who had been replaced with magistrates in the *gaitu guiliu* policy several decades earlier.[18]

Like his father's, Qianlong's approach to the problem of the relationship between the imperial state and lineage leaders mirrored his understanding of the state's relationship to chaste women through the chastity cult. Emphasizing women's fickleness, irrationality, and emotional fragility, he interpreted the role of the cult not as galvanizing chaste women to uphold social order and state orthodoxy but rather as enforcing strict standards of virtue, in part to protect women from the improperly suicidal impulses of their frail and hypersensitive natures.[19] Similarly weak, foolish, and prone to impropriety, lineage leaders required not an expansion of their authority but the paternalistic intervention of the state to show them the path of propriety and coax them to fulfill their already existing duties vis-à-vis lineage members and the state.

Yet despite his more cynical approach to human nature and state building, Qianlong's handling of lineages remained fundamentally contradictory. Pessimism about their moral potential notwithstanding, Qianlong was no more inclined than his father to deny the legitimacy and even utility of lineage leaders arbitrating normative matters for their kin. He never revoked the responsibilities of *zuzheng* for surveillance and reporting of crimes and in fact expanded their powers to detain feuding lineage members, incarcerate the mentally ill, and manage misappropriated lineage property.[20] However, despite all the talk in the latter half of the eighteenth century about expanding the authority of lineage heads to punish their own members, improper arrogation of judicial authority was punishable throughout the dynasty, as it had been in the Ming, as "private settlement" of "public matters." If discovered by the magistrate, it was subject to punishment two degrees less than that of the offender in question, with a maximum penalty of fifty strokes of the light bamboo.[21] The caveat of magistrate discovery would seem to provide tacit state support for lineage punishments for minor offenses if they were accepted as legitimate by the parties involved. However, if an offense of illicit sex or a homicide was at issue, neither this caveat nor the punishment limit applied, and those responsible were subject to even greater punishments.[22] So if a lineage-adjudicated or mediated case ended up in court, the leaders were likely to be punished, especially if the case involved a capital crime.

LINEAGE AUTHORITY IN PRACTICE

While the state was profoundly ambivalent about the proper normative and judicial role of lineage leaders, criminal cases reveal that their authority was regularly challenged by their own relatives as well, suggesting the limitations on their ability to be effective arbiters of morality in local communities. In theory, lineage leaders were arbiters of morality, but in practice their normative authority was only partially acknowledged by the state and by lineage members. The case record is full of lineage leaders who overstepped their authority to punish errant family members.[23] While organized lineages appear in relatively few serious cases involving female virtue, more loosely defined descent groups are highly visible as their leaders intervened to mediate disputes and supervise retribution.[24] When lineage leaders do appear, it is usually because the legitimacy of their authority to punish was questioned or opposed within the lineage or because the matter at hand involved someone outside the lineage, so that they were placed in a mediatory rather than an authoritative role.

Such cases not only placed lineage leaders in direct confrontation with the state but also unraveled any readily assumed congruence between the enforcement of chastity and the interests of patriarchal authority, as an adultery case from Ninghua County, Fujian, illustrates. Leaders of the Zhang lineage intervened when "Old Madame Qiu" (aged sixty-five *sui*), the widowed head of one lineage household, reported to them that in the absence of her son, who was sojourning away from home as a hired hand, her daughter-in-law, Qiu Shi, was having an affair with her dead husband's nephew, Zhang Sipeng. Qiu Shi had taken her quilt, mosquito net, and other belongings and had moved in with Sipeng, the local barber, "wanting to live . . . as husband and wife."[25] According to Sipeng, Qiu Shi had brazenly seduced him. "[Her husband] did wage labor away from home, so the household was very poor. [She] often came to me to borrow money for daily expenses," he testified. "On [the 15th of the month], Qiu Shi came to my house to buy rice on credit and, noticing the razor lying on the table, asked me to shave her face. I flirted with her and we had illicit sex. On the 26th, she suddenly brought her bedding and moved to my house. . . . I didn't dare let her stay." At the request of Old Madame Qiu, the lineage leaders censured *(chize)* Sipeng, and his elder brother instructed his own wife and sister to return Qiu Shi forcibly to her mother-in-law's home.[26]

But this relatively mild punishment failed to satisfy Qiu Shi's husband, Zhang Menglu, who returned home a month later and registered another complaint with the lineage leaders, requesting that they take his wife and Sipeng to the *yamen* for punishment. "Afraid of *yamen* punishment, but willing to submit to a lineage punishment *(wei zui yuan fa),*"[27] Sipeng dispatched his elder brothers to "request punishment *(qiuchu)*" from the lineage branch heads *(zufang)*, a group of three men, aged seventy-seven, seventy-three, and sixty-eight *sui*.[28] According to their collectively collated testimony:

> We consulted together and decided to confiscate Zhang Sipeng's land [as endowment] for sacrifices at the lineage's ancestral hall. The twenty *shi*[29] of land at the place locally known as the Thunder Lord's Mouth were to become sacrificial land for the common ancestors of all three branches of the lineage together. The two *shi* of drained land under the ridge were to be sacrificial land for the first ancestor of Zhang Sipeng's own sub-branch. The remaining four *shi* of land under the ridge were to become sacrificial land for the two branches of Zhang Sipeng and Zhang Sizong, and the cultivation and sponsoring of sacrifices were to be rotated between them every year. Since Zhang Sipeng shared the land at the Thunder Lord's Mouth with his younger brother, Zhang Jihe, four *shi* were given to Zhang Jihe to cultivate, which he was not allowed to misappropriate and sell. Zhang Sipeng's remaining land was sold for fourteen *liang* of silver and 2,700 *wen* of cash, which was used to slaughter pigs and prepare wine for sacrifices at the ancestral hall. Zhang Sipeng signed a contract of compliance, and his elder brothers, Zhang Mengxuan and Zhang Mengke, signed an agreement to remove Zhang Sipeng's name from the lineage register and banish him from

the village. The land contracts are in the possession of the lineage council (*zuzhong*). Qiu Shi was sold in marriage.

This testimony provides a rare glimpse of lineage sanctions at work in a case of moral impropriety. The combined penalty of confiscation of land and expulsion from the lineage and the village for the adulterous man ranked among the most severe punishments for men listed commonly in lineage regulations, while being sold in marriage was the most severe punishment for women.[30] Despite the authoritative tone of the lineage leaders and the severity of the punishment, the judgment rendered here reflects a lineage adjudicatory process that was fundamentally consensual, at least among men. Not only did the branch heads consult together, but they sought a commitment to comply from the male offender and his brothers in the form of written contracts. While the punishments of Sipeng and Qiu Shi were, in a sense, parallel, both involving removal from the lineage, the process of meting out judgment on the two was quite different: lineage leaders sought the open compliance of Sipeng but did not consider Qiu Shi's assent to remarriage necessary.

In the denouement of the case, the reason for attempting to contractualize the punishment becomes clear. For all the ritual formality and meticulous attention to contractual propriety in the elders' decision, Sipeng ultimately refused to recognize the legitimacy of this judgment against him. A year and five months after his banishment from the village, he returned and consulted with his younger brother, Jihe, about the prospect of buying back some land. When word got around about his intentions, lineage members opposed his return. So he accused them in the county court of stealing his property, leading the magistrate to haul several lineage members into court for interrogation. Several lineage members then also filed a counterplaint against Sipeng. On the road home from the *yamen*, they ran into Sipeng and Jihe, and a huge fight broke out among them, in the midst of which Sipeng killed one distant cousin who tried to mediate and severely wounded several others who joined in the melee. Qiu Shi died in childbirth at the home of her new husband before the trial.

This case highlights the limited ability of even a highly organized lineage to instill moral norms, enforce them, and deal with the consequences of transgressions. To begin with, the illicit sex was not discovered until Qiu Shi blatantly moved in with Sipeng. As the record of adultery cases confirms again and again, village life, even in single-lineage communities, did not preclude privacy and the keeping of secrets; hidden trysts and affairs were possible, even within the manor houses of large extended families.³¹ If the lineage leaders could not oversee the private comings and goings of all members, neither could they enforce conformity with moral norms or even command complete respect for sanctions against immoral behavior. Here the judgments of lineage leaders were challenged first by the adulteress's husband, who wanted more severe punishment meted out by the magistrate. The lineage adjudication process then became a negotiation as the offender and his brothers pushed for internal lineage punishment instead.

As in the Chen-Gao case, the fact of the transgression was not in dispute. The problem was how to deal with it. Zhang Sipeng initially accepted his lineage leaders' ruling, no doubt because his relations, including his own brothers, overwhelmingly supported it. But as soon as he could, he made his way back to the village to fight for his place in the community. Given the Qing Code's prohibition of private settlements of criminal cases, his lawsuit was not entirely frivolous. A disgruntled recipient of lineage punishment could try to subvert his elders' ruling by taking them to court with some hope of state redress. Indeed, in this instance, when the case came to trial, not only Sipeng was punished, receiving a death sentence for killing in an affray, but the three branch heads as well, who received eighty strokes of the heavy bamboo in accordance with the statute on "privately settling a case of illicit sex." From the perspective of Qing law the ends of upholding chastity did not justify the misuse of patriarchal authority to infringe upon state prerogative, even when the lineage involved displayed an extraordinary degree of organization and concern for the integrity, if not the legality, of their adjudicatory process. Melissa Macauley has shown how the Qing judicial system offered subordinate actors, including women, tools to challenge the power and authority of those who controlled family and community hierarchies. Disturbed by the subversive uses of lawsuits, counterplaints, and false accusations, Qing officials struggled constantly and unsuccessfully to control access to the courts, most notably by cracking down on the activities of the litigation masters, who facilitated such access for anyone who could pay them.³² What they did not fully comprehend, however, and what this case highlights, was the degree to which their own policies undermined the ability of lineage leaders to check the behavior of their kin and keep intrafamilial disputes out of court.

If anyone could fulfill the expectations of the state about the proper exercise of lineage authority, it would be a family like the Zhangs, who appear to have been a model of lineage integrity when compared to other

Enforcing Gender Order

descent groups, whose punishments of immoral behavior are documented in the case record. It is striking, in this regard, that the branch heads gained nothing materially from the judgment: all confiscated property was designated as sacrificial land, with the exception of the small plot left for Sipeng's brother to cultivate. Care was taken to reserve sacrificial land for Sipeng's own branch ancestors and to deal fairly with his brother in dispensing with the land that the two owned jointly. Even the proceeds of the land sale were used for the sacrifices marking the settlement of the case. Had the case ended simply in a lawsuit and not involved a murder, which obliged the magistrate to send a memorial submitting the transcript of his investigation and trial for the review of his superiors, he might well have condoned the actions of the branch heads.[33]

LINEAGE LEADERS AS VIGILANTES

Many other cases indicate that Qing legislators had good reason to question the effectiveness and legitimacy of lineage leaders. At the opposite extreme from the careful, rule-bound procedures of a highly organized lineage like the Zhangs were descent group punishments that were barely distinguishable from vigilante revenge. A case involving the octogenarian *zuzhang* of the Xu family in Shenzhou, Zhili, typifies the arbitrary and violent potential of lineage adjudication that fulfilled the worst fears of the Qianlong Emperor about the lawless and immoral exercise of patriarchal authority. The elder was informed by one of his nephews that one of his grandnephews had propositioned the nephew's wife by coming into her room drunk in the middle of the night and taking off his clothes. The furious husband wanted to take the offender to the *yamen* for punishment, but the elder replied, "This is a disgraceful matter *(choushi)*, and if word of it gets out, we will be ridiculed by people. It is better to tell his father . . . to punish him himself. . . . He should break his legs and gouge out his eyes." The father complied to the point of breaking his son's legs but then refused to gouge out his eyes, begging the elder instead to request that the offended husband have mercy on his son. When the husband refused, the elder simply left the scene, abdicating any responsibility for the consequences of his judgment. After he left, the husband, several of his male relatives, and his wife's brother, who lived in the same village, all went to complete the gruesome punishment and, in their fury, also beat the offender's father to death.

The nature of this *zuzhang*'s authority was clearly quite different from that of the leaders of the Zhang lineage. The offended husband thought it necessary to appeal to the octogenarian elder when his wife was propositioned and expected him to take charge of the matter, either by taking the culprit to the *yamen* or ordering descent group punishment. But the elder made his judgment alone with no reference to any formalized descent group regulations or custom or any process of consensus building. All parties to the incident initially complied with his orders. Yet when the culprit's father resisted, the elder simply let the matter drop, evading responsibility for the consequences of his decision. He functioned, in effect, as a rabble-rouser, stirring a mob of descent group members to violence from which he then distanced himself.[34]

Even when lineage leaders were less arbitrary and violent, the disruptive potential of challenges to their authority was considerable, especially when illicit sex and other violations of women's virtue were involved. Situations in which people refused to accept lineage punishment for a misdeed provided the context for many assaults and homicides. In one case in 1780, a seven-month-long incestuous affair between a widow and her brother-in-law in Xinfeng County, Jiangxi, was finally discovered after her sister-in-law caught her one evening boiling palm root procured by a female friend to try to induce a miscarriage. She reported the incident, and the octogenarian head of the lineage told his son to bring the adulterer to the ancestral hall for corporal punishment *(zechu)* because he himself had difficulty walking. The adulterer's father objected, saying, "The lineage head is your father.... Even if my son and Wang Shi have had illicit sex, it is your father who should punish him. Why have you come?" The lineage head's son accused him of "siding with a wrongdoer" and hit him. A fight ensued in which the adulterer killed the lineage head's son.[35] The magistrate sentenced the murder as killing in an affray rather than the more serious crime of a guilty person killing someone allowed to make an arrest. He explained that although the adulterer was "a person who had committed a crime," the lineage head's son, as a relative without mourning obligations, did not have the responsibility to arrest him. Moreover, he wanted to bind him to take him to the ancestral hall for private punishment, not to be handed over to the magistrate. Rather than seeing the incestuous adultery as an aggravating factor enhancing the guilt of the murderer, he, in effect, treated the improper aggrandizement of judicial authority by the lineage head's son as a mitigating factor in his murder. He also sentenced the murderer's father to a year in exile for his involvement in the fight, his failure to prohibit his son and daughter-in-law from committing adultery, and his inappropriate protection of his guilty son. The magistrate censured the lineage head

Enforcing Gender Order 77

for not reporting the adultery to the *yamen* but did not punish him because of his age.

As the magistrate attempted to sort out the moral and judicial culpability for the loss of life in this complicated case, he drew upon an array of substatutes intended not just to punish crime but to implicate family authorities in the moral failings of those under their tutelage and hold them accountable for the improper handling of such infractions. Such cases inevitably highlighted the mutual distrust between state and lineage authorities. When confronted with such disgraceful matters, family elders often identified themselves first as guardians of family reputation, preferring to handle them internally, often in ways that evaded state interference and mitigated strict enforcement of norms. Even statecraft thinkers who sympathized with this sentiment, arguing that such matters should ideally be handled by upstanding lineage leaders rather than the state, envisioned that such limited delegation of judicial authority would be under the close supervision of the magistrate to make the policing of social order more effective. For many family authorities, however, maintenance of social order required the concealment of disgraceful matters from all outsiders, including the magistrate, and the avoidance of messy and embarrassing entanglements with the state.

In a case from Guixi County, Jiangxi, for example, a lineage council (*zuzhong*) consisting of five men, aged forty-five, thirty-four, twenty-seven, twenty-five, and twenty-one, confiscated property illicitly as punishment for an attempted rape. The five were meeting one day in the main room of the ancestral hall to calculate lineage expenses for the ancestral sacrifices at the winter solstice when they heard screaming and commotion coming from the house of one of their elder brothers, Zhan Chengxiu.[36] They ran to the house to investigate and were told by Chengxiu's sister-in-law, Xu Shi, that she had been out visiting neighbors and had left her daughter, Heying, at home alone spinning in her bedroom. Xu Shi's husband's nephew, Zhan Erde, came into the house and grabbed her, wanting to have illicit sex. Heying screamed and struggled with him, in the course of which he ripped her clothes. Xu Shi heard the screaming and ran home just as the culprit was running out the door. Justifying his subsequent behavior, Zhan Chengxiu explained to the magistrate, "When we heard that such a thing had happened, ruining the reputation of the family *(baihuai menfeng)*, we found this unacceptable, and we all went to Zhan Erde's house to seize him and take him to the ancestral hall for punishment."

Erde fled his house when he heard that the lineage leaders were looking for him. They told his father, Zhan Zhengshi, "If you can't control your son, then in accordance with the regulations of the ancestral hall, you must slaughter a pig and distribute the meat and make a penalty offering of grain to the ancestral hall." Zhengshi himself fled the scene, since, as he put it, "The collective anger of the lineage members had been aroused and I could only hide myself at my wife's family's house." After he left, the five leaders took his pig for themselves, slaughtered it, and divided the meat amongst themselves. They confiscated twenty *shi* (one *shi* is approximately a bushel) of grain and stored it in the ancestral hall. Defending their actions to the suspicious magistrate, Chengxiu explained, "This has long been our village custom. All those who do illegal things are punished to warn those in the future. This was definitely not plundering."

When Erde heard about the confiscation, he stated in his confession, "In my heart I could not endure it, and I also feared that my lineage people would not be willing to let the matter drop and I would still face *yamen* punishment." Devising a horrifically insane scheme to get back at the lineage leaders by manipulating the magistrate, he murdered his crippled younger brother, then ran to the house of his maternal relatives, where his father was waiting out the conflict, and told them that the lineage leaders had killed his brother and that they should take the lineage leaders to court.[37] Seeing him covered with blood, his family immediately realized what he had done and refused to participate in his false accusation. Erde went to court on his own, but the magistrate quickly uncovered his guilt.[38] The gravity of Erde's crimes notwithstanding, the magistrate also convicted the lineage leaders for stealing Erde's father's pig and grain. The statute on plundering *(qiangdao)* does not mention plundering between relatives but mandates instead that such cases be sentenced according to the statute on "using intimidation to obtain another's property," which specifies punishments for various degrees of relatives, including "senior relatives who offend against juniors." The magistrate therefore ordered the elders to compensate Erde's father for the value of his plundered property, and Zhan Chengxiu, as their leader, was sentenced eighty strokes of the heavy bamboo, reduced one degree to seventy because these were relatives with no mourning obligations. The other members of the *zuzhong* received sixty strokes as his accomplices.[39]

Both Erde and his father feared the power of the lineage leaders. The father humbly expressed his respect for their authority to punish his son and nervously hid himself to avoid more trouble. Erde, though obviously not contrite like his father, explained his attempt at revenge as an act of desperation undertaken out of fear of further punishment from the lineage leaders. Significantly, he feared that they would still take him to the *yamen* for the more severe punishment mandated by law for attempted rape, namely one hundred blows of the heavy bamboo and life exile. The threat of *yamen* involvement hovered over case participants and, from Erde's perspective, augmented the power of the lineage leaders. The *yamen* card, could, however, be played by anyone, as both this and the Zhang lineage case demonstrate. Pervasively present in the minds of villagers as one avenue of redress for an offense or proper punishment for someone who had violated local norms, the county *yamen* represented an important source of symbolic capital in local communities. In a subtle interplay between state and lineage authority, this symbolic function worked in turn to enhance the normative authority of the state, whose punishments were feared above all others.

Perhaps the most ironic result of the contrapuntal play of state and family interests was the creation, in the context of sexual assault cases, of a direct conflict between the defense of chastity and the exercise of patriarchal authority that positioned the state as the defender of chaste women over and against their families. This theme will be addressed in much greater depth in Part Four, but one example here will suffice to demonstrate the state's concern with the potentially tragic consequences of lineage punishments intended to avoid state judgment. After Chen Limei, from Rendai County, Guangdong, flirted with his aunt, Yang Shi, and embraced her while she was out herding cows, her husband informed the Chen lineage elders that he intended to report the incident to the magistrate, as the law required him to do. They pressured him to keep the matter within the lineage, arguing that "it was not good to spread the disgraceful family matters of clan members outside." Punishing the offender according to clan rules instead, the three lineage elders censured the young man, took him to the woman's house, and ordered him to kowtow and make a formal apology to her family. The elders considered the matter closed, but a few weeks later Yang Shi was out drawing water from the village well when she overheard Chen Limei explaining his punishment to another lineage member. "All I did was embrace her briefly and they made me go and beg for forgiveness, " he said dismissively. Furious, Yang Shi grabbed the unrepentant offender and bit his finger. Returning home, she told her husband, "I have repeatedly been humiliated by Chen . . . and cannot face people, so I can only kill myself *(Lü bei Chen . . . xiuru jianbude ren zhihao zi jin)*." She hanged herself a few days later. The magistrate sentenced Chen Limei to strangulation after the assizes for attempted rape leading to the suicide of the victim, noting that his later telling of the story aggravated his offense. The lineage elders were also punished for failure to report a case of illicit sex.[40] Yang Shi was honored with a citation for chastity. As many officials noted in memorials calling for stricter punishments for the private settlement of illicit sex offenses, family avoidance of state judgment also prevented the public vindication of women whose chastity had been impugned, resulting all too often in suicides that implicated the families involved in an even greater crime. As we saw in Part One, the substatutes criminalizing unwanted flirtation and holding family authorities accountable for reporting it evolved amidst widespread concern among mid-Qing emperors and officials about the failure of family leaders to deal justly and effectively with violations of chastity. The particular circumstances leading to Yang Shi's suicide were addressed only one year after her death in a new substatute explicitly stating that causing a woman to commit suicide by ridiculing her in the wake of an unwanted flirtation was a crime.[41]

In the memorials submitting serious cases for the scrutiny and final judgment of the Board of Punishments and the emperor, the state, through its officials, played a central role as the final arbiter of moral matters in local society. Read against the grain of this judicial teleology, however, case histories illustrate the limits of the state's purview and its normative authority. In fact, the state often played a defining role only in the final stages, as cases were adjudicated in the county court. In the Zhang case the state was effectively excluded from dealing with the moral offense of adultery when the lineage leaders, acting at the request of Sipeng's brothers for leniency, decided to reject the demand of Qiu Shi's husband to take him to the *yamen*. The magistrate became involved again only when Sipeng brought suit against his relatives. In the Xu case, the affronted husband also requested *yamen* punishment, but the descent group elder felt that this would augment the disgrace to the family and insisted on internal punishment. In the Zhan case, no one ever even suggested that the matter be taken to the *yamen* until Erde himself made his false accusation, and his intent was not to defer to the moral authority of the court but to manipulate it for his own immoral ends. As in the case of Chen Shiwan killing his wife, Gao Shi, the state was reactive, summoned by those involved in a conflict to play its authoritative role in the midst of the much larger processes of local efforts at resolution. And while the authority of the state and the authority of the descent group could complement and reinforce each other, they were also, paradoxically, in tension. Although judicial practice and rhetoric stressed the importance of letting lineages adjudicate their own minor matters, this "third realm" was to operate at the state's behest.[42] The state refused, at least in principle, to grant automatic recognition of descent group punishments. Meanwhile, descent group leaders wary of submitting their internal disgraces for public scrutiny continued to act autonomously until circumstances forced them to engage with the state.

CHAPTER 4

Divided Loyalties

Natal Families and the Exercise of Patrilineal Authority

The judicial authority of lineage leaders and family patriarchs was debated explicitly in official discourse, social commentary, and social life. But other questions about the nature of patriarchal authority, who had the right to exercise it, and its relationship to the enforcement and defense of women's virtue were contested more indirectly in discourse and social practice, producing subtle shifts in the state's and popular understanding of the nature of patriarchy and its relationship to chastity. James Lee and Cameron Campbell's demographic work on Liaoning Province has strikingly demonstrated that household structure varied tremendously from region to region and from family to family. Each variant carried its own set of consequences for patterns of family politics, the centralization of patriarchal authority within the family, and thus the degree of what the authors call "demographic privilege"—the right to high fertility and low death rates, available to individuals at different points in the kinship system and in the family life cycle.[1] Household structure, kinship practices, and the geographic proximity of relatives all shaped the nature of patriarchal authority in practice, with particularly decisive consequences for women's lives and for processes of dealing with transgressions of female virtue. Many cases of adultery, marital conflict, and other moral crises, for example, featured nuclear or stem families or fragmentary households with only one adult living in isolation from routine relationships with an extended kin community. In most criminal cases, whether or not relatives were involved, neighbors were present in the background and often played a critical role as witnesses, mediators, and parties to conflict. For some families, neighbors provided the only community of any immediate relevance to their lives. Although Qing law and the *baojia* system required neighbors to report crimes, their de facto role in enforcing propriety and mediating family conflicts remained largely unaddressed in statecraft discussions of the civilizing process or in prescriptive literature.[2]

A far greater challenge was posed to the ideal and practice of patriarchal authority by women's natal families, who are pervasive throughout the case record, playing a crucial role in crises and conflicts over women's behavior. If women involved in cases of adultery or marital conflict had natal relatives living anywhere near their marital homes, their testimonies regarding a woman's character and the tenor of her relations with her in-laws were usually included in the case record. Quite often natal family members played a much more central role in resolving social conflicts or causing conflicts between women and their in-laws.[3] While the normative authority of lineage leaders was often diluted by opposition to their judgments or distracted from moral priorities by concerns about reputation, greed, or favoritism, the patriarchal prerogative of the patriline was also challenged by the ritual, legal, and emotional claims of women's natal families. What, precisely, was the role of a woman's natal family in her life, and how did her relationship with her parents mesh with the requirements of the wifely way? In the case record these questions are revealed to have been contentious and pervasive issues for statecraft reformers and ordinary people alike. If the exercise of descent group authority was shaped by contestation with the state over judicial and normative prerogative, the role of natal families was structured by patterns of cooperation and competition between them and women's marital kin.

AFFINAL AFFECTIONS AND THE WIFELY WAY

As he explicated for his sons the responsibilities and prerogatives of family elders, Wang Huizu had in mind the patriarchs of the patrilineally defined family. Tellingly, the first potential threat to patrilineal harmony that he identified was tensions caused by outside women who had married into the family. "Within a family, the tenor of blood ties and marital relationships differs, and temperaments vary from the stubborn to the pliant," he explained, "Only the discipline of family elders can forge unity. Without this, the wanton destruction of propriety will be endless as brothers' wives compare the splendor of their wealth and wives and sisters develop animosities over unfriendliness."[4] Controlling the behavior of women was particularly difficult, he argued, for "wives come from outside and their mothers' teachings are not necessarily thorough. Within one family, if there is one wife who does not respect family supervision and does not uphold the family instructions ... then there will be no unity. Animosities will arise and one day lead to the fomenting of rebellion. This is no trifling matter."[5]

The divisive potential of "outsider" wives and daughters-in-law is an all too familiar trope in late imperial morality handbooks and fiction. But while the concerns of social commentators like Wang Huizu about outside women and affinal politics were not entirely misplaced, as their contentious role in the case record suggests, the fact was that law, ritual propriety, and popular custom all recognized to some extent married women's obligations toward their natal families and their families' responsibilities for their behavior. What made affinal family politics one of the most controversial social issues of the day was that the balance of a woman's loyalties between her natal and marital families was one of the most emotionally charged issues in family life, and interpretations of what was proper varied widely. Ritual protocol explicitly ordained that a woman's primary source of identity was her husband's family: her ancestral tablet could reside only on the altar of her marital family, never on that of her parents.[6] The "Three Obediences" *(sancong)* pithily encapsulated the timeless ritual principle that a woman had to shift the focus of her obedience from father to husband. Commentaries on female virtue and handbooks for women in the mid-Qing all reiterated and elaborated on the notion that filiality to parents-in-law was the heart of the "wifely way" *(fudao)*. Yet they often conceded, if only with disapproval, that natal families would, in fact, continue to participate in the lives of their married daughters in some way. Occasional visits home by a woman to pay respects to her parents on festival days were both ritually proper and expected. But the case record suggests that many, if not most, women had much more extensive contact with their parents and siblings than was ritually required. The role played by natal families in women's lives and attitudes toward their involvement were extremely varied. Incidental references to routine visits home and social interactions with natal relatives abound. Moreover, many families expressed active caring and concern for their daughters long after marriage, intervening on a daughter's behalf when they felt she was being mistreated or even defending and sheltering a daughter accused of adultery.

Between the extremes of limited parental contact on ritually sanctioned occasions and "excessive" devotion that sometimes led parents to condone and defend their daughters' improprieties, the proper boundaries for affinal relationships were often unclear. Continued intimacy with parents was a frequent cause of conflict between women and their husbands and parents-in-law, especially if in-laws perceived it to detract from a woman's filial duties to them. One husband, for example, killed his wife in an argument when she refused to come home to tend his sick father after spending several days with her parents.[7] Another got into a fatal fight with his wife after refusing to allow her to go with her father to an opera performance in his village because it was the busy agricultural season. She walked out the door to go anyway and then, he claimed, cursed his parents when he detained her.[8] Yet another husband stabbed his wife to death in an argument over what he saw to be her preference for her parents. "My wife hated the poverty of my house and often fought with me," he told the magistrate. The incident that triggered their fatal conflict started when he sent her to borrow a mule from his father-in-law for his plowing. When, by the next day, she still had not returned, he went to see what had happened. His wife told him that her parents were going to lend the mule, but since they had already planned to ride it into town to light incense at the temple that day they had asked her to wait a day. So she was unwilling to go back home with her husband. The incensed husband told the magistrate, "We started to argue because my wife prefers to live at her mother's house and doesn't care about her own household affairs." In the ensuing fight, she "cursed his parents" and he stabbed her to death.[9]

Morality handbooks and ethical commentaries all stressed the imperative that a woman's filial feeling for her in-laws should entail something more than superficial deference. As Lan Dingyuan opined in his early eighteenth-century tract "Lessons for Women,"

> [Master Zhu] also says that filial sons whose love is deep will surely be good-natured and have a contented countenance and a genial appearance. Surely the service of wives to their father- and mother-in-law is the same. If they do not desire to do the utmost to please [their parents-in-law] but instead brazenly act on their own without permission, speak hatefully, and display a recalcitrant demeanor, then even if they care for them by fulfilling all their daily needs and offering all the ritual sacrifices, their relatives will not consider them to be filial.[10]

In the background of most cases of marital conflict over a wife's relationship with her parents, there was routine contact between a married daughter and her parents. Such contact was usually accepted, or at least tolerated, by a husband until he perceived it to conflict with his wife's duties and obligations at home or felt that his wife was favoring her own parents and slighting his. A woman's loyalty to her husband's parents and family appears to have been the heart of the wifely way for many men. A wife's preference for her own family therefore constituted a personal betrayal, often alluded to in the testimonies of defensive husbands with the trope of wives cursing their parents-in-law in arguments.[11] As stiff and hackneyed as rhetoric on filiality, like that of Lan Dingyuan, often appeared in moral handbooks and tracts, it thus actually reflected some very real and highly emotional expectations on the part of husbands and parents-in-law that a daughter-in-law would indeed transfer her parental devotion to her new family. Frequent mentions of the problem of wifely loyalty in handbooks like Wang Huizu's and in the testimonies of angered husbands also betrayed a common anxiety that women's loyalties would remain, at best, divided. Men and their parents were not the only ones who felt deeply about the filiality requirements of the wifely way. The subject was often a sensitive one for women and their own parents as well, but for them it involved an unresolvable conflict between emotional bonds and norms of virtue.

The depth of such conflicted feelings on the part of both parents and their daughters is well illustrated by a case from Huaiyuan County, Shaanxi, involving a young woman, named Wang Shi, aged seventeen, and her widowed mother, Sun Shi, who could not bear to part from each other.[12] Married at the age of fourteen, Wang Shi was said by her husband, Wang Guanying, and his father to be lazy and ill-behaved. "She only liked to roam around and play and never helped with anything around the house," her father-in-law testified. "My son realized that she was still young and often admonished her." One day she wanted to go to visit her mother, so Wang went with her and they stayed there together for a few days. When it came time to leave, Wang Shi wanted to stay with her mother. Sun Shi could not bear her daughter's unhappiness. She explained, "My heart ached, and I was afraid that the two of them would fight when they got home." Yet she made her daughter return, accompanying the couple back to their house.

Once there, Wang Shi again balked at staying with her husband. This time her mother suggested to Wang's father, "Your household is poor and you can't really take care of my daughter. Wouldn't it be better if I took her back with me as before? I'm afraid that in the future when you have nothing to eat you will want to sell my daughter in marriage to some-

Divided Loyalties 87

one else." Wang's father retorted angrily, "It wasn't so easy getting my son married. How could I possibly be willing to sell my daughter-in-law? If you want to take your daughter home to stay, then just go ahead and do it." At this, mother and daughter set off to return home. But Wang ran after them. "I was annoyed and impatient because Wang Shi . . . wanted to go home with her mother yet again and Sun Shi said these unendurable words," he told the magistrate. Catching up with them, Wang grabbed his wife and told her to come back with him. She shouted that he could not make a living and had no business trying to take her back, then grabbed her mother's walking stick and began to hit her husband. He grabbed the stick back and in a fury beat her to death.

The magistrate attributed the victim's laziness and her homesickness to her youth. But he rebuked Sun Shi for "ignorantly pampering" *(ni ai buming)* her daughter and failing to control and instruct her, as well as inciting the fight with her in-laws by accusing them of wanting to sell her. Such deep emotional attachments between parents and daughters were quite common, especially in the early years of marriage. Describing the life course of elite women, many of whom expressed their feelings in poetry and memoirs, Susan Mann notes that "for newly married young women the very intimacy of natal family ties compounded the profound loneliness and alienation that followed her [sic] wedding."[13]

Common as they were, women's susceptibility to bias for their own parents and parents' tendency to become too attached to their children were problems of concern to mid-Qing moralists because they posed a subtle challenge to the patrilineal definition of patriarchal authority, muddied women's loyalties, and suggested that their parents had ongoing rights and powers in their daughters' lives. Tang Yi, author of a handbook included in Chen Hongmou's popular anthology, warned that parental pampering was a danger for both daughters and sons. "Those who raise sons and daughters should cherish them, but not too much. If they cherish them excessively, then the result of their love will be harmful."[14] Only daughters, however, would experience the contradiction between their ritual obligations to their parents-in-law and their affection for their own parents. Tang explained,

> There are some daughters-in-law who are incapable of being filial to their mothers-in-law and are prejudicially filial to their own mothers. This truly is not being filial to their mothers. If [a woman] does not serve her mother-in-law filially, she will certainly give her own mother a bad name. How can this be considered showing filiality to her mother? Now, when a girl is at home, she places most importance on her mother, but after she is married

her mother-in-law becomes most important. Today's daughters-in-law must show love and filiality to their fathers and mothers while also planning that later they will give priority to showing filiality and respect to their fathers-and mothers-in-law and their husbands. If a father-in-law is pleased with his daughter-in-law's filiality, then this will surely return merit to her father and mother and augment their virtue. If a husband is pleased with his wife's virtuousness, then he will surely say, "If it were not for the virtuousness of my mother-in-law, how else would my wife become so amiable and yielding?" . . . This, then, is the way for women to benefit and show filiality to their natal families.[15]

Tang's resort to an ethical sleight of hand, reversing ritual logic to justify filiality to parents-in-law as the highest expression of devotion to parents, reflects the intractability of the conflict between the parental bond and the obligation to parents-in-law. Conflicted feelings were sometimes compounded by the ambiguity of the ritual rules. Despite the mandate to place priority on their in-laws, women were still ritually required to show filiality to their own parents through their yearly obeisances and in proper mourning upon their deaths, albeit a lesser level of mourning than that required for husbands or parents-in-law.[16] Husbands were also to treat a wife's parents with respect as senior relatives.

The balance between obligations to parents and in-laws was particularly precarious with only daughters, whose parents had no sons and daughters-in-law of their own to care for them in their old age. Such was the predicament of a young woman, Liu Sun Shi, from Shanghe County, Shandong, who was summoned home by her mother to care for her elderly father, Sun Yin, when he became ill.[17] Her husband came several times to fetch her, but, she testified, since her father's condition remained serious, she ended up staying to nurse him for several months. Finally her father-in-law, Liu Shouchang, came to retrieve her, telling her parents, "When people marry a daughter-in-law she is supposed to serve her father- and mother-in law. How can it be right for her to stay so long at her mother's house to take care of her father?" Sun Yin replied, "Do you mean to tell me that the daughter I brought into this world cannot take care of me?" The two men argued and Sun Yin hit Liu in the head with his ax. Liu Sun Shi's mother calmed them down and told her daughter to return with her father-in-law.

Liu Shouchang then brought suit against Sun Yin for assaulting him, but Sun's illness flared up again, so the magistrate dismissed the case. Some weeks later, Sun Yin, feeling a bit better, told his wife that he missed his daughter and walked the short distance to her house. His daughter saw him coming from the courtyard where she and her husband were working and ran to meet him. "I miss you, so I just came over for a little visit," he said to her. Liu Sun Shi testified, "My father only had me as his child. When I saw Father's thin and frail body and thought how I could not take care of him at home and here he was ill and had come to see me, my heart suddenly ached and I embraced him and started to weep." When her husband saw this display of affection, he said derisively, "Womenfolk can do nothing but cry in the streets. Why aren't you afraid someone will notice and ridicule you?" The old man raised his cane to strike his son-in-law, who pushed him so that he fell to ground and died immediately. "I didn't mean to kill him," he told the magistrate, "but Father-in-Law had been ill for a long time, so his body was very weak and he was unsteady on his feet."

Recognizing the validity of Sun Yin's filial claim of support from his daughter and the obligation of Liu Sun Shi and her husband to show him deference, the magistrate berated the nineteen-*sui*-old son-in-law: "This Sun Yin was a sick man and was, moreover, your father-in-law. If he . . . tried to hit you, you had only to dodge him. Why would you push him . . . and cause his death? Evidently you intended to kill him because he struck your father." Young Liu replied that he did dodge the first blow but pushed him to avoid being hit by the second. "My father had already accused him in court, and the government had examined the case and made its judgment. It was definitely not the case that because he hacked at my father I wanted to kill him." Under a statute that reaffirmed the ritual deference owed by a son-in-law to his father-in-law, Liu was sentenced to decapitation after the assizes for murdering a senior relative.

NATAL FAMILIES AS WOMEN'S ALLIES

The threat posed by women's natal families to notions of patrilineal prerogative was most salient in the many cases in which women's parents, elder brothers, or other senior relatives intervened to defend daughters who had been accused of impropriety by their in-laws. However forcefully the prescriptive literature stressed the need to avoid such interference, the legal implications of such situations were complex. Qing law was not nearly as dismissive of natal family interests as one might expect and in fact explicitly articulated a significant normative role for affinal kin through laws regulating family life and the handling of improprieties. The section on marriage in the Qing Code elaborated the joint responsibilities of the families of the bride and groom for adherence to the dictates of propriety in the arrangement of marriages. It specified punishments, usually flogging, for deceptions or breach of contract by either family. In the 1740 revision of the code, the only substatute added under the statute on arranging marriages addressed the growing phenomenon of brides' families abrogating marriage contracts to betroth their daughters to someone else. This often led to kidnapping of brides by either the family of the first groom or the family of the second after a magistrate ordered the bride returned to the first husband.[18]

The code also contained numerous limitations on the patriarchal privilege of the husband and his family, identifying many actions that effectively nullified their prerogative vis-à-vis a wife. If a husband divorced a wife who had not committed one of the seven offenses deserving divorce *(qichu)*, then the law considered him to have "arrogated [to himself] the authority to divorce *(shanchu)*" and sentenced him to eighty strokes of the heavy bamboo. Even if his wife had committed one of the seven offenses, he could not divorce her if she had performed the three years' mourning for his parents, if he had become wealthy during the marriage, or if she had no family to which she could return.[19] Demotion of a wife to concubine status or the taking of a new wife while the first was living carried punishments of flogging.[20] If the husband forced his wife into prostitution or mortgaged her to another man as wife or concubine and she herself did not consent to the crime, then she could be returned to her natal family.[21]

The degree to which these laws were enforced in court is unclear, since very few such minor cases that did not require review of the higher levels of the judicial system have been preserved. But the record of serious cases indicates that natal families often intervened on a daughter's behalf because of perceived breaches of ritual obligation, propriety, or the law on the part of the husband or parents-in-law, such as incest, wife selling, or pressuring the wife to suicide. One loyal brother in Shandong went storming over to his in-laws' house after he heard that his brother-in-law, Su Shengxing, had severed relations with his sister, Lin Shi, in favor of a concubine and was pressing her to hang herself.[22] The couple had never had any children after many years of marriage, so the sixty-one-*sui*-old husband took a concubine in 1731. Although the concubine never had any children either, he came to prefer her, which led to many quarrels between husband and wife. In 1739, he moved his wife to separate living quarters in the household. Shortly thereafter Su and Lin Shi had an argument during which he threatened her with his adze, a tool of his trade as carpenter. As rumors of the incident floated around the community, the story was embellished to include the notion that Su had handed her a rope and was trying to threaten her with the adze into hanging herself.[23] Catching wind of this story, Su's uncle reported it to Lin Shi's brother Lin Siwang, who was outraged and wanted to "vent fury *(chuqi)*" on behalf of his sister by "fixing things" with his brother-in-law. He recruited two fellow kinsmen to go with him to confront Su, and in the ensuing melee, one of them stabbed Su to death. This is one of many cases in this study that attest to the particular strength of the brother-sister bond, even after one or both had been married. In many cases, a brother was the senior male representing the interests and upholding the reputation of the family. Still, the frequency with which brothers came to a sister's defense, even when they were not family heads and often with lethal results, suggests the emotional intensity of their bond.[24] Although all three defendants were, of course, sentenced for their joint participation in the homicide, with the kinsman who struck the fatal blows receiving the most severe sentence, the magistrate did not find the idea of the brother's interference on behalf of his sister problematic in itself. In his interrogation of Lin Siwang, he noted, "If [Su's uncle] told you that your elder sister's husband . . . took a rope and tried to intimidate [her] with an adze into hanging herself, you should only have gone to reason with him."

Lin Shi claimed she did not solicit her brother's help in defending her rights as first wife, but many women did take the initiative in recruiting their natal families for leverage in conflicts with in-laws, even when the rightness of their position was far less clear. One Li Jia Shi got into a huge fight with her stepbrother-in-law after she failed to wear proper mourning clothes for her stepfather-in-law's funeral. She claimed she was not aware of what she was supposed to wear, but her stepbrother-in-law beat her anyway. The next day she went home to her mother's house *(niangjia)* and reported the incident to her two elder brothers (her parents were deceased). When they heard about it, they were incensed and went to confront him. A fight ensued and they ended up killing the stepbrother-in-law.[25] In another case, a young woman, Zhao Yu Shi, told her visiting maternal cousin that her mother-in-law had beaten her for not knowing how to do needlework properly. The cousin reported this to Zhao Yu Shi's mother, who was also the younger sister of her mother-in-law. The mother immediately marched over to her sister's house with their brothers and yelled at her, "Your daughter-in-law is still young. A mother-in-law should not beat her." Zhao Yu Shi tried to calm her mother, while her husband bought some wine and meat for her to prepare a meal for everyone to eat together to smooth things over. After getting a bit drunk, one of the brothers got into an argument with Zhao Yu Shi's husband, during which her husband declared, "It is a normal thing for a mother-in-law to admonish and instruct a daughter-in-law." The two then came to blows and the husband killed him.[26]

In each of these cases of natal family advocacy on a daughter's behalf, conflict between natal and marital kin, or between a woman's parents and her husband, surrounded the practice of well-established norms governing marital family relationships. Significantly, as in the conflicts involving lineage authority examined in the previous chapter, what was at issue was not the content of the norms themselves: no one in the first case disputed the right of a husband to take a concubine if his wife bore no children or the obligation, in the second, of a daughter-in-law to wear proper mourning clothes for a stepfather-in-law, or the duty of a young bride to apply herself diligently to household chores in the third. The source of the arguments had rather to do with the manner in which the norms were enforced: Who had the right to chastise or punish a wife or daughter-in-law, and how was the censure carried out? What were the obligations of a husband to his first wife after he took a concubine? Did a brother-in-law have the authority to impose corporal punishment on his sister-in-law for failure to wear proper mourning clothes? Was it right for a mother-in-law to beat a young and inexperienced daughter-in-law for incompetence in her household chores? Beyond the letter of ritual propriety and the law, these were the kinds of practical moral issues for which no absolute answers existed and that were therefore widely debated and negotiated in daily life, particularly in the communities formed through marriage.

As we have seen, the normative role of the natal family was itself just such an issue, with its circumscribed ritual relevance belied by its de facto presence in the resolution and redress of moral infractions. The incongruence of ritual norm and practice with regard to the status of the natal family is neatly exemplified in another case involving a brother killing his brother-in-law. Here the prefectural judge of Fengtian explicitly criticized the woman, Fang Zhang Shi, for reporting to her parents that her brother-in-law, Fang Ze, had beaten her in the course of an argument that arose over their children fighting.[27] Her octogenarian father-in-law had stepped in to pacify the two, but Fang Zhang Shi still felt it necessary to go home. The relationship between natal and marital families was particularly close in this case: they lived near each other, and relations between them were said to have been "extremely good." The judge, however, assumed both the illegitimacy and the exceptionality of natal family involvement by chastising her for reporting the incident to them and suggested more sinister motives on her part: "This fight with Fang Ze over the children's quarreling was a small matter, and you were, moreover, told by your father-in-law to break it up, so you should have let it go. Why did you still return to your mother's house to report it to your brother and family? Clearly you bore a grudge, so you went off and told your brother . . . to come and kill Fang Ze."

Defending her behavior, Fang Zhang Shi acknowledged her father-in-law's authority in settling the fight but also affirmed the ordinariness of both her argument with her brother-in-law and her return home to give herself some time and space away from him:

> When Father-in-Law told us to break it up, we all stopped. Since I got into this fight with my brother-in-law and my husband wasn't home, I felt stifled *(juede xinli qimen)*, so I went home to my mother's house to stay for a few days. . . . Fang Ze and I are close relatives, sister- and brother-in-law. If we fight over the children, this is a normal thing. Why would I tell my brother to come and beat him to death?

Threatening her brother, Zhang Beixian, with torture, the judge again suggested that he must have had some prior quarrel with his brother-in-law and had merely used his sister as an excuse to kill him. Beixian also denied this vehemently, insisting that in the ten years they had been related, there had never been any quarrels or resentments between them and that he had unintentionally killed him in the midst of their fight. He said in his confession,

> I thought to myself, my younger sister is a woman and Fang Ze is a man. What's more, they should relate to each other in the roles of younger brother and elder sister-in-law. How could he then lift his hand to beat her? I went intending to talk sense to [him] and make him realize that in the future he should not be so lacking in propriety. If Fang Ze had been willing to admit he was wrong, I would have let it go. I didn't think he would not only be unwilling to admit fault but also quarrel with me. I . . . dragged him out into the street to confront him in front of everyone.

Confident of community support of his right to challenge Fang Ze for violating the hierarchy of elder sister-in-law and younger brother-in-law, Zhang thrust their conflict into the gaze of his fellow villagers. His assumption of village backing suggests that he perceived his claim against his brother-in-law and his engagement in his sister's familial conflicts to be quite ordinary. The reactions of the prefectural judge suggest, on the contrary, that for him the role of the natal family in this case was aberrant. Although he concluded that the killing was unintentional and that Fang Zhang Shi had not asked her brother to beat Fang Ze, he was still uncomfortable with her behavior. He finally settled for rebuking her for causing the conflict by fighting with her brother-in-law in the first place.

Although no one openly condoned it, parents occasionally hid their daughters' adultery to protect them from punishment. After being chastised by her parents for an affair, one woman repented of her transgression and begged them to keep her secret from her husband. After he found her out anyway, her parents convinced him not to divorce her. Finally, when her lover continued to harass her, her father and brother killed him in a fight.[28] Another woman knew that her daughter was carrying on affairs with two men and said nothing because, she testified in court after one lover jealously killed the other, "my daughter implored me not to and I was afraid she would be called to account." Atypically, the adulteress's brother was not so sympathetic, telling the court, "I was furious and cut off all interaction with my sister."[29]

NATAL FAMILIES AS ALLIES OF IN-LAWS

Natal and marital family interests were not always in tension. Affection aside, parents had other reasons for concern about their married daughters. As Tang Yi's advice suggests, the virtue of a married woman, her chastity and her fulfillment of the wifely way, was vitally important for the reputation of her natal family as well as the family of her husband. Parents thus often appeared counseling, persuading, and admonishing their daughters to behave properly in their husbands' homes. Natal relatives were often the first people that a woman turned to for help in dealing with a conflict in her husband's home or for support when she was involved in some "disgraceful matter" *(choushi)* as an adulteress or as the victim of a sexual assault or insult. But because the behavior and reputation of a married daughter continued to affect her parents' reputation, families were not always sympathetic to the plights of daughters who fought with their mothers-in-law or behaved improperly. Indeed, quite frequently natal families appeared in cases because a woman's husband or parents-in-law had summoned their support in admonishing or punishing her.

Women often ran home to their parents when they had conflicts with their husbands or mothers-in-law, but their parents, whether they sympathized with them or not, almost always pushed them to return to their marital families. After his daughter was killed by her husband in a fight over a quarrel with her mother-in-law, one father testified that indeed, "she has always had an obstinate temperament. . . . She often came home saying her mother-in-law was not good, and I encouraged her to be patient."[30] The elder brother of another woman killed by her husband testified that his sister "was always lazy and came running back home on her own many times. I often admonished her."[31] One father even offered a formal apology to his daughter's mother-in-law after he had to retrieve her from her maternal cousin's house, where she had run to escape her husband when he beat her. "Since my daughter was young (she was eighteen *sui*), she often ran home to my house on her own. . . . Because my daughter did not keep to the wifely way, I offered apologies to her mother-in-law for her impropriety."[32]

Even when they felt sorry for daughters who were abused by their husbands, parents were torn between their affection for them on the one hand and their concern for family reputation and sense of obligation to make them fulfill their proper duties on the other. When her daughter came home repeatedly, saying that her husband was abusive and beat her, one sympathetic mother always let her stay for a few days but then had the village elder take her back to her husband. The daughter, who testified to the magistrate that her husband "treated me cruelly and there was never enough to eat," finally shot him with a hunting rifle.[33] Another mother allowed her daughter to stay with her for over two months after she repeatedly ran away from her husband, with whom she fought constantly and who often beat her. The mother explained, "His household was too poor and she didn't want to spend her life in his house." Yet she did finally make her return to her husband, who ended up beating her to death shortly thereafter.[34]

In all of these cases, natal families provided a kind of safety valve for distraught wives, offering some degree of emotional support and a temporary breathing space away from their husbands and in-laws. Yet they ultimately reinforced patrilineal authority by refusing to provide their daughters any leverage against abusive husbands and unreasonable mothers-in-law. In situations where husbands and in-laws were not quite so cruel and daughters-in-law not extremely intransigent or disrespectful, this kind of ongoing, yet noninterventionist, and thus less controversial, role of natal families probably made the isolation and hardships much easier for many women to bear, particularly in the early stages of married life.[35]

The interests of marital and natal kin converged most strikingly in cases of adultery, which often galvanized the two sets of relatives to work together to deal with a disgraceful matter that implicated both families. A woman's natal family had as much, if not more, to lose when their daughter had an affair. The bond of face linking a woman to the reputation of her parents was not severed by her marriage. A wife's humiliation always brought disgrace to her own family as well as her husband's, and the impropriety of a wife always reflected particularly badly on her parents, who were frequently rebuked by in-laws for having raised a shrewish or dissipated daughter. In some cases, when parents-in-law discovered their daughter-in-law's adultery, they allied with a woman's natal kin to apprehend and punish the man who had blemished the reputations of both families.[36] When a woman's husband or in-laws were for some reason incapable of dealing with her adultery, natal relatives sometimes took the lead to protect their own reputation. Chai Lu Shi, for example, carried on affairs with a neighbor and with the man who rented rooms to her and her husband for over a year while her husband, who worked as a hired hand, was away from home. Her brother testified, "Disgraceful rumors of her affairs . . . had spread around and I had long since heard about it." So he and her second brother finally confronted her one day as she sat smoking with her two lovers, threatening, "You have no face and you'd better be careful to protect yourself." That night the brothers attacked her landlord-lover in his quarters with an ax, killing him and then wounding their sister as well.[37]

In some cases, natal kin stepped in to deal with an affair that was tolerated by a poverty-stricken husband because his wife's lover provided the family with money or food. Such was the case with Du Zhu Shi, whose husband, Du Qingru, was blind. She started an affair with Kong Yuxian, the man in whose house the couple rented rooms. Her husband got suspicious when she suddenly served him rice at meals, and she revealed to him that their landlord had given it to her in exchange for illicit sex. Du decided to look the other way, and the affair continued for two years. But then Kong suggested that her husband sell her to him for the price of the rice he had already given them. To this Du also agreed, since he could not support her anyway. Du Zhu Shi returned to her mother's house to inform her father and brothers, but they cursed her impropriety and later convinced her husband to join them in beating Kong to death.[38]

Contrary to the assumptions of *jiaohua* reformers, there was not necessarily a single, clearly identifiable social hierarchy for the state to reinvigorate. Instead, people lived their lives and dealt with their conflicts enmeshed in a complex array of family and community hierarchies. These conflicts emerged despite broad consensus about norms of female virtue: the duties of a wife, the intolerability of adultery and sexual assault, and the impropriety of flirtation and lewd gestures between men and women. The definition of the norms was not at stake, yet the fragmentation of the authorities charged with their enforcement clouded questions of morality with concerns about reputation, compensation, fairness, and vengeance. Such cases further reveal discrepancies between both state and elite discourses and the array of community standards against which people measured their own behavior, documenting a complex interaction between these multiple, and usually overlapping, sets of norms and the sources of normative authority they represented. In the wake of moral transgressions, knowledge of "orthodox" definitions of right and wrong produced normative crises because it often clashed with the priorities of familial affection, honor, community harmony, and social status. Despite widespread consensus about women's duties, the nature of female virtue, and the principles of social hierarchy, conflict could easily arise over who had the authority to deal with the problem and how to pursue its resolution. Apologies and retribution had to be acceptable to those wronged and to the community. And in the tangled processes of negotiation, the norms themselves were subject to reinterpretation and even compromise.

CHAPTER 5

Adultery, Incest, and the Multiple Meanings of Patriarchy

The social complexities and contradictions of patriarchy in practice widened the fissure between the principle of patriarchy rooted in generational hierarchy within the patrilineal kinship group and the principle of patriarchy based on the marital relationship. As patrilineal authority was battered in practice and in principle by diverse social forces, most ironically a distrustful state, the romance of the marital relationship continued to flourish in the popular imagination. Despite imperial bans and increasing criticism of widow suicides,[1] martyrs to conjugal loyalty and devotion continued to be revered as exemplary heroines, notably by women themselves. Through their poetry, many women immortalized widow suicides and left suicide notes explaining the emotions behind their own martyrdom.[2] Yet suicidal conjugal devotion was not the only enduring legacy of the seventeenth-century cult of sentiment *(qing)*. That cult also fostered a more benign and quotidian notion of romance through companionate marriage, inspired by the proliferation of educated elite women whose poetic and scholarly talents allowed them to become the intellectual equals and soul mates of their husbands.[3] Popularized in the early Qing through the new fictional genre of the "scholar–chaste beauty" romance, the ideal of marital intimacy and shared intellectual life became a staple of mid-Qing fiction.[4] Eighteenth-century moralists promoted a rectified version of companionate marriage, founded on shared classical education and moral purpose and cleansed of its late Ming associations with courtesans and "decadent" poetry writing.[5] For increasing numbers of commentators, companionate marriage was the heart of ethical family order. The common depictions of marital intimacy and love in biographical literature and poetry by women and men attest to the resonance of this ideal in social practice, at least among the literate.

Despite its avowed disapproval of conjugal passion as a basis for chastity, the Qing state was compelled by its own logic of individual moral responsibility and its distrust of lineage leaders to grant increasing recognition to the moral prerogatives of the marital unit. One of the most ironic consequences of the Qing state's construction of chastity around the chaste widow was that it promoted the interests of the conjugal unit represented by a man's widow over those of his patriline. The property regime governing widow inheritance and property rights that the Qing had adopted wholesale from the Ming was intended to protect the property interests of the husband's patriline. Assuming the congruence of chastity and patrilineal interests, it gave widows considerable rights to use and manage their husbands' property as long as they remained chaste.[6] However, as numerous scholars have noted, disputes over widows' management of their husbands' property, which, judging by the case record, occurred often, pitted loyalty and obedience to a husband against the interests of his patriline.[7] In the adjudication of disputes over naming heirs, conflicts created by in-laws forcing widows to remarry, and other attempts to deprive widows of their property rights, Qing judicial officials consistently defended chaste widows against their husbands' relatives. Many justified their decisions by citing not only the widows' welfare and distrust of the motives of scheming, greedy in-laws but also the distinct property interests of the husbands' household unit and the prerogative of husband and chaste widow to be succeeded by an heir.[8] The only modifications of the law on widow inheritance in the Qing came in 1775, when two new substatutes codified the chaste widow's prerogative in choosing an heir.[9] Qing rhetoric on chaste widows and their property rights shows how the state's promotion of a new, universal paradigm of chastity resulted in a new emphasis on the marital bond as the primary familial relationship, since chastity meant sexual loyalty to one's husband first and foremost.[10]

During the latter half of the eighteenth century, the conflict between patrilineal and conjugal definitions of patriarchy also became an acute problem for lawmakers addressing adultery and incest. In these realms, as with attacks on widow property rights, we see a subtle shift in the judicial system's working definition of the relationship between patriarchy and chastity, away from emphasis on fathers and family heads and toward the husband as the one to whom a woman owes supreme obedience and loyalty. Long disillusioned with the moral potential of family patriarchs, neither Qianlong nor his officials were immune to the influence of wider cultural trends of sympathy for the bonds created through marriage.[11] But, as we will see in this chapter, although they were beginning to see the conjugal relationship as the most reliable focus for the defense of chastity-centered family hierarchy when it came to defending chaste widows and the punishment of adultery, they revealed their deep unease with the shifting definition of patriarchy in the context of incest cases, where they struggled to uphold the precedence of generational hierarchy over chastity and marital loyalty.

THE RIGHT TO KILL ADULTERERS

Probably the most explicit state definition of patriarchal prerogative vis-à-vis women was given in the section of the code on "killing the adulterer," which detailed punishments for homicides that occurred in the context of people catching adulterers in the act or attempting to apprehend them. According to the statute, carried over from the Ming, "When a wife or concubine has illicit sex with someone and the husband catches the adulterous man and woman in the place of the illicit sex and immediately kills them, there will be no punishment. If [the husband] kills only the adulterous man, then the adulterous woman will be sentenced in accordance with the statute on consensual illicit sex and sold into marriage [with another man] in front of the magistrate, with the body price confiscated by the magistrate."[12] A substatute created in 1725 during the Yongzheng reign out of a clause in the Ming Code's Small Character Commentary added that

> [t]he husband's elder and younger brothers and relatives with mourning obligations, and people living in the same household, and people authorized to make arrests are all allowed to apprehend adulterers. If the wife's parents, paternal uncles, elder and younger brothers and sisters, and maternal grandparents arrest the adulterers and kill or injure the adulterous man, [they will be treated] just like the husband, but junior relatives are not allowed to kill senior relatives.[13]

Identifying relatives, cohabitants, and those officially deputed to arrest criminals as people allowed to apprehend adulterers, the code implied that the kinship group, the household, and the state shared responsibility for the defense of chastity. The substatute continued a long tradition going back to the Tang dynasty of interpreting the killing of the adulterer as a crime that was in principle parallel to killing an intruder who entered the house in the middle of the night.[14] Chastity was understood in this context to be a household and family concern. All members of the household and family, including servants, were considered equally responsible for defending its moral integrity, and all would be exempt from punishment if they immediately killed an adulterous intruder and the woman who betrayed the household. Significantly, the kin of husband and wife were granted equivalent rights to apprehend the adulterers and to kill them with impunity. The fact that the adulterer's relatives were not mentioned implied the assumption that the adultery was taking place in the house of the woman's family or her husband's.

Over the latter half of the eighteenth century, this single substatute was expanded into an entire section with dozens of substatutes elaborating every possible scenario for the apprehension of illicit sex offenders: the killing of the main parties, bystanders, and other relatives by the wronged husband, the adulterers, their immediate relatives, neighbors and others; provisions for young girls, betrothed girls, concubines, and girls betrothed in childhood and raised by their in-laws *(tongyangxi)*; and separate provisions for incest, prostitution, sodomy, rape, and sexual harassment.[15] Describing the varying extent of people's right and responsibility to apprehend illicit sex offenders, this complex body of statutes assessed who had the greatest stake in women's chastity and who had the greatest authority to enforce it and punish its violation. In other words, this section of the code, in essence, defined the relationship between patriarchy and chastity.

Critically, the elaboration of the crime of killing illicit sex offenders into myriad substatutes during the Yongzheng and Qianlong reigns involved a fundamental reassessment of the rights and responsibilities of husbands on the one hand and both his and his wife's relatives and fellow household residents on the other. In the 1740 revision of the code, the phrase "people living in the same household" was dropped from the substatute, and the right of relatives to kill the adulterers without punishment was rescinded. Even if they killed the adulterers at the time and in the place of the adultery, both the husband's and the wife's relatives were now equally subject to three years' banishment and one hundred strokes of the heavy bamboo, the same as the punishment for those who caught and killed a criminal in excess of their authority. In contrast, the statutes continued to give complete immunity to husbands who caught their wives with a lover in the act of illicit sex and killed them immediately on the spot. They actually lessened husbands' punishment for several variants of the crime, including killing either the adulteress or the adulterer but not both and killing either of them at a later time or outside the place of the adultery.[16]

The copious edicts and memorials from judicial commissioners and Board of Punishments officials that created the striking quantity of extremely tedious legislation on killing adulterers explained its necessity in terms of the consistency and completeness of the laws and the relative appropriateness of punishments.[17] Whatever the judicial logic behind the evolution of these statutes, their significance must be measured in the context of the relative rarity of cases in which they could be applied. Although cases in which the husband was granted complete immunity would not appear in the *xingke tiben* case record, many capital crimes were defined in these substatutes. Yet very few central cases fit under their rubric. Not only was it fairly unusual for a husband or relative to catch a couple in flagrante delicto, but even in the few cases when this did happen, the apprehending parties were not necessarily driven to homicide. The statutes were constructed around the assumption that the sight of a woman having illicit sex would be so shocking and upsetting to husbands or close family members that they would not be in control of their actions. The case record suggests, however, that most family members thrown into such situations were not so prone homicidal fury. Indeed, most responded not simply with anger but also with various other reactions centered on concerns about potential disgrace, lingering affection for the woman, fear, or desire for revenge.

One Zhao Wenfu, for example, caught his wife and his landlord's son, Kuang Ziming, having sex while he was out herding cows in the mountains. Zhao allowed Kuang to escape and dragged his wife back home, where his mother decided, "Since you didn't catch him, this disgraceful matter cannot be spread around. After this don't allow Liu Shi to go out by herself." Still furious, Zhao beat his wife. Liu Shi, for her part, told the magistrate, "I was beaten and cursed by my husband. I felt so ashamed and remorseful that I cut off my little finger and swore to reform myself." Seeing her repentance, her husband let the matter drop. Some days later, her parents came to fetch her for a visit home and she told them what had happened. Her father got angry and said to his son-in-law, "Husband and wife should get along amiably. You shouldn't be beating her!" Again the matter subsided. But the following month, Kuang dropped by the Zhao's house to pay respects on the occasion of Zhao's mother's birthday. "Since [his father] was our landlord, it was not good to refuse him," Zhao noted. After talking with Zhao, Kuang wandered into the kitchen where Liu Shi was alone fixing a meal. As she told the magistrate, "He quietly joked with me under his breath and signaled me with his eyes." She ignored him, but her husband noticed and suddenly grabbed a knife and stabbed both of them, Kuang fatally. Even though he had caught the couple in the act once, and stumbled on them flirting, Zhao did not meet the very narrow criteria for leniency. He was sentenced to strangulation after the assizes for unauthorized killing of an adulterer.[18]

The case record contains quite a few forgiving husbands as well. Upon uncovering his wife's affair with a neighbor, Liu Quanren, when he caught her lover leaving the house, Zhang Xiang initially chose to forgive his wife's infidelity after she pleaded with him and promised to end it. His desire to salvage his marriage and fear of potential damage to the family's reputation initially tempered his reaction to the affair. "Since this was a disgraceful matter *(choushi)*, I did not report it to the *yamen* but instructed my wife that she should never again do any such face-losing things," he explained to the magistrate. The matter dropped, but a month later, his wife was walking to her elder sister's house when she encountered her former lover, who flirted with her again. She ran back home to tell her husband. Afraid to confront the lover alone, since he was a "large bully of a man," Zhang devised a plan to trap him. "I told my wife, 'If he approaches you again to harass you, just set a place and time to meet him and inform me; I will go and recruit some of your natal relatives to come and we'll beat the daylights out of him. Then he'll be so afraid he'll never dare to bother my household again.'" According to plan, Zhang rallied his wife's uncle and cousin to help him, and they ended up beating the lover to death. Zhang was sentenced to strangulation after the assizes for the unauthorized killing of Liu. The magistrate noted his failure to report the initial adultery to the *yamen*.[19]

While the first instinct of many husbands or parents who discovered their wives or daughters having illicit sex was to cover up the matter to preserve family reputation, some sought punishment through the *yamen*. When Zhao Bi Shi discovered her married nineteen-*sui*-old daughter having sex with a neighbor's son in her house, she and her husband, Zhao Liancheng, decided to inform the local constable and take their daughter and her lover into town to the *yamen*. But the young lover's father pleaded with them not to report the infraction, letting him punish his son himself instead. Zhao Liancheng testified, "Since this was a disgraceful matter, I agreed to leave it at that, and I immediately sent my daughter home to my son-in-law's house." His son-in-law, however, heard rumors about her tryst and decided to divorce her and send her home. Humiliated by the publicity of his daughter's affair and the added disgrace of her divorce, Zhao recruited his brother to confront the lover and his father to "vent their fury." Arriving at their house with a scythe in hand, Zhao said to the adulterer's father, "Your son has done this thing to ruin my daughter and now my son-in-law has divorced her and you still haven't punished him!" The lover's father replied, "This daughter of yours ruined my son. How can you say my son is the bad one!" The three men came to blows and the lover's father was killed.[20]

The diverse and mixed motivations of families responding to adultery make the judicial construction of their rights and responsibilities appear somewhat superfluous. The very excessiveness of this legislation, however, highlights both the potent anxieties of officialdom about transgressions of chastity and their ambitions to insert the authority of the state with ever greater precision into social processes for handling improprieties. Moreover, like the contradictory mess of legislation on lineage powers, the profusion of rarely applied substatutes defining the prerogatives of the gamut of family authorities in adultery cases reveals the perennial statecraft desire for effective and righteous patriarchs. In this regard, the most striking aspect of these laws is their shift of emphasis away from generationally defined family hierarchy and toward the marital hierarchy as the foundation of the patriarchal authority exercised over women. The deletion of "other members of the household" effectively restricted this right to the kinship groups of husband and wife. By the end of the Qianlong reign, even their right to avenge the violation of familial honor was severely restricted, so that only the husband had the prerogative to kill the adulterers with impunity. On this frontline of the defense of chastity, the rights of his parents and grandparents—placed, not incidentally, on an equal footing in this context with those of his wife—were significantly more limited than his own. In the logic of these substatutes, a woman's chastity was first and foremost her husband's concern. It was the moral integrity of his inner realm that was violated through illicit sex.[21]

The thinking that underlay this shift becomes clear in an exchange between a memorialist and the Qianlong Emperor over one of the more obscure substatutes in this section. In 1760, the judicial commissioner of Henan, Jiang Jianian, suggested a change in the punishments for the husband, or those authorized to apprehend adulterers, and the adulterer himself in cases in which the husband caught the adulterers but accidentally killed a bystander. Jiang suggested that in such cases the defendant should receive immunity. Reviewing all of the relevant substatutes, he noted that they required as a precondition for immunity from punishment that the killing of the adulterers be at the time and place of the adulterous act so as to "uphold proper customs and prevent reckless killing." However, he continued,

> the husband and all of those allowed by the substatutes to apprehend adulterers are powerfully aroused by righteous indignation all of a sudden, or perhaps for that whole night. Grabbing a knife, they enter the room, having deliberated carefully and determined to suppress this evil. But they are in an agitated state of mind, and if the adulterer, in a moment of panic, thinks his life is in danger and tries to defend himself, the situation becomes all the more a matter of life and death. Too agitated to make a wise decision, [the husband or relatives] have already stabbed the adulterer to death. [The killing in this situation] is thus not punished.[22]

If, in the midst of the confusion, there happened to be a relative who rushed to the scene and the avenging husband or relative mistook him or her in the dark for the adulterer or adulteress and killed him or her accidentally, Jiang argued, the same justification for immunity from punishment should apply.

Jiang Jianian offered one of the most thorough descriptions available of the state of mind associated with the righteous indignation that justified impunity for husbands who killed adulterers. Motivated by a visceral ethical revulsion at this most heinous violation of ritual propriety, righteous indignation was the reasoned and moral desire for vindication. It was neither irrational anger nor personalized lust for revenge. Like proper expressions of chastity, acts of indignation were righteous precisely because they were ritually appropriate attempts to restore ethical order, not selfish expressions of uncontrollable passion. In his edict responding to Jiang's suggestion, the Qianlong Emperor further clarified the meaning of righteous indignation, explaining that to be truly righteous and thus justify immunity from punishment, such indignation had to be exercised by appropriate people whose stake in the violation warranted such emotion. He concluded that since only the husband was properly entitled to righteous indignation when his wife abrogated her chastity, only he deserved immunity by extension for killing a bystander. Offering his own interpretation of the logic of exoneration, he explained that in the event that the husband killed only the adulterous wife, he was exonerated and the adulterer was sentenced to strangulation, for "surely, when the husband kills, he is aroused by righteous anger. The death of the adulterous woman is the result of the illicit sex; therefore [the law] is especially lenient with the husband's crime and makes the adulterous man atone with his life." Reasoning that the same principles should apply when the husband accidentally killed a bystander, he agreed to the suspension of punishment for the husband and the increase in punishment for the adulterer to exile. However, the edict continued,

> the statutes only grant the husband the righteous anger to kill the adulterers. Although the relatives with mourning obligations are allowed to apprehend the adulterers, they are not allowed to kill [them]. For human beings are not equal. Close and distant [relatives] differ, and sincerity and falseness are ever changing. I fear the emergence of reckless killings for selfish motives. If [relatives] accidentally kill [a bystander] and are then sentenced just like the husband, this will contravene the established substatutes. Moreover, I fear this will in turn give rise to other undesirable [consequences].[23]

As in his discrimination of appropriate and inappropriate expressions of female martyrdom, Qianlong emphasized that however well intentioned they might be, moral sentiments like righteous indignation or, in the context of women following their husbands in death, suicidal loyalty had to be expressed and enacted in appropriate contexts by the right people to be ritually proper.[24] And here with regard to killing adulterers, as with female suicide, the state reserved the right to decide when righteous indignation was appropriate and for whom.

With characteristic disdain for the foibles and fickleness of his subjects, the Qianlong Emperor asserted that the husband alone had a special prerogative to defend his wife's chastity, implying that the bond between husband and wife was, in fact, closer than other familial bonds. This striking revision of canonical Confucian views of the hierarchy of family relationships went largely undiscussed at the time. However, the implications of the legislation on killing adulterers for the relationship between conjugal and generational definitions of patriarchal authority was not lost on the eminent late-nineteenth-century judicial scholar Xue Yunsheng, one of the most astute commentators on the Qing Code. He noted with chagrin the unequal treatment of the husband and the relatives in these substatutes and the waning priority placed on familial hierarchy. He pointed out the inconsistency between categorizing relatives of the husband and wife along with the husband as "those allowed to apprehend the adulterers" but rescinding their right to kill the adulterer without punishment. Noting that the substatutes on killing the adulterous man were meant to be consistent with the statute on the head of the household killing an intruder who entered the house in the middle of the night, he remarked:

> What if there is no husband or there is one, but he is away from home and the adulterer is killed in the place of the adultery at the time by an elder or younger brother or relative living in the same household? How is this any different from the husband [killing the adulterer]? Yet there is a great difference in the punishment. I really cannot understand this. . . . [It] contradicts the notion of "all are allowed to apprehend adulterers."[25]

Still holding to the old definition of adultery as a crime against the household, Xue argued against the notion of some special privilege for the husband as the chief defender of his wife's chastity. He insisted instead that the killing of the adulterous intruder was the prerogative of whoever was serving as head of household at the moment of the crime. In his view, the narrowing of the patriarchal prerogative to defend chastity was a contradiction that undermined the practical intent of the law to punish licentiousness and uphold virtue.

Xue was also disturbed by the law's implicit emphasis on the violation of chastity as a more serious crime than the violation of family hierarchy. His criticism of the substatutes on killing the adulteress dwelled on their failure to address specifically the problem of the adulteress being killed by a junior relative. The relevant substatute allowed both senior and junior relatives to apprehend adulterers but punished them with one hundred strokes and three years' banishment for killing either the adulterer or the adulteress on the spot. In effect, this allowed a junior relative to kill a senior relative without receiving a death sentence, the punishment for killing senior relatives in any other set of circumstances. Xue adamantly objected to this abrogation of familial hierarchy. "When senior relatives commit other crimes, the statutes permit [junior relatives] to cover up for them. But when a senior relative commits adultery, [junior relatives] are allowed to kill [her]. Does this make any sense?"[26] For Xue, analyzing the code late in the Qing dynasty, adultery was a far less serious crime than the violation of the principles of family hierarchy, let alone the killing of a senior relative. Nearly a century earlier, at the height of the state's obsession with legislating chastity, judicial officials found it much more difficult to assert so decisively that the maintenance of familial hierarchy took precedence over the defense of chastity. Nowhere was the conflict between these core Neo-Confucian values more poignant than in the laws on incest.

THE INCEST CONUNDRUM

The Qing Code defined incest broadly as sex between relatives of the same descent group *(zong)* or between men and the wives of their same-surname relatives. Not surprisingly, the punishments were more severe than those for parallel crimes of illicit sex and increased with the closeness of the relationship. In the original statute inherited from the Ming Code, sex between relatives without mourning obligations was punished with one hundred strokes of the heavy bamboo if consensual, or, in cases of rape, decapitation after the assizes for the man. In 1735, forty days of the cangue were added to the sentence for consensual incest. The punishment for sex between relatives with mourning obligations varied, depending on the closeness of the relationship, from flogging and penal servitude to strangulation or decapitation.[27]

The substatutes on killing adulterers initially made no provision for cases of incest, alluding only indirectly to such situations, with the caveat in the commentary that junior relatives must not kill senior relatives. By the Qianlong reign, this lacuna was troubling many judicial officials. The judicial commissioner of Henan, Shen Qiyuan, argued in a memorial in 1741 that "incest destroys the moral foundation of senior-junior [relationships]" and that it was therefore not appropriate to punish a husband who out of "righteous indignation" killed a senior relative after catching him having sex with his wife under the statute on junior relatives intentionally killing senior relatives. For all such cases except when sons killed fathers, he suggested instead a lessening of punishments according to the closeness of the relationship between the defendant and the adulterer.[28] This memorial resulted in an imperial directive ordering special review of such cases, which in 1756 was finally codified into a new substatute mandating that

> [i]f a senior relative with mourning obligations has illicit sex with a junior female relative and her husband catches the adulterers and kills the adulterous man, then in cases where the defendant was unaware [of the identity of the adulterer], according to the statute, he is not charged. In all other cases, [including those in which the husband] himself catches the adulterous man and woman in the place of the adultery and kills them at that time, or kills them, but not at the time and place [of the adultery], or captures them and kills them later, he is charged according to the statute on junior relatives intentionally killing senior relatives. The appropriate governor will explain the circumstances in a memorandum, and the High Courts, when they review the sentence, will attach a bamboo slip requesting a rescript. Wounding [of the senior relative] will not be punished.[29]

By 1769, the High Courts were required to send such cases for the extraordinary consideration of the Nine Ministers, an advisory group of the highest-level capital officials. Deliberating the cases together with Board of Punishments officials, they could decide to reduce the sentence from immediate decapitation to decapitation after the assizes if the victim was a relative of one-year mourning, or one hundred strokes and life exile at three thousand *li* if the relationship was one of five- or nine-month mourning. If the victim was a senior relative with full three-year mourning, then the [defendant] was still sentenced in accordance with the statute on beating a senior relative to death. The case then went to the emperor for final approval.[30]

We see the new review procedures at work in a case involving a husband's murder of his wife and uncle for adultery that the emperor referred to the Nine Ministers in 1753.[31] The defendant, one Zhang Sansheng, from Daming County, Zhili, left his wife home alone to tend a critically ill aunt in a neighboring village. Having locked her into their quarters, he returned home to find the latch open on the outside. Suspicious, he beat her until she admitted that his paternal uncle, Zhang Qiwu, who shared a compound with them, had come into her quarters demanding sex. According to the secondhand account of her husband, she said nothing and did not scream when he had sex with her. When Sansheng consulted an uncle of Qiwu's about the situation, the uncle insisted that such a disgraceful matter should remain hidden but agreed to help move the offender to live elsewhere. Several weeks went by, and because the uncle was busy nothing happened. One day Sansheng caught Qiwu making eyes at his wife and, according to his testimony, "was even more furious and feared that I would meet with some calamity at his poisonous hands." He decided to kill him and hatched a plot to burn down his quarters and pass it off as an accident. He told another relative about the incest and convinced him to assist with the murder. They waited one night for Qiwu to come home, attacked him, tied him up, and stabbed him to death. Before they could set fire to the house, however, neighbors who had heard Qiwu shouting for help came over and discovered the murder. Sansheng and his accomplice fled the scene. Knowing that he would probably not be able to escape, Sansheng decided to kill his wife, who, he said, had started all the trouble. He returned home, stabbed his wife repeatedly, and was immediately caught by the neighbors, who turned him in. His wife died of her wounds the next day. The magistrate sentenced Sansheng to slow slicing, the mandated punishment for a junior relative killing a senior relative with mourning obligations. He noted that the defendant had waited some weeks to carry out his attack, thus not acting out of spontaneous and uncontrollable fury, and that the only proof of the incest was a faint nod from Sansheng's wife when questioned about it on her deathbed. Although he pointed out a complication in the definition of the kinship bond between murderer and victim (Qiwu had been adopted out as an heir to another uncle), he concluded that since the adoption applied only to Qiwu and not his descendants, it did not affect the closeness of his relationship to Sansheng.

As required, the governor-general of Zhili, Fang Guancheng, submitted a memorandum on the case to the High Courts asking for the attachment of a bamboo slip requesting a special imperial ruling. His memo began by pointing out that "Zhang Qiwu and his niece-in-law, . . . having committed illicit sex, deserve death sentences. Zhang Sanshen's violent actions were caused by Zhang Qiwu's destruction of human relationships. If he is sentenced according to the law to slow slicing, we would be slightly concerned." Obviously none too sympathetic to the defendant, he made the necessary request that a reduction of the sentence be considered. But he then offered his own interpretation of the case, in which he emphasized that despite the incest, "plotting to kill an uncle with mourning obligations is an extreme perversion of human relationships *(shu guai lunji)*." He recommended that the sentence of slow slicing stand. The High Courts concurred with his judgment, but the imperial rescript ordered the case to be reviewed by the Nine Ministers. The final verdict is unknown. Nevertheless, it is striking that despite the extreme violence and premeditation involved in this murder, the state would even consider lenience, which implied that the husband's prerogative to avenge the destruction of his wife's chastity might take precedence over his filial deference to a close family elder.

Xue Yunsheng, for one, was appalled by the possibility for this kind of questioning of the primacy of generational hierarchy. Laying out the many inconsistencies and lacunae of these substatutes, he emphasized the direct conflict between marital patriarchy and generational hierarchy created by incest. He saw the statutory treatment of junior relatives who killed seniors for incest as a flagrant and dangerous violation of the principles of family hierarchy upon which social and moral order was based, and he adamantly opposed them. He argued,

> The husband who kills the adulterers can still be said to be aroused by righteous anger. It is difficult to treat relatives with mourning obligations without distinctions. The designation of senior and junior is of utmost strictness. Therefore the statutes punish severely [juniors who] bring

accusations in court to expose [senior relatives]. So what of arrogating to oneself the right to kill or wound [them]? Bringing accusations in court against senior relatives with mourning obligations . . . is punished, so can beating and wounding go completely without punishment? It would be most fair to punish the senior for the crime of illicit sex and still punish the junior for the crime of killing or wounding [a senior relative]. . . . [The relationship between] husbands and wives is forged by human beings and is unlike natural [relationships with] relatives like uncles, brothers, and so on. Unfortunately, when a senior relative commits illicit sex, the seriousness [of the offense] makes it possible to renounce [him]. But if, because of this, . . . [the junior relative] savagely kills the senior relative, then even if [the senior relative] was absolutely lacking in human ethics *(renli)*, can the junior relative still be said to have human ethics?[32]

The killing of an incestuous senior relative posed an unresolvable conundrum for Qing judicial officials, placing the defense of chastity in direct contradiction to the preservation of familial hierarchy. For Xue Yunsheng, the proper ordering of these two foundational ethical principles was obvious and unquestionable: the bond between senior and junior relatives in the patriline was far more fundamental than that between husband and wife, and thus the principle of family hierarchy should never be violated, even when senior relatives violated other ethical principles like chastity. For judicial officials in the Qianlong era, however, the primacy of generational hierarchy was not necessarily so clear. By taking the highly unusual approach of adding so many cumbersome and extraordinary stages of review to the adjudication process for such cases, judicial officials in effect declined to confront the problem directly by clarifying the state's moral priorities in a new substatute. Instead, each case was to be handled individually, with judgment left ultimately to the subjective moral instincts of the emperor and the highest judicial officials in the realm. The conjugal patriarchy symbolized by chastity and the patrilineal hierarchy symbolized by filiality were increasingly at odds in the mid-Qing, but while the state expanded the legal scope of husbandly prerogative, it stopped short of codifying the primacy of chastity over filiality.

No such compromise was possible in social practice, however. The social, emotional, and ethical realities of incest were such that it resulted either from patriarchal authority being used illicitly to violate chastity or from licentiousness undermining familial hierarchy. As with the killing of adulterers, cases that fell under the rubric of the new substatutes on incest were rare, although incest, defined as broadly as it was in the code, is not uncommon in the case record in general. Incest cases frequently involved consensual sex between relatives, like that of the woman who ran off with her husband's cousin to Hangzhou, where they lived as fugitives for two years before being caught.[33] Another woman, from Changzhou Prefecture in Jiangsu, started an affair with her husband's uncle, who lived next door in the same courtyard, while her husband was away on business. She later also had an affair with a household servant.[34] One widow from Jiangxi had a long-standing affair with her deceased husband's elder brother until she got pregnant and they were discovered.[35] In a very unusual case of brother-sister incest from Jiangxi, the couple began to have sex with each other before she was married, continued their relationship afterwards, and then plotted together to kill her husband, who was poor, allegedly ugly, and some twenty-five *sui* older than she.[36]

Many cases treated as consensual and all cases of coerced incest presented a direct conflict between the preservation of chastity and filial obedience when fathers-in-law, brothers-in-law, or uncles assaulted or propositioned daughters- or sisters-in-law or nieces. Occasionally, if a woman's resistance to incestuous advances or assault resulted in her murder, magistrates pronounced that the senior relative's heinously immoral and violent acts had abrogated the hierarchical family bond. For instance, one father-in-law repeatedly tried to accost his son's wife, cursing her when she resisted him, saying that she was not showing "filial obedience to her elders." When she screamed back at him that she would rather "eat shit than engage in this depravity," he stabbed her to death. The magistrate had no hesitation in rescinding the murderer's judicial privilege as a senior killing a junior relative, sentencing him instead to decapitation after the assizes, the sentence for attempted rape and murder of a nonrelative, because he "brutally severed the righteous bond between father-in-law and daughter-in-law."[37]

But in many other cases judicial officials showed little sympathy for female victims, prosecuting cases as consensual incest even when the woman was clearly an unwilling partner in illicit sex with a senior relative. Even when magistrates recognized that the woman had submitted to the sex under duress, they often concluded that the illicit sex did not meet the statutory criteria for prosecution as sexual assault because the woman was deemed ultimately to have "consented" to the sex.[38] When Liu Wenzuo of Fengtian Prefecture broached the subject of looking for a wife for their son, his wife, Liu Shi, revealed to him that his cousin, with whom they shared a courtyard house, had raped her many times over the past two years.[39] "That Liu Zhong is not an upright person," she told him. "When you aren't home, he often comes to insult me and has raped me many times. Now you want to bring a daughter-in-law here. This will surely be a bad thing. It would be better to delay a bit and then, after the New Year, marry him to someone from [my home village]. Then we can all move there and leave Liu Zhong to avoid having him harass and humiliate us." Without questioning her story in the least, Liu Wenzuo moved his family to the new village and found a bride for his son without letting his cousin know. He testified that he would have liked to confront his cousin but was afraid of him because he was a strong bully and said he worried that other villagers would "laugh at us" if word got around about the impropriety. Some months later, Liu Zhong came to their house to collect on a debt that Wenzuo owed him. He confronted Liu Shi about the money, and she told him that when they had the cash they would pay him. Then he said, "I see you're doing well for yourself. Want to do like we did before?" She ignored him and walked off. He wandered around the house, haranguing various relatives about the debt, then said he was heading home. Since her husband was not home that night, Liu Shi was nervous about his returning and asked her father to spend the night in the house with her and her son and daughter-in-law. Sure enough, Liu Zhong broke into the house in the middle of the night and stormed into her bedroom, screaming, "If you don't give in to me, I'll kill you." She tried to run, but he caught her and stabbed her to death. Throughout his confession, Liu Zhong described his illicit sex with Liu Shi as consensual, though she clearly understood it as rape. Although the magistrate recognized that the sex was, in some sense, coerced, he did not see it as judicially defined rape, despite her murder. Liu Zhong was sentenced only for intentional homicide to decapitation, which, ironically, was also the punishment for incestual rape of a relative outside the mourning relations, though the magistrate does not mention this.[40]

Shaped by the dictates of the code, with its awkwardly expressed balance between upholding family hierarchy and protecting chastity, the adjudication of incest cases was fraught with moral and judicial ambiguity. For victims of incestuous assault and their husbands and other family members, however, moral priorities were often much more clear. Attempts at revenge killing were probably the most common response to incestuous predators. Revenge was often planned after the incestuous encounter, making such murders ineligible for consideration of a lessened sentence under the new substatutes on catching adulterers. In such cases, it was not uncommon for the female victim of incest forced upon her by a senior male relative to whom she owed obedience to end up receiving punishment herself, either for the incest or for participation in the revenge. In one case, the headman of a village in Ningyuan County, Gansu, discovered a woman from his village, Wang Wang Shi, standing on the edge of a ravine about to jump.[41] When he and a neighbor approached her and inquired what the problem was, she told them that her widowed father-in-law had repeatedly tried to rape her while her husband was sojourning away from home for work. When she resisted him, he beat her with a wooden club. She ran out of the house to kill herself by jumping over the cliff. The headman took her home to her natal family's house. There she told her brother, who recruited her sister's husband to go with them to castigate the father-in-law. Accosting him in his bedroom, her brother shouted, "You are in the position of a father-in-law and yet you do such a faceless thing! How can you still be a human being?" Then he and his brother-in-law suffocated the old man. When the headman inquired about the death, the family told him the old man died of an illness, a story he sympathetically accepted. The murder was uncovered only because the local constable was suspicious and reported the death to the magistrate. The two murderers were sentenced to the full punishment of strangulation. Wang Wang Shi, though she had nothing to do with the murder and was herself the victim of sexual assault, was sentenced to one hundred strokes of the heavy bamboo and three years' banishment commuted to a fine for participating in the cover-up of a parent's murder.

As we saw with the sentencing of Zhang Sansheng, even the few cases that were given special consideration under the new substatutes did not necessarily result in mercy shown to the murderer. A steamed-dumpling vendor named Ma Liu, from Pinghu County, Zhejiang, was initially sentenced to slow slicing for beating his elder brother and family head, Ma San, to death after he caught him repeatedly trying to rape his wife, Ma Yao Shi.[42] Ma San, who shared a compound with his brother, was, according to the testimonies of the village headman, several villagers, and relatives, a "violent bully of a man" who "often behaved improperly." Seven years earlier, after his widowed sister-in-law, Wu Shi, refused to "submit to him as a wife," he broke into her chambers and tried to rape her. She fended him off but decided that to preserve her life (and, ironically, her chastity), she had to remarry. She took her younger son and daughter with her, but since Ma San had arranged the marriage and taken the brideprice, she had to leave her eldest son with him. According to Ma Liu, Ma San harassed the wives of all the neighbors as well, but "everybody fears his strength and ferocity so we all had to put up with it and avoid him."

In his first attack on his other sister-in-law, Ma Yao Shi, Ma San grabbed her while her husband was out working, she screamed, and he ran off. She went to tell the neighbors, and he pursued her and started to beat her in front of them, though they intervened to stop him. When her husband came home, she informed him about the incident and asked if they could move. But he said they didn't have the money and suggested that since she had refused him, he should leave her alone. A few months later, when her husband was again working away from home, she was grinding flour in the kitchen when her two-*sui*-old daughter started to cry, ready for a nap. A drunken Ma San came into the room, naked except for his underwear, and embraced her five-*sui*-old daughter. While she put the crying baby to bed in the inner room, Ma San carried her elder daughter outside, then ran into the inner room and grabbed her, tearing her lower clothing. As she struggled to fend him off, her husband walked in. Ma San returned to his quarters, cursing and threatening to kill his brother. As the couple were eating dinner, Ma San returned with a wooden bucket, which he threw at his brother's head. He then picked up a shovel and started to hit Ma Liu. Ma Liu dodged the blow and grabbed Ma San. Furious, Ma Yao Shi grabbed the shovel and started hitting him. Ma San then picked up the bucket to hit Ma Liu, who snatched the shovel from his wife's hands and hit him in the head. The drunken Ma San fell to the ground and passed out. Seeing that he was having difficulty breathing and would probably die, Ma Liu confessed, "I was flustered. . . . If he died and was discovered, . . . I would pay with my life. My elder brother was such an evil bully that if he recovered, he would seek revenge. Either way, it would be hard for my wife and me to escape death." He decided to tie him up, and as he did so, Ma San died. With the help of his nephew, the son of his remarried sister-in-law, he dragged the body to a pond in the middle of the night and threw it in, weighted with rocks. The body floated to the surface and was discovered by the local constable.

The magistrate sentenced Ma Liu to slow slicing for killing his elder brother and sentenced his wife to one hundred strokes of the heavy bamboo and three years' banishment for striking a senior relative. The nephew, under twelve at the time of the murder, had his sentence of flogging and banishment automatically commuted to a fine. Considering the incestuous attempted rape and the violent assault that prompted Ma Liu to kill his brother, however, the magistrate suggested that the board submit a request for a possible lessening of the sentences of Ma and his wife. After weighing the mitigating circumstances, the High Courts recommended that the original sentences be carried out. They concluded, "Although Ma San's repeated attempts to rape his younger brother's wife were a licentiously evil destruction of human relationships, nevertheless, Ma Liu intentionally killed his elder brother. This is a matter of proper relationships, and thus it is difficult for the law to be lenient." The highly unusual imperial rescript on this case ignored the High Courts' advice and lessened Mao Liu's sentence to decapitation, while ordering further deliberation. Read in the context of the many Qianlong-era edicts asserting the special prerogative of the husband to defend his wife's chastity or avenge its loss, this rescript may suggest that the impetus for the increasing recognition of a conjugal definition of patriarchy in the law was coming from the throne.[43] The deliberations over incest cases indicate persistent resistance on the part of judicial officials to allowing the defense of chastity to trump respect for patrilineal family hierarchy. What is clear, though, is that judicial officials' confusion and reticence in the face of the incest conundrum reflected an intensification of the tension between generational and marital patriarchy in both statecraft discourse and social life.

Consistent with this vision of the weakening emphasis on generational patriarchy, Norman Kutcher has argued that the dynasty gradually "disengaged" itself from the Confucian system of mourning practices in its policies on mourning leaves for officials, thereby displacing filial piety as the normative heart of a political order based on the assumed parallelism of family and political values.[44] Analysis of law and ritual policy affirms this provocative observation: the primacy of filial piety as the relevant paradigm of loyalty and hierarchy was being severely challenged by the paradigm of female chastity as loyal and obedient service to the family and the Qing political order. With all the political symbolism and resources that the state invested in its civilizing project, filiality was only rarely at issue in changes to ritual regulations or law or in official discourse on ritual, law, and customs. Yet statecraft discourse was rife with the problems of defining, enforcing, and awarding female chastity. Year-end tallies of state honors registered filiality awards in single digits while recording hundreds, if not thousands, of chastity canonizations.

Yet as we have seen, the state's working definition of patriarchy remained inconsistent. The state's treatment of female suicide itself straddled a widening fissure between marital and generational notions of patriarchy. As the Yongzheng Emperor observed in his edict banning widow suicide, it was a narrow maritally defined notion of chastity that fueled the widow suicide phenomenon to the detriment of the larger family order.

Yet the notion of wifely loyalty remained so politically and emotionally salient that the dynasty was frequently compelled to make exceptions to its own policy.[45] During the Qianlong reign, laws on revenge for adultery and incest were revised to recognize the legitimacy of husbandly prerogative and occasionally its precedence over patrilineal authority and filial obedience. As we will see in the Part Three, the adjudication of rape was also shaped by a notion of marital patriarchy as the heart of the inner realm that was violated in sexual assault by rogue males outside the family system. Yet even in this context, where Qing judicial officials unequivocally defended a chastity-centered conjugal patriarchy, they were confounded by the unexpected complexity of chastity as precept and practice and the ironic unreliability of any patriarchal authority, including husbands, to make the vindication of chastity an overwhelming priority.

PART THREE

Mapping Chastity across Boundaries of Body, Mind, and Space

Prologue: A Compromised Widow Sacrifices Her Body to Defend Inner Virtue

One day in the eighth month of 1753, a sixteen-*sui*-old boy named Du Ming made the daylong journey from his home in the Xiuyan District of Fengtian Prefecture in Manchuria to the village of the local constable *(xiangyue)* to report that his mother had been raped the night before by a stranger who broke into their house while they were sleeping. Afterwards, he said, his mother stabbed the attacker, who grabbed the knife and stabbed her and Du Ming several times before escaping. According to the constable the boy requested that he arrest the culprit to avenge his mother's violation. The constable headed off to Du Ming's home to investigate, bringing along a group of men to search for the offender. Four days later they found a man named Sun Er whose wounds matched the boy's description in an inn down the river from Du Ming's house and took him off to the Xiuyan Banner Headquarters for interrogation. The banner commandant handed him over to the Haicheng County Magistrate Qi Fashang for trial.[1]

Widowed the year before, Du Ming's mother, Du Song Shi, aged thirty-three, lived alone with her three sons in an isolated thatched house on the road to Xiuyan Town. It is highly likely that the rape would never have been discovered by the magistrate had the victim's son not reported it. Yet from the perspective of the judicial officials who tried the case, her vindication was not a foregone conclusion. Having sought the state's intervention, Du Song Shi subjected herself to the intense scrutiny and moral judgment of powerful men whose sympathy was not guaranteed. To them, her life and the circumstances of her violation bristled with contradictory moral messages. She appeared, on the one hand, to be the quintessential chaste widow valorized by the state chastity cult, living a difficult yet righteous life, supporting herself and her three sons, aged sixteen, nine, and three, by spinning cotton. On the other hand, though, her independence from family and neighbors, even if forced upon her by fate, made the adjudicating officials very uncomfortable.

Their suspicions of her character were enhanced by depictions of her response to the alleged assault and the tone of her own testimony. According to her first statement of events, as she lay sleeping one night with her sons, a stranger broke into her house, jumped onto her *kang*, and tried to rape her.[2] At first she screamed, but, she testified,

> I live in an isolated farmstead with no neighbors. Screaming was of no use. My children are still small, so I had to struggle with him myself. He grabbed me around the waist with all his strength. As I struggled, my hand fell against a knife that he carried at his waist, and I was terrified. He told me, "If you move again I will take out my knife and kill you." I was afraid of dying and was raped by him as he held me down. I thought to myself that I had lost my chastity and must get revenge *(shile jie biyao baochou)*, so I tricked him into putting his knife down and slipped it under the straw mat. Then I deceived him, saying, "It is not convenient that the children are still sleeping at my side. Let me go and I will move them and come back and sleep with you again."

He agreed and she then got up, grabbed a knife, and came back to stab him in the scrotum. He fainted and she stabbed him several more times with his own knife. Then she and Du Ming dragged him outside, where he suddenly regained consciousness, snatched the knife back, and stabbed Du Ming. She tried to grab the knife away, but he stabbed her too, so she bit him on the arm, and he finally dropped the knife and crawled frantically away.

In his preliminary statement during the magistrate's first investigation at their house,[3] Du Ming said that he had first laid eyes on the defendant earlier that same day when he showed up at their gate, asking him how to get to the south temple. The boy gave him directions, and the defendant then inquired as to whether the household had a family head or not. "I tricked him," Du Ming said, "telling him that my father had gone to the mountains to cut firewood. Then he left." Later that day, his mother sent him to the temple with two catties of cotton thread she had spun for the temple watchman. The stranger who had asked him directions was sitting with him. Du Ming told the watchman, "Some of the thread got wasted. My mother says you should deduct whatever is appropriate from the payment." He replied, "How could I keep back money from orphans and a widow?" Sun Er then asked the watchman how the boy could have no father when he had earlier heard him say otherwise, and the watchman revealed that Du Song Shi was in fact a widow, "eking out an extremely bitter living with her children."

The magistrate had great difficulty believing the story of the rape despite the victims' wounds and corroborating testimony from the defendant himself and the temple watchman, who called him a "wicked man." Indeed, the twenty-three-*sui*-old Sun Er perfectly fit the common judicial stereotype of a rapist as a rootless male *(guanggun)* cut off from the constraints of family and community and prone to thuggery.[4] In the areas of Manchuria, like Fengtian, that attracted large numbers of Chinese migrants in the mid-Qing, village communities were much more fluid than they were in the Han heartland. The presence of strangers and newcomers was common, and the phenomenon of the rootless male was growing in the late eighteenth century, exacerbated both by the widespread practice of female infanticide to control family size and composition and by adherence to the norms of the chastity cult by the vast majority of widows.[5] Together, these factors meant that about one-tenth of men in the region never married and were likely to be those at the bottom of the familial and social order.[6] Sun Er's lack of family ties and livelihood at his age of twenty-three made it almost inevitable that he would never marry.

He explained in his confession that he was a single migrant from Northern Shandong Province across the Bohai Straits and had been working for over a year as an itinerant laborer in various villages.[7] Unable to find work at the beginning of the eighth month, he was headed off to Xiuyan Town to look for a job in the merchant shops when he passed by Du Song Shi's lonely homestead. Peeking inside the front gate, he noticed only a woman and children but no husband. Scoping out the situation, he then struck up a conversation with Du Ming by asking directions and made his inquiry about the presence of a household head. When he heard from the temple watchman that Du Song Shi was a widow, he stated, "I then got the urge to go and have illicit sex with her." A woman living alone with her children and no close neighbors no doubt appeared to him to offer an opportunity at least for a sexual encounter of some sort, while the added enticement of her widowed status perhaps held out the hope of something more. Sun Er rented a room at the temple but in the middle of the night went to Du Song Shi's homestead. Before he left, he stole several catties of cotton thread and wild mushrooms *(mu er)* along with an old knife that the watchman used to dig them up, presumably to start him off in his commercial ventures. The theft led the magistrate to suspect him of being part of a gang of robbers, a charge he vehemently denied, insisting that he was no criminal and that this was his first and only theft.

If Sun Er fit the expected profile of a rapist, Du Song Shi's rape story contravened most of the judicial requirements for proving that an illicit sexual encounter had been coerced and not consensual. The commentary appended to the statute on "coerced illicit sex" in the Qing Code elaborated in detail on these evidentiary requirements:

> In prosecution for rape there must be evidence of violent coercion, and the situation must have been such that the woman could not struggle free; there must also be persons who were aware and heard what happened, as well as physical injury to skin and body, torn clothing, and other such evidence. Only then shall the offender be sentenced to strangulation. If an offender joins with a woman by coercion but completes the act by means of her consent, then it does not count as coercion.[8]

While the wounds sustained by Du Song Shi, her son, and the defendant clearly pointed to a struggle of some sort, there was no torn clothing. There were no witnesses who heard her scream, nor did she seek help from neighbors after the attack. Although the defendant carried a knife, his threat to kill her was merely verbal, and she admitted that after struggling at first she submitted to him to avoid death. While the degree of her isolation was rather unusual, the paucity of required evidence and the compromising circumstances of her assault were common problems faced by magistrates trying sexual assault cases. In fact, magistrates' handbooks on judicial procedure anticipated such problems and suggested strategies for adjudicating cases that did not fit readily into the judicial paradigm of rape. Huang Liuhong in his popular handbook for magistrates advised that

> [w]hen rapes occur in empty courtyards or deserted places in the wilderness, then the assailant, fearing she will not submit, will surely threaten her with a knife and there will be a struggle that will probably leave wounds on their hands and faces. Anxious to have illicit sex quickly, the assailant will surely tear her underclothes and belt. How could someone break into a village house in broad daylight without worrying about causing noise and commotion, without carrying a weapon, and rape a woman without leaving

any signs of struggle, wounds on her body, and torn clothing? . . . There are also instances where a fierce bully uses brute force to flagrantly rape a woman. She cannot resist, perhaps because she is tied up and gagged. How could she endure this? If she is chaste she will not fear death, and even though she is gagged she will cry out and put up a struggle. Would she really be all alone with no relative or neighbor who would hear her screams and come to her rescue?[9]

Suspecting that this was a case of consensual illicit sex, Magistrate Qi interrogated the defendant and the victim intensively. He asked Du Song Shi, "Did you or did you not know Sun Er on a daily basis? . . . He did not even take out his knife to threaten you. Why did you then submit to him, and after submitting to him, why would you then stab him in the scrotum?" She insisted that they had never met and that she had submitted to him once he threatened to kill her and had then stabbed him to get revenge. Sun Er confirmed her story and elaborated further on her deception to get his knife, quoting her as saying, "'I have already submitted to you. Why do you still need to carry a knife? Give it to me.'" "I thought it was okay and handed the knife over to her," he testified.

The deception scenario made no sense to the magistrate, who queried him further: "You carried along a hidden knife to rape Song Shi. Naturally this was because you intended to use violent force if she did not submit. How then would you not carry the knife in your hand to threaten her? How can you say that that she 'bumped against your waist, felt the knife, and then did not dare to move?' And if you intended not to use violent force, then why would you later stab her and her son?" Sun Er explained, "I carried the knife thinking I would use it to threaten her. When I got to her house and grabbed her . . . she could tell I had a knife, so there was no need to take it out. . . . I told her, 'If you move again I will take my knife and kill you.' So she dared not move." His later stabbing of mother and son, he claimed, happened because he was in a state of shock after being stabbed and was trying to defend himself. The magistrate's line of questioning, common to all sexual assault cases, conformed precisely to models laid out in handbooks for judicial procedure.[10] These questions not only incorporated the evidentiary requirements stipulated in the statute on illicit sex but also moved beyond the code's empirical concerns to open up questions about customs, habits, and state of mind to establish how Du Song Shi came to find herself in a situation where contact with a man outside her immediate family was even possible.

The county magistrate accepted Du Song Shi's assertions of her virtue and sentenced Sun Er to decapitation after the assizes for rape and for stabbing of the victim as she tried to capture him. But the Manchu Prefect of Fengtian, Obao, found this verdict preposterous. In a long critique of the magistrate's judgment, he expressed numerous doubts about the veracity of all of the testimonies. Probing into Sun Er's state of mind and the seeming ease with which he had entered Du Song Shi's house, the prefect implied that there must have been some contact between the two that had emboldened him and caused her to let down her guard. He queried,

> How could [Sun Er] have known that there were no other relatives living with [Du Song Shi and her children]? Moreover, how could he have known that Song Shi had no sons older than Du Ming? . . . Although it took extremely lecherous daring to go openly straight [to her house], still, how could he not have the slightest fear to make him hesitate? . . . Furthermore, such a beautiful woman with small children living alone in an isolated hamlet would certainly bolt the door and take precautions at dusk before going to bed.[11] How could Sun Er push the door open and walk straight in without a sound so that neither Song Shi nor any of her children were startled? This is extremely difficult to believe.

Pressing further, the prefect raised doubts about many elements of the sequence of events in the course of the assault itself, questioning in particular the strangely passive behavior of the sixteen-*sui*-old Du Ming and Sun Er's state of mind as he patiently awaited the return of the woman he had supposedly just assaulted:

> At the moment when Sun Er jumped onto the *kang* . . . Song Shi still did not realize that he had a knife at his waist. Waking up suddenly out of deep sleep to face this violent attack, [she] must have been frightened out of her mind and screamed loudly . . . and struggled. Yet Du Ming was sleeping so heavily that he heard nothing. This is even more preposterous. Also, . . . how could Song Shi, a woman, carry [Du Ming] to another spot, and even if she could, . . . how could she prevent him from waking and asking what was happening? At that moment, Sun Er was blinded by intense lust and in a haze worrying that he would not necessarily be satisfied. If Sun Er believed her without hesitation, then he must have removed his [clothing] and lain there naked. . . . [After being wounded severely], how could he not leave his clothing behind?

Finally, the prefect questioned the moral attitudes of mother and son, suggesting that their behavior was not reflective of a true spirit of chaste humiliation or righteous indignation.

> If Song Shi were a widow who was preserving her chastity and encountered such violence and was polluted and humiliated, then her spirit of indignation would be impossible to quell. Du Ming, knowing that his mother had

been humiliated, would certainly be gnashing his teeth with loathing. As soon as Sun Er had fainted, mother and son could join forces to end his life on the spot. Why did they not make certain that [he] was dead before dragging him outside? . . . Why did they not go to their neighbors for help?

These questions pushed the inquiry beyond accounting for objective markers of rape to the search for expressions of daring lechery and chaste indignation in behavior and demeanor. Here again, the line of questioning and its implied assumptions about the links between intent, moral integrity, and behavior were anticipated in judicial handbooks. Huang Liuhong allotted the bulk of his section on rape cases to the difficulties of decoding the demeanor and testimony of alleged assault victims to assess the quality of their chastity, suggesting that when evidence was lacking or contradictory, accurate reading of the moral character of the victim, her family, and the perpetrator finally offered the best hedge against wrongful prosecution. He advised,

> [The magistrate] must also carefully observe the demeanor of husband and wife as they make their statements to see if they are truly full of righteous indignation. . . . If it is really a case of coerced illicit sex, then the statements in the plea will be straightforward and complete and will coincide with the oral testimony. If it is a case of consensual illicit sex misrepresented as rape, then the statements in the plea will be very disjointed and the oral testimony quite incoherent. In testifying, the husband will not show true righteous indignation but will exhibit evasive demeanor as though concealing something, each time glancing at his wife for fear that she will contradict him. The woman's face will show no sign of humiliation or great shame, and her testimony will be very halting. Under cross-examination she will contradict herself, and when confronted with the accused, she will bow her head and not wrangle with him. The woman originally felt tenderness for him and they were intimate, so she is unable to hide her lingering feelings completely. If the accused does not appear to be fierce and vicious and his answers are clear and fitting and the statements of witnesses do not provide conclusive evidence of coercion, then usually it is a case of consensual illicit sex.[12]

The cogency of a testimony and the forthright demeanor of the person testifying were, for Huang, key measures of its truthfulness. Assuming the useful convergence between behavior, demeanor, intent, and moral quality, he stressed the importance of shame as an external signifier of chaste intent. Only a woman who was without shame could commit adultery, and such a woman would be expected to be incapable even of feigning the "righteous indignation" that a truly chaste woman would be unable to contain as she faced the man who had violated her. Likewise, only a "fierce and vicious" man would end up as the defendant in a sexual assault, presumably because the chaste woman would surely be able to fend off anything less.

Seeking precisely this kind of moral consistency between behavior, courtroom performance, and intent, the Fengtian prefect identified numerous contradictions between and within the testimonies, along with several procedural errors on the part of the magistrate, and concluded that "the case testimonies are full of evasions and ambiguities and are completely disjointed. . . . Obviously there are some other important circumstances that are relevant." He ordered the magistrate to reinterrogate everyone. This time, in response to the questions quoted above, Du Song Shi added significant new details to her story that contradicted her original account at numerous crucial points:

> The house I live in is a very isolated three-room thatched cottage. Ever since my husband died I have felt uneasy living there, but since there was no place else in the area to move to, I had to stay. . . . Even though I locked the gate at night . . . it could never be latched securely. On that night . . . I was already asleep . . . when I heard someone outside knocking. I awoke startled and asked who it was. He said, "I am a passerby and have taken the wrong road. I would like to borrow some lodgings for the night." I told him, "We are a household, so it is not convenient for you to come in." Then he broke into the door, came into the room and jumped onto the *kang*, wanting to have illicit sex. At this point, I did not realize that he had a knife on him, and I did not submit, but screamed curses at him. Then, . . . my hand bumped against his knife . . . and he said, "If you move again, I will take my knife and kill you." I still wanted to resist him but was afraid that he really would kill me. My sons are still small, and I have no neighbors who could have rescued me. Because of this I was scared and had no choice but to be raped by him. My son had already awoken in a fright, but he is young and usually very timid. . . . When he also heard the man say he would stab me, how would he dare to try and save me? Once I had been raped and polluted, my mind was tortured and I wanted to get revenge. So I tricked him into giving me his knife . . . [After he let me go], I came back and saw that he had taken off his clothes. I pretended to caress his scrotum with the knife and then stabbed him and he fainted. I detested him and grabbed his knife intending to stab him again, but my own hands were too weak and I couldn't cut him. So I called my son, Du Ming, to come and he stabbed him several more times. He never moved.

She now claimed that after the scuffle outside her house, Sun Er had said to her, "I have done wrong. If you give me my clothes, I will leave." "I didn't want to return them," she testified, "but I was afraid that he would go back into the house and do something violent again." So she sent Du

Ming to fetch his clothing, and Sun Er crawled off into the fields. "At that point," she said, "Du Ming and I were extremely agitated and did not want to leave each other's side." Finally, she said, it was the middle of the night, each of them had multiple stab wounds, and the gate would not lock securely. "How could I get away to seek help from the neighbors?" Interrogating the defendant for the last time, the magistrate wondered how he could have believed her when she said she would have sex with him again. Sun Er responded that at first he did not dare to remove his clothing completely, but then "since Song Shi spoke so many nice words to me, I finally relaxed and undressed completely. When she came back [to the *kang*] she caressed my body wildly *(luanmo)* with her hands. . . . It didn't occur to me that she was caressing my scrotum with a knife."

Finally, the magistrate asked Du Song Shi why she had left crucial details out of her first testimony. Her disarming reply astutely points up the power relation between official and commoner in the courtroom, which provides an obvious alternative explanation for the equivocating testimony and demeanor that Huang assumed to be indicative of deliberate lying. "These things really happened," she insisted. "We live in the countryside and have never even seen a magistrate before. Suddenly having to come to court and answer questions, it is necessary to conduct oneself with dignity and reserve, to speak up and not be concerned about the consequences. How could I think of absolutely everything and speak completely? Today under detailed questioning, we finally thought of these things and testified clearly."

After his exhaustive review of all the relevant evidentiary standards for proving rape, Huang Liuhong finally admitted that whatever corroborating evidence might or might not exist, because the alleged victim's chaste intent was the key factor in establishing that a sexual assault occurred, the magistrate was ultimately required to make a subjective moral judgment about her mental state based on her demeanor during and after the assault:

> *The ancients judged the intention, not the act.* For example, if a woman confronts the violent coercion of a rapist and her reputation and chastity are at stake, she will be so outraged that she will not care about her safety and will scream at the top of her lungs. Even though the rapist has polluted her, *in her heart she will always hope that someone comes to her rescue,* and if no one comes, then after the rapist has fled, she will cry out to heaven and strike her head on the ground, weeping and shouting for help incessantly. Although she was already polluted, *the chaste intent of this woman never wavered.* . . . When an encounter ends with consent

it is not necessarily the case that at first the woman did not cry out loudly and resist, but after being polluted *she has a change of heart* and the shouting ceases. *In her heart she had already acquiesced,* . . . so how can the man be charged with rape?[13] (italics mine)

Huang asserted that there was a proper mental trajectory for chaste intent, from outrage to hope to humiliation to despair, with each stage of mental anguish expressed in appropriate physical gestures: screams of outrage, tears of humiliation, striking the head on the ground as if in grief. Partial fulfillment of these requirements of chastity raised immediate doubt; if, despite screaming and struggling throughout, the woman failed to express appropriate verbal and physical outrage after the attack, Huang considered her to have acquiesced in her heart.

In the wake of her violation, Du Song Shi expressed her outrage and humiliation, not in the proper form of weeping and shouting, or attempting to kill herself, but by trying to kill her attacker through a deception that required cunning, presence of mind, and sexual savvy. Her testimony was contradictory and perhaps deliberately misleading. Yet the magistrate concluded, again, that appearances aside, her intent was to maintain and vindicate her chastity. This time, the verdict was accepted by the prefect, so the sentence of decapitation after the assizes for rape and wounding of the victim stood.[14] Ironically, Du Song Shi's chastity, the chastity that was vindicated by the legal system, was only a matter of intent—an inner, personal sense of virtue. The circumstances of her life, her behavior in the face of assault, and the tone and construction of her testimony violated all of the other definitions of chastity at play in her case—bodily integrity, wifely loyalty, and chaste demeanor. As a lone widow, she defined her virtue not in terms of her loyalty to a husband but in terms of her duty to her uterine family and her very personal sense of chastity, which transcended what she saw as the lesser chastity of her body.

Du Song Shi's construction of her response to sexual assault is strikingly reminiscent of the ploys of the satirist Li Yu's (1611–80) heroine in "The Female Chen Ping Saves Her Life with Seven Ruses." Asserting that "it is almost impossible to distinguish true virtue from false," he presents the story of Secunda Geng, who, after being kidnapped by bandits, defends her chastity in a most unusual manner.[15] Secunda has been dubbed "the female Chen Ping" by her neighbors because, like the tactician who cleverly defended the newly unified empire of Han Gaozu with six secret stratagems, she is always able to devise solutions for the most intractable problems of her family and neighbors. When her village is besieged by bandits during the chaotic last years of the Ming dynasty, she lives up to her nickname by devising seven ruses to protect her virtue and get revenge on the bandit chief who has forcibly taken her as his wife.

After fawning over him with feigned wifely devotion, she first fends off his sexual advances by pretending that she has her period so that "that erect member of his, poised before the cavity, gave a mighty thrust—and thrust straight into a rag!"[16] After her "period" is over, she manages to feign contraction of an "infection" that causes her genitals to swell to "the size of a bowl," by rubbing them with croton-oil beans that she has secretly brought with her for the purpose. Then, when the desperately disappointed bandit chief tries rubbing against her "eunuch-fashion," she slyly rubs croton-oil on his member, causing it to become "so badly swollen that it looked like a laundry beater made out of crystal."[17] For her fourth ruse, she grinds croton-oil beans and mixes them in his food so he gets severe diarrhea that lasts for days. Her fifth ruse consists of a lie she invents about a hidden family fortune to convince the bandit chief to take her back to her village, where she is able to sneak away from the bed-ridden bandit to run home to her husband for help. The sixth ruse is to convince the bandit to hide his stolen loot in the river, where she and her husband will later be able to find it. With the seventh and final ruse, she contrives to make the bandit describe her stratagems and swear in front of all her neighbors that although all of the other kidnapped village wives willingly succumbed to the bandit's advances, she alone kept her chastity.

Li Yu's play on the notion of "keeping one's chastity" is the crux of his satire in this story. Secunda's ruses dangerously skirt the boundaries of unchastity, as she sleeps in the arms of the bandit every night. The narrator explains, "All of Secunda's ruses and ploys were devoted to preserving her 'insignia of rank,'[18] which she refused to yield to anyone. Everything else she possessed—rosy lips, crimson tongue, soft breasts, tiny feet, and jadelike fingers—she looked upon as inanimate things external to her, and she let him clip, suck, fondle, and pinch them as if unaware of what he was doing. Hers was the expedient of 'saving root and trunk at the expense of branches and leaves.'"[19] This extremely narrow definition of chastity is, on one level, consistent with the letter of Qing rape law, which strictly equated the pollution of chastity with penetration.[20] Yet Secunda's actions, not unlike those of Du Song Shi, defy the spirit of chastity as it was expressed in judicial discourse and in people's everyday notions of gender propriety. Li Yu's ribald humor emerges, of course, from the absurdity of drawing the technical line between chastity and unchastity so thin that instead of posing a dichotomy these moral opposites rub against each other in "eunuch-fashion," touching yet not interpenetrating.

What does it mean when the state vindicates the virtue of a woman whose actions, like those of Secunda, parody the Qing Code's definition of chastity and its violation, and whose case defies almost every established judicial standard for proving rape, including material evidence, behavior during the attack, and courtroom performance? Having dabbled with legal commentaries on the illicit sex statute, Li Yu in this story put his finger on its many ironies, whose ramifications would explode less than a century later in the flurry of lawmaking and statecraft debate that marked the state-building and civilizing projects of the Yongzheng and Qianlong reigns.

CHAPTER 6

The Wages of Wanton Mixing

Violation and Gender Disorder

As they worked to carry out the dynasty's civilizing mission, officials contended not only with the fracturing of patriarchal authority but with what they perceived to be the widespread ignorance and wanton violation of the standards of gender separation that defined moral order. Qianlong-era memorials reporting on local targets for the *jiaohua* campaign were full of shock, outrage, and general hand-wringing about the dismal state of gender relations. As usual, most memorialists suggested that the creation of new substatutes or modification of existing ones was needed to foster propriety in relations between men and women. Lurking beneath concerns about the mixing of the sexes was a pervasive anxiety about illicit sex, which destroyed morality and undermined patriarchal authority. As officials dealt with illicit sex cases, they understood themselves to be promoting a civilized gender order defined by separation between inner and outer realms. The illicit sex statute, the Qing state's clearest defense of husbandly prerogative, assumed an idealized moral universe in which chastity, narrowly construed as absolute sexual loyalty to a present, past, or future husband, was nurtured in the inner quarters of the family, safe from the outside world. Chastity could be threatened only by the moral weakness of women or the predations of criminal elements unhindered by family and community ties. Highlighting the problem of proving the chaste resistance of the alleged victim, the language of the rape statute appeared to put women's chastity on trial as it defended marital patriarchy against external assault and internal betrayal. Yet as numerous judicial commentators throughout the Qing period pointed out, the presumed dichotomies of chaste and unchaste, inner and outer, coercion and consent that structured the rape statute were fundamentally untenable in judicial practice.

GENDER SEPARATION AND IMPERIAL CIVILIZATION

The paradigm of separation or distinction *(fen, bie,* or *bian)* between "inner" and "outer" defined gender difference and gender order in the late imperial period. It framed discussions of women and their proper social roles in morality handbooks, lineage instructions, social commentary, and statecraft discourse.[1] Imagined in spatial, social, and behavioral terms, the inner quarters, governed by proper gender separation, was a preserve of female virtue and family honor. Within it resided the ideal woman of virtue, "sitting quietly in the depths of the women's quarters, cultivating excellent virtue,"[2] meaning that she was secluded, diligently engaged in the appropriately feminine pursuits of needlework, cooking, and household chores, and sheltered from casual contacts with people outside her family. According to the classical logic of distinction between inner and outer, separation was to be accomplished first of all in the patterning of household space, which included both the differentiation of household work and living spaces for male and female family members and a separation of the private family spaces appropriate to women from both the world outside the compound gates and the more public spaces of the household itself in which men interacted with outsiders. Spatial separation within the household was ideally to be reinforced by social customs of early marriage, separation of brothers and sisters after the age of ten, restriction of contact between male and female relatives, and barring of the entry of male servants into the women's quarters. Distinction between inner and outer thus also meant differentiation of work and leisure activities between women and men and separate social circles.

In sanctioned social interactions between men and women within the family, the principle of separation required the maintenance of circumspect decorum in speech and body language: touch, giggling, joking, and appearing in makeup and fancy clothes all constituted breaches of gender separation in the most rigid formulations of literati moralists.[3] Lan Dingyuan noted, "It is better that [women] are cautious and timid than rash and outspoken; better to be overly severe than to frolic and joke."[4] In his section on proper appearance he advised, "When dressing up with clothing and accessories, they should be in accordance with everyday habits: fresh and clean, tidy and modest, so that they could not possibly cause disgrace *(gouhui).*"⁵ Even in relations between husbands and wives, he counseled, tribulation in marriage occurs when there is "excessive familiarity": "[I]ntimacy and yet respect, reverence and yet love: this is what it means to have separateness *(bie)*. . . . To respect each other as guests, with concentrated heart and upright countenance: this is ritual propriety. Those who, on the contrary, have disheveled hair and unkempt appearance, yet feign modesty, are obviously not dignified women. Those who see them will detest them."⁶

Separation also meant avoidance of potentially corrupting contacts with the outside world when women ventured outside the household gates or when they received visitors. Discussions of female virtue in the mid-Qing were not complete without admonitions against women visiting temples, going on pilgrimages, attending the opera, or appearing in public at all with their faces uncovered. So too, warnings about the corrupting influence of the "three nuns and six old women" (Buddhist and Daoist nuns, diviners, brokers, matchmakers, witches, procuresses, medicine women, and midwives) who frequented the inner chambers were clichés of inner quarters etiquette. Advising his sons to prohibit such women from visiting the inner quarters, Wang Huizu caustically explained that with their "ignorant . . . and idle talk about fortune and misfortune," often "wrapped in the guise of scriptures," and their "wagging tongues and shaking lips" they enchanted women, swindled money, and stirred up all kinds of trouble.⁷ Railing at the same time against the noxious influence of Buddhism in the inner quarters, which distracted women from the filial duties of the wifely way, Wang revealed the tangle of cultural and normative assumptions lurking within the rhetoric of the inner-outer distinction.⁸

The most feared corruption was in fact the dilution of the norms themselves, through the insinuation of alternative gender paradigms offered by Buddhism, Daoism, or heterodox religious sects, the perpetuation of entrenched "barbarian customs" among the less civilized segments of the imperial populace, or simply the gradual weakening of standards of gender etiquette. In statecraft and ethical discourse of the High Qing period, proper gender relations patterned by distinction between inner and outer were the foundation of the civilized customs and social order promoted by the imperial state. The inseparability of gender distinction and civilization was, of course, not a new theme. It was, as Lan Dingyuan emphasized in his handbook, the foundational principle of the rites. "[Gender] separateness/distinction *(bie)* is ritual propriety," he argued.

"It is what distinguishes human beings from birds and beasts."⁹ However, in the heyday of Qing imperial expansion, as the imperial state expanded its normative influence in society, the link between gender order and civilization took on a more explicitly political connotation. Transgressions of gender separation norms were a pervasive issue on the empire's many frontiers and became one of the most popular metonyms, matched only by "debauched" mourning rituals, for communities living outside the bounds of civilization because they were barbarian, heterodox, or ignorant. Officials in the frontier provinces of Yunnan and Guizhou reported repeatedly on their efforts to civilize the gender customs of the many non-Han ethnic groups of the region.¹⁰ With the major campaigns to pacify the southwestern tribal regions in the middle of the eighteenth century, consciousness of the imperial dimension of gender order diffused into Qing society far beyond official circles. Examining the life and works of Wanyan Yun Zhu (1771–1833), Susan Mann has suggested the extent of elite women's awareness of how the gender boundaries of inner and outer that structured their lives mapped onto imperial cultural space.¹¹ Yun Zhu's anthology of women's poetry and her history of women pointedly recorded the literary achievements and virtues of non-Han women in border regions as evidence of the fulfillment of the imperial civilizing mission.¹² On a somewhat less highbrow level, the author of a Qing vernacular handbook for women, complaining of "the failure to maintain strict separation *(wubie)*" between brothers-in-law and sisters-in-law, warned that in "failing to avoid suspicion *(bu bixian)*" by observing proper gender etiquette people behaved "like the barbarian tribes of the north and south."¹³ Depictions of the "uncivilized" ignorance of customs of gender separation and chastity among the Miao, noted for the ferocity of their resistance to Qing conquest, appeared even in fiction.¹⁴

As the political salience of chastity-centered female virtue intensified in the latter half of the eighteenth century, signs of the fraying of gender order built on the inner-outer dichotomy proliferated. At the height of the dynasty's civilizing zeal in the early Qianlong years, numerous officials across the empire memorialized on the problem of neglect and ignorance of norms of gender separation and widespread transgressions of the boundaries of the inner quarters. If their observations of social life across the empire were at all accurate, they had good reason to be concerned. Susan Mann and William Rowe have noted the widespread worry among officials about failures to observe a proper gender division of labor, expressed in the campaigns of numerous officials across the country to encourage sericulture and other textile work so as to stop women from working in the fields and promote gender separation in work practice under the rubric "Men plow, women weave."[15]

Even larger concerns about gender chaos were evident in Qianlong-era statecraft discourse. Sichuan civil and military officials, for example, worried in the 1730s about the ongoing threat to gender order posed by shantytowns of migrant "barbarians" (apparently not ethnic minorities but indigent Han people) that sprang up seasonally along river banks in mountain regions where agriculture was difficult. Not only did men and women mix freely in these communities, but prostitution was rampant. In such conditions, the Chongqing Regional Military Commander observed, it was difficult for "good" women who did not come to work as prostitutes to strictly uphold ritual propriety, and they were readily led "outside" by immoral women. Since most of these "immoral women" were young, he suggested, rather unrealistically, attempting to enforce a degree of female seclusion by prohibiting women under forty from migrating far from their home villages.[16]

The multitude of memorials on the problematic customs of Huguang indicate that the region was a hotbed of cultural ignorance and flagrant violation of gender separation and dominant norms of propriety in general. In 1745, the year before the Hunan governor's report on extravagant and improper funerals and weddings among the local elites and common people,[17] the Manchu governor-general of Huguang, Emida, and Hubei's governor, Yan Sisheng, memorialized to present their investigations of violations of gender propriety spawned by the "lack of separation between men and women *(nannü zhi wubie)* resulting in the destruction of the way of knowing shame *(lianchi)*." They singled out as most egregious couples' practice of using unscrupulous brokers to contract their marriages illicitly without their families' involvement and widows' practice of violating their chastity and then remarrying their lovers. Emida called for a concerted effort to "hunt down" and punish the men and women who formed such marriages, along with the brokers and family heads who assisted them, in accordance with the established statutes on proper marriage. In consort with the *jiaohua* campaign's emphasis on strengthening local moral leadership, he further called for local magistrates to admonish and educate lineage leaders and *baojia* heads who were negligent in their duty to supervise marriage contracts and even protected those who engaged in such illicit relations. Yan Sisheng presented these problems as the result of lack of attention to the classic instructions from the Book of Rites *(Liji)* that men and women should not eat and drink at the same table or live in the same rooms. Emida noted, however, that while the well-off families of the literati might not need to be educated in these norms, it was extremely difficult to promote them among the majority of poor households. He thus also recommended that local magistrates become actively involved in providing moral examples and instruction to the populace on matters of gender propriety through propaganda and through primary schools so that the people would be "well versed in [the *Liji*'s] 'Pattern of the Family' and 'Rules of Propriety' for marriage, and [these texts] will illuminate their every action."[18]

As if the mixing of the sexes in ordinary social life were not worrying enough, many officials identified the violation of separation norms in judicial procedures, especially among criminals within the judicial system, as another threat to civilized customs and morals. The statute on women criminals inherited from the Ming Code already stipulated that women who committed offenses other than illicit sex or capital crimes should never be imprisoned but should instead be placed in the custody of their husbands, relatives, or neighbors while awaiting trial. Women who were imprisoned were to be housed in separate quarters.[19] From the early years of the Qing dynasty, women who committed minor crimes had to be represented in court by male relatives, so as to "foster the sense of shame and strengthen customs and morals," as Xue Yunsheng explained. Indeed, male relatives who allowed their mothers, wives, or daughters to file lawsuits in person were to be punished.[20] By the early Qianlong years, many judicial officials perceived these measures to be inadequate defenses of female propriety for various reasons. In 1736, concerns were raised in several memorials from judicial officials that the use of the cangue for women violated the separation of men and women, not only because the convicted women were exposed to public view, but also because mixed-sex crowds gathered to stare at such women. A new regulation was therefore promulgated, allowing the sentence of the cangue to be commuted to a fine for women, so that after first being "punished by flogging for her lack of shame, she is then allowed to pay a fine to preserve her sense of shame." As one commentator put it, "This truly is benevolence in the service of righteousness!"[21]

The lack of separate prison quarters for women and men (described as *nannü wufen*), especially at the county level, was a perennial problem, which, as many memorialists noted, resulted not only in a general breakdown of standards of gender distinction but also in the harassment and even assault of women prisoners by male prison staff and by male prisoners, who also corrupted them by forcing them into the service of prison gangs.²² Among the many memorials calling for better enforcement of the existing regulations, one from Hunan Governor Jiang Pu resulted in the creation of a new substatute in 1744 mandating the construction of separate prisons for women and adding illicit sex to the list of crimes for which women would be remanded to their families' supervision during trial, reserving imprisonment only for capital crimes.²³ Jiang Pu argued in his memorial that in line with the new regulations on the use of the cangue such a policy would allow "women without a sense of shame *(wu lianchi)*" who had committed crimes of illicit sex to "make a slight beginning on the road toward self-renewal." More careful monitoring of facilities for women prisoners, moreover, would "fulfill the way of avoiding suspicion."²⁴ His similar concerns with regard to the transfer of women sentenced to penal servitude up to the prefectural court for reinterrogation resulted in another substatute stipulating that such women also be given over to their families' control while their cases made their way up through the stages of review.²⁵ In 1760, yet another substatute was added in response to observations made by Sichuan Provincial Judicial Commissioner Yong Tai about the impossibility of keeping women prisoners sentenced to strangulation or decapitation after the assizes separated from male prisoners and guards while they were being transported from one *yamen* to the next for reinterrogation as part of the assizes process. He noted the frequency of violent incidents caused by the proximity of men and women and suggested the modification of the assizes regulations for women so that "women prisoners' fear of being humiliated can be somewhat alleviated."²⁶ The new substatute ordered that women being transported for the assizes process be accompanied by female chaperones appointed by the magistrate. It also exempted women from appearing in person for more than one round of the assizes process if the facts of their cases were indisputable.²⁷

The relevance of gender distinction extended not only to women who had already "lost their sense of shame" by committing crimes but also to dead women. The balance of propriety and judicial necessity in the forensic examination of women's bodies was yet another frequent topic of debate during the Qianlong years. Many judicial officials complained that very few local *yamen* adhered to the Board of Punishments regulations mandating the use of female coroners or midwives to examine the bodies of women. Consequently, one memorialist observed, "The naked body of the dead woman of the inner quarters enters the view and the hands of the male coroner. . . . Thus it is difficult to maintain distinction between inner and outer *(neiwai nanbie)* and to speak of honor and shame, and the common people know little of ritual propriety." He requested that the emperor order the employment of female coroners or midwives at every level of the judicial system, thereby "distinguishing inner and outer to prevent the destruction of honor and shame for the benefit of the inner quarters and the rectification of customs."[28]

In statecraft discourse, the mingling of men and women was also a defining feature of heterodox religious sects, which were endemic features of local society in many regions in the mid-Qing, judging from the large number of memorials on the subject. In 1737, for instance, the governor-general of Jiangnan, Qing Fu, reported on his efforts to deal with the emergence of a new sect, whose transgressions of gender separation were threatening customs and morals in Jiangnan, by arresting its leaders and punishing them with the cangue, fines, and flogging. Reviewing a long list of popular Jiangnan sects that "gang together to engage in violence and debauch women," however, his memorial indicated the impossibility of rooting out such popular customs, despite his resolve.[29] Reporting on a similar sect spreading across the northern provinces in 1746, Shaanxi Governor Chen Hongmou noted that regional customs of pilgrimage across province borders in which "men and women mix and the illicit and the good are indistinguishable" fostered the growth of such sects and should be prohibited along with the sects themselves.[30]

Many mid-Qing officials and moral commentators agreed with Chen's feeling that the pervasive practice of women going on pilgrimage and visiting temples was just as aggravating, scandalous, and difficult to stop as the florescence of heterodox sects.[31] In a telling memorial submitted in 1744, the first year of the Qianlong Emperor's *jiaohua* campaign, the investigating censor for the West Capital District, Shu Min, requested that women be prohibited from "traipsing around the hills and temples" to the west of the capital in order to "rectify customs and morals" but readily admitted his helplessness to deal with the problem. Reiterating the familiar orthodoxy, he insisted, "Temples ought to be pure and quiet places to burn incense and discipline oneself. The boundaries of the inner quarters ought to be strictly enforced. Inner and outer both need to be admonished not to tolerate transgressions." Shu noted that the Yongzheng Emperor had prohibited women from lighting incense at any of the temples in the capital region "to preserve the purity and order of the inner quarters." A decade later, however, the temples of the Western Hills were full of "flocks of banner and commoner women, heavily made up and gorgeously dressed, wandering at will across the peaks of the hills, roaming around the temples, and often even staying overnight in the temples

The Wages of Wanton Mixing

under the pretext of curing illnesses." He followed these observations with the familiar warnings about the corrupting influences of monks. But since he already recognized the long-standing popularity of these customs among women across the social spectrum, his moralizing conveyed a tone of nostalgia mixed with realism:[32]

> When the *Liji* says that inner speech should not go outside and outer speech should not come in, this means that men and women should guard against improper intimacy. Inner and outer words still cannot be exchanged. Yet publicly going in and out of temples, not avoiding contact with the monks, and staying overnight in their rooms, [women] learn the dissipated ways of the outside world. If this is allowed to continue without interference, then the harmful Buddhist disciplines of these monks will immeasurably corrupt the virtue of women in the inner quarters.

Moral ideals aside, Shu finally admitted defeat, explaining that although he would like to prohibit such behavior in the districts under his jurisdiction, he worried that sudden prohibitions of such "entrenched customs" by lowly and unknown officials like himself were likely to fail. Having rejected the most fundamental assumption of the *jiaohua* campaign about the civilizing potential of local officials, he requested that the emperor issue a prohibition to deal with this problem, a solution that, given his documentation of the ineffectiveness of past prohibitions, was bound to fail.[33]

William Rowe has argued that when Chen Hongmou engaged in similar unrealistic criticism of transgressions of the inner-outer boundary, he did so in contexts where his real concern was "bigger game," such as popular Buddhism, opera, or extravagant wedding and funeral ceremonies.[34] However, in his systematic association of gender impropriety with these other "evils," Chen was typical of moralists and officials in his day. In statecraft discourse, violation of gender boundaries was an intrinsic and defining aspect of heterodoxy, barbarity, immorality, and social disorder of all sorts, extravagant excess, and even, in some contexts like the memorial on Sichuan migrants, poverty. Gender order founded on the inner-outer distinction was not the only or even the most important item on the *jiaohua* agenda, but at the height of the Qing Empire it was the single most pervasive metaphor for imperial civilization, insinuating itself into unexpected corners of law, policy, and political culture. For as officials surveyed the cultural and moral landscape, they saw rampant and wanton mixing of the sexes *(nannü hunza)* in every corner of the realm at every level of society, from the capital to the frontiers, in temples and prisons, among elites and peasants, Han and non-Han.

ILLICIT SEX IN THE OFFICIAL IMAGINATION

The specter of gender disorder haunted officials as they confronted the most common violation of the inner/outer divide faced by officialdom, illicit sex, which every magistrate dealt with in his judicial caseload on a routine basis. Both Qing law and the officials who applied it assumed that sexual assault and adultery happened essentially because standards of gender separation had been violated. In judicial and nonjudicial discussions, illicit sex was often described as a violation of the inner quarters: the body of the rape victim or adulteress was readily equated with the inner sanctum of the household as the preserve of female virtue and family honor. The assumption that a woman literally embodied her husband's inner realm emerges in the minute elaboration of variations on the crime of illicit sex in the code.[35] The punishment for consensual fornication was one degree more severe for a married woman than for an unmarried woman, and yet another degree more severe if the offending man had lured the woman outside her home to engage in illicit intercourse. The mid-Qing judicial commentator, Yao Run, explained the variation in punishments this way:

> If there is a husband, who is abandoned for debauchery outside, the punishment is one degree higher. [When a woman is] lured outside and does not fear that people will know, the level of dissolute abandonment is particularly high, so [the punishment] is even more severe. The law holds that to debauch another's wife is to ruin his inner quarters *(yin ren funü huai ren guimen)*. While responsibility for the crime of illicit sex originates with the adulterous man, the adulterous woman must be licentiously wicked and without shame *(yinxie wuchi)* for it to be achieved. Therefore, no matter whether the case is one of consensual illicit sex or luring [a woman] into illicit sex, whether the woman is married or not, both man and woman are sentenced equally.[36]

In the legal construction of consensual illicit sex, which assumed the active role of the male and the reactive role of the female, the cuckolded husband was the victim of a transgression of his inner quarters perpetrated at the initiative of an "outside man" with the willing collusion of the "inside" woman. The crime and the degree of moral turpitude was more severe still if the woman left her appointed seclusion in the inner quarters, an action that, in the logic of the commentary, indicated that she was shamelessly unconcerned about concealing her action. What was at stake in the adjudication of illicit sex cases, then, was the integrity of conjugal patriarchy, defined as a husband's sexual monopoly over his wife, which was to be maintained through the separation of inner and outer.

Yao Run's reading of the illicit sex statute suggests that threats to chastity could result only from a violation of the sanctity of the inner quarters by an outside intruder or from a woman's own transgression of the spatial and social boundaries of proper female activity. In other words, beyond the criteria of evidence prescribed literally by the code, only two scenarios of transgression were thinkable: either the woman was unvirtuous to begin with and did not avoid contact with the man, which would amount to consensual illicit sex, or, she was virtuous and fell victim to rape by an unknown predator. Any sex outside marriage was illicit and illegal. Even if consensual, it warranted equal punishments of flogging for the man and the woman. Since judicially defined rape could occur only in a context where the sexual liaison would have been illegal anyway, the critical question in the adjudication of sexual assault cases was not whether a crime was committed but whether the crime was coerced or consensual illicit sex. As the work of Matthew Sommer has shown, while the behavior of the man was one factor judicial officials considered as they distinguished between the two crimes in practice, the behavior and moral quality of the woman were much more critical. It was here, in the adjudication process, that chastity, which was not mentioned in the statute itself, was revealed to be central to the judicial definition of rape. For only a chaste woman could qualify fully as a victim of rape, which judicial commentaries described routinely as a violation of chastity, narrowly and precisely defined as the virtue that inspired women to uphold sexual loyalty to their husbands at all times, even in the face of sexual assault.[37] For the purposes of the illicit sex investigations, the inner realm was thus defined by two concentric barriers: a woman's spatial separation from outside men and her own body, whose penetration defined the fully completed act of rape.[38] The process of investigation and interrogation focused on evaluating a woman's defense of each of these barriers. The first question considered relevant in determining whether a woman had consented to the illicit encounter or been coerced into it was that of how she came to find herself in a context where contact with a man outside her immediate family was possible. The next question was whether the man had used force and, if so, whether the woman had resisted to the best of her ability.

The "evidence of violent coercion" itemized in the commentary accompanying the statute was at once proof of both the man's coercive actions and the woman's chaste resistance. However, after emphasizing the importance of such objective evidence, the commentary stated that "if an offender joins with a woman by coercion but consummates the act by means of her consent, then it does not count as coercion." Furthermore, even when there was evidence of coercion, the commentary explained that "if an offender, seeing a woman engaging in illicit sex with another man, subsequently himself uses coercion to engage in illicit sex with her, then because she is already a woman who has committed an offense of illicit sex, it would be inappropriate to sentence him to the penalty for coercion. Instead, the statute's provision on 'luring a woman to another place for illicit sex' should be applied."[39] Observing that there was no provision in the statutes for dealing with the rape or attempted rape of a woman who had already committed an offense of illicit sex, Xue Yunsheng noted that in practice offenders in such cases were sentenced to life exile, a punishment one degree lower than that for rape.[40] Together these two provisions had the effect of undermining the validity of the objectifiable evidence the statute required. No matter what eyewitness testimony or physical signs of coercion and struggle existed, any accusation of sexual assault could be challenged with evidence of the victim's past lack of chastity or final consent to her attacker. In other words, the code's construction of rape contained a fundamental contradiction: it codified a very clear and narrow definition of rape and a rigid set of objectively verifiable criteria for identifying it but mandated that what had to be proved through this evidence was the essentially subjective moral quality and intent of the woman to consent or resist at various points during the encounter.

The subjective element in the adjudication process was explicitly recognized by many judicial commentators. Some, like Huang Liuhong, did not see it as problematic. But in an odd, yet telling echo of Li Yu's humorous critique of the logic of chastity, many other commentators argued in far more serious tones and contexts that behind its veneer of objectivity the rape statute mired adjudicating officials in a judicial quagmire. The potential for inconsistency of judgments due to the subjective nature of assessments of coercion and consent was deeply troubling to Yuan Bin, author of a mid-Qing commentary on the Qing Code. He elaborated on the multitude of adjudicatory problems posed by the contradictions in the statute, which, he concluded, was not "fair or just." He observed,

> The party who has been violated will surely say that [the illicit sex] ended in coercion. The party using force will surely say that it ended in consent. Which side [should one] believe? When the situation is obscure and the interrogator is uncertain, then he is likely to conclude that [if the woman] commits suicide, it was coercion, but if [she] does not commit suicide, it was consensual. This will generally lead to coercion being interpreted as

consent. . . . When a woman is originally pure and chaste but happens to be polluted through coercive violence, this is like passing clouds obscuring the bright sun, and she has done nothing wrong. Sometimes, she has above her a father and mother-in-law and children below. Her person (body) is extremely important. . . . Unscrupulous men, knowing well that women cannot necessarily die, take the facts of their coercion and falsely claim to the magistrate that [the woman] finally consented. Such strategy is sure to work in the end.[41]

Echoing the Yongzheng Emperor's view of the importance of women's social duties in his argument against widow suicide, Yuan expressed considerable respect and sympathy for women, assuming that they were most likely to be victimized by the confusion caused by the statute. Other commentators who noted the evidentiary problems posed by sexual assault were far less trusting of women's motives. Yao Run explained that the annotations detailing more stringent requirements of evidence in rape cases were necessary because "the law on rape is the most severe, yet the evidence of rape is easily fabricated and the circumstances of the use of force vary."[42]

Without intending to critique the statute, Yao ironically pointed out yet another problem with its evidentiary standards. Such concerns about false accusations of sexual assault and the distrust of women's motives and moral integrity implied by them were quite common among officials discussing the statutes, authors of magistrates' handbooks, and magistrates adjudicating cases. The problems of false testimony and the differing perspectives of victim and defendant were particularly acute in cases fitting under the rubric of beginning with coercion and ending with consent. Yuan Bin remarked,

> [I]f we take torn clothing, wounds, and witnesses who heard as evidence of starting with coercion, then if the clothing seen [by the magistrate] is already mended and the wounds have already healed, is this evidence of final consent? . . . Sometimes . . . the gradual subsiding of the screams and the lack of neighbors who heard something are taken as evidence of final consent. . . . Most of those who engage in coercion dare to behave recklessly only at the houses of the poor with no neighbors within earshot. And if there was a neighbor who heard something, who could distinguish the beginning and ending of the sound? Ultimately, then, there is no evidence for beginning with coercion and ending in consent. . . . [T]he risks of randomness [in judgment] are great.[43]

Indeed, the case record on illicit sex is full of such apparent randomness, fully supporting such criticisms of the fairness, judicial logic, and evidential basis of the code's construction of rape.[44] Since direct eyewitnesses beyond the man and woman in question were almost always lacking and evidence was almost always mixed, every case confronted magistrates with the full array of potential scenarios: rape, attempted rape, coercion ending in consent, flirtation, and false accusation. As Yuan Bin noted, approaches to the interpretation of evidence varied. Some magistrates applied the evidentiary standards with literal precision, even when the testimonies of all parties failed to support the conclusion that the physical evidence suggested. In a case where a woman hanged herself after being propositioned, the magistrate of Wu County in Suzhou Prefecture assumed that a minor scratch and a torn sash indicated rape or attempted rape.[45] The defendant, Xu Da, aged twenty-six, had worked for some five years for the family of the victim, Zhou Xianjie, as a hired hand. Two months before the incident, Xianjie's father fired him because he was loafing on the job, and Xu Da began to support himself by doing odd jobs for various families in the village. One day Xu Da was helping another villager irrigate his fields when, according to his confession, he got thirsty and went to ask for a cup of tea at the Zhou house since it was close by. Questioned by the magistrate about why he would think to go there, he stated, "Even though they fired me, I still went over there all the time, so I just walked right in." He went directly into their kitchen, where Zhou Xianjie, only eighteen and unmarried, was alone. Apparently unconcerned about his presence at first, she handed him a bowl of tea. But then, he confessed, "All of a sudden I got the urge to flirt with her and touched her breast once. She screamed and started to run out. I was afraid people would find out, so in a panic, I grabbed her skirt to stop her. Xianjie scratched open my finger on my right hand. As she struggled to free herself, the sash on her skirt tore. Her mother came in at that moment and I ran off immediately." Her mother told Xianjie to wait until her father came home from the market town the next morning and he would deal with Xu Da. But the next morning, after her mother went out to the fields, Xianjie hanged herself.

Xu Da insisted that he did not try to force her to have sex with him, but the magistrate refused to believe him, concluding, categorically, "If you ripped the belt on Xianjie's skirt and she scratched open your hand, clearly this is evidence of rape. How can you say that you did not intend to go there and merely flirted with her on the spur of the moment? Hurry up and tell the truth if you want to avoid being tortured." Xu Da stuck to his story, replying, "I truly did not want to rape her. Go ahead and torture me and I still won't confess to this." The magistrate questioned him further: "If you were afraid of being caught and grabbed her, you should have grabbed her shoulder or her two hands. Why would you, on the contrary, tear her skirt so that the sash was completely ripped? Clearly you were using force to attempt to rape her. Why do you still not speak the truth?" Xu Da again replied,

> When Xianjie gave me the bowl of tea, she was originally facing me. I took the tea to drink with one hand, and with the other I caressed her breast. When she screamed and cursed me, she turned to run out. I quickly put down the tea bowl and grabbed at her clothing to stop her. She was wearing only a summer garment, so while I pulled the sash around her skirt with my hands, she tore it with her struggling. I really intended only to stop her from going out and shouting. I absolutely did not intend to tear her skirt off and use force to try to rape her. Moreover, the rip in the skirt sash was only four or five inches long. It did not come loose and the skirt did not fall down.

The victim's mother confirmed his story, explaining that the sash was not holding up the skirt so that the skirt did not fall and her daughter "was not polluted."

The intense interrogation surrounding Xu Da's state of mind in this case had no bearing on his immediate sentence: under the relevant substatute, a man who caused a woman to commit suicide through either attempted rape or flirtation received a sentence of strangulation after the assizes. However, the nature of Xu Da's intent would have become quite relevant in the assizes process, during which his case would have been considered for a possible lessening of sentence.[46] Not seeing grounds for leniency here, the Board of Punishments officials who reviewed the sentence dropped the reference to flirtation and stated simply that he had attempted to rape her. Xianjie was officially canonized for defending her chastity.

Narrow reading of the code could work against the victim as well. In a 1780 case from Shandong, another young unmarried woman, named Jiang Chengjie, claimed that she was raped, but the magistrate, lacking the requisite physical evidence, concluded that hers was an assault that began with coercion and ended with consent.[47] According to her testimony,

> Zhang Tianzheng (twenty-nine) was my neighbor, and we ordinarily did not avoid each other *(pingri bu biji)*. At midday on the twenty-second day of the first month, . . . my mother . . . was making lunch and told me to go out to the empty room on the east side of the front courtyard to fetch some firewood. As I went into the room, Zhang Tianzheng happened to be walking by, and he came over, blocked the door to the room, and flirted with *(tiaoxi)* me. I did not submit to him *(bu yi ta)*; I screamed for my mother and cursed him. I didn't expect he would force me onto my back on the

kang. He said, "If you don't submit to me, I will use the knife I carry at my side to kill you." I didn't dare to say a word. He then pulled off my pants and polluted me with illicit sex *(jianwule)*.

By this time, her mother had run over from the kitchen, seen Zhang having sex with her daughter, and started screaming and cursing herself. Zhang hurriedly pulled up his pants and ran off. When her mother chastised her, Chengjie began to cry and told her that "Zhang Tianzheng threatened and intimidated me into having illicit sex *(hehu chengjian)*." That evening, when her elder brother, Jiang Yueyu, came home from the fields (her father had died), her mother told him about the incident. Like many a loyal brother, he wanted to go and beat up Zhang. Like many family elders, however, his mother told him not to, saying, "This is a disgraceful matter. If outsiders find out about it, your little sister will not be able to face people." Yueyu went out looking for Zhang anyway, but an uncle told him that he was in hiding, also counseling that since this was a disgraceful matter, it was best to let it drop.

Four months later, Chengjie testified, "I was sitting alone on the ground at the front gate making shoes when Zhang Tianzheng came by and tossed a piece of dirt at me. I ignored him. Then he came over and grabbed my hand. I started to curse him, and just at that moment, my cousin . . . walked by and saw him, so Zhang. . . . left." That night the cousin came to her house to tell her elder brother about this second incident. Yueyu ran off to Zhang's house "to have it out with him," but Zhang was not home. Zhang's father apologized and begged Yueyu to let him punish his son himself. Several days later, Yueyu was chopping wood in his courtyard when he heard Zhang Tianzheng's voice arguing with someone in the street. He ran out with his ax and attacked him. Two male relatives helped Yueyu hold Zhang down while he chopped up his legs with the ax and gouged out his eyes. Zhang died the next day. Not only did the magistrate sentence Jiang Yueyu to strangulation after the assizes, but he also sentenced Chengjie to a month in the cangue and one hundred strokes of the heavy bamboo, commuted to a fine, under the rape statute's clause on illicit sex that began with coercion but ended in consent. Her recorded testimony, shaped to fit the magistrate's conclusion that the assault ended with her consent, deliberately avoided use of the judicial term for rape *(qiangjian)*, having her instead describe the final act as "intimidating me into having illicit sex."

Although they do not present parallel sets of circumstances, there are some intriguing similarities between the assaults on these two young, single women. Although Xianjie's assailant was a hired hand from another province while Chengjie's was a neighbor, both men were single, members of the village community, with no background of criminal or thuggish behavior, who knew their victims and had regular social interactions with them. Accosted inside their homes, both women screamed for help, and neither was injured in the assault. In many ways, there was more actual evidence of Chengjie's coercion than of Xianjie's attempted rape. While Chengjie's mother arrived on the scene in time to witness the sexual encounter, Xianjie's mother saw only the torn sash and the assailant running out the door. Chengjie's second illicit encounter with Zhang Tianzheng was witnessed by her cousin. With her assailant dead, Chengjie's testimony was critical, and, like Du Song Shi, whose case opened Part Three, her description of her assault involved a verbal death threat and physical coercion. Unlike Du Song Shi, Chengjie never admitted that she decided to submit to her attacker, although she appeared from the record to have made a far less charismatic and sophisticated defense of her actions than Du. Chengjie's emphasis on her immediate and vehement rejection of his advances, his physical overpowering of her, and his terrifying intimidation make it clear that she felt she "could not struggle free," to use the words of the statute. Although her mother initially yelled at her, her brother defended her, insisting that she was "bullied into illicit sex *(qijian)*." Moreover, the assailant's father did not deny the accusations against his son but offered apologies and, worried about publicizing his son's involvement in this disgraceful matter, promised to punish him. The evidence of the encounters themselves, in all three cases, was mixed and could readily be interpreted in different ways.

Spotty evidence aside, there were three critical differences between the cases of Chengjie and Xianjie that help to explain why the former did not win the sympathy of the magistrate while the latter did. The first was that Xianjie committed suicide, confirming Yuan Bin's observation that when evidence was murky, magistrates' sympathies were readily swayed by a suicide. As we will see in Part Four, suicide almost always convinced people of a woman's innocence and chastity. The suicide may well have accounted for the second difference: the divergent interpretations of the victims' interactions with their assailants prior to the attack. Although both women had a history of social interaction with the men, Chengjie was described as failing to "practice avoidance" *(bu biji)* with Zhang. This judicial catch-phrase gave her relationship with him a somewhat improper taint that was absent in the depiction of Xu Da's interaction with Xianjie, who, from the magistrate's perspective, was vindicated by her suicide. The third significant difference was that Chengjie's rapist was brutally murdered by her brother and other relatives. The case thus came to the magistrate as a homicide investigation, which undoubtedly blurred the boundaries of guilt and innocence, not to mention provoking the perennial official annoyance at the private settlement of serious crimes like sexual assault.

The point here is that, as Yuan Bin and other commentators complained, the adjudication of illicit sex cases was more art than science, more about instinct than judicial principle: as they interpreted the evidence, magistrates were swayed by circumstances and personalities that had nothing to do with the code's construction of consent or coercion. In fact, because of its contradictory evidentiary requirements, magistrates often relied on examination of the victim's demeanor, reputation, lifestyle, and community mores to establish circumstantial evidence of her intent, shifting the crux of the inquiry away from questions about consent and coercion to the reconstruction of the social and spatial contours of women's lives. The stringent evidentiary requirements for proving rape have usually been interpreted as fundamentally unsympathetic to the victims' perspectives by burdening them with very high standards of proof and requiring demonstrations of chastity before and during the attack. To be sure, the code expected women to respond to assault not as passive victims but as active moral agents. Yet subjective interpretations of their integrity and agency sometimes worked in favor of women and sometimes did not. While in some cases lack of resistance to the utmost, especially in the context of improper behavior on the part of the woman, resulted in a verdict of consensual illicit sex or coercion ending in consent, in many others, these deviations from the standard judicial construction of rape were not even a cause for comment.[48]

In one case from Qinxian County, Jiangsu, for example, the victim Ju Jiujie's improper foray outside the inner quarters, involving a highly suspicious interaction with men, set the stage for her assault. Though she had already reached the age of twenty-five, she was not yet even engaged because she had been orphaned, and her guardian elder brother, a *shengyuan*, felt that their "family status was too uncertain" to undertake marriage negotiations. Moreover, Jiujie was hardly an exemplar of feminine duty and obedience to family authority. By her own account, she and her brother "did not see eye to eye."[49] One day he reprimanded her for not responding to his request to make a cap for his little boy. In his words, "[B]ecause she has always been spoiled, she flew into a rage and decided to go to stay with our widowed elder sister without telling me." While her brother was out, Jiujie arranged for the servant in charge of the family boats to load her clothing, money, and jewelry into a boat, and she set off with only her teenaged maid and the three male servants in charge of the family's boat to accompany her. The senior servant, deciding to take advantage of the situation, steered the boat to a remote area for several days and raped her twice before dropping her on the shore near her sister's house and stealing her belongings and the boat. In response to the defendant's claim that he was trying to convince Jiujie to run off with him as his wife, the magistrate briefly pursued the theory that, remaining single far beyond the respectable age for marriage, she might have planned to run off with the servant, selling her jewels and clothing for support. Evidence of consistent resistance on her part was missing. Indeed, she herself admitted, like Du Song Shi and Chengjie, that after she screamed and struggled at first, he threatened verbally to kill her, and she concluded that, being isolated on the boat with no one to rescue her, "I was forced to give in to him." Jiujie clearly did not practice proper avoidance as she set off alone with these male servants. Moreover, there was no torn clothing, there were no wounds, and the only immediate witnesses were the co-defendants. In the end, though, the magistrate accepted the rape story, which was corroborated by her maid and the other two collaborating servants, but for which the evidence of any resistance on her part was completely absent. Ultimately, her chaste intent was demonstrated not through physical evidence (indeed contrary to it) but with reference to her gentry status and reputation as a proper, albeit intractable, unmarried woman *(guinü)*, as her kidnapper described her.

Sympathy for the victims of rapes that "began with coercion and ended with consent" was quite common. While upholding a very rigid interpretation of the statute's evidentiary requirements and often disparaging women's moral integrity, Huang Liuhong himself argued for flexible compassion in cases where "a man uses force to intimidate a woman so that she fails to repudiate him virtuously." Although the code did not deem such cases to be rapes, indicating that the woman should be punished, like the man, for consensual illicit sex, Huang noted, "Human feeling finds this situation abhorrent." Thus, he stated, "I feel that it is appropriate to judge such a case by analogy to the statute on illicit intercourse between an official and a women under his jurisdiction, that punishment being more severe than ordinary adultery by two degrees.

The woman should be punished as in an ordinary case of adultery because she was threatened by the adulterer."[50] Yuan Bin took this logic a step farther, suggesting that the woman in such cases was, in fact, still a victim of sexual assault:

> There is no evil greater than a violent rogue who has already insulted a woman and then draws her into [a situation that results in] both of them being flogged, overwhelming her into disgrace with his strength. If the woman's resolve is not firm, she then thinks that she has already been polluted and bears the insult secretly so as to avoid having it spread around. Her mental [anguish] is greatly deserving of pity. In comparison, if [a woman] signals tacit assent with her eyes and the two mutually transgress, [the punishment is the same]. If there is proof beyond doubt of beginning with coercion and ending with consent, then the sentence of flogging for the man is still too light and flogging for the woman is too severe.[51]

Ever concerned about the lacunae and inconsistencies in the code, Xue Yunsheng expressed his concern about the "unavoidable injustice" of this situation by noting that the code did not indicate what the punishment should be for beginning with coercion and ending with consent, implying that such cases should be treated as consensual illicit sex and failing to punish the initial violence. "Supposing a burglar has already broken into the gate and entered the house, and the victim does not dare to make it known and lets him carry things off. Can we also label this as coercion first, then theft? In principle, the crime of coerced illicit sex is even more serious and the circumstances more obscure." He recommended that in such cases the assailant be sentenced to exile and the woman not be punished.[52]

Sympathy aside, since the victim's intent ultimately defined the nature of the crime, magistrates had to pay attention to women's own depictions of their lives, their state of mind, and the circumstances of their assaults. In some cases, like that of Du Song Shi, women's constructions of their chastity and its violation shaped the magistrate's conclusions. In others, like that of Zhou Chengjie, women's views and feelings were ignored. Either way, the contradictions of the law routinely forced judicial officials to compromise legal standards and modify their normative expectations. They inevitably discovered that lack of distinction between inner and outer was not in itself necessarily a moral failing but simply a fact of life. So while the law defined the inner/outer boundary in spatial and bodily terms, the defense of chastity often depended more on women and men's maintenance of decorum in social interactions than on their complete separation. With its insistence on a single, objectifiable paradigm of chastity, the illicit sex statute profoundly misrecognized the reasons for gender disorder. More surprisingly, though, it also significantly underestimated the vitality of the inner/outer paradigm as a rubric for people's lives. For, as we will see in the next chapter, rather than reject the norms, women, like Du Song Shi, articulated them to fit the virtue that they practiced.

CHAPTER 7

"Accommodating Sages"

Gender Separation in Social Practice

The "ethnographic" evidence provided by criminal cases confirms official perceptions of widespread transgressions of norms of gender separation. However, these cases suggest that, contrary to the worst fears of statecraft reformers and moralists, these transgressions worked, not to invalidate the inner-outer paradigm, but rather to shift and complicate its meaning. In their detective work magistrates were confronted with a society that looked quite different from that imagined in morality handbooks.[1] Very few women outside the leisured elite lived and worked in circumstances conducive to strict observance of the inner-outer boundary. While even the simplest of rural houses usually included an inner hearth and sleeping room and an outer courtyard separated from the outside world by a gate, the strict spatial and functional demarcation of inner apartments for women that were standard in the spacious mansions of the wealthy that informed the standards of literati moralists was obviously impossible for most families.[2] There were, moreover, many unorthodox households for which the distinction between inner and outer realms was spatially impossible. Poverty forced many families to leave their home villages and wander in search of work or as beggars. The poor, itinerant or in their home villages, often had to rent rooms in the houses of strangers or unrelated neighbors. In a case from Zhili Province, for example, a woman moved back into her widowed mother's household after her husband left home to beg and she could not support herself. Her mother earned income by renting out half of her house to a bannerman and his wife, whom, she testifies, "we talked to and interacted with every day without trying to avoid each other." The case emerged when the bannerman got drunk and propositioned the daughter one night while the two older women were both away from home visiting relatives. The daughter threw herself into the village well after the offender convinced her mother not to report the incident to the *yamen*.³

Even when meaningful spatial distinctions between inner and outer were possible, they were rarely interpreted in the rigid manner of the morality tracts: the seclusion of women was relative, not absolute. The glimpses of women's lives depicted in cases do indicate that they were far more home centered in their daily activities than men, spending much of their time in their compounds busy with handicraft work and household chores: weaving, spinning, sewing, making baskets or shoes, cooking, and caring for their children and parents-in-law. The potential degree of their seclusion is suggested by occasional comments made in case testimonies to the effect that a particular woman had "never left the gate" or never laid eyes on any male villager, even her husband's closest friends. Yet far more common are casual references to women's work and leisure activities that took them regularly not only outside the confines of their household compounds but outside their villages as well.⁴ Women in many regions routinely worked in the fields alongside their male relatives, and gathered firewood and herded animals in mountain or forest areas outside their villages. They fetched water from wells and streams outside the gates and walked out to far-flung fields to carry the noon meal to their husbands. Some worked in their husbands' shops, restaurants, or inns. Frequent references are made to women's involvement in commercial exchanges. While they usually did not go to markets themselves, sending instead a husband, son, or brother to sell their shoes, thread, or cloth or to purchase handicraft materials and other household goods, women often dealt directly with their fellow villagers in small-scale transactions. Local vendors came to their gates with wares to sell, and women did work for neighbors. One woman, for instance, ground flour for the owner of the dye shop in exchange for the dyeing of her cloth. Their interaction formed the backdrop for her daughter-in-law's suicide, prompted by the unwanted advances of the dye shop owner's son.⁵ Women often visited neighboring women and made overnight journeys to other villages to visit their natal families or married children. And as officials suspected, many went to temples, attended temple fairs and operas, and went on pilgrimages.

Standards of seclusion and toleration of women "outside" varied significantly across regions of the empire and even local communities. Yet customs of family and village sociability as they are depicted in case records typically appear to have sanctioned friendly, casual interactions and exchanges of conversation between relatives outside the immediate family and neighbors of both sexes. Village men and hired hands dropped into neighbors' houses when the men were out working or drinking at the local wine shop to ask for a light for their tobacco or a cup of tea or to borrow tools and farm implements. Often it was said that a woman knew a man because he was her husband's friend or had business with him, so that he frequently came to the house. Some male culprits sneaked or broke into the woman's house to proposition or assault her. Yet in most cases the explanation for contact between parties to cases of unwanted flirtation, adultery, or assault began with the fact that the offending man was a neighbor, a fellow villager, a distant relative, or even an incestuously close relative whom the woman knew or who, at least, knew of her, if indeed she did maintain a fairly cloistered existence and did not know many of her fellow villagers. Most assault and harassment victims were assailed not by strangers but by men that they knew, often neighbors or relatives.[6]

Expectations about gender etiquette varied from one community to the next and from person to person. In one case from Henan, a man dropped by the house of a family in his village that he had formerly worked for as a hired hand to ask for a cup of tea.[7] The woman of the house was sitting in the front room playing with her grandson and told the young man to go back into the kitchen and ask her daughter-in-law for a cup. He did so, but the daughter-in-law ignored him. He flirted with her by offering her a pear, and she started screaming. The case ended with her suicide in humiliation. There may well have been some prior history between culprit and victim that made her so sensitive, but suffice it to say, her mother-in-law saw nothing irregular about sending the man into the "inner quarters" of her house to deal with her young daughter-in-law, while the latter refused even to acknowledge the man.

Two parallel case scenarios from the same province illustrate the potential for local variation in notions of proper interaction between women and men. In one case from Wugong County, Shaanxi Province, in 1753, one Jin Ciying went to the house of a fellow villager and distant relative, Jin Ku, to collect on a debt one evening.[8] Standing outside the door, he called for Jin Ku. His wife, who was standing by the *kang* smoking, told him her husband was not home. Seeing that she was home alone, the visitor went in and caressed her shoulder to flirt with her. She screamed at him and he fled. When the culprit tried to explain himself to a curious neighbor, the neighbor asked him, "What business did you have going to collect on a debt after dark when you knew Jin Ku wasn't home?" After Jin Ciying sued Jin Ku for false accusation of assault, the latter's wife finally hanged herself. Standards of interaction were looser in another very similar case from Xunyang County, Shaanxi, in 1795, in which a carpenter named Liu Bencheng went to the house of Zhang Shibao, an old acquaintance, one evening to collect payment for a job he had done for him.[9] Zhang was out visiting relatives, and his wife and aunt, who were home alone, told Liu to come back another time to collect his payment. Liu asked them if he could spend the night, since it was dangerous to walk home along the mountain road after dark. The women agreed. That night Liu sneaked into the bedroom of Zhang's wife to seduce her. She screamed and he fled. Later her husband killed Liu in a fight while trying to take him to the *yamen* for punishment. In the first case, villagers considered it taboo for a man to even enter the gate of a neighbor's house if the man of the house was not home. In the second, the women did not consider it improper for a male friend of the husband to spend the night in his absence.

However, in most cases, it was not the sociability or the interaction itself that was problematic but rather what was said, gestured, or implied in the course of it. The upshot was not that inner and outer did not matter but that their definitions were in flux. Quite often an improper encounter was said to have happened in the course of "everyday interaction" *(pingri wanglai)* because the woman and man in question did not "maintain the distinction between inner and outer *(bufen neiwai)*" or because the woman "did not practice avoidance *(bu biji)*" in relating to the offending male culprit. Intriguingly, this latter term, *biji*, was also used to talk about avoidance of certain activities on inauspicious days. The term connoted something taboo and unlucky, hinting of feelings of foreboding about the possible consequences of interactions that were not quite proper and thus aroused suspicion. This sense of the ominous in illicit encounters was not necessarily misplaced, for, as we will see in Part Four, the stakes for women and men were often extremely high. In any case, the use of such stock expressions in testimonies indicates that however unrealistic the spatial and social demarcation of an "inner quarters" may have been for people, and whatever variety existed in local customs, the inner-outer paradigm was the working normative standard of gender propriety in the minds of many. In response to the value-laden questions of magistrates, who with their very presence embodied the authority of the state and its orthodoxy, many people felt the need to justify the unorthodoxies in their living situations. "My household is poor and doesn't even have a wall or a gate," said the husband of one victim of attempted rape by a neighbor. His wife explained that the culprit "often came to our house to eat because he had no family ... so I never did avoid him *(bu bi ta)*.[10] The defendant in another rape case was the brother of the victim's sister-in-law, a relatively distant relationship. But he worked at the household compound shared by the victim's husband and his two brothers, so he knew the victim and the other women in the household well. "Since I was related to one of the wives, the women of the household did not hide themselves and avoid me *(bu duobide),*" he explained, as if such interactions were to be expected.[11] In a case in which the concubine of an innkeeper was sexually assaulted by a customer, the innkeeper's wife had to explain that while he was away, she and his concubine had to manage the inn and deal with customers, so "we women knew [the culprit] and did not at all avoid him."[12]

SEPARATION AS A STATE OF MIND

In case after case, women and men asserted the significance of the inner-outer distinction as a mental boundary even when its social and spatial realization was problematic. In a typical case of attempted rape from Nanyang County, Henan, in 1789 the victim, Gao Shi, aged thirty, and her husband, Yin Quan, lived in one half of a compound, the other half of which was occupied by a man named Liang Sihou, who was known in the village as a mean and ferocious bully.[13] One day, Yin was talking to a close friend, Wang Er, who complained that his shoes were old and worn and he had no one to make new ones for him. Wang Er noted that Yin was wearing very well-made shoes. Yin testified, "Because he was such a close friend, I told him that my wife could make some for not too much money if he bought the cloth himself and brought it to me." Yin's defensive explanation of how his wife came to make shoes for his friend reflects the fact that the making of shoes by women for men was an extremely touchy and controversial subject over which misunderstandings were not unusual. Women routinely made shoes for their family members, for sale in the market, and as favors for friends. However, in many people's minds the making of shoes was a gesture of intimacy that transgressed proper gender boundaries.[14] Yin Quan emphasized that his friend gave the cloth to him, he then had his wife make the shoes, and his friend paid him. In other words, this close friend of his never laid eyes on his wife and the transaction was purely commercial.

A few days later, Yin came home from the market and found his wife outside the door weeping and cursing Liang Sihou because, she told him, he had come over to their house and propositioned her, offering her money to make him shoes. "You made shoes for Wang Er and associated with him," he told her. "Now I have two hundred cash and I want you to make me shoes and get together with me. If you are not willing, I will spread the story that you and Wang Er are having an affair and you made him shoes. Then you won't be able to face people *(jianbude ren)*." Gao Shi screamed at him and cursed him and he left. That evening, Liang walked past their door and taunted Yin Quan: "Your wife made shoes for Wang Er but won't get together with me." Gao Shi wanted her husband to confront Liang, but Yin was afraid of his big clan and did not dare to make trouble. So he tried to console his wife to bear the insult patiently and told her they would gradually work things out with him. Gao Shi, however, was deeply upset and refused to eat. That night while her husband was asleep, she drowned herself in the pond behind Liang's house. Liang confessed that he had long felt that Gao Shi was a beautiful woman and wanted to sleep with her. So when he noticed she had made shoes for Wang even though he was not related to them, he decided to try and blackmail her into giving in to him. Since Yin Quan had no relatives, he noted, he felt he had nothing to fear from him.

Gao Shi was, by all accounts, a very proper woman who had never even met her husband's closest friend. Yet she shared a compound with a man all witnesses recognized as the local bully and therefore saw him every day. She and her husband figured there was no problem with her making shoes for his friend, yet Liang interpreted this activity as a sign either of her openness to an affair or of impropriety that provided the opportunity for blackmail. He testified that he had confronted Wang about the shoes, saying, "Gao Shi is not related to you. How come [she] was willing to make you shoes? Isn't it true that [she] and you are having an affair?" Even after Wang denied ever meeting her, Liang stated, "I didn't believe this." The shoemaking also looked suspicious to the magistrate, who questioned everyone about her reputation, forcing her husband to stress again that his wife had never even met Wang and that Liang was slandering her. After intensive interrogation of all parties on the question of the rumored adultery between Wang and Gao Shi, the magistrate concluded that she was indeed chaste, and she was rewarded with the standard chastity citation, money for a memorial arch, and a plaque in the local Shrine to the Chaste and Filial. Gao Shi's case illustrates the typical points of disjuncture between the circumstances of most women's lives and the ideals of a proper female lifestyle. However, it also demonstrates that the ordinariness of bending and breaking the norms of gender separation did not lessen the danger of "suspicions" of impropriety arising from even minor transgressions.

In the High Qing era, the classic Confucian concept of "knowing shame" *(zhichi)*, or "being incorruptible and knowing shame" *(lianchi)*, was an ubiquitous metaphor for civilized and ritually appropriate gender behavior.[15] Implying a relational model of personal virtue, shame was the ethical dynamic that animated the inner-outer paradigm, motivating people to "avoid suspicion" *(bi xian)* in their interactions with the opposite sex. To know shame was to know what was proper and improper but also to care about one's moral image, the way that inner virtue appeared to the outside community. Although both men and women were admonished to know shame, the concept had a particularly complex relevance for women. As "inner people" *(neiren)*, women in late imperial society were in the paradoxical position of being defined by their virtue even as they embodied inner virtue for their families, especially for their husbands and fathers. Chastity-centered female virtue was the measure of public family honor, but it was also integral to women's sense of self and constructs of femininity.[16]

Case testimonies attest to the fact that most women internalized the ethic of shame as an integral part of their identities. The language of personal shame in the stock expressions used by women and their family members to describe the outrage women felt at their violation suggests the intimate connection between reputation, often invoked as "face" *(mianzi)*, and personal moral identity for women. "Being so humiliated, how can I face people?" "Having been insulted like this, I cannot be a person any longer." "Being so mortified, I'm am so indignant I can't go on living!" For these women, face, moral reputation, was inseparable from personal integrity and from the very meaning of being human. Women experienced the physical, verbal, or social violation of the inner-outer boundary as an essentially personal loss of face. To return again to the case of Gao Shi and her shoemaking, it is striking, and typical, that all parties to that case described the nature of the violation committed by Liang's proposition and slander as a personal humiliation of Gao Shi herself, not an offense against her husband. Liang threatened Gao Shi that his slander would "make it so you can never face people." Explaining his wife's outrage, Yin said, "Being insulted and slandered by Liang Sihou like that, what sort of person could she still be *(haizuo shenmo ren)*? She wanted to have it out with Liang." Such women not only knew shame but had a much more personal stake in chastity norms than did men.

CHASTE WOMEN AS SAGES

In eighteenth-century society, women's virtue could not be measured strictly by their adherence to the spatial and social distinctions of inner and outer, yet these distinctions somehow continued to be relevant. The broad resilience and potency of orthodox norms in contexts where social practice appears to have made them irrelevant presents a conundrum that is not readily resolved by the models of elite cultural hegemony or communication between oral and literate culture that have been adduced to explain patterns of cultural transmission and normative consensus in late imperial society.[17] In their seminal work on women in the early and mid-Qing periods, Susan Mann and Dorothy Ko have argued that in the lives of elite women who had the raw materials for conformity to orthodox norms, there was a creative tension between norms of female seclusion and practices of transgression like pilgrimage or publishing that could be justified in terms of other normative priorities like filiality, lineage perpetuation, or classical and aesthetic education. Integral as such transgressions were to the lives of many elite women, particularly in the Lower Yangzi region, they remained highly controversial and limited in scope. They represented a space of negotiated flexibility carved out of the still salient paradigm of distinction between inner and outer.[18] Although the forms and justifications of transgression were usually quite different for nonelite women, this approach helps to explain the ideological and practical significance of gender norms, while accounting for variation in their interpretation and even their transgression in everyday life.

As he concluded his story of Secunda Geng's defense of her chastity, Li Yu comically celebrated the wisdom of such a flexible approach to orthodoxy. But he took the argument one step further to suggest that orthodoxy was not merely flexible, or tolerant, but constructed through women's social improvisation and their own representation of their behavior. Toying irreverently with the notion of moral models that lay at the heart of late imperial ethical discourse, he formulated a typology of female virtue that in light of the complexities of gender relations in the mid-Qing appears to be as realistic as it is humorous. Parodying a passage from Mencius, the narrator pronounces, "Wives who preserve their chastity have always qualified as sages amongst women. Those who vow martyrdom and keep their vows are the pure sages. Those who endure disgrace to gain revenge are the responsible sages. The kind to which Secunda Geng belongs is that of the accommodating sages. Not only was she called the Female Chen Ping, she should also have been dubbed The Distaff Liuxia Hui."[19] In the original passage, Mencius compared the very different sagelike qualities of three men. The first, Bo Yi, maintained absolute moral purity by refusing to serve any but the most upright rulers and shunning the company of commoners. Yi Yin, the second, served any ruler and shunned no one because he believed it his duty to instruct the ignorant and immoral around him. Liuxia Hui, the third type of sage, was "not ashamed to serve an impure prince," yet while doing so "did not conceal his virtue but made it a point to carry out his principles." Far from shunning uncultivated villagers, "he was quite at ease and could not bear to leave them." Known also for his staunch resistance to sexual temptations, he had a saying, "You are you, and I am I. Although you stand by my side with breast and arms bare or with your body naked, how can you defile me?"[20] Thus, Mencius concluded, "Bo Yi among the sages was the pure one; Yi Yin was the responsible one; and Liuxia Hui was the accommodating one."[21]

Nowhere else in the copious discourse on female virtue did anyone attempt to apply such classical typologies of male virtue to suggest similar complexities in the elaboration of ethical standards for women. For despite the practical subtleties of everyday ethics for women and the reality of flexibility in the application of chastity norms in the courtroom, the ideal of chastity-centered virtue, embodied most vividly by the model lives recorded in virtuous women biographies, followed the example of the absolutist, Bo Yi. A few women managed to uphold the most rigid demarcation of the inner-outer boundary as pure sages, some going so far as to kill themselves when their chastity was violated or even besmirched by suspicions of impropriety. Most, however, negotiated the conflicting constraints of law, gender norms, and life circumstances as responsible or accommodating sages. With their lives in a perpetual state of moral compromise, the former endured humiliation or assault in order to vindicate their chastity and punish their assailants through violence, legal sanction, or even suicide.[22] The latter, like Du Song Shi, pushed the boundaries of propriety even farther. Possessing a powerful personal sense of virtue, they were not concerned about suspicions and

"Accommodating Sages" 163

were even willing to risk defilement to save their lives and fulfill their broader duties as wives, mothers, and daughters-in-law.

The virtue of many such responsible and accommodating female sages was eventually vindicated by the judicial system. Yet in the process they all had to answer for their deviations from the expected "pure" model of chaste behavior. Having lain side by side with her alleged attacker "with breast and arms bare [and] body naked," Du Song Shi, like Secunda, had a hard time convincing judicial officials that she remained in her heart undefiled. Li Yu astutely identified Secunda's self-defense, the final representation of her actions to those who would create or destroy her reputation, as a seventh ruse, integral to the strategy of "keeping her chastity." The narrator comments,

> Let me just point out how marvelous this last stroke was. Had she wanted to put the chieftain to death along the road, it would have taken only a few more croton-oil beans. Simple! Instead she persisted in keeping him alive until they got home, so as to use his testimony in vindicating her own conduct. *That* is what makes it so amazing! Had she done him to death along the road and then returned home alone, denying she had lost her honor, no one would have believed her. Even her own husband would have considered her a little disingenuous, for who has ever seen a piece of white cloth pulled from an indigo jar? But once the accolade had been bestowed on her by her enemy, everyone accepted it as fact. This is why she was known as "the Female Chen Ping," even though Chen brought off only six amazing ruses and she managed seven.[23]

The Chen Ping analogy acquires added resonance here, for the story of this early Han military strategist, as constructed by Sima Qian, is not simply about his ingenuity. It is a tale of loyalty that is repeatedly questioned and defended. As a former officer for Xiang Yu who became one of the most trusted of Han Gaozu's advisors, Chen Ping was vulnerable to frequent slander attempts on the part of jealous rivals. In defending himself against the slanders of the emperor's suspicious advisors, he cleverly managed to construct his checkered record of serving many rulers as a justification for his loyalty to the Han, which, in the end, gave him his place in history. Sima Qian praised him, despite his blemishes, for both his ingenuity and his defense of "the dynasty's ancestral temples and the continuance of its altars of the soil and grain."[24]

Li Yu's satire moved beyond parody of the hackneyed analogy between female chastity and male loyalty to suggest, subversively, both the constructed nature of chastity and the critical role played by women in defining it. Since the line between coercion and consent, between "true virtue and false," was so difficult to draw in sexual assault cases, judicial officials routinely resorted to assessments of the moral quality of women's lives and courtroom demeanor to discern the purity of their intent. In effect, they made "the seventh ruse" of appropriate self-representation a required component of "keeping one's chastity" and proving it in court.[25] The rape statute did put women's chastity on trial. But by making the reaction of a woman to a proposition, insult, or assault the crucial factor in determining whether a crime of illicit sex was coerced or consensual and how severe a crime it was, the code not only required women to be active moral agents defending their chastity but also made their own definitions of virtue and its violation integral to the adjudication process.

PART FOUR

"Being a Person"

Female Humiliation and Social Power

Prologue: Male Impropriety and Female Outrage Lead to a Tragic End

Confronted with a homicide that resulted from an unwanted proposition in 1753, Liu Shaobin, the magistrate of Taiyuan County, Shanxi, was vexed by what he saw as an utterly useless loss of innocent life over a matter of face and played the devil's advocate with all parties to the case.[1] The facts of the case were clear and were corroborated fully by the victim, her mother-in-law and brother-in-law, the defendant, members of his family, and neighbors. What bothered Magistrate Liu was that the facts of the case added up not to a clear-cut tale of chastity impugned and requited but to a tragedy of poor judgment, misunderstanding, and blind fury, and he was none too sympathetic to any of the participants.

In the background of this incident, like that of many propositions, assaults, or adulterous affairs, was a woman left home by a sojourning husband, who, in this case, had been away for some three years on business. One day, the twenty-nine-*sui*-old Ren Shi was left home alone while her mother- and brother-in-law went off to visit the mother-in-law's natal family. Toward evening, her husband's cousin, Bai Xian, aged twenty-seven, dropped by her house on his way home from the opera in a nearby village. "My house is only three doors up from Ren Shi's and I go there regularly," he explained in his testimony. "I see her and talk to her all the time." On this particular evening, he admitted, he knew that she was home alone, and, having drunk "many cups of wine," he decided, as he passed her door, "that I would like to have illicit sex with her. So I went into Ren Shi's room, smoked some tobacco, and joked with her, saying, 'My cousin, Bai Bao, is not home. Aren't you cold and bored? How about if I keep you company while you sleep?'" He emphasized, though, that "I only joked verbally with her to sound her out with some suggestive remarks. I didn't use my hands or feet to coerce her."

In a common response to such drunken boorishness, Ren Shi shouted at him, "What sort of nonsense are you talking? Get out of here quickly!" He ran out while she continued shouting. A neighbor came over to see what was happening and berated Bai Xian for his impropriety. Ren Shi was furious, but the neighbor counseled her to calm down and wait for her mother-in-law to come home before doing anything about it. "Since it was a disgraceful matter *(choushi)* and my husband was not home, I let it go," she testified. When her mother-in-law and brother-in-law returned the next day, the latter, as a hot-headed head of household and guardian of the family reputation, wanted to go out immediately and beat the culprit up. But his mother dissuaded him because, as she told the magistrate, "It was a disgraceful matter, so I was afraid that if he beat him up it would lead to an accusation in court and outsiders would ridicule us."

Bai Xian, in the meantime, had gone home and been reprimanded again by his elder brother, who also, as head of household, was concerned that his brother's careless insensitivity would ruin the family name. Not entirely lacking in conscience himself, Bai Xian now felt guilty and ashamed. He explained, "I myself was remorseful. I should never have done this, and I thought I should go to apologize for my wrongdoing." Remembering that the year before Ren Shi's mother-in-law had lent him a silver ornament to pawn when he was short of money, he decided to use the excuse of returning the ornament to visit her house. He redeemed it and went over to see her. He called for her mother-in-law but got no reply, so he went in and took the ornament to Ren Shi's room. According to his testimony, he approached her, saying, "The other day I was joking with you. You didn't go along with me and that was the end of it. What was the use of screaming and cursing? Now let me offer you my apologies." Bai Xian claimed, "Before I had even finished speaking these words, Ren Shi immediately became angry and began to shout and curse me. So I ran out toward my house."

According to Ren Shi's version of this encounter, he came in and tossed the ornament for her to catch. She said nothing, and he then said, "That day you did not go along with me and that was the end of it. What was the use of screaming and cursing?" She explained, "As soon as I saw him coming I started to fume. Then I heard him mention the words about not going along with him and that was the end of it. I was even more furious and couldn't stand it. I started screaming and cursing and finally he ran off." Completing the portrait of the bumbling male, unaware of female sensitivities and unable even to articulate an effective apology without compounding the insult, Bai Xian here fumbled again. Already in no mood to deal with her annoying cousin, Ren Shi heard only the equivocation and not the regret.

She told her mother-in-law, and, after he came home from the market, her brother-in-law, Bai Zhang, that Bai Xian had "again said some improper things" to her. Her brother-in-law, who had gotten drunk on the way home, exploded in anger when he heard this, shouting, "If he insults people like this, how can I let it go and not repay it?" He grabbed a kitchen knife and ran out the door to Bai Xian's house. Bai Xian saw him coming and ducked out of the house to hide. His sister-in-law, in the courtyard turning the millstone, grabbed Bai Zhang, who in his drunken fury began to stab her. Bringing up yet again the escalating impropriety, she shouted, "If Bai Xian wants to sleep with your sister-in-law, why do you come and stab me?" Bai Zhang stated, "My rage was overflowing, and when I heard her scream such disgraceful words I was even more furious and stabbed her two more times. . . . I was drunk and confused." A neighbor eventually grabbed the knife away from him, but the woman died that night.

Although the hapless Bai Xian admitted in his first testimony that "the original cause of all this was me flirting with Ren Shi after I had been drinking," the magistrate found fault on all sides in this tragic case and interrogated everyone ruthlessly. He asked the neighbors about Ren Shi's reputation and why they did not report the first incident of flirtation when they heard about it. Bolstering Bai Xian's description of his sense of shame, they described how he stood by "red-faced without saying anything" while Ren Shi told them that he had said "scoundrel's words of flirtation to her." They claimed, "Originally when we grabbed Bai Xian we wanted to tell the constable to report it, but since Ren Shi's mother-in-law and brother-in-law were not home, we berated him and let him go. We intended to wait until Hao Shi came home to report to the *yamen*. Then when they came back, they said nothing about it, so why would we go and report it?" Defending Ren Shi and expressing suspicion about Bai Xian's motives, they added, "Ordinarily she was a very upright person. . . . After flirting with [her], why would [Bai Xian] set foot in her house again?" Typical of neighbors in many such cases, they deferred to the need to keep disgraceful matters under wraps. While willing to mediate, chastise, and break up fights, even to the dangerous point of grabbing weapons away from combatants, they would never initiate action in court unless rallied to the cause by the family whose reputation was at stake.

The magistrate asked the same questions of Ren Shi's mother-in-law, Hao Shi, who defended her daughter-in-law's reputation: "My daughter-in-law and I have long slept together in the same place, never apart for a moment. [She] has never done anything improper." As for her failure to take Bai Xian to court, she stated, "Because this was a disgraceful matter, I was afraid of stirring up trouble by reporting to the *yamen* so that people would ridicule us. . . . Who could have known it would lead to a homicide?" She also, incidentally, offered the information that she had lent Bai Xian the silver head ornament because he had nothing to live on, suggesting a degree of familial concern and affection between them and confirming the image of Bai Xian as a pathetic, yet benign, ne'er-do-well.

Turning to Ren Shi, Magistrate Liu unsympathetically needled her with the argument that a truly chaste woman would not have found herself in such a compromising situation to begin with. Then, in an apparent shift of interrogation strategy, he contradicted his suggestion of her immorality and blamed her instead for being overly sensitive about the insult and not accepting Bai Xian's apology. He queried,

> If you truly conformed to the way of the wife all the time and were upright, prudent, and self-disciplined, then how could Bai Xian dare to utter a proposition? It is evident that you must have previously had some frivolous moments to make him come and be unduly intimate with you. As for the second time he came to your house, Bai Xian said he was returning the pawned silver ornament as a convenient excuse because he wanted to apologize. He had not even finished speaking before you started screaming. He absolutely did not come to flirt with you again. So why did you stir up all this trouble for no reason?

Unfazed, Ren Shi resolutely defended herself, refusing to be compromised or to admit any responsibility for the murder.

> I live in a village where the houses are narrow and close together. Bai Xian is my husband's cousin with mourning obligations, and he lives nearby. He and Mother-in-Law and Little Brother-in-Law talk all the time, and he drops

by frequently, so we originally had seen each other. But he has never joked with me before. And I myself have never been the least bit improper. Only on that day, Mother-in-Law and Little Brother-in-Law had gone out to her natal family's house, and he came and humiliated me. My sons are still small, I live alone as a single person, and he had also gotten drunk, so he dared to come and jest with me like that. If I had been improper, I would not have screamed and cursed at that point. As for Bai Xian coming over the second time to my house, even though this was to return the silver ornament, when no one responded to him he should have left. How could he again bring up that earlier incident to me? He was wrong to come and flirt with me. Although I didn't know [what he wanted to say], he should not have spoken to me at all. I absolutely did not stir up trouble for no reason. Please check the facts!

Hovering in the background of Ren Shi's exchange with Magistrate Liu was the specter of a suicide that was not committed. Suicide was, to be sure, not the inevitable result of humiliation. Many confident and strong-minded women reacted similarly to insults and even propositions with angry curses, a caustic rebuke, or even sarcastic dismissal. Yet by the 1750s, with the ill consequences of a besmirched reputation at a peak, ritual rewards for the victim assured, and severe punishment for the harasser guaranteed, the phenomenon of female suicide in response to humiliation would seem to have been overdetermined. Indeed, as Yuan Bin had so astutely noted in his critique of the rape statute, many a magistrate, faced with a case of assault in which victim and perpetrator presented opposite interpretations of an illicit encounter, took suicide as proof of the woman's chastity. Incidents of verbal harassment presented magistrates with even more nebulous evidence, and in this case the murder of Liu Shi, an innocent bystander to the conflict over the insult, exacerbated the magistrate's lack of sympathy for Ren Shi.

Luckily for her, however, her cousin Bai Xian did not try to deny his impropriety or malign her reputation, despite his frustration at her fury and his implication in a murder. Equally impatient with him, the magistrate in his interrogation now, ironically, took up the perspective of the wronged woman, even accusing him of intent to rape, which Ren Shi had never suggested herself:

After you first flirted with Ren Shi and she cursed you and then the neighbors also reprimanded you, you ought to have laid low. Why after only a couple of days did you make up the excuse of returning the silver head ornament and dare to go back to her house and then, on seeing Ren Shi, bring up the earlier incident again? This indicates clearly that you have a licentious and evil nature and went again to try and rape her, which stirred up all this trouble. Why do you still prevaricate? If you don't tell the truth, I am definitely going to use the [thumb] press.

Bai Xian also refused to be cowed and defended his version of events, in which he was crude and clueless but not without shame and certainly not criminal. He admitted that after being chastised for his misdeed,

> I should not have set foot again in her house, but I lived so close by and the two of us would see each other constantly. Those two days I did not see Bai Zhang to speak to him. I also did not dare to see Bai Zhang's face. I felt I couldn't stand it at all. On the 22nd, I redeemed and returned the pawned silver ornament as a convenient excuse to go to Ren Shi and apologize to her face so as to ameliorate the situation from before. I didn't think that when I went to her house and called out no one would answer. I saw that Ren Shi was sitting in her room. I said to Ren Shi, "You weren't willing and that was the end of it. What use was there in screaming?" I intended to mollify her. Who could have known that she would not even wait for me to finish speaking my words of apology and that instead I would provoke her angry screaming and stir up this sort of trouble? It's all because I am a stupid and ignorant rustic. But I absolutely would not have dared to think of raping Ren Shi.

Turning finally to Bai Zhang, the magistrate reprimanded him for not reporting the flirtation incidents and then lashing out irrationally before he clarified the situation.

> If Bai Xian really did flirt with your sister-in-law Ren Shi, then you should have reported it to the *yamen* for punishment. Why did you keep your grievance bottled up so that he came to your house a second time? Again you did not report it to the constable but instead grabbed a knife to stab Bai Xian. Vegetable knives are lethal weapons that can kill people. If you pursued him with a knife, you must have intended to kill him. When Liu Shi saw this evil situation and grabbed you, she had good intentions to stop you. You then stabbed her fatally in the back of the head with the knife. . . . Undoubtedly either you and she had some ongoing conflict or you must have momentarily intended to kill her.

Making no apologies for his failure to report the flirtation, Bai Zhang stated, "Because this was a face-losing matter, Mother instructed me to let it go, so I temporarily bottled up my grievance and did not report to the *yamen.*" After the second incident, he stated, "I was a drunk person and suddenly became extremely angry. I didn't think about how I should report it to the constable." The indignant family head tried to justify his rage by appealing to the righteousness of his sister-in-law's grievance: "I had only my sister-in-law's view that Bai Xian had come again and said

Prologue

improper things to her. I myself did not know whether he had propositioned her or not. But since there had been a flirtation incident on the 19th, what business did he have coming back to my house to talk to my sister-in-law?"

In the end, Bai Zhang was sentenced, not surprisingly, to strangulation after the assizes for unintentional killing in an affray. Yet responsibility for the murder did not stop with him. Magistrate Liu found the behavior of both Ren Shi and Bai Xian to be rash and ill-considered, though he ultimately recognized the validity of her outrage and the authenticity of his contrition. He could not ignore that their fateful encounters had resulted in a murder. He decided finally to exonerate Ren Shi completely of any wrongdoing despite the fact that her reaction not only to the proposition but to the apology was the most immediate catalyst for the killing. It was thus Bai Xian, whose proposition started the whole chain of events leading to the murder, who would bear the brunt of the moral responsibility for the needless loss of life. By the 1750s, there were many substatutes that dealt with unwanted propositions, harassment, and assault, and the magistrate carefully reviewed the complex options available to him. The substatute that most accurately addressed the nature of Bai Xian's crime was the one promulgated only eight years earlier in 1745 that mandated the cangue and flogging for flirtation or propositions without accomplishing illicit sex.[2] But it was also possible to apply the substatute on rape that was not accomplished, carrying a much more severe sentence of one hundred strokes of the heavy bamboo and life exile at three thousand *li*. The magistrate concluded that because Bai Xian's proposition led to Liu Shi's killing and because Ren Shi was an incestuously close relative with mourning obligations, the culprit should be sentenced by analogy for the more serious crime of attempted rape. He reasoned that although Bai Xian did not intend to rape Ren Shi and on the second visit did want to apologize, "Bai Zhang's crimes were all gradually brought about by this criminal. Although there is a difference between rape and flirtation without accomplishing illicit sex, flirting with a relative is different from flirting with a stranger. It is not appropriate to be lenient." The 1745 substatute on flirtation detailed punishments for local constables or headmen who failed to report such incidents but did not mention neighbors. So the neighbors who knew of Bai Xian's impropriety and failed to report it to the authorities were sentenced to forty strokes of the light bamboo, commuted to fifteen strokes, by analogy with the statute on doing what ought not to be done. Although Hao Shi had prevented her son from reporting the flirtation, the magistrate excused her from punishment because she was a woman and therefore presumably ignorant of the law.

Every case of violation produced its own array of conflicting opinions and interests, and many resulted in violence of some sort subsequent to the offense against chastity: the case record abounds with suicides, revenge killings, and assaults that indicate the failure of more peaceful methods of mediation and redress in response to disgraceful matters. Drunkenness and misunderstanding functioned here, as in many cases, as catalysts for impropriety and violence. As we have seen in previous chapters, the working definition of violation for magistrates prosecuting cases of unwanted flirtation, insult, and even attempted rape was not, usually could not be, the crossing of a strictly defined spatial or bodily divide. It was rather the transgression of more nebulous boundaries of propriety in the content, tone, and style of social interaction. A multitude of cases like that of Ren Shi and Bai Xian reveal that women's own definition of violation included not only the bodily invasions of rape or an unwanted caress but also social and verbal slights of their virtue. Time after time, men's remarks, in the context of their spatial transgressions, caused women to interpret the interaction, correctly or incorrectly, as an explicit attempt at flirtation. As lawmakers, moralists, and magistrates knew all too well, these kinds of misunderstandings and indiscretions always created the possibility that women would vindicate their chastity by killing themselves, with explosive consequences for everyone involved.

The positions of the various players here present a common spectrum of attitudes toward insults to a woman's virtue: the unquenchable outrage of the insulted woman; the defensive regret of the offender; the embarrassed reticence of family elders; the vengeful fury of the victim's loyal brother; and the active yet measured concern of neighbors and fellow villagers. Each individual had his or her own particular take on the violation. What was at stake for Ren Shi was her personal pride, her moral integrity—in a word, her personhood. In contrast, both her family and the family of the offender were concerned primarily with family reputation. Even within her family, her mother-in-law preferred to preserve the family name by covering up the incident, while her brother-in-law wanted to even the score through public revenge. It was not clear what sort of resolution Ren Shi herself would have preferred; she reported her disgrace to her brother-in-law but then claimed she tried to stop him from violent revenge. The neighbors, concerned with the social stability and mores of their fellow villagers, were willing to chastise wrongdoing and break up fights but again, dissociating themselves from the killing, claimed that they hesitated to initiate mediation or punishment out of respect for a family's interest in dealing with matters of face as inner issues. Hesitant to condone breaches of propriety or extreme responses to insult, many magistrates responded to such seemingly preventable tragedies with dismay at both the oversensitivity of women and the insensitivity of those around them.

CHAPTER 8

The Problem of Female Moral Agency

VALORIZING FEMALE OUTRAGE IN THE LAW

Bai Xian propositioned Ren Shi at a time when the stakes for such rude indiscretions were higher than they had ever been and women's perceptions of insult were given unprecedented weight in law and judicial proceedings. Over the course of the Yongzheng and Qianlong reigns, the Qing state explicitly incorporated women's definitions of violation into a series of substatutes that addressed more subtle transgressions of the boundary between inner and outer than assault. They were part of the plethora of new substatutes promulgated in this period to elaborate every possible variation on the crime of forcing people to commit suicide because of an incident of illicit sex, including the suicides of all possible parties affected by various scenarios of adultery, rape, attempted rape, harassment, incest, and prostitution.[1] In 1733, the Yongzheng Emperor created the first substatute to deal specifically with the suicide of a woman, her husband, or her parents in the wake of rape, attempted rape, or flirtation *(tiaoxi)*.[2] At the same time, he added suicide after flirtation or proposition to the types of female martyrdom eligible for state canonization.[3] This was the first time that the concept of sexual harassment in the form of unwanted propositions or flirtation was recognized in the code or in ritual regulations. If a woman committed suicide in reaction to either an attempted rape or an unwanted proposition, the offending man received a sentence of strangulation after the assizes.[4]

In 1740, in response to a memorial from the vice minister of the Court of Imperial Sacrifice, Tang Suizu,[5] another new substatute was promulgated specifically to address unintentional verbal insults:

> Whenever an ignorant rustic, without intending to attempt illicit sex, and without having seductively touched, intimidated, or harassed and insulted [a woman], but only having spoken with improper familiarity [to her], causes her, upon hearing these obscene words, to take life lightly, [the offender] shall, in accordance with the substatute concerning suicide of the woman after rape that is not accomplished, with a reduction of one degree, be sentenced to one hundred strokes of the heavy bamboo and life exile at three thousand *li*.[6]

According to yet another substatute added in 1785, the impropriety need not even have been directed at the woman herself: "In cases where a woman commits suicide out of shame and anger at someone speaking indecently or joking *(xieyu xixue)*, if there is no other reason [for the suicide], then the one who was disrespectfully familiar by joking in [her] presence *(yixiyan dimian xiangxia)* should be sentenced, in accordance with the substatute on causing a woman to commit suicide through an unwanted proposition, to strangulation after the assizes."[7]

These substatutes explicitly applied the judicial paradigm governing the interpretation of sexual assault to verbal and unintentional violations of chastity. The victims in all these sorts of cases were, moreover, eligible for canonization as chastity martyrs. Contrary to the much touted imperial goal of reducing the numbers of female suicides, the legal and ritual recognition of suicide in response to insult sanctioned a form of suicide that appears to have become increasingly widespread over the mid-Qing and could well be considered more reckless and irrational than the custom of widows following their husbands in death. Moreover, touched off by a woman's interpretation of a man's wording or tone of voice, such suicides represented a powerful, albeit circumscribed, form of female agency. If in the context of sexual assault cases the reaction of the woman was the critical indicator of whether the crime was coerced or consensual illicit sex, in cases of flirtation, verbal insult, or unwitting impropriety, it was the response of the woman that determined whether a crime had been committed at all. Against the background of the concerted efforts of the Qing state to control the practice and interpretation of women's suicide, the codification of these crimes of harassment represented a significant concession to women's own definitions of violation.

Precisely for these reasons, these substatutes were extremely controversial among judicial officials, many of whom expressed an increasingly dim view of women's moral integrity and their ability to make moral decisions. While most commentators agreed that insults, humiliation, and harassment that caused a woman to kill herself were serious matters that threatened moral order, many were deeply troubled by the subjective nature of these crimes. In a trenchant critique of these substatutes, the judicial commentator Yuan Bin argued that blaming a man for the unexpected consequences of remarks that were not intended to offend was profoundly unfair, for "'Propositions' are 'consensual [illicit sex]' that is not accomplished. He who 'propositions' has 'consent' in mind. She who commits suicide tragically does something unexpected." While the offender may well have in mind that consensual illicit sex could result in a punishment of flogging, he contended, he surely does not expect that his proposition could get him a sentence of strangulation. "This is truly pitiable!" he declared. From this perspective, an "ignorant rustic" like Bai Xian was lucky that the object of his flirtation did not express her outrage through suicide, which would have ensured a death sentence for him. For Yuan Bin the injustice of the severe sentences in such cases was compounded by the lack of precision in defining propositions or flirtations, the fickleness and often inappropriateness of women's motives for committing suicide, and the inconsistency between these punishments and other parallel crimes in the code. He continued,

> Now the expression "proposition" refers to many things: sometimes verbal hints, sometimes eye signals, sometimes jokes, sometimes obscene comments, and sometimes grabbing and pulling. [The motivation for] suicide also varies: sometimes it is anger, sometimes shame, sometimes a sullied reputation, sometimes [the woman] does not want to live anyway and uses this as an excuse to proclaim her chastity, and sometimes there is another source of conflict and she uses this as a pretext to incriminate him falsely. If these are all sentenced with strangulation, then the crime of "proposition" is ironically greater than the crime of "coercion" [for illicit sex]. "Coercion" that is not accomplished is punished only with flogging and exile, while "proposition" that is not accomplished receives a death penalty. What is there besides coercion to distinguish the minor from the major crime among those who spread licentiousness? Those who beat and curse people, leading them to commit suicide, are not punished with strangulation, yet those who proposition people, leading to suicide, are punished with strangulation. Why? Beating and cursing and "propositioning" are all crimes in and of themselves, but the suicides all occur unexpectedly. Mencius says, "When it is permissible both to die and not to die, it is an abuse of valor to die."[8] . . . The statutes canonize chaste widows but do not canonize widow martyrs so as to esteem the lives of the people. Sui-

cides [in response to] propositions are not as worthy as widow martyrs who follow their husbands in death. If canonizations are bestowed on them, encouraging such deaths, does this not teach all women under heaven to take life lightly? In my humble opinion, cases of suicide out of humiliation should be judged according to the clause on beating and cursing that leads to a suicide.[9]

In his discussion of the problematic judicial delineation of consent and coercion, Yuan Bin expressed extraordinary sympathy for the plight of women struggling to preserve their chastity, but like many men of his day, he was deeply disturbed by the phenomenon of female suicide caused by humiliation and the implications of its new prominence in the code. Invoking the imperial state's paradigm of appropriate and inappropriate suicides, he echoed common criticisms of female suicide on humanitarian and ethical grounds.[10] Not only did they constitute an unnecessary and ritually and ethically inappropriate loss of life, but in the statutory context of the Qianlong period the impulsive suicides of oversensitive women implicated men in a capital crime merely for their ignorant or boorish behavior.

The creation of these new substatutes and ensuing debates over them were framed by the larger politics of the imperial chastity cult. As the numbers of canonized women proliferated during the Qianlong reign, stretching the resources of the state, officials and even the emperor himself began to question the appropriateness of certain kinds of chastity martyrdom. With a new tone of impatience with what they saw as the fickleness and hypersensitivity of women, they increasingly applied the dynasty's rubric of proper and improper suicides to dissect the motives of would-be martyrs.[11] Whether their critiques were inspired by compassion or by a zealous desire to promote orthodoxy, memorialists and the emperor shared a disparaging view of the purity of intent of women who killed themselves, assuming them to be weak and irrational, or even conniving and self-serving. Yet no matter how disturbing or pathetic they found the female suicide to be, neither emperor nor officials ever suggested abandoning the vision of the chastity suicide vindicated in law and celebrated by the imperial state as one of the highest incarnations of female virtue. After rewriting the criteria for canonization and exalting the official chastity model as an exemplar of the social duty and absolute loyalty it expected of its subjects, the imperial state was inextricably invested in the chastity cult as a vital manifestation of the civilizing mission that was increasingly bound up with its legitimacy. The new ritual and legal legislation on suicide was thus couched in tremendous irony, for it granted unprecedented influence to women's views of chastity at a time when the political significance of female virtue was at its height, yet it affirmed a form of martyrdom that most commentators found to be tragically unnecessary and even abhorrent.

The Qianlong Emperor himself had difficulty reconciling these conflicting interpretations of women's suicides. After the Nine Ministers placed a man sentenced to death for flirtation causing a woman's suicide into the assizes category of deferred execution in 1740, the emperor reprimanded them, saying, "When the death of a chastity martyr is due to the flirtation of the defendant, leniently assigning him to the category of deferred execution does not prioritize ritual propriety and rectify the people's customs."[12] Although he let the more lenient verdict stand in this case, he ordered that in all future such cases the Nine Ministers should adhere strictly to the law and uphold the recommendations of provincial judicial officials when they assigned defendants to the category of circumstances deserving of death. By 1742, however, the emperor had softened his stance a bit, noting that when women committed suicide after a flirtation or attempted rape, "the circumstances varied." He began his edict by opining, "Chaste widows and chastity martyrs receive sacrifices in their local areas in order to honor virtue, rectify customs, and cultivate civilization. Punishments are to foster the transformation of customs. The law cannot be lenient with criminals who cause the death of a woman." But he now decided that when assessing during the Autumn Assizes process whether these defendants deserved to die, he would "give them careful consideration," so that "if there is the slightest indication that [the defendant's behavior] was pardonable, he will avoid the hook [the emperor's mark indicating that his death sentence was to be carried out]." Moreover, the emperor continued, after going through this process once and avoiding the hook, these defendants were to have their sentences changed to deferred execution, meaning that they would be reduced to some form of exile.[13]

Unease about the social and moral consequences of the new substatutes continued to plague judicial officials through the end of the century. Observing the social effects of the law in the 1745 memorial that resulted in the new substatute on flirtation, Zhang Ruoai, head of the capital Office of Transmission, treated female suicide as a tragic and preventable social problem caused by women's oversensitivity and the mishandling of sexual harassment by family and state authorities. Noting that many women delayed their suicides for days after an insult, he suggested that additional sanctions against local constables who failed to report cases of flirtation or attempted rape and against magistrates who failed to deal with them could save the lives of many humiliated women and the hapless men who insulted them. Though he was more circumspect in his criticism than Yuan Bin, he implied that the new substatutes covering suicide in the wake of flirtation or insult exacerbated women's propensity to take life lightly and that the punishments were too severe.[14] Henan Judicial Commissioner He Wei took this disparagement of women's motives for suicide a step further, suggesting in a 1765 memorial that many women killed themselves for reasons that had nothing to do with vindicating their chastity. He requested that honors for women who killed themselves in response to a proposition or harassment be limited to those who acted purely out of humiliation or desire to prove their chastity. In response, the Qianlong Emperor refused to accept this cynical perspective. He called for greater attention to the details of individual cases but declined to make a hard and fast rule, declaring that

> women who take life lightly may perhaps do so because they wish to assuage their fury and use this as a pretext to obtain hidden merit. But they are not so different from those who become vegetarians and recite Buddhist scriptures. Within the women's quarters sincerity and insincerity are obscured. There is no consistent pattern. Sometimes wives and daughters originally do not want to die but are pressured by husbands or parents to do so. And we cannot protect them from doing so. How is it benevolent to promulgate a statute to distinguish [these motivations] clearly?[15]

The emperor asserted that precisely because women were incapable of consistent moral reasoning and often unclear or mixed in their motivations, one should approach their suicides with compassionate benefit of the doubt. Though they disagreed about the best way to deal with feminine foibles, memorialist and emperor shared a dim view of women's moral integrity, while still upholding the ideals of the chastity cult.

The paternalistic and disdainful tone of Qianlong-era statecraft discourse on female suicide revealed an important shift in the state's relationship to its female subjects from the days when Yongzheng called upon women to take up their social duties in service of the empire. The female suicide caught in the zealous gaze of late-eighteenth-century moral reformers was more than ever the object of bureaucratic intervention seeking to deconstruct her motives, alter her behavior, and control the public interpretation of her death. If Yongzheng's chaste widows and heroic martyrs were ideal loyal subjects participating in the civilizing project, Qianlong's chastity martyrs were either victims or ignorant woman acting out of pathetic desperation and in need of the state's civilizing charity.

THE FICKLENESS OF THE CHASTE

Policy makers were not the only men who held such disparaging and contradictory assumptions about women's moral capacity and behavioral tendencies. In handbooks, social commentary, and fiction, cautionary criticism of women's propensity to commit suicide in overreaction to humiliation was often intertwined with condescending assessments of women's potential for independent moral judgment. Most observers, including magistrates confronting these suicides in criminal proceedings, talked about such deaths as preventable tragedies, the extreme response of hypersensitive women whose families had failed to comfort and reason with them. Nothing confirms more clearly that the new suicide substatutes expressed a woman's perspective than this overwhelming criticism of humiliation suicides by elite men of the day. In his handbook for women's education Chen Hongmou articulated a sentiment reflected widely in the questions and commentaries of magistrates when he warned of the propensity of wronged women to kill themselves:

> Now, womenfolk of the inner quarters who are fully attentive to the dictates of propriety will sometimes suffer unintended [compromises of their virtue]. In such cases, if parents, elderly aunts, husbands, and brothers offer the woman instruction and guidance on how to react, and seek calmly to resolve the situation, and perhaps if some elderly matron of the community steps forward to offer the woman comfort and consolation, the calamitous event [her suicide] may be avoided. . . . If menfolk bring up their women right, there will be no suicides at all.[16]

Chen resolutely condemned the suicide of the insulted woman as an irrational and inappropriate act of blind fury. Yet, like many of his male contemporaries, he juxtaposed his revulsion at women's suicides with unrealistic standards for gender propriety and a disparaging view of women's capacities as moral agents, both of which worked to produce the social and emotional pressures that motivated women to kill themselves. He promoted stringent standards of separation between the sexes to avoid the suspicion of impropriety, yet also criticized women for being overly sensitive and prone to suicide at the slightest provocation. Chen warned that "suspicions *(xianyi)* about men and women are especially entangled in family honor or disgrace. Never say they are harmless, for the calamity they cause can only escalate."[17] In the very same passage from his handbook, he disdainfully dismissed women's sensitivity to insult: "Residing deep within the inner apartments, women know nothing of the affairs of the world or its hardships. They develop haughty and truculent dispositions . . . and unavoidably become humiliated at the slightest suspicion *(xianyi)*."[18]

Huang Liuhong also maligned women's moral maturity as he justified strict adherence to norms of gender separation, although as a man of seventeenth-century sensibilities he readily granted more legitimacy to human emotions and passions than his more prudish eighteenth-century counterparts. Transgressions were all too common, he argued, for "what man or woman is without sexual desire?" The slightest lapses of propriety led all too easily to wanton or merely imprudent behavior in all segments of society. "In wealthy families too much leisure gives rise to evil desires, while in poor households, the need for food and clothing leads to a loss of the sense of shame. Tough bullies develop lustful intentions when they catch a glimpse of a beautiful woman, while frivolous types take delight in a charming face and, suddenly forgetting their proper role, begin to flirt, which leads to the swearing of covenants of love."[19] Thus, he concluded, "The only way to avoid transgression is to use ritual to discipline oneself."[20] Even the most upright and chaste of women, however, were incapable of rigorous self-discipline and succumbed readily to temptations:

> When seduction is achieved through artful words, it may be the case that [the woman's husband] is poor and she is enticed by [the seducer's] wealth, or [the husband] is old and ugly and she is beguiled by [the seducer's] youth and beauty, or [the husband] is vulgar and fierce and she is enticed by [the seducer's] gentleness. Women have fickle temperaments. Who among them would not be moved by such talk? Even though a resolutely chaste woman would rebuke him before hearing his voice, causing him to retreat hastily in shame, if the words but enter her ears, they will be so compelling that she will be unable to control herself.[21]

To keep women chaste, he insisted, strict observance of gender separation was essential to eliminate both the inspiration and opportunity for casual or accidental contact between the sexes so that "suspicions *(xianyi)* will be kept at a distance and undue intimacies *(xiexia)* will not arise."[22]

In his household instructions for his sons, Wang Huizu similarly distinguished the moral capacities of men and women. He pointedly advised his sons that "mishaps" occurred when one "has no sense of shame." "If one cares about shame, one must have scruples. If one has scruples, then one is capable of discipline. And one who is capable of discipline is a noble man, and not a small person."[23] In another section, entitled "Knowing How to Become a Person after Suffering Humiliation," he counseled his sons that while insult was most difficult to bear, maintaining one's temper and cultivating a capacity for tolerance was the best way to handle humiliation.[24] The moral education of women, though, was complicated by the fact that women and men required and responded to different sources of normative authority. Wang noted that the reason he emphasized the behavior of women was that "women obey family elders; sons and nephews individually follow the principles learned from their inquiry into what is fundamental." It was not that men were not subject to familial authority, as Wang made clear in the subsequent section, entitled "Filiality Begins with Obedience." But while morality for men was based on the understanding of principles gained through study of the classics, women learned propriety by following the dictates and behavioral examples of their mothers, husbands, and mothers-in-law. Thus "morally transforming men is easy, but transforming women is difficult. For women to be morally transformed, men must obviously guide and educate them."[25]

Even Yuan Mei (1716–98), an outspoken critic of the gender norms of the Qianlong era who, as a patron of women poets, expressed his great respect for women's intellectual abilities, found the suicidal sensitivity of women to insult excessive and even ridiculous. Although he did not dismiss the value of chastity entirely, he encouraged casual interactions among the sexes, especially in the context of elite poetry circles, and explicitly condemned the suicides of rape victims, the custom of widow chastity, and even footbinding as unnecessarily extreme expressions of virtue.[26] His collection of tales of the strange included a story that is one of the most trenchant critiques of the perverse effects of the twinned phenomena of the chastity obsession and female outrage. Entitled "The Shame Disease" *(xiuji),*[27] the tale introduces a brilliant young scholar named Shen who suddenly contracts a strange illness: "Whenever he ate a meal, he would raise his hands to scratch his face and say, 'Shame, shame.' Whenever he went to the toilet he would scratch his buttocks and say, 'Shame, shame.'" He tells his family that in these moments of insanity there is a girl dressed in black who grabs his hands and forces him to do this, beating him if he hesitates. The young man becomes weak and emaciated, and after a series of doctors fail to cure him, his family consults a Daoist priest, who reports the matter to the City God for investigation.

Some days later, the City God reports through a judicial officer that

Shen was, in a former life, the wife of a man named Ye and that the girl in black was her younger sister-in-law who was engaged to a poor scholar. To facilitate his passing the examinations before their marriage, Ye invited him to live in their household. Strolling in the garden one evening, the young sister noticed her fiancé still studying and had her maid take him a cup of tea. The maid reported the affectionate gesture to the elder sister-in-law, who, in front of the household, slapped the hapless young woman and said, "Shame, shame!" Humiliated, the fiancée hanged herself. In death, she reported the incident to the City God, requesting that he avenge her death by taking Shen's life. He replied, "As a young virgin of the inner quarters, you brought suspicion on yourself by walking in the moonlight and sending tea [to your fiancé]. How can you . . . frivolously request a person's life? I will not allow it."

Unsatisfied, the young woman then went to the Grand Emperor of the Eastern Peak, Mount Tai, who told her,

> The judgment of the City God is indeed wise. You ought to reflect on [your behavior]. However, if this Shen so-and-so was your elder sister-in-law in a former life, then in principle she ought to have been tolerant. If her younger sister-in-law committed a small transgression, she ought to have admonished her privately. Why did she need to slander her in front of people? Now if I bring him here to confront you, his life will certainly be harmed. His guilt is not great enough to deserve that. Therefore, I will allow you to seek recompense yourself. You can just cause him a bit of vexation.

The Celestial Master advises the family, "This is a small matter and you can simply invite a high-ranking monk to assist the passage of the younger sister-in-law's soul toward salvation so that she can be reborn." The family follows these instructions, and Shen is soon cured.

With characteristically caustic satire and a keen eye for human foibles, Yuan in this tale dramatized the absurd extremes to which the ideal of chastity was taken in his day, suggesting with his title that they were pathological, driving both women and family authorities to inhumane actions. It was the severe and doctrinaire approach to female virtue, not the value of chastity itself, that was the focus of the satire. Although the cosmic powers-that-be affirmed the value of gender separation, chastising the fiancée for her improper behavior, they also pointed out that her transgression was minor and did not deserve such harsh and humiliating punishment. At the same time, they found her suicide to have been an excessive expression of her shame and her demand for revenge disproportionate. Finally, imagining the metamorphosis of female shame into the demeaning psychological disorder of a promising young literatus, involving self-mutilation and embarrassing toilet habits, Yuan brilliantly implicated literati moralists and officials in the production of the chastity pathology, suggesting that while suicide was a female compulsion, shame was a male obsession.

GENDERED INTERPRETATIONS OF INSULT

Elite literati and officials were not the only men who held contradictory views of the significance of chastity and female outrage. The existence of similar views among the wider population was attested in the countless testimonies of fathers, husbands, and even mothers who tried to cover up suspicious improprieties to avoid damaging family reputation, yet readily expressed their disbelief when women killed themselves after a compromising encounter. Men convicted under the new substatutes often insisted that they were completely unaware of the nature of an insult or were merely joking when their words inspired fury or suicidal humiliation in a woman. One 1767 case of such tragic misunderstanding from Xinyu County, Jiangxi, involved a young unmarried military student named Zhang Juguang, aged twenty-three, and a young married woman named Hu Shi, aged twenty-five *sui,* who had been raised together as "practically brother and sister," since she recognized his mother as a "godmother."[28] One day the man accidentally walked in on the woman in the toilet. "I was flustered," he testified, "and laughed a little and said, 'Oh are you using the toilet here? I also wanted to use the toilet.' Hu Shi blushed and started screaming that I was trying to flirt with her." The ruckus brought several neighbor women running to the scene. He denied the accusation, but they chastised him and tried to console her, saying, "You are a person who reads books, how could you still be so lacking in ritual propriety and not recognize your wrongdoing? Quick, get out of here! What are you still standing around for?" When the young man's mother later questioned him about the incident, he refused to discuss it. The following day, she marched over to her goddaughter's house and asked her what had happened. When her goddaughter told her about the flirtation, Zhang's mother testified, "Since this was a matter involving face *(guanxi lianmian),* I told her she should not make accusations falsely, and we argued." Again the neighbor women tried to mediate, but the next day Hu Shi hanged herself. Zhang was sentenced to strangulation after the assizes for flirtation that caused a woman's suicide. That such a grave misunderstanding could occur between people who knew each other so well is indicative of the degree to which men underestimated the depth and intensity of women's concern for their virtue and their awareness of social and spatial boundaries.

In 1780, after a misunderstanding with his neighbor, Kang Shi, aged thirty-three, a willow basket vendor named Feng Youcai, aged twenty-nine, from Taiyuan Prefecture in Shanxi, was sentenced to one hundred strokes of the heavy bamboo and life exile under the 1740 substatute on "ignorant rustics" who caused a woman's suicide by "speaking with improper familiarity."[29] One morning, Kang Shi went to Feng's house to request payment for a basket that she had woven for him. He was not home but later that afternoon came over to her house to pay her. He said, "It is I who owe you money, so you needn't have come to my house to fetch it." She replied that she was putting together some cash to buy rice. He reached into a jar of money he had brought and took out two copper cash. Then he rubbed the mouth of his jar and said, "Don't I have a lot of money?" She suddenly began to shout, "If you have a lot of money, what does that have to do with me?" In a state of consternation, he dropped the two cash and ran out the door.[30] After her husband came home that evening from the fields and saw her crying, she told him the story and said that since Feng had humiliated her she would "never again have the face to be human." Her husband beat up the defendant and set off to the county seat to file a plaint but was stopped along the road by several fellow villagers who talked him out of it and offered to make Feng apologize formally with a kowtow. The apology failed to mitigate his wife's sense of humiliation, and after weeping and threatening suicide for a week, she finally went to Feng's house while her husband was in the fields and took arsenic in his mother's bed. When her husband found her there, vomiting, as she died, she said, "When Feng Youcai insulted me, I got so indignant that I couldn't stand it anymore, so I ate . . . arsenic out of desperation." The hapless Feng insisted to the magistrate that "I merely made a casual joke. I didn't think she would get so furious and start cursing. . . . Really, I didn't mean to flirt with her." The magistrate believed him and sentenced him for unintentional insult, not intended flirtation, which would have resulted in a death sentence. Kang Shi was canonized as a chastity martyr.

Not all husbands and family members were as sympathetic to women's suicidal fury as Kang Shi's. Many a man failed to understand the depths and nature of his wife or daughter or daughter-in-law's feelings after being propositioned or touched or even assaulted. The disbelief of a husband explaining his wife's suicide in a case from Xuzhou Prefecture, Jiangsu, is typical:

I came home in the evening and my mother and wife told me that [the neighbor] had come over and caressed my wife's shoulder to flirt with her. My wife screamed and he ran off. Because this was a matter concerning face, I comforted my wife and did not speak out about it. My wife said she had been humiliated by [him] and could no longer be human. My mother and I repeatedly consoled her, but my wife only wept and wailed. My mother was afraid she would kill herself and kept watch over her at home. [A few days later] I thought my wife's fury had subsided and went out to plow.... In the afternoon I came home ... and to my surprise my wife had hanged herself from a beam.[31]

Often, family members tried to reason with women whose outrage over a careless remark seemed excessive to them. When Gao Wang Shi from Baoding Prefecture, Zhili, interpreted the drunken rambling of her husband's nephew, Gao Huoer, as a proposition, her husband tried to convince her that however rude Gao had been, he had not meant to be lewd.[32] Gao Huoer, who was a frequent visitor to her home, had stumbled into her house drunk one night, asked for a light, and vomited on her floor. She screamed, "What do you think you're doing coming to my house drunk to degrade *(zaota)* me?" He replied, "I came to grab a light to smoke some tobacco." She retorted, "You can well enough draw a light at your own house! Get out of here now!" Then he said, "If you won't let me smoke, I won't smoke *(chou)*. Why do you have to curse?" And he left. Offended at this reply, she ran after him, screaming with rage. Later she told her husband, "I think this line was clearly intended as a proposition.... I am a woman. Since I've been subjected to his vulgarity like this, it is truly difficult to be a person *(Wo shi nüren. Bei ta zheyang sacun shizai nanyi zuoren)*. I want to have it out with Gao Huoer." Her husband, failing to understand the intensity of her fury, tried to calm her down, saying, "Gao Huoer did not mean anything by it. Why take it so seriously?" Then, her husband testified, "My wife saw that I was unwilling to go and express outrage on her behalf and walked out the door. I thought she was going to make trouble and pursued her to call her back. Little did I know that she would run to Gao's gate and jump in his well." He tried to rescue her, but she was already dead. He noted, finally, "As for what Gao said about 'If you won't let me smoke, I won't smoke,' this is local dialect."[33] When she jumped in the well, Gao Huoer testified, "I was still in a drunken haze ..., but I was extremely sad. Truly, I absolutely did not intend to flirt [with her]." He was convicted, like Feng Youcai, of unintentional insult resulting in suicide. In accordance with ritual regulations, the magistrate recommended Gao

Wang Shi for canonization, noting, "as soon as she heard obscenities, she sacrificed her life to proclaim her chastity. How commendable!"

Like the case of Ren Shi and Bai Xian, these cases bristled with inconsistent assumptions, not only about proper interactions between the sexes, but also about the appropriateness of women's responses to insult. The clueless distress of defendants was often paired with the aggrieved disbelief of relatives and neighbors, whose anger at the assailant's impropriety was mixed with regret at what they perceived to be overreaction on the part of the victim. The law explicitly recognized that these crimes were unintentional, yet by punishing them severely and rewarding the victims, the state emphatically validated the propriety and even valor of women's suicidal outrage. At the same time, the new regulations on handling harassment cases required magistrates to work to stem the tide of humiliation suicides by informing people that it was the duty of family members "to try to comfort [women who have been insulted] and refrain from exacerbating their humiliation" and that they could face punishment for doing "anything to incriminate her and cause her to take life lightly."[34] Guarding a woman determined to sacrifice her life to vindicate her virtue was no easy task. It required constant vigilance for prolonged periods of time and could thus present a real burden for busy farm families. After a neighbor she knew well grabbed her hand to flirt with her, one young chaste widow was so determined to die, even after her brother-in-law beat up the offender, that she deceived her family.[35] Her father-in-law testified, "We all took turns keeping watch over her day and night. [A few days later] we were busy in the fields, so I told my daughter-in-law to come with us and pick flowers. She said she was no longer angry and would watch over things at home and told us to go ahead and pay attention to our work. I thought she was sincere and let down my guard and we went to the fields. I didn't expect that she had tricked us and after we left she would hang herself in her room."

Since inquiry into how family members dealt with the initial insult was a mandated component of suicide investigations, every case report contained similar accounts of the precise circumstances leading to the suicide. Magistrates thus enforced a state-defined notion of the proper way for families to handle the outrage of their wives and daughters, just as they enforced state models of the "proper" way for women to express and defend chastity. Confronted in the courtroom with these expectations, husbands, parents, and parents-in-law were at pains to prove that they had done their utmost to console and "watch over" *(kanshou)* their suicidal women. Underlying these encounters between officials and family authorities was a common tone of condescending concern for women who were supposedly so impulsive and ignorant of ritual propriety that they were incapable of figuring out for themselves what course of action was most proper or was in their best interest.

Given the prevalence of such low expectations of women's ability to make sound moral judgments and of worries about rampant transgressions of gender boundaries, it is hardly surprising that, as Susan Mann notes, "Chastity was the focus of the grooming process [for women]. Keeping a daughter chaste and ensuring that not even a hint of rumor besmirched her reputation required vigilance on the same level accorded her brothers' classical training."[36] But even the most well-educated and well-intentioned women still had to cope with fundamentally contradictory expectations about their chastity and serious doubts about their ability to meet the moral challenges posed by the norms of the chastity cult. They were supposed to conform to rigid standards of chaste behavior, yet they could not avoid the suspicion that their weak moral fiber made chastity difficult, if not impossible, to maintain. They were expected to express moral outrage at violations of their chastity and indeed were often chastised for not expressing their outrage in appropriate ways, yet they were seen to be irrationally sensitive to insults. They were required to defend their chastity vigorously whenever it was threatened or challenged, but they were assumed to be incapable of moral reasoning and independent moral agency.

CHAPTER 9

The Logic of Female Suicide

In the context of an intense politics of chastity fraught with contradictions and conflict, women's suicides in the wake of sexual assault or harassment became profoundly assertive, public, and political acts that placed women at odds with state, family, and community authorities and the dominant gender orthodoxy they represented.[1] Pervasive rhetoric about the importance of chastity and the dangers of gender disorder fueled a fervid moral climate in the eighteenth century. Meanwhile, as the case record reveals, the unavoidable gap between moral ideals of inner and outer distinction and the muddled realities of women's lives, shaped by skewed sex ratios, male sojourning, poverty, economic change, and shifting social practices, produced enormous anxiety on the part of many women about their moral image and integrity. While the humanitarian concerns and admonishments of literati moralists and officials, fathers, and husbands sounded like the voice of cool-headed reason amidst the heated rhetoric on female chastity, women in fact had good reason to be extremely and even suicidally sensitive about slights to their virtue. The vast majority of female victims of sexual assault or insult were young married women between the ages of sixteen and thirty, whose children, if they had any, were still small, whose status in the families and communities of their husbands was still quite low, and whose reputation was still taking shape.[2] Their assailants were most often of a similar age, unmarried, and usually known to them as neighbors or relatives. Rumors of trysts and illicit affections arose easily, especially when the victim was a widow or her husband was sojourning elsewhere. Poverty, business, bureaucratic postings, or the search for opportunity led many men in all social classes to sojourn for long periods of time away from home as merchants, magistrates, teachers, or itinerant laborers. They left their wives, parents, and children home alone in what became essentially female-headed households in which wives took on responsibility for family business and household chores.[3]

Many cases of adultery or assault at every level of society started with the fact of the husband's long-term absence from the household. While her husband was on a four-month business trip to Beijing, Xu Wang Shi, the wife of a Shanxi merchant with a purchased *jiansheng* degree, was propositioned by her husband's cousin Xu Jinxi.[4] He came into her quarters asking to borrow a broom, then grabbed her and flirted with her, saying, "Since my elder cousin is not home, I'll buy you a little something over the New Year holiday if you want." She screamed at him and he ran off, but her mother-in-law heard the noise and came asking what happened. When Xu Wang Shi told her, she advised her not to say anything about such a "disgraceful matter." Xu Wang Shi kept the incident secret until the day after her husband returned, when he said he wanted to pay a visit to his cousin. Xu Wang Shi blurted out, "Xu Jinxi cannot be considered human [because he is so immoral]. There's no need to pay respects to him!" After confirming the story of the proposition with his mother, her husband grabbed a stick and confronted his cousin out on the street. "Since this was a disgraceful matter, it was not good to speak of it to outsiders, so without saying a word, I . . . hit him in the head." Xu Jinxi died that evening, and Xu Wang Shi's husband was sentenced to strangulation after the assizes for homicide after not reporting the incident and taking matters into his own hands.

If improper interactions were common, so too was illicit sex. Indeed, the case record contains at least as many instances of women responding to flirtation by assenting to an affair as of women resisting harassment, assault, or rape.[5] While her husband was working away from home as a tutor, a Hunan woman failed to "separate inner and outer," starting an affair with the local doctor, who had flirted with her when he was treating her.[6] One remarried widow from Zhejiang, who sold tea, fruit, and warm wine to passersby in front of her gate, gave in to the charms of a handsome traveler who asked to stay the night and then became a frequent guest of her husband's when he passed by on his way to and from the prefectural capital.[7] Many poverty-stricken women, like the wife of a day laborer from Zhili who was propositioned by the village sesame cake maker, agreed to illicit sex because they owed money to the seducer.[8] Others hoped to get money, free lodging, or food in exchange for sex. It was not uncommon for husbands to tolerate or even encourage such affairs. After his wife was propositioned by the landlord from whom they rented a room when she asked to borrow rice, the blind Du Qingru from Shanxi agreed to their affair in exchange for a regular supply.[9] Shen Gui, from Anhui, who barely made a living as a day laborer, accepted payments from a neighbor after discovering him in bed with his wife.[10]

Seemingly casual and innocent interactions were readily seen to be suspicious by neighbors, relatives, and magistrates, largely because, as Huang Liuhong noted, the same kinds of questionable encounters and flirtatious remarks that initiated cases of sexual assault or insult were also the starting point for adulterous affairs. The frequency of transgressions exacerbated the confusion and disagreement over norms of proper etiquette, which led so often to misinterpreted words or gestures, even between people who knew each other well. But it also produced a set of expectations on the part of many men about the sexual availability of women who were young, living without their husbands, or poor enough to be tempted by the prospect of material gain, especially if such women appeared in public. Such assumptions formed the backdrop for a flirtation suicide case from Puzhou Prefecture, Shanxi, in which the town ne'er-do-well sneaked into the house of the young Zhou Shi, whose husband had been away for over a year on business, to try and seduce her.[11] Only nineteen *sui* old, Guo Zhou Shi was described by all of her natal and marital relatives as being a "very proper person" with an "absolutely upright nature," living a quiet life alone with her three-*sui*-old son and spending her days diligently spinning and weaving. Her assailant, Zhou Sijia (no relation), was the quintessential rogue male: still single at the age of fifty-three, he had pursued a career as a petty burglar until he was caught and tattooed in 1738, at which point, he claimed, he reformed himself and took up farming. But since Guo Zhou Shi's husband had left, he admitted, he often saw her pass his gate on her way to visit her natal family and, "noticing that she had grown into a beautiful young woman, I had long thought about having illicit sex with her." Though they knew of each other, Zhou had never had any interaction with her, and since she lived next door to her husband's many relatives, who were charged with looking out for her in her husband's absence, he did not dare to approach.

Then one night in 1750, when the Guo men were all away at a family funeral and after drinking several cups of wine, Zhou sneaked into the house and found Guo Zhou Shi sitting on her *kang* spinning cotton

The Logic of Female Suicide

in the lamplight. The moment she saw him, she shouted, "What are you doing, coming into my house in the middle of the night!" Zhou confessed, "I thought I would take advantage of her youth, so I laughed, went over to the *kang* and pulled on her little leg a bit, saying, 'Tonight there is no one around to find out, so how about if I give you a little money and you sleep with me?'" She shoved him away and began screaming at the top of her lungs that there was a thief in the house. Zhou ran out the door and was caught by the Guo men as they were returning from the funeral. He immediately admitted that he was at fault for having "insulted" her, and they broke his legs on the spot. Left alone in her room amidst the commotion, Guo Zhou Shi hanged herself from a beam. Although he had pulled her leg and propositioned her, Zhou Sijia was convicted of flirtation resulting in suicide rather than attempted rape, since he did not use any force against her. She, of course, was canonized.

Explaining his thinking, the culprit stated, "I figured that since she was a young woman whose husband had long been away from home and was very poor, if I offered her a few copper cash she would naturally be willing to give in to me. So I had the nerve to walk in without even carrying a weapon." When she screamed for help, she mentioned only that there was a thief, but to the relatives who came to her rescue, it was obvious that he had come for other reasons, even though there were no wounds or ripped clothing to indicate rape. "Clearly," they told the magistrate, "he knew there was no one at her house, that she was a young woman living alone, and he assumed he could trick her into having illicit sex. We think she committed suicide because [the defendant] dared, in the middle of the night, to come into her house and humiliate her. She was at pains to report this outright, so, in her shame and outrage, she killed herself." Given her solid reputation for staunch virtue, Guo Zhou Shi's extreme sensitivity about the incident, to the point that she could only say that there was thief, not a sexual assailant, might seem unwarranted. Yet her reputation did not preclude Zhou Sijia from thinking he could seduce her. Even her relatives, without questioning her virtue, discussed his prurient assumptions matter-of-factly, as though they were to be expected given her circumstances. They were not surprised either that this kind of insult would fill her with such shame that she had to kill herself.

CHOOSING SUICIDE

Examination of patterns of women's reactions to various forms of assault or proposition suggests that there was more method in the seemingly mad suicidal fury of insulted women than at first meets the eye. To begin with, not every woman was obsessed with her chastity. Plenty of women carried on adulterous affairs for years without worrying about their reputations. Women whose chastity was important to them made deliberate and considered choices about how to respond when their virtue was impugned. Suicide was hardly the automatic or universal response of women to verbal or physical compromise of their virtue. As Board of Punishments memorials *(xingke tiben)*, all the cases in this study are serious cases involving sentences of capital punishment or exile for rape, attempted rape, driving a person to suicide, homicide, or killing in an affray, all of which required review by capital officials. Nevertheless, they illustrate a wide array of responses to verbal or physical violations on the part of women and their families, ranging from the victim's caustic chastisement to suicide, from silence to murderous revenge. Moreover, absent from the already incomplete judicial record are unreported assaults and instances of sexual insult or unwanted flirtation that were instantly dismissed by the woman or dealt with successfully through apologies, monetary compensation, or community or clan punishment that bypassed the courts entirely. Even when women did commit suicide, they often did so days or weeks after the assault or insult, suggesting, as Zhang Ruoai astutely observed, that some sort of aggravating circumstances often came into play, pushing them to a death they would not initially have sought. It was, moreover, rare for a woman to kill herself in spontaneous outrage before telling the story of her violation to a family member or neighbor.

For every Guo Zhou Shi who immediately killed herself, there was a woman like Liu Zou Shi, who, though also young and left home alone, did not even contemplate suicide after she was raped. After only a year of marriage to a government student *(shengyuan)* in Anyang County, Henan, her husband went off to the prefectural capital to sit for the second level of the examinations.[12] Since her mother fell ill, Liu Zou Shi returned home by herself to care for her. One day her mother had a craving for wild jujubes, so she took her five-*sui*-old brother and went off to a spot outside the village behind a tomb to pick some. One of her parents' neighbors, a man she knew well from her childhood, accosted her there, first offering her a jujube and then, when she refused it, flirting with her, saying that he could see her flesh through her pants. She cursed him, but he knocked her to the ground and raped her, ripping her pants. She screamed, her brother cried, and another neighbor came running to rescue her and hit the assailant a couple of times before he ran off. Her father reported the incident to her husband in the prefectural capital, and the husband returned home to report the rape to the authorities. The prospect of suicide was never even raised in this case, nor did anyone attempt to hide the disgraceful incident, although one might expect such a young gentry woman and her upwardly mobile literatus husband to be quite sensitive to threats to their reputation. So what made Liu Zou Shi able to withstand the loss of her chastity while Guo Zhou Shi found the shame of her pollution to be unbearable?

Obviously, many factors of personality, the tenor of family relationships, and women's personal histories contributed to their individual responses but remain hidden from the judicial record. Still, correlating the incidence of suicide with the type of assault or insult and the nature of family reaction to it is revealing of the kinds of choices women made in response to an attack on their virtue. Most rape victims (29 out of 34 cases in my total sample of 182 sexual assault and harassment cases), even those who suffered extreme violence or were the victims of gang rapes, did not commit suicide. The few who did were unusually vulnerable to accusations of impropriety, like widows, or were assaulted in highly compromising situations—for example, while stealing fruit. Suicides were much more common in cases of attempted rape (44 out of 101 cases) and harassment or sexual insult (27 out of 47 cases). Among attempted rape victims who did not commit suicide, 15 were avenged by the murder of their assailants by a member of their families, and 23 were killed by their attackers.[13] Among those victims of harassment who did not commit suicide, 16 were avenged through the murder or assault of their assailants, and 3 killed their attackers themselves.[14] Such patterns suggest that when an assault or insult was avenged in some manner, the victim usually did not kill herself. Intriguingly, requital almost always involved violence. It could be violence enacted on the assailant as state punishments of execution or flogging or retribution in the form of beating or murder. But the requiting violence could also take the form of suicide on the part of the offended woman or her own wounding or murder in the course of the attack. For many women, once the boundaries of the chaste body, the virtuous reputation, the proper interaction, or the inner quarters had been violated, only a publicly known and violent vindication of the chastity that was destroyed could restore the moral integrity that was integral to so many women's sense of self.[15] When requital was not provided for them, many women took matters into their own hands, killing themselves to publicize their humiliation and ensure vindication.

Many, if not most, women suicides thus killed themselves not as an impulsive expression of unreasoned and uncontrolled outrage but to redeem their ability "to be a person" or "to face people," when their violation was not recognized and requited. This sense of personhood was, in large part, about moral integrity. While the burden of proof of a woman's virtue always lay with her or her family, the routine unorthodoxies of everyday life made verification of her chaste character, intent, and actions extremely tricky and made her vulnerable to slanders and rumors about improprieties. As Yuan Bin astutely noted in his critique of the illicit sex statute, given the impossibility of discerning consent from coercion in any systematic and objective way, a woman's suicide was all too often taken by adjudicating magistrates as proof of her chaste intent, while women who did not kill themselves in the wake of humiliation were likely to face suspicions about their chastity. Failure to commit suicide, he noted, often made a woman vulnerable to slander by her assailant and to suspicions about the true nature of her intent and of the alleged assault. Illustrative of common magistrates' assumptions about suicide was the question put to one defendant in an attempted rape case, "If you really did not coerce and rape [her], then why did she commit suicide?"[16] The victims of convicted rapists were fully vindicated because in judicial terms they were, by definition, chaste women who had resisted their attackers virtuously. Women who were wounded in the course of an attempted rape also had solid proof of their resistance. It was much harder for a woman to prove her virtuous conduct in cases of attempted rape and insult, where evidence of coercion was usually lacking and the circumstances of the encounters were often murky and known only to the two parties. Victims of insult or sexual assault whose husbands, fathers-in-law, or brothers confronted their violators and killed them received not only revenge but the passionate belief in and defense of their reputations by their families.

In the cases in which women did commit suicide, on the contrary, family members had usually failed to take action to dispel doubts about the victim's behavior, and there was no vindication from either a court judgment or revenge. (This was true in 23 out of 27 harassment suicides and 27 out of 44 attempted rape cases.) Usually this was not because the women did not make their wishes known: most demanded that their husbands take the offender to court or confront him to "express outrage *(chuqi)*." As one woman explained to her husband when he and her father-in-law refused to take a neighbor to court after he had flirted with her and grabbed her, "He humiliated me like this, but you are not willing to express outrage on my behalf. I can only take the path of seeking death."[17] Ever concerned about attempts to hide illicit sex or illegally pursue private settlements or punishments to avoid *yamen* involvement, magistrates routinely questioned victims and their families and neighbors about failures to report even minor incidents of harassment or improper flirtation, let alone more serious assaults. When women committed suicide out of humiliation, many magistrates attributed the death, in part, to failure to report the insult or assault. In one case, for instance, a young woman hanged herself even after the harasser's mother promised punishment and a formal apology. The magistrate harangued family members, neighbors, and the local constable with questions like "Why did you fail to send him to the *yamen* for punishment, thereby causing Wu Shi to harbor pent up anger and kill herself?"[18]

Women's passion about their chastity stood in sharp contrast to the concerns of family members, neighbors, and magistrates about social harmony, reputation, fair compensation, and expedient conflict resolution. Husbands, parents-in-law, parents, and other family members of victims and perpetrators often resisted the pursuit of legal action or public redress, explicitly linking chastity to family reputation. They encouraged the victim to "endure the humiliation *(yinren),*" saying that the assault was "a disgraceful matter" or "a matter of face" and should not be made known. Particularly if the victim had not actually been raped, they were often more worried about the effects of a public airing of a violation of their inner quarters than about the violation itself, even if, as was often true, they assumed the innocence of their wives, daughters, or daughters-in-law in the disgraceful encounter or assault. One husband testified that his wife, after being caressed by a man who worked as a servant in the same house where she was the cook, told him she was so humiliated she no longer felt like a person and wanted him to have it out with the offender. He replied, "If you were not raped and polluted by him, then this is a disgraceful matter, and you shouldn't go again to argue with him and make trouble or we will be ridiculed by people. I will go and reason with him." But, he testified, his wife remained furious and would not agree. She committed suicide the next day.[19] This husband drew a distinction between rape, which would have constituted a clear enough and severe enough violation to warrant the kind of vindication his wife sought, and an indecent advance, which was merely a disgraceful matter best dealt with through quiet remonstrance.

Families of culprits in these improper encounters, local headmen or constables, and other community members often initiated attempts to deal with the offense privately through a formal apology or compensation in order to forestall the involvement of the *yamen* or pursuit of violent revenge. Sometimes, if the offender was a local bully or came from a large or powerful family, the motivation for such intervention was fear of the consequences of reprisals. Thus in one case from Zhejiang in which an unmarried, eighteen-*sui*-old woman was raped by a local thug, her mother, concerned about her marriage prospects, sought a verdict from the local *yamen*. But the assailant, who routinely harassed women, forced them to have affairs with him, and picked fights with people, had sufficiently cowed the leaders of the community that at his request they sent a delegation, including representatives of the local degree-holding family, to stop the women on the road to the *yamen* and bribe them to let the case go. Now that the culprit had drawn them into the case, they argued, he would surely seek revenge on them all. The women accepted the money and then proceeded anyway to the *yamen*. Appalled that an entire community would allow such a thug to continue in their midst and then prevent a brave woman whose chastity had been violated from seeking justice, the magistrate sentenced the members of the delegation to flogging.[20]

In most instances of attempted mediation, neighbors, local leaders, or the family of the assailant argued for quiet settlement in the interests of preventing the loss of face that would ensue for both the victim's and the culprit's families if the disgraceful matter was publicized. Although husbands and parents of victims were often willing to accept such settlements, wronged women themselves were rarely contented with anything less than the public retribution and redemption of their reputations that a legal judgment or revenge would bring. For example, after being assaulted and almost raped in a sorghum field by a distant cousin of her husband's on the way to visit her mother, one Henan woman ran immediately to her attacker's house and hurled curses at his door.[21] Unwilling to face his accuser, the culprit told his wife to offer her 1,700 copper cash and seven *qian* and five *fen* of silver (one-hundredth and one-tenth of a tael, respectively). She did so, admitting that her husband had "done this face-losing thing" and asking her not to say anything about the assault. Unmoved, the victim refused the money and returned home, telling her husband she wanted to kill herself: "Even though I was not raped and polluted by him, I still can no longer be a person." Her husband reported the crime to the *yamen*, but his wife took no comfort from this, saying, "Even though you filed a plaint, I still have no face." That night she hanged herself. The assailant then offered bribes to her husband and to the *yamen* to hide the real cause of the suicide, which was only finally revealed when the husband's grief and conscience got the better of him and he reported the case again.

In an attempted rape case from Guilin Prefecture, Guangxi, the *bao* headman intervened to encourage the culprit to offer the victim's father, a distant cousin of his, sixty *liang* of meat as an apology in return for concealing the offense and not reporting to the *yamen*. Neither the victim nor her husband was willing to accept this, and they determined to file charges anyway, though she died after they went to the *yamen* of wounds sustained during the assault.[22] In another case from Taiyuan Prefecture, Shanxi, it was the culprit's father who, hearing of his neighbor's intent to file a plaint against his son for attempting to rape his wife, told him, "This is a disgraceful matter. You really don't want to file a plaint. Please let me have this beast come to kowtow to you and apologize." The neighbor and his wife, who, incidentally, never even mentioned suicide as an option, accepted this, but days went by with no sign of an apology, so the husband took his own revenge and beat the culprit to death.[23]

In some cases, doubts about the victim's virtue and the nature of the encounter were exacerbated by the assailant's attempts to slander the woman, his denials of wrongdoing, or his accusations that the woman was trying to slander him. In a case from Yongning County, Henan, for example, when one Zhao Shi expressed her determination to commit suicide after her neighbor sneaked up on her while she was sleeping and caressed her, her husband promised to "express outrage" on her behalf. But the culprit's father, unaware of his son's guilt, accused Zhao Shi's husband of slander and attacked him. He then went to the *yamen* to file a plaint, and the son was duly arrested. A few days later he escaped and came back telling everyone that he had raped Zhao Shi and that prosecuting him was "merely telling a brothel's tale." Outraged anew, Zhao Shi told her husband, "I waited at first for the *yamen*'s inquiry before seeking death. Now there has not even been a judgment yet, and he has come again to humiliate me. Why should I continue to wait to seek death?"[24] In another case from Tongzhou, a victim of attempted rape and her husband gave up their plan to report the case under pressure from neighbors who reminded them of the scandal it would cause. But the assailant, afraid they would eventually turn him in, sued them for accusing him falsely of adultery. When the victim found out about the suit, she said to her husband, "I did not say a word, yet he goes and files a plaint. I can't stand this life anymore."[25] Both of these women hanged themselves. In another similar case, from Quanzhou Prefecture, Fujian, a woman refused to believe that her son had flirted with a neighbor's wife. Hearing that they intended to file a plaint, she took her son to confront the victim and accused her of slander, with the result that the victim committed suicide that same night.[26]

The views and words of women who killed themselves were always expressed through the testimonies of their husbands or other family members. It is thus intriguing that in their testimonies, the ultimately personal meaning for women of the distinction between inner and outer and its violation stands in contrast to the familial, in some sense more public, definition of face expressed in the reactions of their families. Cases affirm again and again the vital and incontrovertible importance of women's virtue for family reputation and thus for family status in the community.[27] In a handful of cases, husbands or parents actually experienced an insult to a woman's chastity as such a devastating and personal humiliation that they themselves committed suicide.[28] More often, however, family members distinguished between the "humiliation" and "mortification" of the victim and their own anger and anxieties about "disgraceful affairs spreading outside" and threats to family face. They thus admitted that on the experiential level of violation chastity belonged, in the first place, to individual women to define and defend. When husbands, brothers, or fathers did seek revenge or retribution for the violation of their inner quarters, they frequently described their actions as "expressing outrage on behalf of" the victim. The element of personal humiliation that marked the responses of violated women is largely absent in the testimonies of the men describing the anger that drove them to pursue redress in their names.[29]

These divergent reactions of women and their family authorities (usually men) to sexual violations highlight the particular importance of chastity in structuring many women's identities.[30] For women, chastity was not simply about moral reputation or social status but also about dignity and self-respect. With the widespread recognition of her virtue by family and community members, Ren Shi, whose case introduced Part Four, was not embarrassed to be implicated in an impropriety. Rather, she was angry that her boorish cousin had insulted and demeaned her with his propositions. Gao Wang Shi (insulted by her nephew's lewd pun on smoking) encapsulated the complicated meanings of humiliation for women when she told her husband, "I am a woman. Since I've been subjected to his vulgar lewdness like this, it is truly difficult to be a person."

She told the culprit that he had "degraded" *(zaota)* her, using a term that can also mean "to waste, ruin, debase, or trample down" and is commonly used to describe the effects of slander.[31] It suggests both a sense of shame at the destruction of one's public image and a loss of dignity and self-respect. Whether they were infuriated, ashamed, disgusted, or all three, most women who cared at all about chastity (and there were plenty who did not) felt deeply that it was integral to their sense of being human. To insult a woman's chastity was to deny her humanity. The English-language etymology of the words *humiliation* and *mortification* that are the standard translation for the most common term used to describe the effects of insult on women, *wuru*, are very apt in this context. *Humiliation* implies abasement, while *mortification* literally means loss of life or vitality as well as embarrassment. Women may well have represented the inner realm in some sense for men and for family authorities, including mothers and mothers-in-law, who were often instrumental in discussions of how to deal with insults and assaults. Yet parties to these cases differentiated clearly between the disgrace that befell the family and the violation of an individual woman's inner sense not only of moral integrity but of self-respect and dignity. As their canonizations demonstrated, the martyrdom of humiliated women redeemed their chaste reputations in the eyes of the state and their communities, but for the women themselves, suicide, by restoring chastity, was also a profound assertion of personhood.

SUICIDE AS AN AGGRESSIVE ACT

The meanings and potential effects of chastity suicides were manifold and powerful. Qing law and ritual regulation, of course, shored up the social, symbolic, and political efficacy of suicide. A woman's death ensured that her natal family or in-laws would pursue redress; indeed, it would make it nearly impossible to cover up the original incident or keep it out of court. If suicide was often seen as proof of a woman's virtue, it concomitantly exacerbated the defendant's crime and, in subtle cases where he claimed he meant no offense, became the critical proof of his guilt. In a sense, then, by choosing to commit suicide, a woman chose to charge her harasser or attacker with the most severe crime carrying the heaviest punishment that the law made possible.[32] The imperial state also rewarded the victim with canonization as a chastity martyr, which brought not only vindication but glorious honor for herself, her family, and her posterity in the form of a public arch, an imperially inscribed plaque on the gate, and a tablet in the Shrine to the Chaste and Filial. Moreover, the reputation of the offender's family would be damaged, if not ruined, and they would face the opprobrium of the community.

The degree to which the specific legal and ritual consequences of suicide colored women's motivations is often difficult to discern; however, quite a few women clearly had revenge on their minds, choosing forms and venues for their deaths that magnified their emotive and even supernatural impact and focused it on their assailant. According to prevalent popular beliefs, a suicide became a malevolent ghost who could torment her attacker and the local community, seeking revenge for years to come. The terrifying supernatural power wielded by such ghosts is indicated by their commanding presence in fiction and drama.[33] The disruptive power of wronged women was powerfully deployed in the most viscerally terrifying part of the widely popular Mulian operas: the scene depicting the vindication of the "hanged woman" who had been wrongfully accused of adultery by her husband and had resolved to commit suicide to protest her chastity.[34] This hanged-ghost scene was often performed as an exorcistic rite in communities where there had been a suicide.[35] In the eighteenth-century novel *The Story of the Stone,* the suicides of several women tainted by suspicions of impropriety, some of whom appeared as ghosts, became disturbing harbingers of the Jia family's decline.[36]

The inauspicious power of the female suicide was a particularly prominent theme in tales of the strange.[37] Yuan Mei played on the notion of the strange and disturbing potency of female outrage in his tale "The Chaste Woman Tian," featuring the ghost of a chaste widow who hanged herself when her husband's elder brother forced her to remarry. After she appears to the local prefect in the middle of the night to remonstrate for justice, he arrests and punishes the brother-in-law and vindicates her chastity publicly with an inscribed stone stele extolling her virtue. Although the governor reprimands the prefect for using ghosts to solve a criminal case, the prefect's action brings him local acclaim, and he later becomes a governor himself. Some years later, the ghost intervenes again, causing the death of a highway robber who was going to kill him. The story plays with the unsettling incongruity of the chaste victim of forced remarriage returning to the world as a powerful ghost who controls not only life and death but the careers of powerful men. Yuan Mei accentuated the irony here by depicting the widow as the epitome of chaste self-effacement: veiled in black, she demurely refuses to rise from her kneeling position to present her grievance, and when she speaks, her voice is weak and childlike.[38]

The "strangeness" of such tales emerged, in part, from the unsettling effect of weaving orthodox values into narratives of the unconventional, placing the language of chastity, for example, in the mouths of ghosts, monsters, and reincarnations of the unrequited dead. Such strange beings appeared as vehicles for the vindication of wronged women, representing their virtue to the conventional world when other avenues of salvaging their reputations or requiting injustice done to them were closed. Often malevolent, or at least aggressive, these incarnations of female outrage were disturbing also because they imposed their self-representations upon living men and women by wielding power over life and death. In the universe of the strange, becoming a ghost or speaking through a reincarnation was an aggressive means of defending one's virtue. Like Li Yu's story of Secunda Geng's defense of her chastity, Yuan Mei's tale of Chaste Woman Tian also emphasized the fundamentally dialogic and public nature of the upholding and defense of virtue, making the courtroom the venue for vindication and referencing the public monuments of the Qing state chastity cult.

It was not only fictional officials who dealt with the problem of ghosts. Although routine memorials were completely devoid of any references to supernatural beliefs, which were forbidden by the regulations governing the structure and editing of testimonies, they did appear in local legal documents, and the memoirs of several well-respected model magistrates from the Qing included discussions of their manipulation of such beliefs in the adjudication of legal cases.[39] Huang Liuhong, for instance, alluded to this problem in his section on suicide: "Women who hang themselves with ropes and sashes become ghosts who haunt village lanes and dark rooms."[40] The pervasiveness of supernatural beliefs in late imperial society made it highly likely that most wronged women were aware of their potential power as ghosts.[41] Some forms of suicide appear more obviously to be calculated for maximum effect as revenge than others. Motives of posthumous revenge were most powerfully suggested when a woman hanged herself in the offender's house or drowned herself in his family's well. Women who hanged themselves in their harasser's house or yard were sure to haunt the property as vengeful ghosts. After confronting her rapist with a knife and being chased off by his mother, one Zhengzhou woman hanged herself later that night from a persimmon tree in the orchard of her attacker, which was also the scene of her violation.[42] When Li Chengwen of Qiu County, Shandong, attempted to rape

Li Zhang Shi, she took her baby and hanged herself in his house while her husband was out looking for him.[43] After a neighbor flirted with her and touched her hand one day when he came over to borrow a ladder, Su Li Shi, of Jianli County, Hubei, confronted him several times for an apology before finally slamming her head against a beam in his house to kill herself.[44] Many women jumped into community wells or those on the offender's property, thus defiling the water.[45] Having told her husband that after her nephew's degrading comments she could no longer be a person, Gao Wang Shi, of Ansu County, Zhili, threw herself into the well outside her nephew's door.[46]

Nothing more clearly illustrates the public and aggressive potential of female suicide than these deaths calculated to disturb the cosmic order. Ironically, in her most unsettling guise, the wronged woman of virtue aggressively pursuing vindication came to resemble her moral opposite: the shrew. If the chaste woman was quintessentially a conforming and self-sacrificing woman, then the shrew represented, on the contrary, the epitome of antisocial self-assertion. The combination of feminine virtue with unfeminine aggression and even physical prowess was not in itself unusual or taboo: the Chinese literary tradition abounds with portrayals of unconventional women warrior types. Yet, as many literary historians have pointed out, the potential of such model female heroes to disrupt gender boundaries and challenge the patriarchal socioethical order was effectively contained by the use of their prowess to promote orthodox values.[47] The aggressive woman vindicating her chastity was thus much more disturbing than the woman warrior, for while her grievance was legitimized by state and family authorities, the disgrace that created it and frequently its requital posed a threat to the interests, the reputation, and even the legitimacy of those very authorities.

But do these powerful and transgressive consequences suggest that suicide was a form of female agency? Sometimes the intent of the victim to use her suicide for revenge was explicit, but when it was not, the symbolic, social, and judicial consequences of suicide were the same, no matter how or where she killed herself and whether she acted with conscious intent to get revenge or simply out of outrage or despair at her violation. Paola Paderni has argued that the suicides of humiliated women demonstrate their "perfect internalization" of a value system that recognized them only for chastity and made martyrdom the only vindication of that chastity in many situations.[48] Numerous other scholars have argued that in certain situations women's suicides were not only acts of defiance against men who wronged them but expressions of autonomy and a means of controlling the circumstances and significance of their deaths. Examining the portrayal of female suicide in late imperial fiction, Paola Zamperini places the phenomenon within the long Chinese tradition of venerating the good or honorable death. She argues that for fictional heroines who were wronged or alienated by their inability to fulfill their desires in life, suicide was "a revitalizing self-assertion" that signified "a moment of control and power, . . . an act of self-construction."[49] Grace Fong identifies a similar form of agency in the notes and poems that women wrote to explain their suicides for posterity. She argues that the ethic these women internalized was that of "a long tradition that placed certain values of righteousness, loyalty, and courage above the value of preserving one's finite life. In this tradition, injustices may occur, . . . but the public recording of the injustice redeems it by giving a voice to the victim, a voice that helps transform the victim into a heroine."[50]

The illiterate women whose suicides are recorded in the criminal case record could not inscribe their motives and the significance of their deaths for posterity. Yet in the traces of their voices left in the testimonies of their families, there are echoes of the principled self-assertion of the elite women whose deaths Fong describes. One woman writes in her last poem,

> Since ancient times to become humane one always kills oneself.
> Why should I myself shrink back from this?
> I will return the boundless breath to Heaven and Earth,
> And keep company with the chaste spirits at Heaven's gate.[51]

When they insisted on suicide to redeem their personhood, women, like this poet, clearly accepted the notion that chastity was vitally important to their lives. Yet the chastity that women died to redeem was, as we have seen, very different from the chaste duty that the state deemed proper and from the chaste reputation that their families defended. Female suicide, as an almost instinctual assertion of personal integrity and interests, was thus neither an act of resistance against dominant gender norms nor an expression of accommodation to them. In suicide and in myriad other ways, women struggled to define chastity for themselves and to defend their own sense of morality against the standards of propriety asserted by family authorities and the state. Their agency in this regard was not unlike the creative interpretation of the inner/outer paradigm that marked the writings and lives of educated elite women, as Dorothy Ko and Susan Mann have shown. To be sure, their choices, like those of most men, were circumscribed. Still, the case record richly illustrates the many ways in which ordinary women of varying statuses and stages of life, like their elite sisters, had enormous stakes in the gender values of the age and used them to enhance their own interests and quality of life. Their outrage was directed not at the system itself but at men who had failed to treat them with the respect and decorum they knew to be their due.

Ultimately, this study looks beyond the complex and diverse motives of individual women to suggest the larger collective effects of women's agency in the development of the Qing state's gender orthodoxy and its normative ambitions to transform society. This book began with the state attempting to control the meaning and practice of female martyrdom as part of its project to rectify customs and promote gender hierarchy and patriarchal social order. It ends with the state canonizing women's suicides that contravened the dynasty's rubric of proper martyrdom, legitimated women's personal definitions of violation, defied patriarchal authority, and undermined community order. Indeed, with its substatutes on forcing a woman to commit suicide, the state exacerbated the disruptive effects of these deaths by mandating severe punishments not only for the men who caused them but for family and community members who failed to deal with them properly. There is one very simple explanation for this apparent paradox. The Qing state called upon women to be model subjects, taking personal responsibility for the defense of their chastity, and when they did, the state was compelled by its deep investment in chastity to affirm their actions. Emperors and officials assumed that the perfection of personal virtue was compatible with proper social hierarchy. What they did not expect, or fully understand, was that this emphasis on individual moral responsibility eroded the prerogatives of the very patriarchal authority it hoped to strengthen.

This paradoxical outcome was produced by many factors that tell us a great deal not only about how gender norms worked in social life but about how the state interacted with society and the nature of its normative influence on its subjects. For all its hubris about being the arbiter of gender norms and morality more generally, the state's implementation of its priorities and values through law, ritual regulation, and social policy was fraught with unintended consequences, contradictory impulses, and misunderstandings of how morality was defined and enforced in local communities. Policy makers were often astute observers of the society they hoped to reform, frequently recognizing the weaknesses of patrilineal authority, the tensions between generational and marital definitions of patriarchy, the elusiveness of chaste intent, and the chaotic effects of state-sanctioned martyrdom. Yet despite their ambitiously activist vision of the state's normative role, they failed to see how their strategies for reaching into the lives and minds of their subjects were beginning to shift the balance of social power in irrevocable ways.

Epilogue

As the mid-Qing state engaged itself with its subjects through the canonization system, education, propaganda, social reform policies, and, most directly, the judicial system, it was never able to impose a coherent gender orthodoxy without challenge or compromise. As officials tried to implement the civilizing agenda, they were frustrated by the contradictory constructions of family authority, female agency, and chastity itself that were embedded in imperial law and ritual regulation. Confounded by the ambiguities and paradoxes of their own mandate, officials then also found themselves engaging in continual processes of negotiation with local people as they responded to their values, priorities, and the vagaries of virtue in their social practice. Violations and transgressions of chastity almost always implicated family authority for being too weak to prevent them, too contested to deal with them effectively, or, as in incest cases, too corrupt and abusive to care about them at all. The defense of chastity all too often required the recognition of the authority of women's natal families, their husbands, and themselves over and against that of the husband's patriline. Unwilling to admit compromise of its commitment to either chastity or patrilineal family hierarchy, the mid-Qing state waffled. Sometimes it conceded the primacy of the conjugal bond, as in the legislation on catching adulterers, and sometimes it clung to the sanctity of patrilineal hierarchy, as in the legislation on incest killings. As a result, the mid-Qing state's implementation of its gender policies unintentionally perpetuated and exacerbated the very tensions between patrilineal and conjugal notions of patriarchy that they were meant to overcome and enhanced the chastity cult's potential to subvert patriarchal principles.

Whatever the limits of its effectiveness in influencing behavior at the local level, the new legislative apparatus for the promotion of a politicized normative agenda systematically associated state legitimacy with its role as moral arbiter and social reformer. Indeed, the most significant legacy of the mid-Qing chastity cult was the forging of a new relationship between ruler and subject. The most striking manifestation of this process was the state's evolving relationship with women as officials adapted policies toward women's suicides to respond to women's own perspectives on the nature of chastity, its violation, and its proper vindication. As chastity-centered gender norms permeated the heart of Qing political culture and state-building processes, women participated in the evolution of public discourse on chastity through their catalytic suicides, their daily enactment of virtue in social life, and their courtroom testimonies. As they fought to maintain their chastity and vindicate its violation, women were in fact among the most consistent advocates of state intervention in family and community life. Women's "voices" were publicly and politically influential through their odd alliance with state officials in the chastity cult. These voices were heard because women had become the dominant icons of the dynasty's ideal subjects—the quintessential objects of the imperial state's civilizing paternalism.

The larger historical implications of the entanglement of state legitimacy with female chastity emerge in the fate of the state chastity cult during the last century of Qing rule, when the state's resources and legitimacy dwindled along with its ability to manage society. Already in the Qianlong reign, the success of the new chastity system began to produce strains on the state's fiscal and personnel resources as the numbers of awardees exploded. As early as 1749, the huge increase in the numbers of women qualifying for imperial canonization every year led the governor of Jiangsu to memorialize the throne, suggesting that the award of money for a personal commemorative arch be restricted to only the poorest and most hardship-ridden of widows. The rest, "ordinary chaste widows," as he labeled them, would have their names inscribed on a collective arch.[1] The Qianlong Emperor agreed, noting both the high cost of individualized awards and their practical consequences. "In Jiangsu Province alone," he stated, "there are over two hundred people [eligible for awards] every year. If we order tablets placed in [local chastity] shrines for all of them, then as time goes by, . . . there will be no more room." From this point on, "ordinary chaste widows" were no longer entitled to a personal arch or a tablet in the local chastity shrine but only to a plaque for their family's gate and a spot for their name on a collective arch outside the shrine. With this adjustment, the system functioned effectively for almost a century with few complaints from emperors or provincial officials charged with overseeing its administration.

However, in 1845 the collective arch policy was extended to all chaste widows, leaving individual arches only for chastity martyrs.[2] Two years later, the policy was extended to martyrs as well.[3] By the early nineteenth century, the scaling back of awards reflected not the continued success of the system but the mounting pressures of population growth and social unrest, which were echoed in the changing tenor of state chastity discourse. Beginning in the early Jiaqing reign, requests for honors for women, often many at one time, who died defending their chastity in the midst of bandit attacks or rebellions appear with striking frequency, having been completely absent from the record prior to this. In 1800, new procedures were implemented in the wake of banditry in Miao areas of Hunan to deal with such massive assaults on chastity. Local magistrates were to search out all the victims of such attacks and construct a collective community arch inscribed with the names of all the victims "at a site on a public highway, or major road."[4] Eighteen women were honored in this way in one Hubei community in 1801. After the Eight Trigrams Rebellion in 1814, over thirty women were thus honored in one Henan county, and an imperial edict ordered further investigations to uncover more chastity victims.[5] In 1825, the governor of Shaanxi reported the construction of a special shrine to honor the 4,799 people, women and men, who were killed in attacks by "heterodox bandits" during the previous reign.[6]

While the numbers of martyrs grew, the state steadily lowered the standards for chastity canonization. In 1803 the ban on honors for rape victims who had been violated was lifted.[7] From this point on, requests for awards that contravened dynastic rules and precedents were routinely granted without debate or special justification. The state bestowed honors on increasing numbers of chaste widows who died before their twentieth year of chastity or were from titled or official families or previously excluded non-Han peoples. Regulations were also ignored to honor the suicides of widows, concubines, women forced into prostitution, and those committing *gegu*. In contrast with the often tedious debates about eligibility in the eighteenth century, throughout the nineteenth, not a single request for an exception was denied.

In 1851, as the Taiping Rebellion was gathering force, the Xianfeng Emperor issued an edict overturning the ban on honors for widow suicides, with eligibility extended the following year to concubines as well. The emperor prefaced this reversal of a policy that had, despite frequent granting of exceptions, long been a defining element of the dynasty's approach to chastity with an unusual description of ominous weather patterns and their implications for the cosmic legitimation of the dynasty:

> Since last year's winter solstice, there has been very little moisture from melting snows. The weather has been very parched and dry. Since the beginning of spring, cold and hot have come in unseasonable fashion. Yesterday we passed the vernal equinox with dense sleet and freezing cold. Today it is finally beginning to be warm and clear. We are acutely aware that the people depend upon Us, and have constantly examined Our conscience, being deeply afraid that Our policies are not yet appropriate, and We are not able to induce a harmonious response from Heaven above.[8]

Neither the emperor's anxious tone nor his admission of the tenuous hold of the dynasty's mandate has any precedent in Qing imperial discourse on the chastity cult. Indeed, such expressions of insecurity contrast dramatically with the self-assured pronouncements of the Yongzheng and Qianlong Emperors as they asserted the state's prerogative to distinguish proper and improper expressions of chastity and its potency in transforming customs and rectifying morals. Xianfeng went on to excuse this major relaxation of award standards by pointing out that only twenty to thirty such widow suicide cases were submitted for canonization every year. "If we bestow honors on them, it will be sufficient to revive weakened customs and encourage the Three Bonds." Thus he recommended canonization "to comfort their chaste souls," a phrase used occasionally by eighteenth-century emperors when they granted state honors to women who were technically ineligible but whose suffering was particularly moving. Widow suicides canonized under the new rules carried a completely different political meaning and served a different political function from that of chastity models of the High Qing era. These women, like those caught up in bandit attacks and rebellions, were constructed as pathetic victims, not purposeful heroines. By canonizing such women, the state made them models, not of virtue to be emulated, but of its own benevolent concern for its helpless subjects, trapped, like the dynasty itself, in situations of crisis beyond their control. In the High Qing, it was the chaste widow with her fancy private arch outside her gate who epitomized the civilized and dutiful subject of a powerful and glorious empire. By the late Qing the chastity martyr was the predominant female icon of the realm. Publicized in the hundreds on collective arches on the public highways, chastity martyrs embodied the noble righteousness of a besieged country, asserting the dynasty's moral legitimacy despite military and economic crisis.

Taiping-era discourse on the state cult was consumed with the problems of maintaining an effective award system in the midst of social chaos and dislocation, declining state control, and wartime conditions that created unprecedented numbers of martyrs. Concerns about the effectiveness and integrity of the system were expressed in a desperate tone that suggests the degree to which the High Qing chastity bureaucracy effectively linked dynastic legitimacy to its normative function to promote proper gender and moral order. In 1854, the Xianfeng Emperor simplified procedures and extended responsibility for searching out martyrs to military authorities in order to manifest state recognition of martyrs as quickly as possible. He stipulated that rather than waiting to submit rosters of eligible women for Board of Rites approval at the end of each year, local military and civil officials should immediately construct collective arches and enter tablets for martyrs (gentry and commoners) in local chastity shrines and then report to the Board of Rites.[9] Concerned that the massive dislocations of people during the rebellion would result in worthy women being overlooked, the dynasty in 1864 issued new procedures for dealing with martyrs and those eligible for chastity or filiality honors among refugee families. Displaced families of people martyred in the conquest of their hometowns were to submit requests for state honors to officials in the area they had fled to, who were to forward them to local officials in their home counties for investigation. In accordance with the expedited procedures laid down in 1854, they were to have their names inscribed on collective arches and tablets in the local shrine without going through the board approval process. Ordinary chaste widows, widow suicides, and filial children among refugees were to be considered for canonization together with those from the local area in which they sojourned, their hometowns inscribed with their names on collective arches and tablets.

Not surprisingly, decentralization of the award system, the lessening of oversight by board officials, and the effective anonymity of awardees discovered far from home led to new problems with cheating, corruption, and dereliction of duty on the part of local officials. In 1861, prompted by reports of widespread extortion in the award process in Guangdong Province, the dynasty called for strict punishments for local officials or *yamen* clerks who demanded bribes and special fees for recognition of chastity martyrs.[10] The Tongzhi Emperor issued new punishments for submitting false reports or names of nonexistent or undeserving women and made a point of emphasizing punishments for extortion of bribes from refugees.[11] In a striking demonstration of the critical function of the chastity cult in reproducing state legitimacy, the emperor in 1868 warned officials overwhelmed by postrebellion chaos not to "hope to avoid trouble and shirk responsibility" for maintaining the chastity cult and reminded them of the procedures for reporting on chastity awards. Faced with the daunting challenges of post-Taiping restoration, local defense forces were told to take charge of administering the award system and to give priority to reconstruction of local chastity shrines, arches, and stelae in accordance with the old construction guidelines stipulated by the Yongzheng Emperor when he first established the network of local shrines in more peaceful and prosperous times.[12]

Such was the context for the dynasty's final lowering of the standards for qualification as a chaste widow to a mere six years in 1871, putting state canonization within the reach of the mass of widows.[13] Mark Elvin has described the nineteenth-century chastity award system as "an assembly line,"[14] a term that certainly captures the effects of the streamlining of procedures and the phenomenal numbers of women awarded, often en masse. Yet if the system was geared up to canonize as many women as possible in every corner of the empire, its political function was hardly routine. As the Qing state lost its grip on local society, it created ever larger numbers of chastity models who served as local incarnations of the dynasty's legitimacy and its potency as the central arbiter of the normative order. Some scholars have interpreted state efforts to expand the chastity cult in this period as an attempt to promote orthodoxy in a context of growing social and economic chaos that made adherence to Neo-Confucian gender norms increasingly difficult.[15] But the perpetual lowering of standards in the last decades of the dynasty suggests not a fixation with orthodoxy but rather a desire to maintain and even enhance the vitality of the state's normative presence in society at all costs—even if this entailed substantial compromises of the dynasty's cherished principles.

The last edicts entered into the Qing administrative statutes for chastity awards in the early years of the Guangxu reign called for special measures to sleuth out chastity martyrs in families wiped out by the North China famine of 1877–78 and reiterated award procedures and time limits for investigations. By this time, however, the central government had already lost the initiative in making chastity awards to local bureaus for the investigation of chastity *(caifang zhongjie ju)* or loyalty *(caifang zhongyi ju)* managed and funded locally by gentry and county-level officials. These bureaus compiled and published lists and biographies of local martyrs and worthies based on their own research. Although they also submitted all eligible names for canonization by the Board of Rites, they pointedly recorded the names and deeds of those who did not qualify for imperial honors.[16] From the reign of Jiaqing onwards, local gentry played an increasing role in the maintenance of local Shrines to the Chaste and Filial, as they did in funding other local infrastructure and charitable institutions like homes for chaste widows. While magistrates took charge of the renovation of county chastity shrines in Hangzhou Prefecture during the Qianlong years, for example, repairs in the Jiaqing, Daoguang, and Xianfeng reigns and rebuilding after destruction by the Taipings were funded by donations from local gentry or locally resident officials.[17] In 1851, local gentry founded their own provincial shrine to chaste women, initiated searches for eligible women, and submitted rosters of their names for state canonization. The stele commemorating the shrine's founding expressed their view of the local functions of the state cult. "The bandit forces are spreading day by day throughout the mountains and rivers valleys. Therefore, now is the time to show unity and righteousness sufficient to prop up the Five Relationships and foster proper customs." Emphasizing how "our dynasty has flourished by emphasizing proper customs," the stele narrated the development of the Qing chastity cult and highlighted the stakes local elites had in it in such times of crisis.

The tenor and import of the state's interactions with local people in the nineteenth century, not to mention the dynamics of family and community conflicts over female virtue in the midst of war and economic collapse, have yet to be examined in any detail by historians. But it is striking that these local philanthropists identified the chastity cult as quintessentially a state institution, vital to the dynasty's legitimacy and firmly embedded in local society. In their view, the chastity models honored in local shrines manifested the normative presence of the state in local communities even as their own patronage of such state institutions diminished the state's role. They assumed that promotion of female virtue through the creation of chastity models was essential to the maintenance and defense of the political order. Even as the focus of the Qing chastity cult shifted from creating model subjects to commemorating model victims, officials and elites continued to link female virtue to state legitimacy and gave virtuous women a prominent place in political discourse, a place they continued to occupy well into the twentieth century.

The long-term effects of the political apotheosis of chastity in the eighteenth century, which gendered political discourse and political culture to an unprecedented degree, were subtle, complicated, yet unmistakable. State policies toward women and their virtue became integral to dynastic legitimacy to such an extent that as the dynasty collapsed at the turn of the twentieth century, chastity suicides and the chastity cult in general were among the most powerful symbols of the backward and authoritarian society held in place by the Qing state. As revolutionaries and reformers formulated new visions of a modern civilization, they saw the transformation of the family and gender order centered on chastity as a catalytic first step that would lay the proper foundation for the new society. Inspired by the New Culture radicals' articulation of the normative role of the state in creating a civilized citizenry for a strong modern nation, the Nationalist and Communist regimes intruded purposefully into family life, facilitating the predominance of the conjugal over the patrilineal model of patriarchy in the law, social practice, and popular imagination.[18] The vast common ideological ground underneath the political differences of these groups speaks to the perpetuation of Chinese expectations about the relationship between state and society and the role of gender within it. Despite their rejection of the content of Qing gender norms, modern intellectuals' and state builders' expectations about the catalytic importance of gender ideals and the potential and responsibility of the state to "awaken" its citizens by reforming, civilizing, and regulating them were shaped by Qing political culture and practice of state-subject relations.[19]

Notes

INTRODUCTION

1. Liu Jihua, "Zhongguo zhenjie guannian de lishi yanbian" [The historical evolution of the chastity concept in China] (1934), reprinted in *Zhongguo funüshi lunji, siji* [Collected essays on Chinese women's history, vol. 4], ed. Bao Jialin (Taibei: Daoxiang chubanshe, 1995), p. 128. This first generation of historical discourse on the late imperial chastity cult includes Chen Dongyuan, *Zhongguo funü shenghuo shi* [A history of the lives of Chinese women] (1937; reprint, Taibei: Taiwan shangwu yinshuguan, 1997), especially pp. 177–83, 241–46; Gao Mai, "Woguo zhenjietang zhidu de yanbian" [The evolution of the system of chaste widow halls in our country] (1935), reprinted in *Zhongguo funüshi lunji* [Collected essays on Chinese women's history], ed. Bao Jialin (Taibei: Daoxiang chubanshe, 1979), pp. 205–11; Dong Jiazun, "Lidai jiefu lienü de tongji" [Historical statistics on chaste widows and chastity martyrs] (1937), reprinted in Bao Jialin, *Zhongguo funüshi lunji*, pp. 111–17.

2. Susan Mann, *Precious Records: Women in China's Long Eighteenth Century* (Stanford, Calif.: Stanford University Press, 1997), and "Widows in the Kinship, Class, and Community Structures of Qing Dynasty China," *Journal of Asian Studies* 46, no. 1 (1987): 37–56; Katherine Carlitz, "Shrines, Governing-Class Identity, and the Cult of Widow Fidelity in Mid-Ming Jiangnan," *Journal of Asian Studies* 56, no. 3 (1997): 612–40, and "The Daughter, the Singing Girl, and the Seduction of Suicide," in *Passionate Women: Female Suicide in Late Imperial China*, ed. Paul S. Ropp, Paola Zamperini, and Harriet T. Zurndorfer (Leiden: E. J. Brill, 2001), pp. 22–46; Dorothy Ko, *Teachers of the Inner Chambers: Women and Culture in Seventeenth-Century China* (Stanford, Calif.: Stanford University Press, 1994); T'ien Ju-k'ang, *Male Anxiety and Female Chastity: A*

Comparative Study of Chinese Ethical Values in Ming-Ch'ing Times (Leiden: E. J. Brill, 1988).

3. Yuasa Yukihiko, "Shindai ni okeru fujin kaihō ron: Rikyō to ningen teki shizen" [On women's emancipation in the Qing: *Lijiao* versus human nature], *Nippon-Chūgoku gakkaihō* 4 (1952): 111–25; Yamazaki Jun'ichi, "Shinchō ni okeru setsu-retsu zokuhyō ni tsuite" [On awards for virtuous widowhood in the Qing dynasty], *Chūgoku koten kenkyū* 15, no. 12 (1967): 46–66; Paul S. Ropp, "The Seeds of Change: Reflections on the Condition of Women in the Early and Mid-Ching," *Signs* 2, no. 1 (1976): 5–23; Ann Waltner, "Widows and Remarriage in Ming and Early Qing China," in *Women in China: Current Directions in Historical Scholarship*, ed. Richard W. Guisso and Stanley Johannesen (Youngstown, N.Y.: Philo Press, 1981), pp. 129–46; Mark Elvin, "Female Virtue and the State in China," *Past and Present* 104 (August 1984): 111–52; Mann, "Widows."

4. These arguments are developed in Chow Kai-wing, *The Rise of Confucian Ritualism in Late Imperial China: Ethics, Classics, and Lineage Discourse* (Stanford, Calif.: Stanford University Press, 1994). See also Mann, *Precious Records*; Matthew H. Sommer, *Sex, Law, and Society in Late Imperial China* (Stanford, Calif.: Stanford University Press, 2000); and Harriet T. Zurndorfer, "Han-Hsüeh, 'Evidential Research,' and Female Chastity: A Re-examination of Intellectual Attitudes and Social Ideals in 18th Century China," in *Thought and Law in Qin and Han China: Studies Dedicated to Anthony Hulsewe on the Occasion of His Eightieth Birthday*, ed. W. L. Idema and E. Zürcher (Leiden: E. J. Brill, 1990), pp. 208–24.

5. See especially Sommer, *Sex, Law, and Society*, and T'ien Ju-k'ang, *Male Anxiety and Female Chastity*.

6. Ko, *Teachers of the Inner Chambers*, pp. 292–93.

7. Mann, *Precious Records*, p. 221.

8. The years are Qianlong (QL) 4 (1739), 5 (1740), 18 (1753), 32 (1767), 45 (1780), and 60 (1795). The Qianlong reign is the first for which we have large numbers of extant cases. I collected these cases during a year of research in the archive in 1994–95. Due to the vagaries of archival copying, I have a rather skewed distribution of cases over these years. I collected 30 cases from QL 4; 141 from QL 5; 417 from QL 18; 131 from QL 32; 80 from QL 45; and 67 from QL 60.

9. Most extant case memorials are of two types, reflecting two different stages of the review process. The first type, provincial memorials *(tongben)* from provincial governors or governors-general, presented cases that had made their way up the levels of the judicial bureaucracy to the Board of Punishments and were rescripted for further review by the Three High Courts of Adjudicature *(sanfasi)*. The second type, called board memorials *(buben)*, were the product of this next stage of joint review by the Three High Courts, which recommended acceptance or rejection of the governor's sentence to the emperor. Usually the rescript on these presented a final confirmation of the sentence, but occasionally it recommended further deliberation by the board or the Nine Ministers, a group composed of leading advisors to the emperor. See Zhang Jinfan, *Zhongguo fazhi shi* [A history of the Chinese legal system] (Beijing: Zhonghua shuju, 1998), pp. 586–87; Silas Wu, *Communication and Control in Late Imperial China: Evolution of the Palace Memorial System, 1693–1735* (Cambridge, Mass.: Harvard University Press, 1970), pp. 27–33; Silas Hsiu-Liang Wu, "The Memorial Sys-

tems of the Ch'ing Dynasty (1644–1911)," *Harvard Journal of Asiatic Studies* 27 (1967): 7–75; Shiga Shūzō, "Criminal Procedure in the Ch'ing Dynasty—with Emphasis on Its Administrative Character and Some Allusion to Its Historical Antecedents (I)," *Memoirs of the Research Department of the Tōyō Bunko* 32 (1974): 1–45, and "Criminal Procedure in the Ch'ing Dynasty—with Emphasis on Its Administrative Character and Some Allusion to Its Historical Antecedents (II)," *Memoirs of the Research Department of the Tōyō Bunko* 33 (1975): 115–38.

10. These processes of editing have been traced in Yasuhiko Karasawa, "Between Speech and Writing: Textuality of the Written Record of Oral Testimony in Qing Legal Cases," *Chūgoku shakai to bunka* 10 (1995): 212–50.

11. Natalie Zemon Davis was a pioneer in reading the social and cultural history between the lines of legal records constructed according to narrative and judicial conventions in her *Fiction in the Archives: Pardon Tales and Their Tellers in Sixteenth-Century France* (Stanford, Calif.: Stanford University Press, 1987).

12. Although criminal cases do not represent typical behavior or moral attitudes, they offer glimpses of the larger social and cultural landscape that is the context for this extreme behavior. Moreover, the participants in cases of sexual assault, domestic violence, and homicide arising out of adultery were not career criminals but ordinary people whose conflicts spun out of control. The violence that got them entangled with the state was often an extreme form of more routine encounters. Studies that use these memorials to examine aspects of social history include Thomas M. Buoye, *Manslaughter, Markets, and Moral Economy: Violent Disputes over Property Rights in Eighteenth-Century China* (Cambridge: Cambridge University Press, 2000), and Melissa MaCauley, *Social Power and Legal Culture: Litigation Masters in Late Imperial China* (Stanford, Calif.: Stanford University Press, 1998).

13. The flexible and even experimental approach of Yuan dynasty rulers to Chinese gender norms, kinship rules, and property arrangements has been explored in Bettina Birge, *Women, Property, and Confucian Reaction in Sung and Yüan China (960–1368)* (New York: Cambridge University Press, 2002). The complex interplay between Chinese civilization and Manchu cultural priorities and values has been the central theme of much of the recent scholarship on Qing political culture and identity. See, for example, Evelyn S. Rawski, *The Last Emperors: A Social History of Qing Imperial Institutions* (Berkeley: University of California Press, 1998); Pamela Kyle Crossley, *A Translucent Mirror: History and Identity in Qing Imperial Ideology* (Berkeley: University of California Press, 1999); and Mark Elliot, *The Manchu Way: The Eight Banners and Ethnic Identity in Late Imperial China* (Stanford, Calif.: Stanford University Press, 2001).

14. This element of cultural flexibility figures prominently in accounts of the Qing conquest such as Frederic Wakeman, Jr., *The Great Enterprise: The Manchu Reconstruction of Imperial Order in Seventeenth-Century China*, 2 vols. (Berkeley: University of California Press, 1985).

15. In addition to presiding over public rites honoring virtuous women and men at state shrines, magistrates sponsored public readings and performances of the Kangxi Emperor's Sacred Edict, which, with its generalized injunctions to esteem filial piety and promote propriety and obedience to superiors, was a favored touchstone for advocates of moral transformation *(jiaohua)*. Victor H. Mair, "Lan-

guage and Ideology in the Written Popularizations of the *Sacred Edict*," in *Popular Culture in Late Imperial China*, ed. David Johnson, Andrew J. Nathan, and Evelyn S. Rawski (Berkeley: University of California Press, 1985), pp. 325–59.

16. Sommer, *Sex, Law, and Society*, p. 309.

17. Ibid., p. 10.

18. Disputes between widows and their in-laws over property have been examined extensively by Kathryn Bernhardt, *Women and Property in China, 960–1949* (Stanford, Calif.: Stanford University Press, 1999), pp. 47–72, and Sommer, *Sex, Law, and Society*, pp. 166–209.

PART ONE PROLOGUE

1. XKTB, QL 18.2.19, 181.8 and QL 18.7.10, 194.1.

2. For an elaboration of the notion of "chastity-centered virtue," see Janet M. Theiss, "Femininity in Flux: Gendered Virtue and Social Conflict in the Mid-Qing Courtroom," in *Chinese Femininities/Chinese Masculinities: An Introductory Reader*, ed. Susan Brownell and Jeffrey Wasserstrom (Berkeley: University of California Press, 2002).

3. Wang Yuelin, comp., *Puan zhou zhi* [Gazetteer of Puan District] (n.p., 1758), *juan* 22, p. 7b. This gazetteer, compiled by the district magistrate, provided extensive and derisive descriptions of this and other local Miao customs that did not conform to Han notions of propriety. It noted, in particular, that local Miao wives made long visits home during the busy agricultural season to help their families. This was precisely the context for Aguan's visit home on this occasion. Regular, short visits home were common among Chinese women, but they were frequently a source of familial and spousal conflict (see Chapter 4). The classic study of delayed-transfer marriage in South China is Marjorie Topley, "Marriage Resistance in Rural Kwangtung," in *Women in Chinese Society*, ed. Margery Wolf and Roxane Witke (Stanford, Calif.: Stanford University Press, 1975), pp. 67–88. A more in-depth examination of the subject is provided by Janice E. Stockard, *Daughters of the Canton Delta: Marriage Patterns and Economic Strategies in South China, 1860–1930* (Stanford, Calif.: Stanford University Press, 1989). For a critique of Topley and Stockard's assumptions about the origins, nature, spread, and implications of the practice, see Helen F. Siu, "Where Were the Women? Rethinking Marriage Resistance and Regional Culture in South China," *Late Imperial China* 11, no. 2 (1990): 32–62.

4. *Jian* (illicit sex) is a judicial, not a colloquial, term, the use of which highlights the fact that quoted testimony in such criminal case memorials is not verbatim, though it simulates vernacular speech. Instead, it represents an edited version of investigative interrogations or courtroom testimony. In this case, the testimonies of the Miao participants probably had to be translated into Chinese as well. On the process of recording and creating judicial testimony, see Yasuhiko Karasawa, "Between Speech and Writing: Textuality of the Written Record of Oral Testimony in Qing Legal Cases," *Chūgoku shakai to bunka* 10 (1995): 212–50. For a discussion of the bureaucratic rules shaping judicial reports of homicide in particular, see Thomas Buoye, "Suddenly Murderous Intent Arose: Bureaucratization and Benevolence in Eighteenth-Century Qing Homicide Re-

ports," *Late Imperial China* 16, no. 2 (1995): 66–68. On the judicial construction of *jian* in the Qing, see Matthew H. Sommer, *Sex, Law, and Society in Late Imperial China* (Stanford, Calif.: Stanford University Press, 2000).

5. Wang Yuelin, *Puan zhou zhi, juan* 3, p. 7b. Central state control over the entire province of Guizhou was tenuous and frequently contested or resisted through rebellion throughout the Qing. On the Qing conquest of the region and resistance to it, see Herold J. Wiens, *Han Chinese Expansion in South China* (originally published in 1954 as *China's March to the Tropics*; reprint, Hamden, Conn.: Shoe String Press, 1967), and Robert D. Jenks, *Insurgency and Social Disorder in Guizhou: The "Miao" Rebellion, 1854–1873* (Honolulu: University of Hawaii Press, 1994). The development and implementation of the *gaitu guiliu* policy have been discussed extensively. See, for example, Feng Erkang, *Yongzheng zhuan* [A biography of the Yongzheng Emperor] (Beijing: Renmin chubanshe, 1985), pp. 377–416; Huang Pei, *Autocracy at Work: A Study of the Yung-cheng Period, 1723–1735* (Bloomington: Indiana University Press, 1974), pp. 273–301; Kent C. Smith, "Ch'ing Policy and the Development of Southwest China: Aspects of Ortai's Governor-Generalship, 1726–1731" (Ph.D. diss., Yale University, 1970); and Charles Patterson Giersch, "Qing China's Reluctant Subjects: Indigenous Communities and Empire along the Yunnan Frontier" (Ph.D. diss., Yale University, 1998).

6. Within the Chinese kinship system, the closeness of relationships was described in terms of five degrees of mourning, ranging from the three-year mourning that children were supposed to perform for parents or wives for their husbands to the three-month mourning performed, for example, for distant cousins. The mourning system also reflected family hierarchy. Thus, for example, while a son performed the first degree of mourning for his father, a father performed only the second degree of mourning for his son. The Qing Code, like its predecessors, used the system of mourning relationships to assess the severity of not only crimes of incest but also other crimes committed between relatives. Crimes perpetrated by senior relatives against juniors were punished less severely than crimes committed by juniors against seniors. For an explanation of the judicial use of the system of mourning relationships, see Derk Bodde and Clarence Morris, *Law in Imperial China Exemplified by 190 Ch'ing Dynasty Cases, Translated from the Hsing-an hui-lan* (Philadelphia: University of Pennsylvania Press, 1967), pp. 35–38.

7. The contexts and motivations for women's suicides will be addressed in detail in Part Four.

8. Wang Yuelin, *Puan zhou zhi, juan* 19, pp. 1b–2a. This request came in the context of Zhang's many programs to consolidate Qing control of Guizhou after he successfully led the suppression of the huge Miao rebellion in the province between 1735 and 1737. Arthur W. Hummel, ed., *Eminent Chinese of the Ch'ing Period* (1943; reprint, Taibei: SMC Publishing, 1991), p. 44. In 1738, Zhang also requested imperial honors for a mother and daughter who died defending themselves from the "Miao bandits" in this rebellion. DQHDSL, *juan* 404, QL 3.

9. Melissa Macauley has demonstrated just how widespread knowledge of the judicial system was among ordinary peasant families and the frequency with which they took their grievances and conflicts to court. Melissa Macauley, *Social*

Power and Legal Culture: Litigation Masters in Late Imperial China (Stanford, Calif.: Stanford University Press, 1998).

10. The family's emphasis on concerns of honor and face stands in contrast to descriptions of the materialism of the Miao, who, according to the Han authors of the district gazetteer, in cases of illicit sex simply "hand over silver to ameliorate [the situation]." Wang Yuelin, *Puan zhou zhi, juan* 22, p. 7b. Paola Paderni has explored the complexities of the definition of honor in Qing China and its social implications for women in two articles: "An Appeal Case of Honor in Eighteenth Century China," in *Ming Qing Yanjiu* [Ming Qing studies] (Naples: Istituto Universitario Orientale, 1992), pp. 87–97, and "Le rachat de l'honneur perdu: Le suicide des femmes dans la Chine du XVIII siècle" [The recovery of lost honor: Female suicide in eighteenth-century China], *Études Chinoises* 10, nos. 1–2 (1991): 135–60.

11. Wang Huizu, "Lun qinmin," in *Huangchao jingshi wenbian* [Statecraft compendium from the Qing dynasty], comp. He Changling (1826; reprint, Taibei: Guofeng, 1963), *juan* 22, p. 7a. This essay is part of Wang's classic handbook on local administration, *Xuezhi yishuo*. First published in 1793 and republished numerous times throughout the nineteenth century, this handbook was considered a model of its genre for the rest of the dynasty. For a history of its publication, see Pierre-Etienne Will, "Official Handbooks and Anthologies of China: A Descriptive and Critical Bibliography," unpublished manuscript, pp. 167–68.

12. Wang Yuelin, *Puan zhou zhi, juan* 9, pp. 8b–9a.

CHAPTER 1. DEFINING GENDER ORTHODOXY

1. Bettine Birge, *Women, Property, and Confucian Reaction in Sung and Yüan China (960–1368)* (New York: Cambridge University Press, 2002). See also Beverly J. Bossler, *Powerful Relations: Kinship, Status, and the State in Sung China (960–1279)* (Cambridge, Mass.: Harvard University Press, 1998).

2. Birge, *Women, Property*, pp. 200–282.

3. Katherine Carlitz, "Shrines, Governing-Class Identity, and the Cult of Widow Fidelity in Mid-Ming Jiangnan," *Journal of Asian Studies* 56, no. 3 (1997): 612–40, and "The Daughter, the Singing Girl, and the Seduction of Suicide," in *Passionate Women: Female Suicide in Late Imperial China*, ed. Paul S. Ropp, Paola Zamperini, and Harriet T. Zurndorfer (Leiden: E. J. Brill, 2001), pp. 22–46; Fei Si-yen, *You dianfan dao guifan: Cong Mingdai zhenjie lienu de bianshi yu liuchuan kan zhenjie guannian de yangehua* [From model to standard: The development and rising popularity of increasingly rigid views on female chastity in the Ming dynasty] (M.A. thesis, National Taiwan University, 1996).

4. Fei Si-yen provides the first comprehensive examination of the Ming chastity cult as a state, social, and cultural phenomenon. The lack of Ming parallels for the kinds of sources I use in this study makes it impossible to do a full comparison of the two dynasties' policies on chastity. Nevertheless, Fei's reading of Ming ritual regulations suggests the limited nature of the Ming state's aims: to promote chastity by providing exemplary models for women to follow. There is no indication that concerns about chastity permeated Ming policies the way they did in the Qing, nor did the Ming state have the Qing's ambitions about the

potential for the state to morally transform the populace. See Fei Si-yen, *You dianfan dao guifan*.

5. For an analysis of the origins of the chastity cult in the late fifteenth and early sixteenth centuries, its meaning for Ming literati, and its links with the cult of *qing*, see Carlitz, "Shrines" and "The Daughter." Paola Zamperini also explores the significance of *qing* for the portrayal of female suicide in late imperial fiction in an article entitled "Untamed Hearts: Eros and Suicide in Late Imperial Chinese Fiction," in Ropp, Zamperini, and Zurndorfer, *Passionate Women*, pp. 77–104.

6. On the Qing notion of universal rulership and its diverse inspirations in Buddhist, Confucian, and Central Asian political thought, see Pamela Kyle Crossley, *A Translucent Mirror: History and Identity in Qing Imperial Ideology* (Berkeley: University of California Press, 1999).

7. Ibid.; Norman Kutcher, *Mourning in Late Imperial China: Filial Piety and the State* (New York: Cambridge University Press, 1999); Mark C. Elliot, *The Manchu Way: The Eight Banners and Ethnic Identity in Late Imperial China* (Stanford, Calif.: Stanford University Press, 2001).

8. Petitions for Han commoner awardees passed through review at each level of the bureaucracy, while those for bannerwomen were reviewed by the various levels of the banner command structure. For both, awards consisted of a testimonial of merit *(jingbiao)*, thirty taels *(liang)* of silver for the family to construct a memorial arch *(paifang)*, and, after 1661, rice for chaste widows. Awards for members of the imperial clan were reviewed by the Imperial Clan Court and consisted of sacrificial wine, mutton, paper, and differential quantities of silver and satin depending on rank. DQHDSL, *juan* 403, SZ 9, 10, 11.

The Qing also promoted, and in some cases enforced, different norms of propriety, chastity, inheritance rights, marriage practices, and dress for Manchu and Han women. See Elliot, *The Manchu Way*, pp. 246–55, and "Manchu Widows and Ethnicity in Qing China," *Comparative Studies in Society and History* 41, no. 1 (1999): 33–71.

9. Footbinding was banned by the Shunzhi Emperor in 1645 and again by Kangxi in 1664. These bans appear to have failed completely and were abandoned. Widow suicide was banned in 1688, *gegu* in 1652. Both of these bans appear to have been much more effective and were not rescinded until the nineteenth century (DQHDSL, *juan* 403, KX 27 and SZ 9).

10. On Qing attitudes and policies toward female suicide, see Elliot, "Manchu Widows," and Janet M. Theiss, "Managing Martyrdom: Female Suicide and Statecraft in Mid-Qing China," in Ropp, Zamperini, and Zurndorfer, *Passionate Women*, pp. 47–76.

11. DQHDSL, *juan* 403, KX 27.

12. DQHDSL, *juan* 403, KX 11, 51, 52, 54.

13. DQHDSL, *juan* 403, YZ 11. In the same year the Yongzheng Emperor issued an edict initiating criminal penalties for men whose propositions led to such suicides. DQHDSL, *juan* 806, YZ 11.

14. On this orthodox revival and the role of gender norms within it, see Chow Kai-wing, *The Rise of Confucian Ritualism in Late Imperial China: Ethics, Classics, and Lineage Discourse* (Stanford, Calif.: Stanford University Press, 1994).

15. On Yongzheng's reforms, see Feng Erkang, *Yongzheng zhuan* [A biography of the Yongzheng Emperor] (Beijing: Renmen chubanshe, 1985); Huang Pei, *Autocracy at Work: A Study of the Yung-cheng Period, 1723–1735* (Bloomington: Indiana University Press, 1974); Madeleine Zelin, *The Magistrate's Tael: Rationalizing Fiscal Reform in Eighteenth-Century China* (Berkeley: University of California Press, 1984); and Pierre-Etienne Will, *Bureaucracy and Famine in Eighteenth-Century China* (Stanford, Calif.: Stanford University Press, 1990). On the increasing bureaucratization of the dynasty's approach to managing official mourning leaves, see Kutcher, *Mourning in Late Imperial China.*

16. Both the civilizing project and the statecraft agenda to improve the practical effectiveness of governmental bureaucracy have a long history in Chinese political discourse. What was new in the Qing, as William Rowe has argued, was the linkage of the two goals in an approach to statecraft that combined, as he puts it, "pragmatism and moralism." Rowe argues that Chen Hongmou typified this new approach to statecraft thinking. As we will see in subsequent chapters, mid-Qing policies to reform gender order were very much part of this statecraft discourse linking moral transformation to the improvement of the institutional relationship between state and society. On statecraft thinking in the Qing, see William T. Rowe, *Saving the World: Chen Hongmou and Elite Consciousness in Eighteenth-Century China* (Stanford, Calif.: Stanford University Press, 2001), pp. 2–3 and passim. On the civilizing mission of the Qing, see also R. Bin Wong, *China Transformed: Historical Change and the Limits of European Experience* (Ithaca, N.Y.: Cornell University Press, 1997), pp. 114–22. For an overview of the history of the concept of "civilizing" *(jiaohua)* in Chinese political thought, see Wang Gungwu, "The Chinese Urge to Civilize: Reflections on Change," *Journal of Asian History* 18, no. 1 (1984): 1–34.

17. Mark Elvin traces the evolution of these policies in "Female Virtue and the State in China," *Past and Present* 104 (August 1984): 111–52.

18. DQHDSL, *juan* 403, YZ 1.

19. DQHDSL, *juan* 403, YZ 1.

20. On the development of Hunan in the Qing, see Peter C. Perdue, *Exhausting the Earth: State and Peasant in Hunan 1500–1850* (Cambridge, Mass.: Council on East Asian Studies, Harvard University, 1987).

21. *Shanhua xian zhi* [Gazetteer of Shanhua County] (1818), *juan* 11.

22. *Wuxi Jinkui xian zhi* [Gazetteer of Wuxi and Jinkui Counties] (1881), *juan* 11–12.

23. Susan Mann has convincingly demonstrated the effectiveness of Qing bans on widow suicide in "Suicide and Survival: Exemplary Widows in the Late Empire," in *Chūgoku no dentō shakai to kazoku: Yanagida Setsuko sensei koki kinen ronshu* [Family and society in traditional China: Essays in honor of Professor Yanagida Setsuko] (Tokyo: Kyuko shoin, 1993), pp. 23–39.

24. DQHDSL, *juan* 403, YZ 6. My translation of this passage varies somewhat from that in Elvin, "Female Virtue."

25. Yongzheng's emphasis on the practical social effects of virtue rather than fulfillment of particular orthodox but perhaps socially disruptive ideals may also help to explain the disdain he showed for excessive attention to female chastity in Manchu documents. See Elliot, *The Manchu Way,* p. 253.

26. The contrast between the passionate devotion of the chastity martyr and the duty-bound loyalty of the chaste widow appears to reflect the competing visions of morality that Maram Epstein traces within Qing philosophy and fiction: as the enactment of orthodoxy or as an expression of emotional authenticity. See Maram Epstein, *Competing Discourses: Orthodoxy, Authenticity and Engendered Meanings in Late Imperial Chinese Fiction* (Cambridge, Mass.: Harvard University Asia Center, 2001).

27. See Zelin, *The Magistrate's Tael*, pp. 79–82, for a detailed discussion of Yongzheng's practical evaluation of the circumstances that created official corruption.

28. Meltage fees were collected by local officials to make up for the loss of silver that resulted when silver tax payments were melted down into larger ingots for transport to central government coffers. The Yongzheng reforms stipulated that these fees remain at the local level to be spent on local needs rather than being remitted to the central government. See Zelin, *The Magistrate's Tael*, for an exhaustive examination of the development of these reforms and their effects. Feng Erkang identifies emphasis on loyalty, prioritization of concrete practical results, and optimism about the perfectibility of "governance by people" *(renzhi)* as hallmarks of Yongzheng's policies. All of these themes are evident in his approach to female chastity and moral reform more broadly. Feng Erkang, *Yongzheng zhuan*, pp. 82–86.

29. The term often appears in contexts describing a Qing ruler's paternalistic relationship with his closest officials. It was also used prominently in the Yongzheng Emperor's "Great Righteousness Resolving Confusion" *(Dayi juemi lu)*, a collection of documents compiled to respond to the anti-Manchu writings of Zeng Jing (1679–1736) in 1730. For a discussion of Yongzheng's usage of the term and its Manchu connotations, see Crossley, *A Translucent Mirror*, pp. 140–41 n. 15.

30. On the differences between Manchu and Confucian concepts of loyalty and hierarchy, see Kutcher, *Mourning in Late Imperial China*, pp. 153–94, and Crossley, *A Translucent Mirror*, pp. 125–27, 138–41.

31. DQHDSL, *juan* 403, YZ 6.

32. DQHDSL, *juan* 403, YZ13. Li Wei was one of Yongzheng's closest advisors and a point man in his fiscal reform policies and anticorruption campaigns. See Zelin, *The Magistrate's Tael*, pp. 160–61, and Arthur W. Hummel, ed., *Eminent Chinese of the Ch'ing Period* (1943; reprint, Taibei: SMC Publishing, 1991), pp. 720–21. Gao Qizhuo was twice governor-general of Yunnan-Guizhou under Yongzheng and was a critical player in the conquest of the Southwest. His wife, Cai Wan, was a well-known poetess and daughter of a Han bannerman who played a major role in the Manchu conquest in the Shunzhi-Kangxi periods. It is said that she wrote many of his memorials. Her mother may have been a former concubine of Wu Sangui, captured by her father. See Hummel, *Eminent Chinese*, pp. 721, 735, 920, and Charles Patterson Giersch, "Qing China's Reluctant Subjects: Indigenous Communities and Empire along the Yunnan Frontier" (Ph.D. diss., Yale University, 1998).

33. DQHDSL, *juan* 403, YZ 13.

34. DQHDSL, *juan* 403, YZ 1.

35. Investigations for chastity canonization among nomadic peoples who had moved from Heilongjiang to garrisons in Yili were forbidden in 1767 (DQHDSL, *juan* 403, QL 32). However, an edict of 1799, though noting the difficulties of investigating chaste widow claims among nomads, suggested that canonizations be granted to certain tribal *(buluo)* women of the Soluns, Chahars, Oirats, and (Turkic) Muslims in the Yili garrisons "in order to demonstrate Our intention to show benevolence uniformly among subjects of all tribes" (DQHDSL, *juan* 403, JQ 4). The specific criteria for making chastity awards among such women is not clear in the DQHDSL, but this aspect of Qing chastity policies deserves further research. I am indebted to James Millward for sorting out the status of the peoples referred to in these edicts.

36. DQHDSL, *juan* 403, YZ 4.

37. DQHDSL, *juan* 403, QL 3.

38. DQHDSL, *juan* 403, QL 39. On the Wang Lun Uprising, see Susan Naquin, *Shantung Rebellion: The Wang Lun Uprising of 1774* (New Haven, Conn.: Yale University Press, 1981).

39. DQHDSL, *juan* 403, QL 47, 48.

CHAPTER 2. STATECRAFT AND GENDER ORDER

1. On state promotion of "proper" women's handicrafts, see Susan Mann, "Household Handicrafts and State Policy in Qing Times," in *To Achieve Security and Wealth: The Qing Imperial State and the Economy 1644–1911*, ed. Jane Kate Leonard and John R. Watt (Ithaca, N.Y.: Cornell University East Asia Program, 1992), pp. 75–95.

2. Pierre-Etienne Will maps the trajectory of this campaign in "The 1744 Annual Audits of Magistrate Activity and Their Fate," *Late Imperial China*, 18, no. 2 (1998): 12–14. William Rowe interprets its significance as a manifestation of the intertwined agendas of *jiaoyang* and bureaucratic reform and notes the critical role of Chen Hongmou in the conceptual development and implementation of this project of "state activism as an instrument of sociocultural reform." William T. Rowe, *Saving the World: Chen Hongmou and Elite Consciousness in Eighteenth-Century China* (Stanford, Calif.: Stanford University Press, 2001), p. 361.

3. On the maturation of the Grand Council at the beginning of the Qianlong reign and its impact on the policy-making process, see Beatrice S. Bartlett, *Monarchs and Ministers: The Grand Council in Mid-Ch'ing China, 1723–1820* (Berkeley: University of California Press, 1991), pp. 137–99.

4. Despite the many differences between the approaches of Yongzheng and Qianlong to matters like fiscal and frontier policy, the latter fully embraced his father's civilizing mission and his view of the vital role of the bureaucracy in its implementation. William Rowe has recently reviewed the differences between the two emperors, suggesting, contrary to my own view here, that Qianlong retreated from pursuit of his father's cultural ambitions for the state, envisioning it to be far less intrusive in the affairs of local society. While this may have been true of his approach to economic and fiscal policy, I would argue that it most decidedly was not the case with his approach to the state's role as normative authority ex-

pressed in these reform policies and in the law. See Rowe, *Saving the World*, pp. 47–49.

5. This edict was reprinted in the first section of the 1758 edition of the gazetteer for Puan District, Guizhou Province, which recorded the canonization of the Miao woman Wang Aguan, who was featured in the Prologue to this section. Its prominent inclusion in the gazetteer for this newly constituted district, along with a series of other edicts from the Kangxi, Yongzheng, and Qianlong reigns on the governance and cultural reform of frontier regions, highlights the importance of moral transformation as a tool for imperial expansion. See Wang Yuelin, comp., *Puan zhouzhi* [Gazetteer of Puan District] (n.p., 1758), *juan* 1, pp. 10b–12a.

6. Memorial of Shi Jiqi, QL 8.12.11, LFZZ, doc. #0073–032, reel 5, pp. 0392–97.

7. Philip Kuhn documents Qianlong's particular paranoia about the loyalty and competence of his officials in *Soulstealers: The Chinese Sorcery Scare of 1768* (Cambridge, Mass.: Harvard University Press, 1990). Similarly paradoxical assumptions underlay Chen Hongmou's experiments with granting limited judicial powers to lineage heads in Jiangxi in 1742, and Chen arrived at similar conclusions about the importance of the state's role in local society. See Rowe, *Saving the World*, pp. 393–404.

8. QSL, QL 9.1, *renwu* day, *juan* 208.

9. Pierre-Etienne Will presents the contents of this edict in Will, "1744 Annual Audits," pp. 11–12.

10. For a detailed analysis of Nuoqin's memorial and the implementation of the campaign, see Will, "1744 Annual Audits," pp. 12–15.

11. Memorial of Ou Kanshan, QL 9.5.22, LFZZ, doc. #1456–020, reel 99, pp. 1098–1105.

12. Memorial of Zhou Renji, QL 11.12.11, ZPZZ, *lülilei, bao* 36, *juan* 56, and LFZZ, doc. #0283–017, reel #19, pp. 0403–6.

13. Ibid.

14. Will has suggested, on the basis of the limited number of extant memorials responding explicitly to Qianlong's edict, that the effects of this campaign were limited. But if we consider the manifestations of the *jiaohua* project in law, the impact appears much greater. Will, "The 1774 Annual Audits."

15. For an overview of substatutes dealing with adultery, see M. J. Meijer, *Murder and Adultery in Late Imperial China* (Leiden: E. J. Brill, 1991).

16. Janet M. Theiss, "Managing Martyrdom: Female Suicide and Statecraft in Mid-Qing China," in *Passionate Women: Female Suicide in Late Imperial China*, ed. Paul S. Ropp, Paola Zamperini, and Harriet T. Zurndorfer (Leiden: E. J. Brill, 2001), pp. 47–76.

17. DQHDSL, *juan* 403, QL 43.

18. DQHDSL, *juan* 403, QL 30.

19. Dai Yi emphasizes this contrast between Yongzheng and Qianlong in *Qianlongdi ji qi shidai* [Qianlong and his era] (Beijing: Zhongguo renmin daxue chubanshe, 1992), pp. 98–118. He finds rhetoric on the importance of compassion in imperial policies throughout Qianlong's own writings and pronouncements.

20. His paranoia is evident in his reversal of Yongzheng's lenient verdict on

the traitor Zeng Jing, his handling of the soul-stealing crisis, and his censorship policies, for example. See Pamela Kyle Crossley, *A Translucent Mirror: History and Identity in Qing Imperial Ideology* (Berkeley: University of California Press, 1999), Huang Pei, *Autocracy at Work: A Study of the Yung-cheng Period, 1723–1735* (Bloomington: Indiana University Press, 1974), Kuhn, *Soulstealers,* and R. Kent Guy, *The Emperor's Four Treasuries: Scholars and the State in the Late Ch'ien-lung Era* (Cambridge, Mass.: Harvard University Press, 1989), for extensive treatments of these policies.

21. On his attitudes toward management of officials, see Dai Yi, *Qianlongdi ji qi shidai,* pp. 124–54. On his views of local elites, see Zhu Yong, *Qingdai zongzu fa yanjiu* [A study of lineage law in the Qing] (Changsha: Hunan chubanshe, 1987), pp. 162–71.

22. The expansion of the Qing code to promote the policies of *jiaohua* and the chastity cult is an example of a larger trend in the Qing described by the legal scholar Zheng Qin as the "legalization of imperial policies" whereby "rules [were devised] to guarantee the implementation of the policies in question." Zheng Qin, "Pursuing Perfection: Formation of the Qing Code," *Modern China* 21, no. 3 (1995): 331. For a comparative discussion of the ways in which putative state builders envisioned the social and economic effects of the law, see Melissa Macauley, "A World Made Simple: Law and Property in the Ottoman and Qing Empires," *Journal of Early Modern History* 5, no. 4 (2001): 331–52.

23. Memorial of Chen Hongmou, QL 12.5.15, ZPZZ, *qita lei, bao* 34, *juan* 57.

24. Although Chen certainly exaggerated the relative culpability of women compared to their male partners in the crime of adultery, the case record shows that many women did initiate elopements or, at the very least, were willing partners in the abandonment of their husbands. See Paola Paderni, "I Thought I Would Have Some Happy Days: Women Eloping in Eighteenth-Century China," *Late Imperial China* 16, no. 1 (June 1995): 1–32.

25. Memorial of Chen Hongmou, QL 12.5.15, ZPZZ, *qita lei, bao* 34, *juan* 57. Male attitudes toward women's moral agency will be discussed in much greater depth in Part Four.

26. He Changling, comp., *Huangchao jingshi wenbian* [Statecraft compendium from the Qing dynasty] (1826; reprint, Taibei: Guofeng, 1963), *juan* 54, pp. 7b–8a.

27. Legalism emerged as a rival school of thought to Confucianism in the third century B.C.E. There were numerous differences between the two schools' approaches to governance and law. Most relevant for my purposes here was that Confucians assumed the inherent goodness and moral perfectibility of human beings and thus emphasized the efficacy of education and moral example as tools for the state's promotion of social harmony and moral reform. Legalists assumed that human beings were, for the most part, morally imperfectible and thus that moral suasion of any sort was useless. They argued instead that the state could achieve social stability and conformity with its aims only through a strict system of laws and regulations, including severe punishments for wrongdoing and specific rewards for fulfillment of one's duties. Although Confucianism eclipsed Legalism to become the dominant framework for Chinese social ethics and political

culture, Legalist ideas continued to be relevant in the development and implementation of law codes throughout Chinese history. For a discussion of Confucian and Legalist influences in the Qing Code, see, for example, Derk Bodde and Clarence Morris, *Law in Imperial China Exemplified by 190 Ch'ing Dynasty Cases, Translated from the Hsing-an hui-lan* (Philadelphia: University of Pennsylvania Press, 1967), pp. 17–51.

28. DQHDSL, *juan* 806.

29. Although anachronistic in some senses, the term *sexual harassment* is an accurate description for the behaviors covered in these substatutes, including unwanted verbal and physical gestures like propositions, flirtation, caressing, groping, and so on. Not unlike sexual harassment today, these gestures were understood to have potentially significant and dire consequences for the reputation of the women who were their objects. This topic is discussed at length in Part Four.

30. For an overview of the substatutes dealing with female suicide, see M. J. Meijer, "The Price of a P'ai-lou," *T'oung Pao* 67 (1981): 288–304.

31. The cangue *(jia hao)* was a large, heavy, rectangular collar worn around the neck as a form of punishment for a specified number of days, weeks, or months.

32. Memorial of Zhang Ruoai, QL 10.11.2, ZPZZ, *neizheng lei, bao* 33, *juan* 46.

33. DQHDSL, *juan* 825.

34. DQHDSL, *juan* 403, QL 24.

35. Matthew H. Sommer, *Sex, Law, and Society in Late Imperial China* (Stanford, Calif.: Stanford University Press, 2000). William Rowe, in his recent book on Chen Hongmou, argues for a strain of "protoindividualism" in his views, citing, among other elements, Chen's emphasis on the personal dignity of every individual and his preference for relying on individual moral autonomy in the pursuit of cultural and moral reform. Rowe, *Saving the World*, p. 323.

36. This theme will be addressed at much greater length in later chapters.

PART TWO PROLOGUE

1. This was the punishment mandated by the Qing Code for a husband who killed his wife, intentionally or unintentionally. Xue Yunsheng, *Duli cunyi* [Lingering doubts after reading the substatutes], ed. Huang Jingjia (Taibei: Chinese Materials and Research Aids Service Center, 1970), *juan* 36, p. 929, article 315.

2. XKTB, QL 32.5.18, 226.2.

3. This phrase is one of many formulaic descriptions that appear in case memorials of wives who did not follow the "wifely way."

4. Although the status of Chen's family as "lower gentry" by virtue of his father's possession of the *shengyuan* degree makes this case somewhat unusual, it is otherwise unremarkable: the archival record of criminal cases for the eighteenth century abounds with thousands of similar wife-killing cases, most of which also involved the husband's assertion that his wife failed to fulfill the wifely way and resulted in the same sentence. See Janet M. Theiss, "Dealing with Disgrace: The Negotiation of Female Virtue in Eighteenth-Century China" (Ph.D. diss., University of California, Berkeley, 1998), pp. 254–72.

5. Judging from the evidence provided by the case record, such large age differences between husband and wife were relatively unusual.

6. These included new books like Lan Dingyuan's *Nüxue* [Lessons for women] (n.d. [early eighteenth century]; reprint, n.p., 1897); Wang Huizu's *Shuangjietang yongxun* [Simple precepts from the Hall Enshrining a Pair of Chaste Widows] (1794; reprint, Taibei: Huawen shuju, 1970), and anthologies and reprints of classic texts like Chen Hongmou's *Jiaonü yigui* and the many editions of Yan Zhitui's *Yanshi jiaxun* from the Six Dynasties period and Yuan Cai's *Yuanshi shifan* from the Song. On women's education in the eighteenth century, see Susan Mann, *Precious Records: Women in China's Long Eighteenth Century* (Stanford, Calif.: Stanford University Press, 1997), "Grooming a Daughter for Marriage: Brides and Wives in the Mid-Ch'ing Period," in *Marriage and Inequality in Chinese Society*, ed. Rubie S. Watson and Patricia Buckley Ebrey (Berkeley: University of California Press, 1991), pp. 204–30, and "The Education of Daughters in the Mid-Ch'ing Period," in *Education and Society in Late Imperial China, 1600–1900*, ed. Benjamin A. Elman and Alexander Woodside (Berkeley: University of California Press, 1994), pp. 19–49. On the rising popularity of lineage instructions and handbooks for family life in this period, see also Charlotte Furth, "The Patriarch's Legacy: Household Instructions and the Transmission of Orthodox Values," in *Orthodoxy in Late Imperial China*, ed. Liu Kwang-ching (Berkeley: University of California Press, 1990), pp. 187–211.

7. Tang Yi's handbook is anthologized in Chen Hongmou's much-published collection of advice books for women, *Jiaonü yigui* [Bequeathed guidelines for instructing women], in *Wuzhong yigui* [Five sets of bequeathed guidelines] (1742; reprint, Shanghai: Jingwei jiaoyu lianhe chubanshe, 1935), p. 44.

8. Philip Huang, *Civil Justice in China: Representation and Practice in the Qing* (Stanford, Calif.: Stanford University Press, 1996), pp. 103–4, 110–37.

9. Philip Huang defines this "third realm" as an "intermediate realm" of "semiformal justice" between "the informal justice of community and kin mediation and the formal justice of court adjudication" where the two met and interacted. Ibid., p. 110.

CHAPTER 3. ENFORCING GENDER ORDER

1. This "map" of overlapping hierarchies, with the imperial court propagating orthodox values from the top of a huge bureaucracy down through mediating local elites, has long been the dominant paradigm for describing state-society relations in late imperial scholarship. Assessments of the effectiveness of imperial and elite hegemony have varied. Ch'ü T'ung-tsu, for example, presented a fairly optimistic view of a "status quo" that allowed the most powerful groups in society—officials, sub-bureaucratic *yamen* staff, and local gentry—to pursue their interests successfully and thus functioned effectively to maintain stability. Ch'ü T'ung-tsu, *Local Government in China under the Ch'ing* (1962; reprint, Cambridge, Mass.: Harvard Council on East Asian Studies, Harvard University, 1988). Hsiao Kung-chuan emphasized, on the contrary, the limits of the state's and elites' penetration of local society and thus their ability to maintain ideological control

at the local level. Hsiao Kung-chuan, *Rural China: Imperial Control in the Nineteenth Century* (Seattle: University of Washington Press, 1960).

Later critiques of this model of state-society relations have pointed out the vast variation in substate social structures and in the composition, power, and functions of local elites but have largely maintained the notion of elite hegemony within the framework of linear social hierarchy to describe the lines of communication and control in late imperial society. In the view of most scholars, the key cultural dynamic of the Ming and Qing periods was cultural integration through the popularization of elite values, most importantly female chastity, filial piety, patrilineal identity, and ritual orthodoxy. While granting that differences of dialect, gender, social position, and literacy levels created complex patterns of variation in the form, context, and content of expressions of cultural values and religious beliefs, scholars have, by and large, argued for the essential uniformity of core moral values, particularly those associated with family relationships and the conduct of everyday life. See, for example, the essays in *Popular Culture in Late Imperial China,* ed. David Johnson, Andrew J. Nathan, and Evelyn S. Rawski (Berkeley: University of California Press, 1985). Summarizing the findings of contributors to this seminal volume, Evelyn Rawski, for example, concludes simply, "In the late imperial period, all Chinese shared a common social vocabulary based on the acceptance of orthodox cultural models concerning the family." Evelyn Rawski, "Problems and Prospects," in Johnson, Nathan, and Rawski, *Popular Culture,* p. 405.

2. Memorial of Yinjishan (calling for the dissemination of Zhu Xi's manual on family ritual, the *Jiali*), QL 1.5.8, LFZZ, doc. #0293-002, reel 19, pp. 2109-12.

3. On family instructions, see Charlotte Furth, "The Patriarch's Legacy: Household Instructions and the Transmission of Orthodox Values," in *Orthodoxy in Late Imperial China,* ed. Liu Kwang-ching (Berkeley: University of California Press), 1990. On morality handbooks, particularly those dealing with women, see Susan Mann, "Grooming a Daughter for Marriage: Brides and Wives in the Mid-Ch'ing Period," in *Marriage and Inequality in Chinese Society,* ed. Rubie S. Watson and Patricia Buckley Ebrey (Berkeley: University of California Press, 1991), pp. 204-30, "The Education of Daughters in the Mid-Ch'ing Period," in *Education and Society in Late Imperial China, 1600-1900,* ed. Benjamin A. Elman and Alexander Woodside (Berkeley: University of California Press, 1994), and *Precious Records: Women in China's Long Eighteenth Century* (Stanford, Calif.: Stanford University Press, 1997). On ledgers of merit and demerit, see Cynthia J. Brokaw, *The Ledgers of Merit and Demerit: Social Change and Moral Order in Late Imperial China* (Princeton, N.J.: Princeton University Press, 1991).

4. On the role of ritual in conveying moral values, see Chow Kai-wing, *The Rise of Confucian Ritualism in Late Imperial China: Ethics, Classics, and Lineage Discourse* (Stanford, Calif.: Stanford University Press, 1994), and Patricia Buckley Ebrey, "The Liturgies for Sacrifices to Ancestors in Successive Versions of the 'Family Rituals,'" in *Ritual and Scripture in Chinese Popular Religion,* ed. David Johnson (Berkeley, Calif.: Publications of the Popular Culture Project,

1995), pp. 104–36. On the importance of ritual opera as a vehicle for moral education, see David Johnson, ed., *Ritual Opera, Operatic Ritual: "Mu-lien Rescues His Mother" in Chinese Popular Culture* (Berkeley: Publications of the Popular Culture Project, 1989), and Guo Qitao, "Huizhou Mulian Operas: Conveying Confucian Ethics with 'Demons and Gods'" (Ph.D. diss., University of California, Berkeley, 1994).

5. Janet M. Theiss, "Dealing with Disgrace: The Negotiation of Female Virtue in Eighteenth-Century China" (Ph.D. diss., University of California, Berkeley, 1998).

6. Lan Dingyuan, *Nüxue* [Lessons for women] (n.d. [early eighteenth century]; reprint, n.p., 1897), preface, p. 2a. Patricia Buckley Ebrey elaborates the key elements of what she labels the "classicist" view of the role of the family, which emphasized in particular that well-ordered families were the foundation of a well-ordered state. See Patricia Buckley Ebrey, *Family and Property in Sung China: Yüan Ts'ai's Precepts for Social Life* (Princeton, N.J.: Princeton University Press, 1984), pp. 30–32.

7. Lan Dingyuan, *Nüxue*, preface, p. 4b.

8. Wang Huizu, *Shuangjietang yongxun*, pp. 54b–55a.

9. Ibid., pp. 51a, 54b–55a.

10. Ibid., p. 18b.

11. William T. Rowe, *Saving the World: Chen Hongmou and Elite Consciousness in Eighteenth-Century China* (Stanford, Calif.: Stanford University Press, 2001), p. 394.

12. Zhu Yong, *Qingdai zongzu fa yanjiu* [A study of lineage law in the Qing] (Changsha: Hunan chubanshe, 1987), pp. 157–62.

13. To assist with maintaining public security and social order, the late imperial Chinese government implemented the so-called *baojia* system, which divided the population into local units of one thousand households called *bao*, each run by a headman, appointed by the local magistrate, who was supposed to keep tabs on potential sources of unrest or criminal activities and report them to the magistrate.

14. Ibid., p. 160; DQHDSL, *juan* 811, YZ 25.

15. See Part One and Janet M. Theiss, "Managing Martyrdom: Female Suicide and Statecraft in Mid-Qing China," in *Passionate Women: Female Suicide in Late Imperial China*, ed. Paul S. Ropp, Paola Zamperini, and Harriet T. Zurndorfer (Leiden: E. J. Brill, 2001), p. 57.

16. Zhu Yong, *Qingdai zongzu fa yanjiu*, pp. 163–64.

17. DQHDSL, *juan* 811, QL 5.

18. Zhu Yong, *Qingdai zongzu fa yanjiu*, p. 169; QSL, QL 54.7, *gengwu* day, *juan* 1335.

19. The shift in views of the agency of women as subjects from the Yongzheng to the Qianlong era is traced in Theiss, "Managing Martyrdom." We will return to the theme of Qianlong-era doubts about women's capacity for moral agency in Part Four.

20. Zhu Yong, *Qingdai zongzu fa yanjiu*, p. 170.

21. This statute was carried over from the Ming Code. See Xue Yunsheng, *Duli cunyi* [Lingering doubts after reading the substatutes], ed. Huang Jingjia

(Taibei: Chinese Materials and Research Aids Service Center, 1970), *juan* 44, p. 1109, article 381.

22. Such punishments included flogging with the heavy bamboo and banishment, depending on the specific crime and the relationship to the victim of those engaging in private settlement. The subsection of the statute on illicit sex dealing with private settlement was carried over from the Ming. See Xue Yunsheng, *Duli cunyi, juan* 43, pp. 1079, 1086. On the private settlement of homicides of all types, see Xue Yunsheng, *Duli cunyi, juan* 34, pp. 884–86, under the statute on "private agreements on the killing of superior or older relatives," which was carried over from the Ming Code. On the discussions of changes to the judicial role of lineages, see Rowe, *Saving the World*, pp. 397–98.

23. Zhu Yong, *Qingdai zongzu fa yanjiu*, p. 166.

24. The scarcity of highly organized lineages in cases involving the behavior of women was perhaps a sign of their success in handling their own domestic disputes and disgraceful matters internally. Presumably the judgments and punishments of lineage leaders were often accepted and worked to redress wrongs and mitigate conflicts. Effective lineage punishments would be invisible in the judicial record.

25. XKTB, QL 32.12.22, 208.12.

26. According to Fei Chengkang, this term refers to public censure and the culprit's expression of repentance in front of assembled lineage members. See extended discussion of lineage punishments in Fei Chengkang, *Zhongguo jiafa zugui* [Family and clan regulations in China] (Shanghai: Shanghai shehui kexue yuan chubanshe, 1998), pp. 98–102. Terms for these punishments are discussed in Hui-chen Wang Liu, *The Traditional Chinese Clan Rules* (New York: J. J. Augustin, 1959), pp. 25–30. The content of such instructions and their particular popularity in the mid-Qing period are discussed in Furth, "The Patriarch's Legacy."

27. Fei Chengkang, *Zhongguo jiafa zugui*, pp. 98–102. On the meaning of the final character here, *fa*, see Liu, *Traditional Chinese Clan Rules*, pp. 40–41. She suggests that the term carried different meanings in different genealogies but usually indicated some form of ritual penalty, like bowing and kneeling in apology in the ancestral hall or in front of the offended party or chanting a liturgy for a certain number of days. It often also included a fine of some sort payable to the lineage, which might entail offerings of incense, candles, silver or rice, or perhaps preparation of a banquet for the offended party.

28. In translating kinship terminology, I have attempted in this chapter to follow the lead taken by contributors to Patricia Buckley Ebrey and James L. Watson, eds., *Kinship Organization in Late Imperial China 1000–1940* (Berkeley: University of California Press, 1986). *Descent group* is the general term used to refer to agnatic groupings with or without formal corporate activities or land, while the term *lineage* refers strictly to descent groups with corporate property and regular corporate ritual activity. For the detailed classification of kinship terms, see ibid., pp. 4–9.

29. The term *shi*, also pronounced *dan*, is a dialect term for measuring land equivalent to 6.3 *mu* of land (about one acre). *Hanyu dacidian* [The great dictionary of the Chinese language] (Beijing: Hanyu dacidian chubanshe, 1993), vol. 7, p. 980.

30. In most lineage regulations, this was the most severe punishment possible within the lineage. Expulsion involved removal of one's name from the lineage register and genealogy, confiscation of property for incorporation into the lineage's common holdings, and the curtailment of all rights to lineage participation, including voting, holding lineage office, sacrificial rights, and access to welfare. Zhu Yong, *Qingdai zongzu fa yanjiu*, p. 100, and Fei Chengkang, *Zhongguo jiafa zugui*, pp. 98–102.

31. To give but one other example: a woman from Yanghu County, Jiangsu, carried on an affair with her husband's cousin for eight years. It began while he was living next door to her in a large family compound but continued after his uxorilocal marriage to a woman from nearby Wuxi whenever he visited home. The affair only came to the attention of the lineage head after the cousin discovered her in bed with a family servant, with whom she had also been having an affair for over year, and killed the servant (XKTB, QL 32.*run*7.3, 222.4).

32. Melissa Macauley, *Social Power and Legal Culture: Litigation Masters in Late Imperial China* (Stanford, Calif.: Stanford University Press, 1998), pp. 146–94.

33. For examples of magistrate acceptance and even encouragement of private settlement of such cases, see Philip C. C. Huang, *Civil Justice in China: Representation and Practice in the Qing* (Stanford, Calif.: Stanford University Press, 1996), pp. 123–25, and Zhou Guangyuan, "Beneath the Law: Chinese Local Legal Culture during the Qing Dynasty" (Ph.D. diss., University of California, Los Angeles, 1995), pp. 118–23.

34. XKTB, QL 32.10.2, 211.6.

35. XKTB, QL 45.5.24, 152.6. The pregnant adulteress committed suicide upon hearing of her lover's death.

36. XKTB, QL 5.11.18, 146.8.

37. Although Erde's plot was particularly extreme, the use of false accusations as a preemptive defense against prosecution was quite common in the Qing. See Macauley, *Social Power and Legal Culture*, pp. 140–42.

38. After hearing Erde insist that he was not guilty of either the attempted rape or the murder, the magistrate, in the fashion of the legendary Judge Bao, launched a rhetorical onslaught against him, confronting him with the litany of his own relatives' testimonies confirming his every move on the day of the assault and murder. He then had him remove his spotless outer clothing in front of the court to reveal his still bloodstained undergarments, thus forcing him to confess.

39. Oddly, the magistrate did not even raise the possibility of punishing these lineage leaders for private settlement of a case of illicit sex, despite explicitly labeling Erde's first crime as an attempted rape. Since the memorial for this case still had to undergo the review of the Board of Punishments before the suggested sentences were finalized, it is possible that this apparent oversight was later addressed.

40. XKTB, QL 32.*run*7.9, 210.9.

41. Xue Yunsheng, *Duli cunyi*, *juan* 34, p. 881, article 299.

42. See Huang, *Civil Justice in China*, pp. 110–37, on the operation of the third realm.

CHAPTER 4. DIVIDED LOYALTIES

1. James Z. Lee and Cameron Campbell, *Fate and Fortune in Rural China: Social Organization and Population Behavior in Liaoning, 1774–1873* (New York: Cambridge University Press, 1997), especially pp. 103–56.

2. On the role of neighbors in family conflicts over women's behavior, see Janet M. Theiss, "Dealing with Disgrace: The Negotiation of Female Virtue in Eighteenth-Century China" (Ph.D. diss., University of California, Berkeley, 1998), pp. 99–113.

3. The importance of uterine family ties—that is, the bonds between a woman and her children—within the Chinese family system was first recognized by Margery Wolf, *Women and the Family in Rural Taiwan* (Stanford, Calif.: Stanford University Press, 1972). Married women's relationships with their parents in the late imperial period has recently been explored in Beverly J. Bossler, "'A Daughter Is a Daughter All Her Life': Affinal Relations and Women's Networks in Song and Late Imperial China," *Late Imperial China* 21, no. 1 (2000): 77–106.

4. Wang Huizu, *Shuangjietang yongxun* [Simple precepts from the Hall Enshrining a Pair of Chaste Widows] (1794; reprint, Taibei: Huawen shuju, 1970), p. 18b.

5. Ibid., pp. 21b–22a.

6. See Susan Mann, *Precious Records: Women in China's Long Eighteenth Century* (Stanford, Calif.: Stanford University Press, 1997), p. 54.

7. XKTB, QL 45.12.14, 157.3.

8. XKTB, QL 32.2.19, 222.3. Intriguingly, the potential impropriety of the young woman's going to the village opera was not an issue at all in this case.

9. XKTB, QL 45.4.3, 150.2.

10. Lan Dinyuan, *Nüxue* [Lessons for women] (n.d. [early eighteenth century]; reprint, n.p., 1897), *juan* 5, p. 3a. "Master Zhu" refers to the Song dynasty Neo-Confucian scholar Zhu Xi.

11. The accusation that a wife cursed her husband's parents as he beat her is an extremely common trope in the confessions of men convicted of killing their wives. It was one of several testimonial strategies to mitigate the murderer's guilt by casting the victim as a woman who violated the wifely way. See Theiss, "Dealing with Disgrace," pp. 258–59.

12. XKTB, QL 32.8.20, 226.7.

13. Mann, *Precious Records,* pp. 60–61.

14. Chen Hongmou, *Jiaonü yigui* [Bequeathed guidelines for instructing women], in *Wuzhong yigui* [Five sets of bequeathed guidelines] (1742; reprint, Shanghai: Jingwei jiaoyu lianhe chubanshe, 1935), p. 46.

15. Ibid., p. 44.

16. Women mourned their husbands and parents-in-law for three years but wore only the one-year mourning for their own parents. Susan Mann points out that the dictates of ritual propriety for a woman mourning natal relatives have been found by anthropologists to be highly ambiguous, reflecting the unclarity of the overall relationship between a married woman and her own parents. Mann, *Precious Records,* p. 250 n. 83.

17. XKTB, QL 32.5.16, 223.1.

18. Xue Yunsheng, *Duli cunyi* [Lingering doubts after reading the substatutes], ed. Huang Jingjia (Taibei: Chinese Materials and Research Aids Service Center, 1970), *juan* 11, p. 292, article 101. The substatute, which specified punishments for kidnapping by either husband, was created in response to a memorial from Huguang Judicial Commissioner Yan Yaoxi. Such marriage kidnappings appear to have been a serious and ongoing problem, especially in Huguang, which, newly repopulated with migrants after the conquest, probably had many more men than women. Six years later it was still a major source of social conflict according to Hunan Judicial Commissioner Zhou Renji, whose memorial on the subject was discussed in Part One.

19. Ibid., *juan* 12, p. 312, article 116. The seven grounds for divorce were failure to produce a son, adultery, unfiliality to her husband's parents, loquaciousness, stealing, jealousy, and contraction of a contagious disease.

20. Ibid., *juan* 11, p. 294, article 103.

21. Xue Yunsheng, *Duli cunyi, juan* 43, article 367, p. 1087.

22. XKTB, QL 5.4.24, 153.2.

23. Scenarios of wives committing suicide after being displaced by a concubine were common in fiction and no doubt fueled the popular imagination.

24. The story of one brother's identification with his sister's honor will be told in detail in Part Four. The importance of brother-sister bonds in the case record has also been noted by Melissa Macauley, *Social Power and Legal Culture: Litigation Masters in Late Imperial China* (Stanford, Calif.: Stanford University Press, 1998), pp. 159, 361 n. 18.

25. XKTB, QL 45.4.9, 152.3.

26. XKTB, QL 45.3.2, 170.1.

27. XKTB, QL 32.4.3, 216.10.

28. XKTB, QL 60.5.28, 166.9.

29. XKTB, QL 32.12.22, 208.11.

30. XKTB, QL 60.11.4, 163.4.

31. XKTB, QL 60.10.2, 164.5.

32. XKTB, QL 45.4.2, 160.1.

33. XKTB, QL 32.6.9, 224.3.

34. XKTB, QL 60.2.13, 168.9.

35. For discussion of the texture of married life in its different phases based on the experiences of elite women, see Mann, *Precious Records*, pp. 59–69.

36. See, for example, XKTB, QL 5.5.4, 144.5.

37. XKTB, QL 32.10.13, 216.11.

38. XKTB, QL 60.12.16, 162.10.

CHAPTER 5. ADULTERY, INCEST

1. In the eighteenth century, critiques of widow suicide, especially that of betrothed maidens, and of the ideal of widow fidelity in general were articulated by a wide range of male scholars, including Yuan Mei (1716–97), Ji Yun (1724–1805), Dai Zhen (1724–77), Qian Daxin (1728–1804), Wang Zhong (1745–94), Zang Yong (1767–1811), Yu Zhengxie (1775–1840), and fiction writers like Wu Jingzi, author of the satire on literati life and mores *Rulin waishi*

[The scholars]. For one of the earliest analyses of the implications of this "protofeminist" trend in eighteenth-century elite culture, see Paul S. Ropp, *Dissent in Early Modern China: Ju-lin Wai-shih and Ch'ing Social Criticism* (Ann Arbor: University of Michigan Press, 1981), and "The Seeds of Change: Reflections on the Condition of Women in the Early and Mid-Ch'ing," *Signs* 2, no. 1 (1976): 5–23. Many of these critics of widow chastity were evidential scholars, a phenomenon examined by Harriet T. Zurndorfer, "Han-Hsüeh, 'Evidential Research,' and Female Chastity: A Re-Examination of Intellectual Attitudes and Social Ideals in 18th Century China," in *Thought and Law in Qin and Han China: Studies Dedicated to Anthony Hulsewe on the Occasion of His Eightieth Birthday*, ed. W. L. Idema and E. Zürcher (Leiden: E. J. Brill, 1990), pp. 208–24.

2. Susan Mann conveys the poignant relevance of ideals of martyrdom for eighteenth-century women in *Precious Records: Women in China's Long Eighteenth Century* (Stanford, Calif.: Stanford University Press, 1997), pp. 211–18 and passim. On widow suicide notes, see Grace Fong, "Signifying Bodies: The Cultural Significance of Suicide Writings by Women in Ming-Qing China," in *Passionate Women: Female Suicide in Late Imperial China*, ed. Paul S. Ropp, Paola Zamperini, and Harriet T. Zurndorfer (Leiden: E. J. Brill, 2001), pp. 128–35. For women commemorating the martyrdom of other women in poetry, see Maureen Robertson, "Changing the Subject: Gender and Self-Inscription in Authors' Prefaces and 'Shi' Poetry," in *Writing Women in Late Imperial China*, ed. Ellen Widmer and Kang-I Sun Chang (Stanford, Calif.: Stanford University Press, 1997), p. 213.

3. See Dorothy Ko, *Teachers of the Inner Chambers: Women and Culture in Seventeenth-Century China* (Stanford, Calif.: Stanford University Press, 1994), pp. 68–112.

4. This includes, most famously, *Shitou ji* or *Honglou meng* [The story of the stone], but also *Yesou puyan* [A country codger's words of exposure] by Xia Jingqu and many other mid-Qing novels. Keith McMahon traces the elaboration of the scholar-beauty theme in *Misers, Shrews, and Polygamists: Sexuality and Male-Female Relations in Eighteenth-Century Chinese Fiction* (Durham, N.C.: Duke University Press, 1995), pp. 53, 159–60, 219–20 and passim.

5. See Susan Mann, "Grooming a Daughter for Marriage: Brides and Wives in the Mid-Ch'ing Period," in *Marriage and Inequality in Chinese Society*, ed. Rubie S. Watson and Patricia Buckley Ebrey (Berkeley: University of California Press, 1991), pp. 204–30, and *Precious Records*.

6. The social status, property rights, and moral reputation of widows in the Qing have received a great deal of attention from scholars, including Ann Waltner, "Widows and Remarriage in Ming and Early Qing China," in *Women in China: Current Directions in Historical Scholarship*, ed. Richard W. Guisso and Stanley Johannesen (Youngstown, N.Y.: Philo Press, 1981), pp. 129–46; Jennifer Holmgren, "The Economic Foundations of Virtue: Widow-Remarriage in Early and Modern China," *Australian Journal of Chinese Affairs* 13 (1985): 1–27; Susan Mann, "Widows in the Kinship, Class, and Community Structures of Qing Dynasty China," *Journal of Asian Studies* 46, no. 1 (1987) 37–56; Kathryn Bernhardt, *Women and Property in China, 960–1949* (Stanford, Calif.: Stanford University Press, 1999), pp. 47–72; Matthew H. Sommer, "The Uses of Chastity:

Sex, Law, and the Property of Widows in Qing China," *Late Imperial China* 17, no. 2 (1996): 77–130, and *Sex, Law, and Society in Late Imperial China* (Stanford, Calif.: Stanford University Press, 2000), pp. 166–209.

7. Disputes between widows and their in-laws over property have been examined extensively by Bernhardt, *Women and Property in China*, pp. 47–72, and Sommer, *Sex, Law, and Society*, pp. 166–209.

8. See Bernhardt, *Women and Property in China*, pp. 65–72, and Sommer, "The Uses of Chastity" and *Sex, Law, and Society*, pp. 179–82.

9. Bernhardt, *Women and Property in China*, pp. 71–72.

10. Sommers's analysis in *Sex, Law, and Society* recognizes the link between this new mode of gender performance and a conjugal definition of patriarchy but does not note that this constitutes a shift in definitions of patriarchy.

11. Qianlong himself had passionate and intimate relationships with two of his favored consorts over the many years of his reign. See Norman Kutcher, *Mourning in Late Imperial China: Filial Piety and the State* (New York: Cambridge University Press, 1999), pp. 153–59, and James Millward, "A Uyghur Muslim in Qianlong's Court: The Meanings of the Fragrant Concubine," *Journal of Asian Studies* 53, no. 2 (1994): 427–58.

12. DQHDSL, *juan* 801, p. 762, and Xue Yunsheng, *Duli cunyi* [Lingering doubts after reading the substatutes], ed. Huang Jingjia (Taibei: Chinese Materials and Research Aids Service Center, 1970), *juan* 32, article 285, p. 783.

13. DQHDSL, *juan* 801, p. 763, and Xue Yunsheng, *Duli cunyi, juan* 32, article 285, p. 784.

14. Xue Yunsheng, *Duli cunyi, juan* 32, article 285, p. 802. See also M. J. Meijer, *Murder and Adultery in Late Imperial China* (Leiden: E. J. Brill, 1991), pp. 39–40.

15. The complexities of these developments and their significance in terms of judicial philosophy have been admirably mapped out in Meijer, *Murder and Adultery*.

16. DQHDSL, *juan* 801, pp. 762–63. For a detailed explication of these changes, see Meijer, *Murder and Adultery*, pp. 51–53, 69–71, 100–103.

17. One of numerous examples is a memorial from a Board of Punishments vice-minister suggesting a lessening of punishment for relatives who catch an adulterer in flight and kill him after he resists with weapons as opposed to resisting without them. The change was adopted. Memorial of Qian Weicheng, QL 27.9.30, LFZZ, doc. #1198–004, reel #86, pp. 0655–57.

18. XKTB, QL 32.12.11, 225.1.

19. XKTB, QL 32.12.22, 217.4.

20. XKTB, QL 32.5.29, 224.2.

21. Part Three will address in much greater detail the articulation of the inner-outer paradigm with notions of chastity and violation.

22. Memorial of Jiang Jianian, QL 25.7.4, LFZZ, doc. #1197–036, reel 86, pp. 0573–74.

23. DQHDSL, *juan* 80, p. 773.

24. On the state hermeneutics of female suicide, see Part One and Janet M. Theiss, "Managing Martyrdom: Female Suicide and Statecraft in Mid-Qing China," in Ropp, Zamperini, and Zurndorfer, *Passionate Women*, especially the

discussion of Qianlong's criticism of the inappropriateness of loyalty suicides by daughters and concubines, pp. 70–71.

25. Xue Yunsheng, *Duli cunyi, juan* 32, article 285, p. 802.
26. Ibid., *juan* 32, article 285, p. 803.
27. Ibid., *juan* 43, article 368, pp. 1087–89. To these provisions, carried over from the Ming, new substatutes were added in 1795 to cover attempted rape of a relative (punished with military exile to a distant frontier) and in 1811 the unwanted proposition of a relative (sentenced with one hundred strokes and life exile at three thousand *li*) (DQHDSL, *juan* 825, pp. 992–93). These additions paralleled additions made to the substatutes on illicit sex in general. These are discussed in Parts Three and Four.
28. Memorial of Shen Qiyuan, QL 6.5.16, ZPZZ, *lüli lei, bao* 33, *juan* 48.
29. DQHDSL, *juan* 801, pp. 766–67. See also Xue Yunsheng, *Duli cunyi, juan* 32, article 285, p. 799. Meijer, *Murder and Adultery,* charts the development of these substatutes and the issues surrounding them on pp. 111–13.
30. DQHDSL, *juan* 801, pp. 766–77, and Xue Yunsheng, *Duli cunyi, juan* 32, article 285, p. 799–800.
31. XKTB, QL 18.3.5, 200.1.
32. Xue Yunsheng, *Duli cunyi, juan* 32, article 285, p. 801. Xue ends his very long critique of this substatute with the thought-provoking comment that "[d]ivorce is clearly codified in the statutes but is seldom considered. No wonder the cases of murder because of adultery increase day after day!"
33. XKTB, QL 60.4.12, 168.7.
34. XKTB, QL 32.*run*7.3, 222.4.
35. XKTB, QL 45.5.24, 152.6.
36. XKTB, QL 45.4.8, 168.3.
37. XKTB, QL 45.10.13, 153.4.
38. The judicial definition of rape will be dealt with at length in Part Three.
39. XKTB, QL 45.11.19, 159.1.
40. Incest between relatives of the same clan with no mourning relations was punishable by one hundred strokes of the heavy bamboo if consensual.
41. XKTB, QL 45.8.28, 165.2.
42. XKTB, QL 18.4.7, 195.5.
43. In 1768, the year before the Qianlong Emperor issued the edict mandating that the Nine Ministers review cases in which a junior relative caught a senior relative having illicit sex with his wife and killed him, he also rejected a suggestion for the revision of the ritual regulations on canonization of chastity martyrs in cases of incestuous assault. Ou Yang Yongqi, the Provincial Administration commissioner for Guangdong Province, had memorialized about a case in which a father-in-law tried to rape his daughter-in-law and then hacked her to death with an ax when she resisted. He had been sentenced to death and she had been canonized for defending her chastity to the death. Ou Yang felt that it was improper that the funds to build memorial arches for such women go to their husbands or in-laws, as they would in all other canonization cases. He requested that the regulations be modified to allow the funds to be disbursed to the dead woman's own family instead or, if that was not possible, to the local magistrate so that he could build the arch on her behalf. The emperor's rescript summarily

rejected the idea without providing any hint of his reasoning, so it is difficult to interpret its significance. One could argue that Qianlong was upholding the conjugal notion of patriarchy here by protecting the husband's status as the keeper of his wife's chastity. But one could also read this decision as a reflection of the assumption that her husband's patriline had a greater stake in a woman's chastity than did her natal family. Memorial of Ou Yang Yongqi, QL 33.7.18, LFZZ, doc. #0298–070, reel #20, p. 0760.

44. Kutcher, *Mourning in Late Imperial China.*

45. See Part One and Theiss, "Managing Martyrdom."

PART THREE PROLOGUE

1. XKTB, QL 18.10.19, 198.12. It is not clear why the constable first took Sun Er to the banner headquarters, which handled only cases involving bannermen. Sun Er and all the other participants in this case were Han Chinese settlers who, over the course of the seventeenth and early eighteenth centuries, migrated in significant numbers into this region of the traditional Manchu homeland. The Qing state mandated that the region's Chinese commoners and bannermen live in separate villages under separate administrative systems. Cases involving Chinese commoners were tried first by the county magistrate, as they would be elsewhere. Thus Sun Er had to be transferred to the civil administrative system for trial. The complexities of local administration in Manchuria in the mid–Qing period are examined in Robert H. G. Lee, *The Manchurian Frontier in Ch'ing History* (Cambridge, Mass.: Harvard University Press, 1970), pp. 71–74. See also Christopher Mills Issett, "State, Peasant and Agrarian Change on the Manchurian Frontier, 1644–1940" (Ph.D. diss., University of California, Los Angeles, 1998).

2. The *kang,* a typical feature of houses in regions of north China with cold winters, is a heated platform used for sleeping and daytime activities.

3. In the initial round of court proceedings, Du Ming did not show up with his mother to testify. The magistrate asked Du Song Shi why he was absent, and she stated that he had to stay home because there was no one else to watch over the house and his two brothers while his mother was away.

4. For a discussion of judicial officials' construction of the *guanggun,* see Matthew H. Sommer, *Sex, Law, and Society in Late Imperial China* (Stanford, Calif.: Stanford University Press, 2000), pp. 96–101 and passim.

5. Christopher Issett makes this point about the fluidity of Manchurian villages in Issett, "State, Peasant and Agrarian Change," p. 215. Widow-headed households and even households composed only of married couples and their children were probably not very common in Haicheng County. The spacing and sex of her children suggest that like most poor, simple household families in Liaoning, Du Song Shi and her late husband had practiced female infanticide to control the overall size of their family and ensure that they had only boys. James Z. Lee and Cameron Campbell, *Fate and Fortune in Rural China: Social Organization and Population Behavior in Liaoning, 1774–1873* (New York: Cambridge University Press, 1997), pp. 101, 90–102.

6. Ibid., pp. 48, 84–90, and 138–39.

7. On the phenomenon of migration to Manchuria, see Thomas Gottschang

and Diana Lary, *Swallows and Settlers: The Great Migration from North China to Manchuria*, Michigan Monographs in Chinese History, vol. 87 (Ann Arbor: Center for Chinese Studies, University of Michigan, 2000).

8. Xue Yunsheng, *Duli cunyi* [Lingering doubts after reading the substatutes], ed. Huang Jingjia (Taibei: Chinese Materials and Research Aids Service Center, 1970), *juan* 43, article 366, p. 1079, and Yao Run et al., ed., *Da Qing lüli zengxiu tongcuan jicheng* [Revised comprehensive compilation of the Qing Code] (n.p., 1878), pp. 1a–b, quoted in translation in Sommer, *Sex, Law, and Society*, p. 324.

9. Huang Liuhong, *Fuhui quanshu* [A complete book concerning happiness and benevolence] (n.p., 1699), *juan* 19, 24a–b. Parts of this handbook have been translated by Djang Chu, trans. and ed., *A Complete Book Concerning Happiness and Benevolence: "Fu-hui ch'uan-shu": A Manual for Local Magistrates in Seventeenth Century China* (Tucson: University of Arizona Press, 1984).

10. Huang Liuhong, spells out the necessary questions explicitly: "What was the relationship between the victim and the rapist? Were they relatives? Did they usually have contact with each other and know each other well as neighbors or fellow villagers? When did the rape occur? Where did the rape occur? Did the assailant threaten her with a lethal weapon? Did the victim have physical injuries or lost or ripped underclothes? Was the rape accomplished or not? Did the victim shout for help? Were the screams loud at first and then quieter or did they cease altogether? If there is only the word of the woman that she was raped, were there relatives who heard any noise and came to see what happened? Did the victim's husband capture the assailant or did he escape? According to the confessions, were clothes or other belongings left behind? Each of these questions should be investigated carefully to determine whether the encounter was coerced or consensual." Huang Liuhong, *Fuhui quanshu, juan* 19, p. 23b.

11. The characters used here are *wufu*, meaning "beautiful or charming woman," but given the context, it is almost certain that the intended characters were instead *lifu*, which means "widow." Although it is impossible to know at what stage of the transcription process this mistake was made, one cannot help but wonder if the substitution, which occurs twice in the magistrate's second report as he quotes the prefect's questions, was perhaps an unconscious reference to Du Song Shi's being a very attractive woman. Case memorials rarely contain such impressions of physical appearance, although magistrate's handbooks indicate how important judgments about appearance were in the adjudication process. Could this magistrate's sympathy for Du Song Shi despite the paucity of acceptable evidence of the rape have been inspired in part by her charm?

12. Huang Liuhong, *Fuhui quanshu, juan* 19, pp. 23b–24a.

13. Ibid., *juan* 19, pp. 25a–b.

14. We do not know the final assessment of the Board of Punishments.

15. Li Yu, *Silent Operas* [Wusheng xi], ed. Patrick Hanan (Hong Kong: Chinese University of Hong Kong, 1990), pp. 77–78.

16. Ibid., p. 84.

17. Ibid., p. 89.

18. A reference to the *Zuo Zhuan*, Duke Zhao, year 23.

19. Li Yu, *Silent Operas*, p. 90.

20. Having penned several essays on judicial questions, especially adultery

and homicide, Li Yu was thoroughly familiar with the intricacies of this law. See Patrick Hanan, *The Invention of Li Yu* (Cambridge, Mass.: Harvard University Press, 1988), p. 25.

CHAPTER 6. THE WAGES OF WANTON MIXING

1. Much work has been done to evaluate the voluminous eighteenth-century discourse on gender norms and female virtue. See, for example, Susan Mann, "The Education of Daughters in the Mid-Ch'ing Period," in *Education and Society in Late Imperial China, 1600–1900*, ed. Benjamin A. Elman and Alexander Woodside (Berkeley: University of California Press, 1994); Charlotte Furth, "The Patriarch's Legacy: Household Instructions and the Transmission of Orthodox Values," in *Orthodoxy in Late Imperial China*, ed. Liu Kwang-ching (Berkeley: University of California Press, 1990), pp. 187–211; William T. Rowe, "Women and the Family in Mid-Qing Social Thought: The Case of Chen Hongmou," *Late Imperial China* 13, no. 2 (1992): 1–41; and Chow Kai-wing, *The Rise of Confucian Ritualism in Late Imperial China: Ethics, Classics, and Lineage Discourse* (Stanford, Calif.: Stanford University Press, 1994).

2. Lan Dingyuan, *Nüxue* [Lessons for women] (n.d. [early eighteenth century]; reprint, n.p., 1897), *juan* 5, pp. 5a–b.

3. For discussion of the practice of gender separation and the significance of the inner/outer divide within elite family life, see Susan Mann, *Precious Records: Women in China's Long Eighteenth Century* (Stanford, Calif.: Stanford University Press, 1997), pp. 56–57.

4. Lan Dingyuan, *Nüxue, juan* 5, p. 5b.

5. Ibid., *juan* 5, p. 19b.

6. Ibid., *juan* 5, pp. 2b–3a.

7. Wang Huizu, *Shuangjietang yongxun* [Simple precepts from the Hall Enshrining a Pair of Chaste Widows] (1794; reprint, Taibei: Huawen shuju, 1970), p. 45b. Similar admonitions about such improper women are standard in morality handbooks, family instructions, and other ethical writings in late imperial times. See also Huang Liuhong, *Fuhui quanshu* [A complete book concerning happiness and benevolence] (n.p., 1699), *juan* 19, p. 16b. For discussion of eighteenth-century preoccupations with threats to the inner chambers, see Mann, *Precious Records*, pp. 194–200. Such rhetoric was largely, but not entirely, driven by paranoia. My case sampling includes a handful of examples of married women having affairs with a servant (XKTB, QL 3.*run*7.3, 222.4), with a doctor attending her bed-ridden husband (XKTB, QL 32.6.16, 221.1), and with Buddhist and Daoist monks (e.g., XKTB, QL 32.9.19, 214.5).

8. Wang Huizu, *Shuangjietang yongxun*, pp. 45a–b.

9. Lan Dingyuan, *Nüxue, juan* 5, p. 2b.

10. William Rowe has documented in detail Chen Hongmou's efforts in his various provincial posts to promote the cult of chastity and customs of gender separation through proper marriage practices and labor divisions. As governor of Yunnan in the 1730s, Chen vigorously pursued such reforms among non-Han peoples with the conviction that they were vital to the larger civilizing project of the empire. See William T. Rowe, *Saving the World: Chen Hongmou and Elite*

Consciousness in Eighteenth-Century China (Stanford, Calif.: Stanford University Press, 2001), pp. 313–22, 423–26. This activist vision of the significance of the transformation of gender customs in the empire's larger *jiaohua* project was widely shared by mid-Qing officials on the southwestern frontier. See, for example, the similar agenda articulated in a memorial of the regional commander of Zhaotong in Yunnan, Xu Chengzhen, which outlines strategies for civilizing Yunnan and Guizhou, including enhanced state administration at the local level, promotion of appropriate economic activities, and cultural education (QL 2.10.19, LFZZ, doc. #1455–006, reel #99, pp. 0849–58).

11. See Mann, *Precious Records*, on her work (pp. 94–98) and on her placement of women's culture within the Qing civilizing project (pp. 214–18).

12. Wanyan Yunzhu, comp., *Guochao guixiu zhengshi ji* [Correct beginnings: Women's poetry of our august dynasty] (Hongxiangguan edition, comp. 1831), *Liyan* section, pp. 4a–4b.

13. This handbook is anthologized by Chen Hongmou in *Jiaonü yigui* [Bequeathed guidelines for instructing women], in *Wuzhong yigui* [Five sets of bequeathed guidelines] (1742; reprint, Shanghai: Jingwei jiaoyu lianhe chubanshe, 1935), p. 42.

14. The extensive descriptions of the Miao people in the eighteenth-century novels *Yesou puyan* and *Rulin waishi* are two prominent examples. The former is particularly noteworthy because it portrays the acceptance of Qing imperial rule as inseparable from the adoption of Chinese marriage practices. See Maram Epstein, *Competing Discourses: Orthodoxy, Authenticity and Engendered Meanings in Late Imperial Chinese Fiction* (Cambridge, Mass.: Harvard University Asia Center, 2001), pp. 225–26.

15. Susan Mann, "Household Handicrafts and State Policy in Qing Times," in *To Achieve Security and Wealth: The Qing Imperial State and the Economy, 1644–1911*, ed. Jane Kate Leonard and John R. Watt (Ithaca, N.Y.: Cornell University East Asia Program, 1992), pp. 75–95. On Chen Hongmou's efforts to promote sericulture as a component of the civilizing project, see Rowe, *Saving the World*, pp. 235–43.

16. Memorial of Zhang Shijun, QL 1.11.6, ZPZZ, *qita lei, bao* 33, *juan* 54.

17. This memorial is discussed in Chapter 2.

18. Memorial of Emida, QL 10.12.4, LFZZ, doc. #0339–058, reel 23, pp. 0196–99.

19. Xue Yunsheng, *Duli cunyi* [Lingering doubts after reading the substatutes], ed. Huang Jingjia (Taibei: Chinese Materials and Research Aids Service Center, 1970), *juan* 49, article 420, p. 1280.

20. Ibid., *juan* 49, article 420, p. 1281.

21. Memorial of Liu Fangai, QL 4.11.28, ZPZZ, *qita lei, bao* 21, *juan* 44, and memorial of Zhao Cheng, QL 5.4.3, ZPZZ, *qita lei, bao* 31, *juan* 47.

22. See, for example, the memorial of Liu Fangai, QL 4.11.28, ZPZZ, *qita lei, bao* 21, *juan* 44. These problems were no doubt exacerbated by the increasing caseload and stretched resources that magistrates increasingly contended with at the end of the eighteenth century, but it is also entirely possible that there were unprecedented numbers of women in prisons and convicted of crimes given the criminalization of prostitution (see Matthew H. Sommer, *Sex, Law, and Society*

in Late Imperial China [Stanford, Calif.: Stanford University Press, 2000]) and the proliferation and heightened enforcement of substatutes dealing with illicit sex and other crimes.

23. Xue Yunsheng, *Duli cunyi, juan* 49, article 420, p. 1281.

24. These issues are raised in the context of imprisonment of women sentenced to death and awaiting the assizes process in a memorial of Jiang Pu, QL 9.6.25, ZPZZ, *luli lei, bao* 33, *juan* 47, and LFZZ, doc. #1195–041, reel #86, pp. 0341–45.

25. Xue Yunsheng, *Duli cunyi, juan* 49, article 420, p. 1282.

26. Memorial of Yong Tai, QL 25.6.28, ZPZZ, *luli lei, bao* 21, *juan* 50. The moral and logistical problems posed by women accompanying their husbands into exile were also the subject of a flurry of memorials from provincial judicial officials across the empire during 1743–44. See, for example, the memorial of Chang An, QL 8.2.27, ZPZZ, *luli lei, bao* 43, *juan* 48. The code mandated that the wives and concubines of those sentenced to exile accompany them and allowed other family members to accompany if they wished. Xue Yunsheng, *Duli cunyi, juan* 2, article 15, p. 39. Women who were sentenced to penal servitude or exile had their sentences automatically commuted to one hundred strokes of the heavy bamboo and a fine. There were also special rules for the flogging of women (their pants were left on), and women were never to be tattooed. Xue Yunsheng, *Duli cunyi, juan* 3, article 20, p. 75.

27. Xue Yunsheng, *Duli cunyi, juan* 49, article 420, p. 1282.

28. Memorial of Liu Fangai, QL 4.11.28, ZPZZ, *qita lei, bao* 21, *juan* 44. This same memorial cited above raised the problem of assault of female prisoners and their impressment into gangs, resulting from lack of separate quarters. On debates over examinations of bodies of female suicide victims by coroners, see also the memorial of Han Guangji and other Board of Punishments officials, QL 6.3.2, ZPZZ, *luli lei, bao* 33, *juan* 48.

29. Memorial of Qing Fu, QL 2.9.28, ZPZZ, *qita lei, bao* 28, *juan* 52.

30. Memorial of Chen Hongmou, QL 11.8.22, ZPZZ, *luli lei, bao* 36, *juan* 56.

31. On women pilgrims and eighteenth-century fictional imaginings of their transgressions, see Glen Dudbridge, "Women Pilgrims to T'ai Shan: Some Pages from a Seventeenth-Century Novel," in *Pilgrims and Sacred Sites in China*, ed. Susan Naquin and Chün-Fang Yü (Berkeley: University of California Press, 1992), pp. 39–64.

32. The tone of Shu Min's observations is strikingly similar to that of Chen Hongmou in his oft-quoted diatribe on the same subject. Chen wrote, "A woman's proper ritual place is to be sequestered in the inner apartments. When at rest, she should let the screen fall [in front of her]; when abroad, she must cover her face to distance herself from any suspicion or doubt and prevent herself from coming under observation. But instead we find young women accustomed to wandering about, all made up, heads bare and faces exposed, traveling in the mountains. Some ascend to pavilions and gaze at the evening moon. In the most extreme cases, we find them traveling around visiting temples and monasteries." Quoted in Rowe, *Saving the World*, p. 320, and in Mann, *Precious Records*, p. 195. Rowe notes that what is striking about this commentary is not Chen's defense of female seclusion, which was a common theme in his own

writings and was typical of moralizing elite men in his day, but rather his perception of rampant transgression of the spatial and social boundaries that defined proper gender relations.

33. Memorial of Shu Min, QL 9.11.4, LFZZ, doc. #0281-052, reel 14, pp. 0121-23.

34. Rowe, *Saving the World*, p. 320.

35. These are examined in detail in Sommer, *Sex, Law, and Society*, pp. 26–108.

36. Yao Run et al., eds., *Da Qing lüli zengxiu tongcuan jicheng* [Revised comprehensive compilation of the Qing Code] (n.p., 1878), *juan* 33, p. 2a.

37. Sommer uncovers this line of reasoning underlying the rape statute in his comprehensive discussion of its evolution and application. See Sommer, *Sex, Law, and Society*, pp. 66–113.

38. Physical penetration by the rapist's penis, which meant that the rape was "accomplished," was also crucial for the definition of rape. Incomplete penetration, or penetration by anything other than the man's penis, could, at most, be defined as attempted rape. For a discussion of the meaning of "accomplishing" rape in the Qing Code, see Sommer, *Sex, Law, and Society*, pp. 62–74. See also Vivien Ng, "Ideology and Sexuality: Rape Laws in Qing China," *Journal of Asian Studies* 46, no. 1 (1987): 57–70. Ritual regulations prior to 1803 echoed this bodily definition of violation: rape victims who were killed or committed suicide, no matter how virtuous their reputation or how determined their resistance, were ineligible for canonization as chastity martyrs because they had been penetrated by the rapist. However, women who were killed resisting a rape attempt or who committed suicide after an attempted rape were rewarded with canonization. See Sommer, *Sex, Law, and Society*, p. 209 n. 2.

39. Xue Yunsheng, *Duli cunyi, juan* 43, article 366, p. 1079. See also Yao Run et al., *Da Qing lüli zengxiu tongcuan jicheng*, pp. 1a–b, quoted in translation in Sommer, *Sex, Law, and Society*, p. 324.

40. Xue Yunsheng, *Duli cunyi, juan* 43, article 366, p. 1086. Sommer traces the evolution of this view that the rape victim must be chaste for her attacker to receive full punishment; see Sommer, *Sex, Law, and Society*, pp. 67–77.

41. Quoted in Xue Yunsheng, *Duli cunyi, juan* 43, article 366, p. 1080.

42. Yao Run et al., *Da Qing lüli zengxiu tongcuan jicheng, juan* 33, p. 2b.

43. Quoted in Xue Yunsheng, *Duli cunyi, juan* 43, article 366, p. 1080.

44. Similar official doubts about the workability of the rape statute, especially its delineation of the difference between coercion and consent, are quoted in Sommer, *Sex, Law, and Society*, p. 90. It should be noted, though, that cases of coercion ending in consent, if they did not involve other offenses, like murder or forcing a person to commit suicide, that were "serious crimes" requiring death sentences, would not be sent up for review and thus would not be present in the Board of Punishments case record. It is thus impossible to assess their frequency or get a sense of how magistrates typically handled them.

45. XKTB, QL 18.4.2, 181.7.

46. During the Autumn Assizes, the emperor and the Nine Ministers reviewed all sentences of strangulation or decapitation after the assizes and decided which cases deserved death, which merited a reduced punishment (usu-

ally banishment) due to mitigating circumstances in the crime itself, and which deserved complete amnesty due to extraordinary life circumstances deserving compassion, like having a parent over seventy. For a description of the assizes process and the reasoning behind it, see Thomas Buoye, "Suddenly Murderous Intent Arouse: Bureaucratization and Benevolence in Eighteenth-Century Qing Homicide Reports," *Late Imperial China* 16, no. 2 (1995): 80–90. See also Derk Bodde and Clarence Morris, *Law in Imperial China Exemplified by 190 Ch'ing Dynasty Cases Translated from the Hsing-an hui-lan* (Philadelphia: University of Pennsylvania Press, 1967), pp. 134–43. It should be pointed out as well that in a case like this both the defendant and the victim's family had reasons to prefer that the crime be labeled as flirtation only. Not only would this possibly spare the defendant's life, but it also meant, for some people, that the damage to the victim's chastity was not as severe. For some people, as we will see in Part Four, the distinction between physical and verbal violation mattered in assessing a woman's chastity, while for others it did not. For Xianjie, the difference was clearly irrelevant, but for her mother it was clearly important that she "was not polluted."

47. XKTB, QL 45.5.4, 161.3.
48. Arguing, contra my views here, that the rape statute was applied more rigidly in judicial practice, Sommer presents a case prosecuted as a rape without the evidence mandated by the code, arguing that it is an "exception which proves the rule." But I have come across many cases of rape and attempted rape in which suspicions might well have been raised by the magistrate but were not. Sommer, *Sex, Law, and Society,* pp. 100–104.
49. XKTB, QL 18.12.8, 175.1.
50. Huang Liuhong, *Fuhui quanshu, juan* 19, p. 21b.
51. Quoted in Xue Yunsheng, *Duli cunyi, juan* 43, article 366, p. 1080.
52. Xue Yunsheng, *Duli cunyi, juan* 43, article 366, pp. 1080–81.

CHAPTER 7. "ACCOMMODATING SAGES"

1. Memorials often included the magistrate's detailed firsthand investigation of the spatial and social layout of the scene of the illicit sex: the arrangement of rooms in the house, the distance to neighbors' houses, the remoteness of a path or a field, and the living and socializing patterns of relatives and neighbors. For a pioneering close reading of a case of adultery, see Jonathan Spence, *The Death of Woman Wang* (New York: Penguin Books, 1978).
2. Francesca Bray describes some of the prescribed methods of demarcating a "women's quarters" and provides some ethnographic evidence of various sorts of divisions in the modest houses of the middle and lower strata of society, like the use of curtains in single-roomed houses. She points out that divisions of labor that placed men outside in the fields most of the day and women at home imposed a de facto gendering of work space. "Ethnographic" evidence appearing in cases suggests that such makeshift and circumstantial segregation of women was far less strict than she assumes. Francesca Bray, *Technology and Gender: Fabrics of Power in Late Imperial China* (Berkeley: University of California Press, 1997), pp. 128–33. Even in elite households with the means to maintain a truly

cloistered women's quarters, distinctions between inner and outer were fluid and challenged by women's social networks and publishing activities. See Dorothy Ko, *Teachers of the Inner Chambers: Women and Culture in Seventeenth-Century China* (Stanford, Calif.: Stanford University Press, 1994).

3. XKTB, QL 32.*run*7.24, 215.4.

4. For evidence of the types of work women did inside and outside the home, see Bray, *Technology and Gender*, pp. 132, 206–36.

5. XKTB, QL 45.4.24, 170.3.

6. Contrary to Matthew Sommer, I do not see the judicial stereotype of the rogue male sexual predator from outside the family system *(guanggun)* showing up in very many cases. Many assailants were unmarried, but most were very much part of their family and community systems. On the stereotype, see Matthew H. Sommer, *Sex, Law, and Society in Late Imperial China* (Stanford, Calif.: Stanford University Press, 2000), pp. 93–103.

7. XKTB, QL 32.11.18, 219.6.

8. XKTB, QL 18.7.7, 176.11.

9. XKTB, QL 60.9.8, 163.8.

10. XKTB, QL 18.3.25, 195.11.

11. XKTB, QL 18.5.12, 185.8.

12. XKTB, QL 60.2.27, 168.15.

13. XKTB, QL 45.10.27, 157.4.

14. On the manifold erotic and private meanings of women's shoes, which were intimately bound up with their identity, their femininity, and their sexuality, see Dorothy Ko, *Every Step a Lotus, Shoes for Bound Feet* (Berkeley: University of California Press, 2001).

15. William Rowe discusses the importance of "knowing shame " as a rubric for the civilizing project among Qing officials serving in non-Han areas, like Chen Hongmou, who decried the lack of this quality among "barbarian" peoples. See William T. Rowe, "Education and Empire in Southwest China: Ch'en Hong-mou in Yunnan, 1733–38," in *Education in Late Imperial China (1600–1900)*, ed. Benjamin A. Elman and Alexander Woodside (Berkeley: University of California Press, 1994), pp. 417–57, and *Saving the World: Chen Hongmou and Elite Consciousness in Eighteenth-Century China* (Stanford, Calif.: Stanford University Press, 2001), pp. 319, 424–25.

16. On the multivalent significance of chastity-centered female virtue for women's identity, family reputation, and notions of femininity and even masculinity, see Janet M. Theiss, "Femininity in Flux: Gendered Virtue and Social Conflict in the Mid-Qing Courtroom," in *Chinese Femininities/Chinese Masculinities: An Introductory Reader,* ed. Susan Brownell and Jeffrey Wasserstrom (Berkeley: University of California Press, 2002).

17. Elite hegemony has been assumed among scholars of traditional China for decades. Classic formulations of this approach include Hsiao Kung-chuan, *Rural China: Imperial Control in the Nineteenth Century* (Seattle: University of Washington Press, 1960), and Chang Chung-li, *The Chinese Gentry* (Seattle: University of Washington Press, 1955). More recently the hegemony approach has been elaborated upon to take into account other forms of cultural division besides social stratification, like dialect and gender: see, for example, David Johnson,

Andrew J. Nathan, and Evelyn S. Rawski, eds., *Popular Culture in Late Imperial China* (Berkeley: University of California Press, 1985).

18. This dynamic view of the inner/outer paradigm also allows Mann and Ko to begin to account for shifts in the interpretation of the boundary, in particular the emergence of a morally conservative attitude toward the role of women in society, their education, and writing in the eighteenth century as compared to the seventeenth. See Susan Mann, *Precious Records: Women in China's Long Eighteenth Century* (Stanford, Calif.: Stanford University Press, 1997), pp. 19–44 and passim; Ko, *Teachers of the Inner Chambers*, pp. 295–96.

19. Li Yu, *Silent Operas* [Wusheng xi], ed. Patrick Hanan (Hong Kong: Chinese University of Hong Kong, 1990), p. 95.

20. James Legge, *The Works of Mencius: Translated, with Critical and Exegetical Notes, Prolegomena, and Copious Indexes* (New York: Dover Publications, 1970), pp. 369–71.

21. Translation adapted from Legge, *The Works of Mencius*, pp. 371–72.

22. The use of suicide as revenge will be discussed in Chapter 9.

23. Li Yu, *Silent Operas*, pp. 95–96.

24. Sima Qian, *Records of the Grand Historian of China*, trans. Burton Watson (New York: Columbia University Press, 1961), p. 152. Sima Qian also notes in the commentary concluding the biography that Chen Ping was surprisingly feminine in appearance. I am indebted to an anonymous reviewer for the press for pointing out that in Chinese popular literature the figure of Chen Ping is invoked as an example of male beauty characterized by feminine looks, complicating the gender implications of the notion of a female Chen Ping.

25. In her analysis of depictions of litigation masters in fictional trickster tales, Melissa Macauley observes that such trickery in the service of the weak (like women) is a common theme and is portrayed as having a particular moral cachet in times of moral disorder and official misrule. See Melissa Macauley, *Social Power and Legal Culture: Litigation Masters in Late Imperial China* (Stanford, Calif.: Stanford University Press, 1998), p. 318.

PART FOUR PROLOGUE

1. XKTB, QL 18.12.3, 199.9.

2. Xue Yunsheng, *Duli cunyi* [Lingering doubts after reading the substatutes], ed. Huang Jingjia (Taibei: Chinese Materials and Research Aids Service Center, 1970), *juan* 43, article 366, pp. 1086–87. The context for the creation of this substatute is discussed in Chapter 2 and below.

CHAPTER 8. THE PROBLEM OF FEMALE MORAL AGENCY

1. Between 1733 (YZ 11) and 1821 (DG 1), approximately twenty substatutes were added or modified to deal with the myriad configurations of suicide due to illicit sex. The vast majority of these additions came in the Qianlong years. See DQHDSL, *juan* 806, pp. 804–15. See also Xue Yunsheng, *Duli cunyi* [Lingering doubts after reading the substatutes], ed. Huang Jingjia (Taibei: Chinese Mate-

rials and Research Aids Service Center, 1970), *juan* 34, article 299, pp. 869–84. For a discussion of the evolution of the body of Qing substatutes dealing with rape and harassment, see M. J. Meijer, "The Price of a P'ai-lou," *T'oung Pao* 67, nos. 3–5 (1981): 292–94.

2. DQHDSL, *juan* 806, pp. 807, 810.
3. DQHDSL, *juan* 403, YZ 11.
4. Xue Yunsheng, *Duli cunyi, juan* 34, p. 878. See also Meijer, "The Price of a P'ai-lou," p. 293.
5. Thirteen years later, Tang Suizu would be the judicial commissioner of Shanxi Province who reviewed the case of Bai Xian and Ren Shi.
6. Xue Yunsheng, *Duli cunyi, juan* 34, p. 877. Translation adapted from that of Meijer, "The Price of a P'ai-lou," p. 293.
7. Xue Yunsheng, *Duli cunyi, juan* 34, p. 881. Translation adapted from that of Meijer, "The Price of a P'ai-lou," p. 293.
8. Translation of quote from D. C. Lau, *Mencius* (New York: Penguin Classics, 1970), p. 132.
9. Quoted in Xue Yunsheng, *Duli cunyi, juan* 34, article 299, pp. 879–80.
10. In his commentary on the illicit sex statute, Yuan Bin reiterated these views even more succinctly: "In my humble opinion, if the statute's intent is to treat execution with reverence, then in cases of rape, it is appropriate for the woman to die, but in cases of harassment, it is not appropriate for the woman to die. However, whether she dies or not, the nature of her victimization varies. The intent of a man who commits coercion is already to compel her to die, so even if she does not commit suicide, his crime is severe. The harasser does not really want to compel her to die, so even if the woman commits suicide, his crime is minor." Quoted in Xue Yunsheng, *Duli cunyi, juan* 43, article 366, p. 1080.
11. The evolution of legislation on female suicide and its relationship to shifting official views of women is discussed at length in Janet M. Theiss, "Managing Martyrdom: Female Suicide and Statecraft in Mid-Qing China," in *Passionate Women: Female Suicide in Late Imperial China*, ed. Paul S. Ropp, Paola Zamperini, and Harriet T. Zurndorfer (Leiden: E. J. Brill, 2001).
12. Those sentenced to strangulation or decapitation after the assizes were placed in different categories during the assizes process: deferred execution, worthy of compassion, remaining at home to care for parents or carry on ancestral sacrifices, or circumstances deserving of death. Only the last category continued them along the path toward execution. For a detailed description of the Autumn Assizes procedures, see Derk Bodde and Clarence Morris, *Law in Imperial China Exemplified by 190 Ch'ing Dynasty Cases Translated from the Hsing-an hui-lan* (Philadelphia: University of Pennsylvania Press, 1967), pp. 134–43, and Thomas Buoye, "Suddenly Murderous Intent Arouse: Bureaucratization and Benevolence in Eighteenth-Century Qing Homicide Reports," *Late Imperial China* 16, no. 2 (1995): 80–81.
13. People sentenced to death and placed in the assizes category of "circumstances deserving of punishment" usually went through the emperor's review process for several years in a row. The policy of special consideration during the

assizes for defendants in flirtation-suicide cases was in force beginning in 1742. It was incorporated into the substatute in 1767 but then removed in 1772 pursuant to a memorialist's suggestion. DQHDSL, *juan* 806, p. 807, and Xue Yunsheng, *Duli cunyi, juan* 34, article 299, p. 878.

14. This memorial is discussed at greater length in Chapter 2. It resulted in a new substatute requiring relatives or village headmen to report such cases and then requiring local magistrates to investigate them. Memorial of Zhang Ruoai, QL 10.11.2, ZPZZ, *neizheng lei, bao* 33, *juan* 46.

15. DQHDSL, *juan* 403, QL 30.

16. Chen Hongmou, *Peiyuan tang oucun gao* [Draft writings from the Peiyuan studio] (1896), quoted in translation in William T. Rowe, "Women and the Family in Mid-Qing Social Thought: The Case of Chen Hongmou," *Late Imperial China* 13, no. 2 (1992): 21.

17. Chen Hongmou, *Jiaonü yigui* [Bequeathed guidelines for instructing women], in *Wuzhong yigui* [Five sets of bequeathed guidelines] (1742; reprint, Shanghai: Jingwei jiaoyu lianhe chubanshe, 1935), p. 40.

18. Ibid.

19. Huang Liuhong, *Fuhui quanshu* [A complete book concerning happiness and benevolence] (n.p., 1699), *juan* 19, pp. 16b–17a.

20. Ibid., *juan* 19, p. 21a.

21. Ibid., *juan* 19, p. 21b.

22. Ibid., *juan* 19, p. 16b.

23. Wang Huizu, *Shuangjietang yongxun* [Simple precepts from the Hall Enshrining a Pair of Chaste Widows] (1794; reprint, Taibei: Huawen shuju, 1970), p. 13a.

24. Ibid., pp. 58a–b.

25. Ibid., p. 22a.

26. On Yuan Mei's views of women, see Paul S. Ropp, *Dissent in Early Modern China: Ju-lin Wai-shih and Ch'ing Social Criticism* (Ann Arbor: University of Michigan Press, 1981). See also Arthur Waley's biography, *Yuan Mei: Eighteenth Century Chinese Poet* (New York: Grove Press, 1956).

27. Yuan Mei, *Zibuyu* [What the master didn't speak of] (Beijing: Zhongguo guoji guangbo chubanshe, 1992), pp. 29–30.

28. XKTB, QL 32.6.22, 214.8.

29. XKTB, QL 45.5.2, 168.4.

30. Though the case record does not explain this, Kang Shi may have thought he was offering her money and understood the gesture of rubbing the mouth of the jar to be obscene.

31. XKTB, QL 45.10.13, 153.3.

32. XKTB, QL 45.7.12, 159.4.

33. He did not explain fully what the precise nature of the misunderstanding was, but it would appear that in the local dialect there was a lewd pun on the verb used for smoking, *chou,* a verb that can also mean "to pull," "to whip," or "to suck." *Chou* is a standard term for a man's thrusting action in the midst of sexual intercourse in erotic literature of the late imperial era. My thanks to an anonymous reviewer for the press for pointing this out.

34. The 1759 edict formulating these new rules on family responsibility was

part of a series of measures, including new substatutes, stemming from Zhang Ruoai's 1745 memorial on the preventability of humiliation suicides. The edict appears in DQHDSL, *juan* 403, QL 24.

35. XKTB, QL 32.11.24, 216.1.

36. Susan Mann, *Precious Records: Women in China's Long Eighteenth Century* (Stanford, Calif.: Stanford University Press, 1997), p. 54.

CHAPTER 9. THE LOGIC OF FEMALE SUICIDE

1. The transgressive meanings of women's suicides in late imperial society have been explored by many scholars of history and literature, including Paola Paderni, "Le rachat de l'honneur perdu: Le suicide des femmes dans la Chine du XVIII siècle" [The recovery of lost honor: Female suicide in eighteenth-century China], *Études Chinoises* 10, nos. 1–2 (1991): 135–60; and Paola Zamperini, "Untamed Hearts: Eros and Suicide in Late Imperial Chinese Fiction," in *Passionate Women: Female Suicide in Late Imperial China*, ed. Paul S. Ropp, Paola Zamperini, and Harriet T. Zurndorfer (Leiden: E. J. Brill, 2001).

2. Examining ethnographic and statistical evidence from the twentieth century, Margery Wolf identifies this as a crisis age for young Chinese women, when they had strikingly high rates of suicide for all sorts of reasons, especially conflicts with mothers-in-law. She notes the powerful and frightening consequences of women's suicides for their families and communities. See Margery Wolf, *Women and the Family in Rural Taiwan* (Stanford, Calif.: Stanford University Press, 1972), pp. 163–64.

3. The destabilizing social effects of sojourning are explored through an examination of cases of abduction and elopement in Lai Huimin and Chu Chingwei, "Funü, jiating yu shehui: Yong Qian shiqi guaitao an de fenxi" [Women, family, and society: A study of abduction and elopement cases in Imperial China (1723–1741)], *Jindai Zhongguo funüshi yanjiu* 8 (June 2000): 1–40.

4. XKTB, QL 32.10.16, 208.1.

5. For an examination of the social contexts and consequences of adultery in the Qing, see Lai Huimin and Hsu Szu-ling, "Qingyu yu xingfa: Qing qianqi fanjian anjian de lishi jiedu (1644–1795)" [Passion and punishment: Historical interpretation of adultery cases in the early Qing dynasty], *Jindai Zhongguo funüshi yanjiu* 6 (August 1998): 31–73.

6. XKTB, QL 32.6.16, 221.1.

7. XKTB, QL 45.2.14, 171.1.

8. XKTB, QL 45.10.17, 160.3.

9. XKTB, QL 60.12.16, 162.10.

10. XKTB, QL 60.11.6, 169.2.

11. XKTB, QL 18.2.28, 202.11.

12. XKTB, QL 32.12.21, 219.8.

13. In the rest of the attempted rape cases without suicide the victim was herself wounded (four), one of her family members or neighbors was killed in an ensuing fight after the assault (seven) or the victim killed the attacker herself (two).

14. It should be noted that statistical analyses of *xingke tiben* cases are always problematic because we do not know what percentage of various types of

cases were preserved in the archive. Thus, we cannot be sure how representative any given sample of a few hundred cases is.

15. I explore the importance of chastity-centered virtue for women's identity in Janet M. Theiss, "Femininity in Flux: Gendered Virtue and Social Conflict in the Mid-Qing Courtroom," in *Chinese Femininities/Chinese Masculinities: An Introductory Reader,* ed. Susan Brownell and Jeffrey Wasserstrom (Berkeley: University of California Press, 2002), pp. 47–66.

16. XKTB, QL 18.1.30, 179.5.
17. XKTB, QL 18.3.23, 189.11.
18. XKTB, QL 18.6.15, 200.6.
19. XKTB, QL 32.5.7, 226.5.
20. XKTB, QL 32.*run*7.9, 211.1.
21. XKTB, QL 18.8.21, 198.8.
22. XKTB, QL 18.5.28, 183.11.
23. XKTB, QL 18.5.2, 204.10.
24. XKTB, QL 18.12.16, 198.7 and QL 18.9.17, 209.1.
25. XKTB, QL 18.3.22, 178.3.
26. XKTB, QL 32.8.20, 216.5.

27. In one unusual case, the defendant even admitted that he spearheaded a gang rape in order to sully the reputation of the victim's family: he rallied his male relatives to beat up a man he suspected (wrongly, it turned out) of having an affair with his own wife. When he burst into the man's house and found his sister home alone, he said, "Since Long Wang is not home, let's humiliate his sister to make him lose face!" (XKTB, QL 18.4.18, 187.8).

28. An example of a husband who committed suicide in reaction to his wife's humiliation is given in XKTB, QL 32.6.18, 220.4; an example of a father in XKTB, QL 18.7.5, 191.2; and an example of a mother in XKTB, QL 18.3.27, 200.9.

29. Paola Paderni's examination of women's suicides, in "Le rachat de l'honneur perdu," foreshadows many of the arguments I make here. She also finds that affronts to women's virtue put them at odds with their families, since the women demanded public vindication while their families were often willing to accept private apologies or amends to keep the matter from becoming public. Women killed themselves to prove their chastity when their families refused to take their cases to court. While I see these differing reactions as expressions of two very different understandings of the significance of chastity, she sees them as an indication that communities were "willing to sacrifice the honor of their weakest members in order to preserve social harmony," while women themselves had "perfectly internalized the moral code that required them to be the accomplices and instruments of their destiny as sacrificial victims for social stability" (p. 154).

30. I also explore this topic in Theiss, "Femininity in Flux."

31. See the *Hanyu dacidian* [The great dictionary of the Chinese language] (Beijing: Hanyu dacidian chubanshe, 1993), vol. 10, p. 1151.

32. Melissa Macauley presents the case of one widow suicide who clearly was "more powerful in death than in life." Melissa Macauley, *Social Power and*

Legal Culture: Litigation Masters in Late Imperial China (Stanford, Calif.: Stanford University Press, 1998), pp. 153–54.

33. Avenging ghosts of those who die wrongful deaths are, of course, extremely common in Chinese fiction. For a discussion of fictional ghosts and their significance, see Anthony C. Yu, "'Rest, Rest, Perturbed Spirit!' Ghosts in Traditional Chinese Prose Fiction," *Harvard Journal of Asiatic Studies* 47, no. 2 (1987): 397–434. Paola Zamperini describes the particular potency of vengeful female ghosts in "Untamed Hearts: Eros and Suicide in Late Imperial Chinese Fiction," in Ropp, Zamperini, and Zurndorfer, *Passionate Women*, pp. 87–96.

34. For detailed descriptions of the performance of the hanged-ghost scene in different regional versions of the Mulian operas, see David Johnson, "Actions Speak Louder Than Words: The Cultural Significance of Chinese Ritual Opera," in *Ritual Opera, Operatic Ritual: "Mu-lien Rescues His Mother" in Chinese Popular Culture*, ed. David Johnson (Berkeley: Publications of the Popular Culture Project, 1989), pp. 20–25.

35. See ibid., p. 27. For a description of the exorcistic qualities of the scene as it was performed in Huizhou in late imperial times, where hanged ghosts were particularly problematic because there were so many female chastity martyrs, see Guo Qitao, "Huizhou Mulian Operas: Conveying Confucian Ethics with 'Demons and Gods'" (Ph.D. diss., University of California, Berkeley, 1994), pp. 278–79.

36. For a discussion of the theme of female chastity in the novel, see Louise Edwards, *Men and Women in Qing China: Gender in The Red Chamber Dream* (Leiden: E. J. Brill, 1994), pp. 51–67 and passim.

37. Many scholars have described how authors like Pu Songling (1640–1715) and Yuan Mei (1716–98) were able to use the vehicle of the supernatural or the bizarre to explore the contradictions of gender norms and play with unconventional images of femininity. See, for example, Judith T. Zeitlin, *Historian of the Strange: Pu Songling and the Chinese Classical Tale* (Stanford, Calif.: Stanford University Press, 1993), pp. 98–131, and Allan Barr, "Disarming Intruders: Alien Women in *Liaozhai zhiyi*," *Harvard Journal of Asiatic Studies* 49, no. 2 (1989): 501–17.

38. Yuan Mei, *Zibuyu* [What the master didn't speak of] (Beijing: Zhongguo guoji guangbo chubanshe, 1992), pp. 29–30.

39. One such magistrate, Wang Huizu, even claimed that over the course of his long career, he dreamed several times that he was taken to the underworld court of King Yama by the ghosts of women who had committed suicide after being sexually harassed. Zhou Guangyuan, "Beneath the Law: Chinese Local Legal Culture during the Qing Dynasty" (Ph.D. diss., University of California, Los Angeles, 1995), p. 319. Qing officials did express concern over the cosmologically disruptive effects of wrongful deaths that were not requited. See ibid., pp. 152–53.

40. Huang Liuhong, *Fuhui quanshu* [A complete book concerning happiness and benevolence] (n.p., 1699), *juan* 15, p. 18b.

41. Lu Xun, in a twentieth-century description of the hanged-ghost scene as he remembered seeing it as a child in Shaoxing, describes how women made use of this terrifying image: "She wore a red jacket and a long black sleeveless coat,

her long hair was in disorder, and two strings of paper coins hung from her neck. With lowered head and drooping hands she wound her way across the stage, tracing out the character for 'heart,' according to those in the know.... Even today, some of the women of Shaoxing powder their faces and change into red gowns before hanging themselves [to ensure that their ghosts will be more malign]." Translated in Johnson, "Actions," p. 23.

42. XKTB, QL 18.4.29, 175.4.
43. XKTB, QL 45.9.30, 169.3.
44. XKTB, QL 18.3.27, 200.9.
45. XKTB, QL 32.12.20, 215.4 and QL 45.7.17, 151.6.
46. XKTB, QL 45.7.12, 159.4. This case is discussed extensively in the previous chapter.
47. For analysis of the literary significance of women warriors, see Edwards, *Men and Women in Qing China*, pp. 87–112; Keith McMahon, *Misers, Shrews and Polygamists: Sexuality and Male-Female Relations in Eighteenth-Century Chinese Fiction* (Durham, N.C.: Duke University Press, 1995), pp. 265–82, passim; and Zeitlin, *Historian of the Strange*, pp. 116–27. On literary constructions of the shrew, see also Yenna Wu, *The Chinese Virago: A Literary Theme* (Cambridge, Mass.: Harvard University, Council on East Asian Studies, 1995).
48. Paderni, "Le rachat de l'honneur perdu," p. 154.
49. Zamperini, "Untamed Hearts," pp. 94–95.
50. Grace Fong, "Signifying Bodies: The Cultural Significance of Suicide Writings by Women in Ming-Qing China," in Ropp, Zamperini, and Zurndorfer, *Passionate Women*, pp. 141–42.
51. Quoted in ibid., p. 126.

EPILOGUE

1. DQHSL, *juan* 403, QL 14.
2. DQHSL, *juan* 404, DG 25.
3. DQHSL, *juan* 404, DG 27.
4. DQHSL, *juan* 404, JQ 4.
5. DQHSL, *juan* 404, JQ 19.
6. DQHSL, *juan* 404, DG 5.
7. DQHSL, *juan* 404, JQ 8. Matthew Sommer has pointed out that this made the policies on canonization consistent with the emphasis on the intent of the victim. Matthew H. Sommer, *Sex, Law, and Society in Late Imperial China* (Stanford, Calif.: Stanford University Press, 2000), p. 313.
8. DQHSL, *juan* 404, XF 1; translation adapted from that of Mark Elvin, "Female Virtue and the State in China." *Past and Present* 104 (August 1984): 129.
9. DQHSL, *juan* 404, XF 4.
10. DQHSL, *juan* 404, XF 11.
11. DQHSL, *juan* 404, TZ 1 and 3.
12. DQHSL, *juan* 404, TZ 8.
13. DQHSL, *juan* 404, TZ 10.
14. Elvin, "Female Virtue," 135.

15. See Angela Leung, "To Chasten Society: The Development of Widow Homes in the Qing," *Late Imperial China* 14, no. 2 (1993): 1–32.

16. See, for example, the editorial principles of one such accounting from the Lower Yangzi region, the *Liangjiang caifang zhongyi lu* [Records of the Bureau for Investigation of Loyalty in Jiangsu and Zhejiang] (n.p., 1887), unpublished, undated translation by Tobie Meyer-Fong.

17. See, for example, *Hangzhou fuzhi* [Gazetteer of Hangzhou Prefecture] (n.p., 1922), *juan* 11, pp. 391–92. Tobie Meyer-Fong gives examples of this kind of interplay between local elites and local officials in the post-Taiping reconstruction of monuments, widow halls, and schools in Yangzhou in an unpublished paper entitled "Civil War and Urban Form: The Taiping Rebellion in Yangzhou," 2003.

18. Susan Glosser explores modern Chinese ideas about the normative role of the state in creating family and gender order, revealing the shared assumptions and goals underlying the agendas of New Culture radicals and both the Nationalist and Communist states. See Susan L. Glosser, *Chinese Visions of Family and State, 1915–1953* (Berkeley: University of California Press, 2003).

19. There are compelling similarities between the High Qing civilizing mission and the twentieth-century notion, examined by John Fitzgerald, of the state's mission to awaken the people. The genealogy of this link remains to be explored. See John Fitzgerald, *Awakening China: Politics, Culture, and Class in the Nationalist Revolution* (Stanford, Calif.: Stanford University Press, 1996).

A Note on Archival Sources

Archival documents from the Number One Historical Archives in Beijing are cited to facilitate their location by future researchers. References to Board of Punishments routine memorials *(xingke tiben)*, all of which come from the archival category of marriage and illicit sex cases *(hunyin jianqing)*, contain their Chinese date, followed by the document bundle *(juan)* number and a unique identification number chosen by myself. So XKTB QL 18.7.10, 194.1 refers to a memorial dated the tenth day of the seventh month of the eighteenth year of the Qianlong reign, from bundle 194 of marriage and illicit sex cases for that year. Rescripted palace memorials *(Zhupi zouzhe*—ZPZZ) are referenced with the name of the memorialist, followed by the memorial's date, category, bundle *(bao)* number, and document *(juan)* number. Copies of rescripted palace memorials *(Lufu zouzhe*—LFZZ) are referenced with the name of the memorialist, followed by the memorial's date, archival document number, microfilm reel number, and microfilm page numbers.

Character List

aiyang 愛養
anchasi 按察司
baihuai menfeng 敗壞門風
bao 保
baojia 保甲
bian 辨
bie 別
bijiao 弼教
buben 部本
bu bixian 不避嫌
bu duobide 不躲避的
bu yi ta 不依他
Cai Wan 蔡琬
Chen Hongmou 陳宏謀
Cheng Hao 程顥
chize 斥責
chou 抽
choushi 醜事
chuqi 出氣
congsi 從死
congsizhe 從死者
Emida 鄂彌達
fa 罰
fanfu 番婦
fen 分
fudao 婦道
gaitu guiliu 改土歸流

Gao Qizhuo 高其倬
gegu 割股
gouhui 垢穢
guanggun 光棍
guanxi lianmian 關係臉面
guinü 閨女
haizuo shenmo ren 還做什麼人
hehu chengjian 嚇唬成姦
He Wei 何煒
hunyin jianqing 婚姻姦情
jiahao 枷號
jian 姦
jianbude ren 見不得人
Jiang Jianian 蔣嘉年
Jiang Pu 蔣溥
jiansheng 監生
jiao 教
jiaohua 教化
jiaoyang 教養
jingbiao 旌表
juede xinli qimen 覺得心理氣悶
kang 炕
kanshou 看守
Lan Dingyuan 籃鼎元
lianchi 廉恥
liang 兩
lifu 嫠婦

Liu Fangai 劉方藹
Li Wei 李衛
Li Yu 李漁
luanmo 亂摸
Lü bei Chen... xiuru jianbude ren zhihao zi jin 屢被陳...羞辱見不得人只好自盡
lufu zouzhe 錄副奏摺
lunchang 倫常
manye 蠻野
mianzi 面子
mu er 木耳
nannü hunza 男女混雜
nannü wufen 男女無分
nannü zhi wubie 男女之無別
neiren 內人
neiwai nanbie 內外難別
ni ai buming 溺愛不明
niangjia 娘家
Nuoqin 訥親
Ortai 鄂爾泰
Ou Kanshan 歐堪善
paifang 牌坊
pingri bu biji 平日不避忌
pingri wanglai 平日往來
qiangduo 搶奪
qiangjian 強姦
qichu 七出
qijian 欺姦
Qing Fu 慶復
qingli 情理
qingsheng 輕生
qingsheng congsi 輕生從死
qiuchu 求處
renli 人理
renzhi 人治
run 閏
shanchu 擅出
shengyuan 生員
Shen Qiyuan 沈起元
shenxun 身殉
shi 石
Shi Jiqi 史積琦
shile jie biyao baochou 失了節必要報讎
shu guai lunji 殊乖倫紀
Shu Min 舒敏

Tang Suizu 唐綏祖
tiaoxi 調戲
tongben 通本
tongyangxi 童養媳
tusi 土司
wang 妄
Wang Huizu 汪輝祖
Wanyan Yunzhu 完顏惲珠
wei zui yuan fa 畏罪願罰
wenmiao 文廟
Wo shi nuren. Bei ta zheyang sacun shizai nanyi zuoren 我是女人。被他這樣撒村實在難以做人
wubao 伍保
wubie 無別
wufu 嫠婦
wu lianchi 無廉恥
xiangyue 鄉約
Xiaodemen yumiao wuzhi. Zhiqiu kai en. 小的們愚苗無知。只求開恩。
xieyu xixue 褻語戲謔
xiuji 羞疾
Xue Yunsheng 薛允升
xunjie juanqu 殉節捐軀
xunnan 殉難
xunsi 殉死
yang 養
Yan Sisheng 晏斯盛
Yao Run 姚潤
Yinjishan 尹繼善
yinren 隱忍
yin ren funü huai ren guimen 淫人婦女壞人閨門
yinxie wuchi 淫邪無恥
yi si xunfu 以死殉夫
yixiyan dimian xiangxia 以戲言覿面相狎者
Yong Tai 永泰
Yuan Bin 袁濱
yuan fei jilie qingsheng 原非激烈輕生
Yuan Mei 袁枚
zaota 遭塌
Zhang Guangsi 張廣泗
Zhang Ruoai 張若靄
Zhang Shijun 張士俊
Zhang Tingyu 張廷玉

Character List

Zhang Zai　張載
Zhao Cheng　趙城
zhenjie guan　真節觀
zheng renxin hou fengsu　正人心厚風俗
zhichi　知恥
zhi zunbei　治尊卑

Zhou Renji　周人驥
zhupi zouzhe　硃批奏摺
zong　宗
zufang　族房
zuzhang　族長
zuzheng　族正
zuzhong　族眾

Bibliography

SOURCES CITED BY ABBREVIATION

DQHDSL   *Da Qing huidian shili* [Collected statutes of the Qing, with substatutes based on precedent]. 1899.
LFZZ   *Lufu zouzhe* [Copies of imperially rescripted palace memorials].
QSL   *Da Qing Gaozong Chun Huangdi shilu* [Veritable records of the Qing Emperor Gaozong]. In *Qing shilu* [Veritable records of the Qing]. Beijing: Zhonghua shuju, 1986.
XKTB   *Xingke tiben* [Board of Punishments routine memorials].
ZPZZ   *Zhupi zouzhe* [Imperially rescripted memorials].

OTHER SOURCES

Ahern, Emily M. "The Power and Pollution of Chinese Women." In *Women in Chinese Society,* edited by Margery Wolf and Roxane Witke, pp. 193–214. Stanford, Calif.: Stanford University Press, 1975.
Alford, William P. "Arsenic and Old Laws: Looking Anew at Criminal Justice in Late Imperial China." *California Law Review* 72, no. 5 (1984): 1180–1256.
Barr, Allan. "Disarming Intruders: Alien Women in *Liaozhai zhiyi.*" *Harvard Journal of Asiatic Studies* 49, no. 2 (1989): 501–17.
Bartlett, Beatrice S. *Monarchs and Ministers: The Grand Council in Mid-Ch'ing China, 1723–1820.* Berkeley: University of California Press, 1991.
Bernhardt, Kathryn. *Women and Property in China, 960–1949.* Stanford, Calif.: Stanford University Press, 1999.
Birge, Bettina. *Women, Property, and Confucian Reaction in Sung and Yüan China (960–1368).* New York: Cambridge University Press, 2002.
Bodde, Derk, and Clarence Morris. *Law in Imperial China Exemplified by 190*

Ch'ing Dynasty Cases Translated from the Hsing-an hui-lan. Philadelphia: University of Pennsylvania Press, 1967.

Bossler, Beverly J. "'A Daughter Is a Daughter All Her Life': Affinal Relations and Women's Networks in Song and Late Imperial China." *Late Imperial China* 21, no. 1 (2000): 77–106.

——. *Powerful Relations: Kinship, Status, and the State in Sung China (960–1279).* Cambridge, Mass.: Harvard University Press, 1998.

Bray, Francesca. *Technology and Gender: Fabrics of Power in Late Imperial China.* Berkeley: University of California Press, 1997.

Brokaw, Cynthia J. *The Ledgers of Merit and Demerit: Social Change and Moral Order in Late Imperial China.* Princeton, N.J.: Princeton University Press, 1991.

Buoye, Thomas, M. *Manslaughter, Markets, and Moral Economy: Violent Disputes over Property Rights in Eighteenth-Century China.* Cambridge: Cambridge University Press, 2000.

——. "Suddenly Murderous Intent Arose: Bureaucratization and Benevolence in Eighteenth-Century Qing Homicide Reports." *Late Imperial China* 16, no. 2 (1995): 62–97.

Cai Linghong. "Cong funü shoujie kan zhenjieguan zai Zhongguo de fazhan" [The development of the concept of female chastity in China]. *Shixue yuekan* 4 (1992): 24–30.

Cao Dawei. "Zhongguo lishi shang zhenjie guannian de bianqian" [Changes in the concept of chastity in Chinese history]. *Zhongguoshi yanjiu* 2 (1991): 24–30.

Carlitz, Katherine. "Desire, Danger, and the Body: Stories of Women's Virtue in Late Ming China." In *Engendering China: Women, Culture, and the State,* edited by Christina Gilmartin, Gail Hershatter, Lisa Rofel, and Tyrene White, pp. 101–24. Cambridge, Mass.: Harvard University Press, 1994.

——. "Shrines, Governing-Class Identity, and the Cult of Widow Fidelity in Mid-Ming Jiangnan." *Journal of Asian Studies* 56, no. 3 (1997): 612–40.

——. "The Daughter, the Singing Girl, and the Seduction of Suicide." In *Passionate Women: Female Suicide in Late Imperial China,* edited by Paul S. Ropp, Paola Zamperini, and Harriet T. Zurndorfer, pp. 22–46. Leiden: E. J. Brill, 2001.

Chang Chung-li. *The Chinese Gentry.* Seattle: University of Washington Press, 1955.

Chen Dongyuan. *Zhongguo funü shenghuo shi* [A history of the lives of Chinese women]. 1937. Reprint, Taibei: Taiwan shangwu yinshuguan, 1997.

Chen Hongmou. *Jiaonü yigui* [Bequeathed guidelines for instructing women]. In *Wuzhong yigui* [Five sets of bequeathed guidelines]. 1742. Reprint, Shanghai: Jingwei jiaoyu lianhe chubanshe, 1935.

——. *Peiyuan tang oucun gao* [Draft writings from the Peiyuan studio]. (1896).

Chin Seihō (Chen Qingfeng). "Shinchō no fujo zokuhyō seido ni tsuite—setsufu, retsujo o chūshin ni" [Concerning the system of commemorative tablets for chaste women in the Qing dynasty—especially chaste widows and martyrs]. *Tōyōshi ronshu* 16 (1988): 101–31.

Chow Kai-wing. *The Rise of Confucian Ritualism in Late Imperial China: Ethics, Classics, and Lineage Discourse.* Stanford, Calif.: Stanford University Press, 1994.

Ch'ü T'ung-tsu. *Local Government in China under the Ch'ing.* 1962. Reprint,

Cambridge, Mass.: Harvard Council on East Asian Studies, Harvard University, 1988.
Crossley, Pamela Kyle. *A Translucent Mirror: History and Identity in Qing Imperial Ideology.* Berkeley: University of California Press, 1999.
Dai Yi. *Qianlongdi ji qi shidai* [Qianlong and his era]. Beijing: Zhongguo renmin daxue chubanshe, 1992.
Davis, Natalie Zemon. *Fiction in the Archives: Pardon Tales and Their Tellers in Sixteenth-Century France.* Stanford, Calif.: Stanford University Press, 1987.
Dong Jiazun. "Lidai jiefu lienü de tongji" [Historical statistics on chaste widows and chastity martyrs]. *Xiandai shixue* 3, no. 2 (1937): 1–5. Reprinted in *Zhongguo funüshi lunji,* edited by Bao Jialin, pp. 205–11. Daoxiang chubanshe, 1979.
Du Fangqin. "Shanglie yu changjie: Ming Qing zhenjie de tedian ji qi yuanyin" [Praise and encouragement of chastity: The characteristics of Ming Qing chastity and its origins]. *Shanxi shifan daxuebao* 4 (1997): 41–46. Reprinted in *Zhongguo shehui xingbie de lishi wenhua xunzong,* edited by Du Fangqin. Tianjin: Tianjin shehui kexue yuan chubanshe, 1998.
Ebrey, Patricia Buckley. *Family and Property in Sung China: Yüan Ts'ai's Precepts for Social Life.* Princeton, N.J.: Princeton University Press, 1984.
———. "The Liturgies for Sacrifices to the Ancestors in Successive Versions of the 'Family Rituals.'" In *Ritual and Scripture in Chinese Popular Religion,* edited by David Johnson, pp. 104–36. Berkeley: Publications of the Popular Culture Project, 1995.
Ebrey, Patricia Buckley, and James L. Watson, eds. *Kinship Organization in Late Imperial China 1000–1940.* Berkeley: University of California Press, 1986.
Edwards, Louise. *Men and Women in Qing China: Gender in the Red Chamber Dream.* Leiden: E. J. Brill, 1994.
Elliot, Mark C. "Manchu Widows and Ethnicity in Qing China." *Comparative Studies in Society and History* 41, no. 1 (1999): 33–71.
———. *The Manchu Way: The Eight Banners and Ethnic Identity in Late Imperial China.* Stanford, Calif.: Stanford University Press, 2001.
Elvin, Mark. "Female Virtue and the State in China." *Past and Present* 104 (August 1984): 111–52.
Epstein, Maram. *Competing Discourses: Orthodoxy, Authenticity and Engendered Meanings in Late Imperial Chinese Fiction.* Cambridge, Mass.: Harvard University Asia Center, 2001.
Fei Chengkang. *Zhongguo jiafa zugui* [Family and clan regulations in China]. Shanghai: Shanghai shehui kexue yuan chubanshe, 1998.
Fei Si-yen. *You dianfan dao guifan: Cong Mingdai zhenjie lienü de bianshi yu liuchuan kan zhenjie guannian de yangehua* [From model to standard: The development and rising popularity of increasingly rigid views on female chastity in the Ming dynasty]. M.A. thesis, National Taiwan University, 1996.
Feng Erkang. *Yongzheng zhuan* [A biography of the Yongzheng Emperor]. Beijing: Renmin chubanshe, 1985.
Fitzgerald, John. *Awakening China: Politics, Culture, and Class in the Nationalist Revolution.* Stanford, Calif.: Stanford University Press, 1996.
Fong, Grace. "Signifying Bodies: The Cultural Significance of Suicide Writings

by Women in Ming-Qing China." In *Passionate Women: Female Suicide in Late Imperial China*, edited by Paul S. Ropp, Paola Zamperini, and Harriet T. Zurndorfer, pp. 105–42. Leiden: E. J. Brill, 2001.

Furth, Charlotte. "The Patriarch's Legacy: Household Instructions and the Transmission of Orthodox Values." In *Orthodoxy in Late Imperial China*, edited by Liu Kwang-ching, pp. 187–211. Berkeley: University of California Press, 1990.

Gao Mai. "Woguo zhenjietang zhidu de yanbian" [The evolution of the system of chaste widow halls in our country]. *Dongfang zazhi* 32, no. 5 (1935): 101–4. Reprinted in *Zhongguo funüshi lunji*, [Collected essays on Chinese women's history], edited by Bao Jialin, pp. 205–11. Taibei: Daoxiang chubanshe, 1979.

Giersch, Charles Patterson. "Qing China's Reluctant Subjects: Indigenous Communities and Empire along the Yunnan Frontier." Ph.D. diss., Yale University, 1998.

Glosser, Susan L. *Chinese Visions of Family and State, 1915–1953*. Berkeley: University of California Press, 2003.

Gottschang, Thomas, and Diana Lary. *Swallows and Settlers: The Great Migration from North China to Manchuria*. Michigan Monographs in Chinese History, vol. 87. Ann Arbor: Center for Chinese Studies, University of Michigan, 2000.

Guo Qitao. "Huizhou Mulian Operas: Conveying Confucian Ethics with 'Demons and Gods.'" Ph.D. diss., University of California, Berkeley, 1994.

Guy, R. Kent. *The Emperor's Four Treasuries: Scholars and the State in the Late Ch'ien-lung Era*. Cambridge, Mass.: Harvard University Press, 1989.

Hanan, Patrick. *The Invention of Li Yu*. Cambridge, Mass.: Harvard University Press, 1988.

Hangzhou fuzhi [Gazetteer of Hangzhou Prefecture]. N.p., 1922.

Hanyu dacidian [The great dictionary of the Chinese language]. Beijing: Hanyu dacidian chubanshe, 1993.

He Changling, comp. *Huangchao jingshi wenbian* [Statecraft compendium from the Qing dynasty]. 1826. Reprint, Taibei: Guofeng, 1963.

Holmgren, Jennifer. "The Economic Foundations of Virtue: Widow-Remarriage in Early and Modern China." *Australian Journal of Chinese Affairs* 13 (1985): 1–27.

Hsiao Kung-ch'uan. *Rural China: Imperial Control in the Nineteenth Century*. Seattle: University of Washington Press, 1960.

Huang Liuhong. *A Complete Book Concerning Happiness and Benevolence: "Fu-hui ch'uan-shu": A Manual for Local Magistrates in Seventeenth Century China*. Translated and edited by Djang Chu. Tucson: University of Arizona Press, 1984.

———. *Fuhui quanshu* [A complete book concerning happiness and benevolence]. N.p., 1699.

Huang Pei. *Autocracy at Work: A Study of the Yung-cheng Period, 1723–1735*. Bloomington: Indiana University Press, 1974.

Huang, Philip C. C. *Civil Justice in China: Representation and Practice in the Qing*. Stanford, Calif.: Stanford University Press, 1996.

Hummel, Arthur W., ed. *Eminent Chinese of the Ch'ing Period.* Washington, D.C.: U.S. Government Printing Office, 1943. Reprint, Taipei: SMC Publishing, 1991.

Issett, Christopher Mills. "State, Peasant and Agrarian Change on the Manchurian Frontier, 1644–1940." Ph.D. diss., University of California, Los Angeles, 1998.

Jenks, Robert D. *Insurgency and Social Disorder in Guizhou: The "Miao" Rebellion, 1854–1873.* Honolulu: University of Hawaii Press, 1994.

Johnson, David. "Actions Speak Louder Than Words: The Cultural Significance of Chinese Ritual Opera." In *Ritual Opera, Operatic Ritual: "Mu-lien Rescues His Mother" in Chinese Popular Culture,* edited by David Johnson, pp. 1–45. Berkeley: Publications of the Popular Culture Project, 1989.

———, ed. *Ritual Opera, Operatic Ritual: "Mu-lien Rescues His Mother" in Chinese Popular Culture.* Berkeley: Publications of the Popular Culture Project, 1989.

Johnson, David, Andrew J. Nathan, and Evelyn S. Rawski, eds. *Popular Culture in Late Imperial China.* Berkeley: University of California Press, 1985.

Karasawa, Yasuhiko. "Between Speech and Writing: Textuality of the Written Record of Oral Testimony in Qing Legal Cases." *Chūgoku shakai to bunka* 10 (1995): 212–50.

———. "Legal Plaints and Their Writers in the Qing." *Chūgoku shakai to bunka* 13 (1998): 306–30.

Ko, Dorothy. *Teachers of the Inner Chambers: Women and Culture in Seventeenth-Century China.* Stanford, Calif.: Stanford University Press, 1994.

———. *Every Step a Lotus, Shoes for Bound Feet.* Berkeley: University of California Press, 2001.

Kuhn, Philip H. *Soulstealers: The Chinese Sorcery Scare of 1768.* Cambridge, Mass.: Harvard University Press, 1990.

Kutcher, Norman. *Mourning in Late Imperial China: Filial Piety and the State.* New York: Cambridge University Press, 1999.

Lai Huimin and Chu Ching-wei. "Funü, jiating yu shehui: Yong Qian shiqi guaitao an de fenxi" [Women, family and society: A study of abduction and elopement cases in imperial China (1723–1741)]. *Jindai Zhongguo funüshi yanjiu* 8 (June 2000): 1–40.

Lai Huimin and Hsu Szu-ling. "Qingyu yu xingfa: Qing qianqi fanjian anjian de lishi jiedu (1644–1795)" [Passion and punishment: Historical interpretation of adultery cases in the early Qing dynasty]. *Jindai Zhongguo funüshi yanjiu* 6 (August 1998): 31–73.

Lan Dingyuan. *Nüxue* [Lessons for women]. N.d. (early eighteenth century). Reprint, n.p., 1897.

Lau, D. C. *Mencius.* New York: Penguin Classics, 1970.

Lee, James. "Homicide et peine capitale en Chine a la fin de l'empire: Analyse statistique préliminaire des données." *Études chinoises* 10, nos. 1–2 (1991): 115–16.

Lee, James Z., and Cameron Campbell. *Fate and Fortune in Rural China: Social Organization and Population Behavior in Liaoning, 1774–1873.* New York: Cambridge University Press, 1997.

Lee, Robert H. G. *The Manchurian Frontier in Ch'ing History.* Cambridge, Mass.: Harvard University Press, 1970.
Legge, James. *The Works of Mencius: Translated, with Critical and Exegetical Notes, Prolegomena, and Copious Indexes.* New York: Dover Publications, 1970.
Leung, Angela. "To Chasten Society: The Development of Widow Homes in the Qing." *Late Imperial China* 14, no. 2 (1993): 1–32.
Li Yu. *Silent Operas* [Wusheng xi]. Edited by Patrick Hanan. Hong Kong: Chinese University of Hong Kong, 1990.
Liu, Hui-chen Wang. *The Traditional Chinese Clan Rules.* New York : J. J. Augustin, 1959.
Liu Jihua. "Zhongguo zhenjie guannian de lishi yanbian" [The historical evolution of the chastity concept in China]. *Shehui xuejie* 8 (1934):19–35. Reprinted in *Zhongguo funüshi lunji, siji* [Collected essays on Chinese women's history, vol. 4], edited by Bao Jialin, 101–30. Taibei: Daoxiang chubanshe, 1995.
Macauley, Melissa. *Social Power and Legal Culture: Litigation Masters in Late Imperial China.* Stanford, Calif.: Stanford University Press, 1998.
———. "A World Made Simple: Law and Property in the Ottoman and Qing Empires." *Journal of Early Modern History* 5, no. 4 (2001): 331–52.
Mair, Victor H. "Language and Ideology in the Written Popularizations of the *Sacred Edict.*" In *Popular Culture in Late Imperial China,* edited by David Johnson, Andrew J. Nathan, and Evelyn S. Rawski, pp. 325–59. Berkeley: University of California Press, 1985.
Mann, Susan. "Widows in the Kinship, Class, and Community Structures of Qing Dynasty China." *Journal of Asian Studies* 46, no. 1 (1987): 37–56.
———. "Grooming a Daughter for Marriage: Brides and Wives in the Mid-Ch'ing Period." In *Marriage and Inequality in Chinese Society,* edited by Rubie S. Watson and Patricia Buckley Ebrey, pp. 204–30. Berkeley: University of California Press, 1991.
———. "Household Handicrafts and State Policy in Qing Times." In *To Achieve Security and Wealth: The Qing Imperial State and the Economy, 1644–1911,* edited by Jane Kate Leonard and John R. Watt, pp. 75–95. Ithaca, N.Y.: Cornell University East Asia Program, 1992.
———. "Suicide and Survival: Exemplary Widows in the Late Empire." In *Chūgoku no dentō shakai to kazoku: Yanagida Setsuko sensei koki kinen ronshū* [Family and society in traditional China: Essays in honor of Professor Yanagida Setsuko], pp. 23–39. Tokyo: Kyuko shoin, 1993.
———. "The Education of Daughters in the Mid-Ch'ing Period." In *Education and Society in Late Imperial China, 1600–1900,* edited by Benjamin A. Elman and Alexander Woodside, pp. 19–49. Berkeley: University of California Press, 1994.
———. *Precious Records: Women in China's Long Eighteenth Century.* Stanford, Calif.: Stanford University Press, 1997.
McMahon, Keith. *Misers, Shrews, and Polygamists: Sexuality and Male-Female Relations in Eighteenth-Century Chinese Fiction.* Durham, N.C.: Duke University Press, 1995.
Meijer, M. J. "The Price of a P'ai-lou." *T'oung Pao* 67, nos. 3–5 (1981): 288–304.

———. *Murder and Adultery in Late Imperial China.* Leiden: E. J. Brill, 1991.
Meyer-Fong, Tobie. "Civil War and Urban Form: The Taiping Rebellion in Yangzhou." Unpublished paper, 2003.
Millward, James. "A Uyghur Muslim in Qianlong's Court: The Meanings of the Fragrant Concubine." *Journal of Asian Studies* 53, no. 2 (1994): 427–58.
Naquin, Susan. *Shantung Rebellion: The Wang Lun Uprising of 1774.* New Haven, Conn.: Yale University Press, 1981.
Naquin, Susan, and Chün-Fang Yü, eds. *Pilgrims and Sacred Sites in China.* Berkeley: University of California Press, 1992.
Ng, Vivien. "Ideology and Sexuality: Rape Laws in Qing China." *Journal of Asian Studies* 46, no. 1 (1987): 57–70.
Ocko, Jonathan K. "I'll Take It All the Way to Beijing: Capital Appeals in the Qing." *Journal of Asian Studies* 47, no. 2 (1988): 291–315.
Paderni, Paola. "Le rachat de l'honneur perdu: Le suicide des femmes dans la Chine du XVIII siècle" [The recovery of lost honor: Female suicide in eighteenth-century China]. *Études Chinoises* 10, nos. 1–2 (1991): 135–60.
———. "An Appeal Case of Honor in Eighteenth Century China." In *Ming Qing Yanjiu* [Ming Qing studies], pp. 87–97. Rome: Dipartimento di Studi Asiatici, Istituto Universitario Orientale, 1992.
———. "I Thought I Would Have Some Happy Days: Women Eloping in Eighteenth-Century China." *Late Imperial China* 16, no. 1 (June 1995): 1–32.
———. "Between Constraints and Opportunities: Widows, Witches, and Shrews in Eighteenth-Century China." In *Chinese Women in the Imperial Past, New Perspectives,* edited by Harriet Zurndorfer, 258–85. Leiden: E. J. Brill, 1999.
Perdue, Peter C. *Exhausting the Earth: State and Peasant in Hunan, 1500–1850.* Cambridge, Mass.: Council on East Asian Studies, Harvard University, 1987.
Rawski, Evelyn S. *The Last Emperors: A Social History of Qing Imperial Institutions.* Berkeley: University of California Press, 1998.
Robertson, Maureen. "Changing the Subject: Gender and Self-Inscription in Authors' Prefaces and 'Shi' Poetry." In *Writing Women in Late Imperial China,* edited by Ellen Widmer and Kang-I Sun Chang, pp. 171–217. Stanford, Calif.: Stanford University Press, 1997.
Ropp, Paul S. "The Seeds of Change: Reflections on the Condition of Women in the Early and Mid-Ch'ing." *Signs* 2, no. 1 (1976): 5–23.
———. *Dissent in Early Modern China: Ju-lin Wai-shih and Ch'ing Social Criticism.* Ann Arbor: University of Michigan Press, 1981.
Ropp, Paul S., Paola Zamperini, and Harriet T. Zurndorfer, eds. *Passionate Women: Female Suicide in Late Imperial China.* Leiden: E. J. Brill, 2001.
Rowe, William T. "Women and the Family in Mid-Qing Social Thought: The Case of Chen Hongmou." *Late Imperial China* 13, no. 2 (1992): 1–41.
———. "Education and Empire in Southwest China: Ch'en Hong-mou in Yunnan, 1733–38." In *Education in Late Imperial China (1600–1900),* edited by Benjamin A. Elman and Alexander Woodside, pp. 417–57. Berkeley: University of California Press, 1994.
———. *Saving the World: Chen Hongmou and Elite Consciousness in Eighteenth-Century China.* Stanford, Calif.: Stanford University Press, 2001.
Shanhua xianzhi. [Gazetteer of Shanhua County]. 1818.

Shiga Shūzō. "Criminal Procedure in the Ch'ing Dynasty—with Emphasis on Its Administrative Character and Some Allusion to Its Historical Antecedents (I)." *Memoirs of the Research Department of the Tōyō Bunko* 32 (1974): 1–45.

———. "Criminal Procedure in the Ch'ing Dynasty—with Emphasis on Its Administrative Character and Some Allusion to Its Historical Antecedents (II)." *Memoirs of the Research Department of the Tōyō Bunko* 33 (1975): 115–38.

Sima Qian. *Records of the Grand Historian of China.* Translated by Burton Watson. New York: Columbia University Press, 1961.

Siu, Helen F. "Where Were the Women? Rethinking Marriage Resistance and Regional Culture in South China." *Late Imperial China* 11, no. 2 (1990): 32–62.

Smith, Kent C. "Ch'ing Policy and the Development of Southwest China: Aspects of Ortai's Governor-Generalship, 1726–1731." Ph.D. diss., Yale University, 1970.

Sommer, Matthew H. "The Uses of Chastity: Sex, Law, and the Property of Widows in Qing China." *Late Imperial China* 17, no. 2 (1996): 77–130.

———. *Sex, Law, and Society in Late Imperial China.* Stanford, Calif.: Stanford University Press, 2000.

Spence, Jonathan. *The Death of Woman Wang.* New York: Penguin Books, 1978.

Stockard, Janice E. *Daughters of the Canton Delta: Marriage Patterns and Economic Strategies in South China, 1860–1930.* Stanford, Calif.: Stanford University Press, 1989.

Sutton, Donald. "Myth Making on an Ethnic Frontier: The Cult of the Heavenly Kings of West Hunan, 1715–1996." *Modern China* 26, no. 4 (2000): 448–500.

Theiss, Janet M. "Dealing with Disgrace: The Negotiation of Female Virtue in Eighteenth-Century China." Ph.D. diss., University of California, Berkeley, 1998.

———. "Managing Martyrdom: Female Suicide and Statecraft in Mid-Qing China." In *Passionate Women: Female Suicide in Late Imperial China*, edited by Paul S. Ropp, Paola Zamperini, and Harriet T. Zurndorfer, pp. 47–76. Leiden: E. J. Brill, 2001.

———. "Femininity in Flux: Gendered Virtue and Social Conflict in the Mid-Qing Courtroom." In *Chinese Femininities/Chinese Masculinities: An Introductory Reader,* edited by Susan Brownell and Jeffrey Wasserstrom, pp. 47–66. Berkeley: University of California Press, 2002.

T'ien Ju-k'ang. *Male Anxiety and Female Chastity: A Comparative Study of Chinese Ethical Values in Ming-Ch'ing Times.* Leiden: E. J. Brill, 1988.

Topley, Marjorie. "Marriage Resistance in Rural Kwangtung." In *Women in Chinese Society,* edited by Margery Wolf and Roxane Witke, pp. 67–88. Stanford, Calif.: Stanford University Press, 1975.

Wakeman, Frederic, Jr. *The Great Enterprise: The Manchu Reconstruction of Imperial Order in Seventeenth-Century China.* 2 vols. Berkeley: University of California Press, 1985.

Waley, Arthur. *Yuan Mei: Eighteenth Century Chinese Poet.* New York: Grove Press, 1956.

Waltner, Ann. "Widows and Remarriage in Ming and Early Qing China." In *Women in China: Current Directions in Historical Scholarship*, edited by Richard W. Guisso and Stanley Johannesen, pp. 129–46. Youngstown, N.Y.: Philo Press, 1981.

Wang Gungwu. "The Chinese Urge to Civilize: Reflections on Change." *Journal of Asian History* 18, no. 1 (1984): 1–34.

Wang Huizu. *Shuangjietang yongxun* [Simple precepts from the Hall Enshrining a Pair of Chaste Widows]. 1794. Reprint, Taibei: Huawen shuju, 1970.

Wang Yuelin, comp. *Puan zhou zhi* [Gazetteer of Puan District]. N.p., 1758.

Wanyan Yunzhu, comp. *Guochao guixiu zhengshi ji* [Correct beginnings: Women's poetry of our august dynasty]. Hongxiangguan edition, 1831.***ch. 6bn***

Wiens, Herold J. *Han Chinese Expansion in South China*. Originally published in 1954 as *China's March to the Tropics*. Reprint, Hamden, Conn.: Shoe String Press, 1967.

Will, Pierre-Etienne. *Bureaucracy and Famine in Eighteenth-Century China*. Stanford, Calif.: Stanford University Press, 1990.

———. "The 1774 Annual Audits of Magistrate Activity and Their Fate." *Late Imperial China* 18, no. 2 (1998): 12–14.

———, ed. "Official Handbooks and Anthologies of China: A Descriptive and Critical Bibliography." Unpublished manuscript.

Wolf, Marjorie. *Women and the Family in Rural Taiwan*. Stanford, Calif.: Stanford University Press, 1972.

———. "Women and Suicide in China." In *Women in Chinese Society*, edited by Margery Wolf and Roxane Witke, pp. 111–41. Stanford, Calif.: Stanford University Press, 1975.

Wong, R. Bin. *China Transformed: Historical Change and the Limits of European Experience*. Ithaca, N.Y.: Cornell University Press, 1997.

Wu, Silas. *Communication and Control in Late Imperial China: Evolution of the Palace Memorial System, 1693–1735*. Cambridge, Mass.: Harvard University Press, 1970.

Wu, Silas Hsiu-Liang. "The Memorial Systems of the Ch'ing Dynasty (1644–1911)." *Harvard Journal of Asiatic Studies* 27 (1967): 7–75.

Wu, Yenna. *The Chinese Virago: A Lierary Theme*. Cambridge, Mass.: Harvard University, Council on East Asian Studies, 1995.

Wuxi Jinkui xianzhi. [Gazetteer of Wuxi and Jinkui County]. 1881.

Xue Yunsheng. *Duli cunyi* [Lingering doubts after reading the substatutes]. Edited by Huang Jingjia. Taibei: Chinese Materials and Research Aids Service Center, 1970.

Yamazaki Jun'ichi. "Shinchō ni okeru setsu-retsu zokuhyō ni tsuite" [On awards for virtuous widowhood in the Qing dynasty]. *Chūgoku koten kenkyū* 15, no. 12 (1967): 46–66.

Yao Run, Ren Pengnian, Tao Jun, and Tao Mianlin, eds. *Da Qing lüli zengxiu tongcuan jicheng* [Revised comprehensive compilation of the Qing Code]. N.p., 1878.

Yu, Anthony C. "'Rest, Rest, Perturbed Spirit!' Ghosts in Traditional Chinese Prose Fiction." *Harvard Journal of Asiatic Studies* 47, no. 2 (1987): 397–434.

Yuan Mei. *Zibuyu* [What the master didn't speak of]. Beijing: Zhongguo guoji guangbo chubanshe, 1992.

Yuasa Yukihiko. "Shindai ni okeru fujin kaihō ron: Rikyō to ningen teki shizen" [On women's emancipation in the Qing: Lijiao versus human nature]. *Nippon-Chūgoku gakkaihō* 4 (1952): 111–25.

Zamperini, Paola. "Untamed Hearts: Eros and Suicide in Late Imperial Chinese Fiction." In *Passionate Women: Female Suicide in Late Imperial China*, edited by Paul S. Ropp, Paola Zamperini, and Harriet T. Zurndorfer, pp. 77–104. Leiden: E. J. Brill, 2001.

Zeitlin, Judith T. *Historian of the Strange: Pu Songling and the Chinese Classical Tale*. Stanford, Calif.: Stanford University Press, 1993.

Zelin, Madeleine. *The Magistrate's Tael: Rationalizing Fiscal Reform in Eighteenth-Century China*. Berkeley: University of California Press, 1984.

Zhang Jinfan. *Zhongguo fazhi shi* [A history of the Chinese legal system]. Beijing: Zhonghua shuju, 1998.

Zheng Qin. "Pursuing Perfection: Formation of the Qing Code." *Modern China* 21, no. 3 (1995): 310–45.

Zhou Guangyuan. "Beneath the Law: Chinese Local Legal Culture during the Qing Dynasty." Ph.D. diss., University of California, Los Angeles, 1995.

Zhu Yong. *Qingdai zongzu fa yanjiu* [A study of lineage law in the Qing]. Changsha: Hunan chubanshe, 1987.

Zurndorfer, Harriet T. "Han-Hsüeh, 'Evidential Research,' and Female Chastity: A Re-examination of Intellectual Attitudes and Social Ideals in 18th Century China." In *Thought and Law in Qin and Han China: Studies Dedicated to Anthony Hulsewe on the Occasion of His Eightieth Birthday*, edited by W. L. Idema and E. Zürcher, pp. 208–24. Leiden: E. J. Brill, 1990.

Index

adultery: apprehending adulterers, 100–107, 211; cases, 71–75, 76–77; circumstances of, 192–94; incest and, 108–11; natal family reaction to, 94–97; as social problem, 48–49
aiyang (loving support), 35–37, 44
apology, as response to insult or assault, 92–93, 95, 196, 200, 201
assizes. *See* Autumn Assizes
attempted rape, cases, 17–23
Audit Campaign. See *jiaohua* campaign
Autumn Assizes, 147, 181, 247–48n46

banditry, and canonization, 213, 217
baojia system, 83; bao headmen, 68, 137
barbarian: in reference to uncivilized customs, 135–36; as term for non-Han people, 9, 21, 38, 46
Bian. See gender separation
Bie. See gender separation
Biographies, female virtue portrayed in, 26–27, 98–99
Birge, Bettine, 26
Bo Yi, 162
Board of Rites, 215, 217
Board of Punishments, 80, 109; regulation of forensic examination of women, 139, 220n9
Book of Rites (Liji), 137–38, 141
brother–sister bond, 91, 92–94, 168–75
bureaucratization: of chastity cult, 30, 37; and the Yongzheng Emperor, 34

Bureau for the Investigation of Chastity *(caifang zhongjie ju)*, 217
Bureau for the Investigation of Loyalty *(caifang zhongyi ju)*, 217

Cai Wan, 227n32
Campbell, Cameron, 82
cangue *(jiahao)*, and women, 138
canonization: corruption and, 215–16; rules for, 27–33, 47–48, 177, 182–83, 212–17; social effects of, 22–23; as vindication for women, 203–5
Carlitz, Katherine, 26
censure *(chize)*, 72
chaste widows *(jiefu)*: as ghosts, 204–5; Ming period chastity cult and, 26; Qing imperial canonization of, 25–38, 216; in the Song, 25–26; in Yuan law, 26
chastity: constructed nature of, 152–53, 163–64; and filiality, 110–12, 116–17; and intent, 127–30, 198; multiple definitions of, 130–32; political significance of, 211–18; and the rape statute, 142–53; social practice of, 133–41, 154–64; in tension with patriarchal authority, 10, 52, 71, 74, 79, 98–117, 211; women's definition of, 121–32, 192–203
chastity arch *(paifang, pailou)*, 22, 28, 31, 212–13

275

chastity award system, canonization system: in the Ming, 26–27; in the Qing, 25–38, 177; in the Yuan, 26
chastity-centered female virtue, 2, 13, 34, 62, 160
chastity cult: local significance of, 17, 20–23; in the Ming, 26–27; in the Qing, 7, 25–38; after the Taiping Rebellion, 216–17
chastity martyrs *(liefu)*: elite male views of, 183–87; family and community views of, 187–91, 192–209; judicial treatment of, 17–23, 177–83; Ming chastity cult and, 26–27; rules for canonization in the Qing, 25–38, 177; social significance of, 20–23; women's views of martyrdom, 192–209
Chen Hongmou, 48–49, 66–67, 87, 140, 141, 183, 244n10, 246n30, 246–47n32
Chen Ping, 162
Cheng Hao, 42
chize. See censure
choushi. See disgraceful matters
civilizing mission: gender separation and, 133–41, 160; in Qing political discourse, 7–8, 10, 21–23, 27–28; in the Qianlong reign, 39–54; role of lineage leaders in, 69; Yongzheng Emperor's view of, 33–38
clan punishment, lineage punishment, 65–81, 196
clan rules, lineage regulations, 72–73, 76, 78, 134
coercion ending in consent, 143–52
commemorative stone arch *(pailou, paifang). See* chastity arch
Communists, 218
companionate marriage, 11, 98–99
compensation, as response to insult or assault, 196, 200–201
concubines, 47, 90–91, 101; canonization of, 213
confiscation of property, as a lineage punishment, 73, 78
Confucius Temple *(wenmiao)*, in relation to state chastity shrines, 21, 31–32
conjugal bond, 98–99, 211
coroners, handling of women, 139–40
corporal punishment *(zechu)*, 76
counterplaint, 19, 21, 73–74
county magistrate: adjudication of harassment cases, 52–53, 182; adjudication of rape cases, 19–23, 124–30, 167–75; and family authority, 66–67, 80; role in mediation, 59, 61, 63; role in moral transformation, 21–23, 42–43

daughters-in-law: obligations of, in prescriptive literature, 83–89; tensions with mothers-in-law, 57–60, 91–92
delayed-transfer marriage, 18
descent group *(zong)*, role in adjudication, 61, 65–81
disgraceful matters *(choushi)*, 4, 6, 13, 62, 75–76, 79, 94, 103, 168, 169, 193, 199, 202
divorce, 60–61, 104; seven offenses as grounds for, 90
domestic violence, wife-killing, cases, 57–63, 95
dowry, 26
drunkenness, as circumstance for impropriety, 168–69, 172, 189, 194–95

education: and the civilizing mission, 7, 44; vs. punishments, 50; for women, 161, 185
Eight Trigrams Rebellion, 213
Elvin, Mark, 216
Emida, 137–38, 245n18
eulogies, 26–27
expulsion from lineage, as form of punishment, 73
extrajudicial punishment, 68–71

face. *See* reputation
false accusation, 74, 78–79
false testimony, 145
family elders, 10, 43, 52, 174
family head, 168, 172
family instructions, 59, 65–66
family life cycle, 82
Fang Guancheng, 110
Fei Si-yen, 26
female seclusion. *See* inner/outer paradigm
femininity, 13, 160
fen. See gender separation
Fengtian, 92–94, 112–13, 121–32
fertility, 82
fiction: conjugal intimacy in, 98–99; female ghosts in, 204–5, 207; maintaining chastity in, 130–32, 161–64; non-Han people in, 136; treatment of women's outrage in, 185–87
filial piety: and the civilizing mission, 7, 28, 39, 41, 65; in conflict with chastity, 112–17; and daughters-in-law, 85–86, 87–89, 161; filial obedience, 62, 112; as political metaphor, 110, 116–17

Index

flirtation *(tiaoxi)* leading to suicide: cases, 17–23, 29, 75–76, 79–80, 156–57, 158–61, 167–75, 193, 194–95; in law and ritual regulations, 29, 51–53, 177–83

Fong, Grace, 207

footbinding, 185; Qing ban on, 28

forensic examinations, and women, 139–40

fudao. See wifely way

Fujian, 71–75, 202

funerary rituals: propriety of as social problem, 40, 44–46, 49–50, 136, 141; as source of family conflict, 91–92; women's duties in, 88

gaitu guiliu policy, 19, 70

Gansu, 114

Gao Qizhuo, 36

Gegu: and canonization policies, 213; Qing ban on, 28

gender division of labor, 40, 134, 136–37

gender performance, vs. status performance, 8, 53

gender separation *(bian, bie, fen)*: and civilization, 44, 133–41, 152–53; as foundation of gender order, 11, 183–84; in social practice, 154–64

ghosts, 185–87, 204–6

Guangdong, 79–80, 215–16

Guanggun. See rogue male

Guangxi, 201

Guangxu Emperor, 216–17

Guinü, 151

Guizhou, 17–23, 32, 136

Han Gaozu, 130, 163

Han Guangji, 217

Hangzhou, 217

He Wei, 47–48, 182

Henan, 156, 158–61, 196–97, 201, 205

heterodox religious sects, gender impropriety and, 7, 40, 135, 140

homicide: role of lineage leaders in adjudicating, 68–69, 71, 167–75; wife-killing, case 57–63

household structure, 82

Huang Liuhong, 124–25, 127–28, 129–30, 144, 151–52, 184, 194, 205

Huang, Philip, 61

Hubei, 206

Huguang, 137

humiliation *(wuru)*: defined, 203; as female reaction to assault or insult, 177–91; as motivation for female suicide, 192–209

Hunan, 32, 137, 139, 193

illicit sex *(jian)*: coerced versus consensual, 143–52, 164; as judicial term, 19, 222n4; and Qing gender order, 8; substatutes on, 48–49, 142–53

imperial clan, canonization policy and, 28

impropriety, unintentional forms of, 187–91

incest: coerced, 112–16; consensual, 19, 76, 108; and contradictions of Qing gender ideology, 10, 11, 108–17; and substatutes on killing adulterers, 101, 108–9, 211

individualism, 53–54

infanticide: as form of birth control, 242n5; as target for moral reform, 39

inner/outer paradigm *(nei/wai)*: behavioral aspects of, 134–35, 150, 152; psychology of, 202–3; and Qing gender order, 11–12, 133–41; in social practice, 192, 154–64; spatial dimensions of, 123, 134, 150, 152, 154

inner people *(neiren)*, 160

inner quarters: demarcation of, 248n2; equated with women's bodies, 142

itinerant laborers, 123, 149

jiahao. See cangue

jian. See illicit sex

Jiang Jianian, 104–5

Jiang Pu, 139, 246n24

Jiangnan (Lower Yangzi region), 140, 146, 161

Jiangsu, 32–33, 36, 57–63, 150–51, 188–89

Jiangxi, 76–80

jiaohua (moral transformation), 21–23, 35–36, 39–54, 61–62, 66, 96, 133–41

jiaohua campaign (Audit Campaign), 39–54, 133–41

jiaoyang, 35–36, 49

Jiaqing Emperor, 213

Jiefu. See chaste widows

jiexiao ci. See Shrine to the Chaste and Filial

jingbiao. See canonization

jingshi. See statecraft

judicial procedure: educational effects of, 21–22; women in, 138–40

Kangxi Emperor, 7, 28, 34; view of lineage judicial authority, 68

kidnapping for marriage, 40, 46, 48–49, 90

killing the adulterer: in Ming Code, 100; Qianlong Emperor's approach to, 101–2, 104–6; substatutes on, 100–107; in Tang Code, 100–101; Yongzheng Emperor's approach to, 100–101
knowing shame (zhichi). See shame
Ko, Dorothy, 2, 161, 207
Kutcher, Norman, 116

Lan Dingyuan, 66–67, 85–86, 134–36
law, as tool for moral transformation, 7, 21–22, 46–54
lawsuits: as judicial problem, 39, 41, 44; as strategy in social conflict, 74
laziness, of wives as source of marital conflict, 86
Lee, James, 82
Legalism, 50, 230–31n27
Levirate, 26
Li Wei, 36
Li Yu, 30–32, 144, 161–64, 205
liangchi. See shame
Liaoning, 82
Liefu. See chaste widows
Liji. See Book of Rites
lineage branch heads (zufang), 92–93
lineage council (zuzhong), 73, 77–79
lineage head (zuzhang): judicial role of, 68, 75–76; role in moral transformation, 10, 43, 65–81; vs. zuzheng, 68, 70
literati elites: as case protagonists, 57–63, 150–51, 196–97; as moralists, 98–99; as promoters of chastity cult, 26–27, 33; and ritual revival, 29; views of female moral agency, 183–87
litigation masters, 7
Liu Fangai, 245n21, 246n28
Liu Jihua, 1
Liuxia Hui, 162
local bullies, 41, 158–61
local constable (difang), 121, 172, 173, 181, 199
Lower Yangzi region. See Jiangnan
loyalty: Chinese vs. Manchu definition of, 35; as political principle, 27–28
Lu Xun, depiction of female ghost, 255–56n41

Macauley, Melissa, 74
magistrate's handbooks: advice for adjudicating rape cases, 124–25, 145, 184; portrayal of the supernatural, 205

Manchuria, 121–32
Mann, Susan, 3, 59, 87, 136, 161, 191, 207
marriage: conflict in, 82–97; sale into as lineage punishment, 73
marriage rituals: extravagance of, 141; and law, 89–90; matchmakers, 40; propriety of, 137–38; role of women's natal families in, 89–90; as social problem, 40, 44–46, 49–50
Mencius, 162, 179
merchants, 193
mianzi. See reputation
Miao people: as examples of impropriety, 46, 136; in cases, 17–23; in fiction, 245n14
Miao Rebellion, 38
midwives, and forensic examinations of women, 139–40
migrants, to Manchuria, 123
Ming Code: on incest, 108; on killing adulterers, 100; on women criminals, 138
Ming dynasty, chastity cult in, 2, 26–27
mixing of the sexes, 40, 45, 133–41
monks, Buddhist and Daoist, 45, 135, 140–41
moral agency, of women, 12, 150, 161–64, 177–91
morality handbooks, for women, 59, 65–66, 134–36, 183–85
moral models, 161–64
moral transformation. See jiaohua; jiaoyang
mother's house (niangjia), 91
mothers-in-law: and daughters-in-law, in prescriptive literature, 83–89; tensions with daughters-in-law, 57–60, 91–92
mourning rituals. See funerary rituals
mourning system: political symbolism of, 116; use in law, 19, 223n6
Mulian opera, 66, 204

natal families: vs. patriline, 82–97; ritual propriety and, 83–84, 87–88; role in marital disputes, 57–63; as source of normative authority, 10, 57–63, 82–97; visits to natal families and inner/outer paradigm, 155
Nationalists, 218
native officials (tusi), 38, 70
neighbors, role in family conflicts, 82–83, 156–57, 169, 173, 174, 199
neiren. See inner people
neiwai. See inner/outer paradigm

New Culture Movement, 1, 218
niangjia. See mother's house
Nine Ministers, 108–10, 181, 220n9, 247–48n46
non-Han peoples: canonization policies and, 136, 228; and Qing gender politics, 7, 17–23
North China famine, 216–17
Nuoqin, 43

opera, propriety of for women, 39–40, 135, 141, 155
Ortai, 37
Ou Kanshan, 44
Ou Yang Yongqi, 241–42n43

Paderni, Paola, 206
paifang, pailou. See chastity arch
patriarchal authority: challenges to, 57–63, 65–81; vs. chastity, 10, 52, 71, 74, 79, 101; judicial construction of, 89–90
patriarchy: generational vs. conjugal definitions of, 4, 11, 27, 98–117; judicial construction of, 98–117, 142
patrilineal family: vs. affinal family, 82–97, 211; and chastity, 25–26, 62; vs. conjugal family unit, 27, 34; normative authority of, 57–63, 55–81; and the state, 65–81
penetration, and judicial definition of rape, 143, 247n38
personhood, being a person, 13, 160–61, 174, 189, 198, 200, 203, 207–8
pilgrimage, 135, 140–41, 155, 161
poetry: marital intimacy in, 98–99; suicide in, 207; women poets, 185
poverty: and impropriety, 154–55, 192–93; as source of marital tension, 85–87, 192–94
practicing avoidance, 147, 157–58
prison system, women in, 7, 40, 138–40
private settlement of crimes, 71, 74, 80
prostitution, 40, 90, 101; and canonization, 213
publishing, and inner/outer paradigm, 161

qiangjian. See rape
Qianlong Emperor: and the *jiaohua* campaign, 40–54; and the state chastity cult, 7; and tightening criteria for canonization, 212–13; treatment of incest cases, 108, 241–42n43; view of conjugal bond, 100; view of female suicide, 181–82; view of patriarchal authority in re killing adulterers, 104–6; view of ruler-subject relations compared to Yongzheng's, 48; views of lineage authority, 69–71
qing. See sentiment
Qing Fu, 140, 246n29
Qing Code: constructions of patriarchy in, 98–117; definition of rape, 142–53; revision of as part of jiaohua campaign, 48–50; treatment of female suicide, 177–83; treatment of marriage, 89–90

rape: cases, 121–32, 146–51, 196–97; contradictions of rape statute, 142–53; evidentiary requirements for, 124–25; incestuous, 112–16; and inner/outer paradigm, 142–43; profile of rapists, 123–24; and suicide, 197
rebellions, canonizations and, 38, 213–15
refugees, canonization of, 215
reputation: and face *(mianzi)*, 199; of families, 21, 77, 94, 174; and suicide, 204; vs. women's sense of personhood, 187, 199, 202
revenge: and adultery, 102–3; and lineage punishment, 75; vs. righteous indignation, 105–6
righteous indignation, 105–6, 108
ritual revival, 2, 29
rogue male *(guanggun)*, 10, 11, 123
Rowe, William, 67, 136, 141
ruler-subject relations, 35–38, 212

Sacred Edict, 7, 39, 221n15
sanfasi. See Three High Courts of Judicature
sentiment *(qing)*, 27, 98
servants, 150–51
sex ratios, 192
sexual assault. *See* flirtation; rape; sexual harassment
sexual desire, 184
sexual harassment: and suicide, 51–53, 177–82, 197–98; judicial treatment of, 12, 51–53, 171, 177–82
Shaanxi, 86–87, 140, 156–57
shame: knowing *(zhichi)*, 12, 137, 160–61; sense of, 139, 142, 184, 195, 203
Shandong, 88–89, 90–91, 123, 147–48, 205–6

Shanxi, 167–75, 188, 193, 194–95, 201
Shen Qiyuan, 108
Shi Jiqi, 41–43
shrews, 206
Shrine to the Chaste and Filial *(jiexiao ci)*, 21, 22, 30–33, 38, 204, 216–17
Shrine to the Loyal, Righteous, and Filial *(zhongyi xiaodi ci)*, 31
Shu Min, 140–41, 246n32
Shunzhi Emperor, 28
Sichuan, 137, 139
Sima Qian, 163
slander, 40
sodomy, 101
sojourning, 154, 167, 192–93
Sommer, Matthew, 8, 53, 143
Song dynasty: definition of chastity in, 25–26; statecraft thinkers, 42
state: gender orthodoxy, 7, 10, 33, 208; vs. family authority, 65–81
state building, 4, 30, 212
statecraft *(jingshi)*, 226n16; chastity cult and, 39–50
state-society relations, 35, 48–50, 70–71, 217
step-mothers, 40, 57
strangers, 156
suicide: as aggressive act, 203–9; canonization regulations for, 177–83; circumstances of, 197–99; consequences of, 203–6; humiliation and, 17–23, 156–57, 159, 171; incidence of, 197–98; motivations for, 192–209; as proof of chastity, 203–4; as proof of rape, 144–45, 149; sexual harassment and, 51–53, 79–80; substatutes on, 3, 12–13, 177–83
Sun Zongpu, 49–50
suspicion, avoidance of, 12, 136, 139, 160, 183

Taiping Rebellion, 214–17
Tang dynasty, laws on killing adulterers, 100–101
Tang Suizu, 178
Tang Yi, 60, 87–88, 94
Temples, women visiting, 40, 155
third realm of justice, 61, 81
Three High Courts of Judicature *(sanfasi)*, 5, 108–10, 115–16, 220n9
Three Obediences *(sancong)*, 84
tiaoxi. See flirtation
tongyangxi, 101
Tongzhi Emperor, 216
tusi. See native officials

uterine family, 237n3

village headman, 114

Wang Huizu, 21–22, 66–67, 83–84, 86, 135, 184–85
Wang Lun Uprising, 38
Wanyan Yunzhu, 136
wenmiao. See Confucius Temple
widow chastity: in the Ming, 26–27; in the Qing, 25–38; in the Song, 25–26
widows: inheritance rights of, 99; property rights of, 11; remarriage of, 204–5
widow suicide: ban on canonization for, 28, 98, 179, 213–15; in law and ritual regulation, 25–38
wifely way *(fudao)*: 57, 84, 94–95
wife-selling, 90
women, elite, 154, 161, 207
women's quarters, demarcation of, 248n2
women's work: and inner/outer paradigm, 134, 155; commercial activities, 155, 158–61, 188, 193; field work, 18; household chores, 155; making shoes, 158–61; needlework, 91; textile work, 122, 194
wuru. See humiliation

Xianfeng Emperor, 214–15
Xiang Yu, 163
xingke tiben (Board of Punishments routine memorials): ethnographic evidence in, 154; nature of case record, 102, 196; structure of, 3, 4–6; types of, 220n9
Xue Yunsheng: on distinguishing coercion from consent, 144, 152; on incest, 110–11; on killing adulterers, 106–7; on women criminals, 138;

yamen, as source of punishment, 72, 75, 78–79, 103, 172, 199, 201
Yan Sisheng, 137–38
Yao Run, 142–43
Yi Yin, 162
Yong Tai, 139, 246n26
Yongzheng Emperor: and the civilizing mission, 33–40; contrast with Qianlong, 48; and female pilgrimage, 140; and female suicide, 182; and lineage authority, 68–69; and state chastity cult, 30–37
Yuan Bin, 144–46, 152, 171, 179–80, 182, 198
Yuan Mei, 185–87, 204–5
Yuan dynasty, 1, 6; widow chastity in, 26

Index

Yunnan, 136

Zamperini, Paola, 207
Zhang Guangsi, 20, 38
Zhang Ruoai, 51–52, 181–82, 196
Zhang Shijun, 245n16
Zhang Tingyu, 51
Zhang Zai, 42
Zhao Cheng, 245n21
Zhejiang, 114–15, 193–94, 200
zhichi. See under shame
Zhili, 36, 75–76. 110, 154–55, 189, 206
zhongyi xiaodi ci. See Shrine to the Loyal, Righteous, and Filial
Zhou Renji, 44–46
Zhu Xi, 85
Zhu Yong, 68

Compositor:	Integrated Composition Systems
Text:	10/13 Sabon
Display:	Sabon
Printer and binder:	Sheridan Books, Inc.